# Praise for *The Ten Worlds*

"*The Ten Worlds* is one of the most insightful modern books on the pursuit of happiness I've ever read. Alex and Ash expertly weave interesting research, ancient wisdom, and real world examples to create a better framework for understanding how we pursue happiness and what's really getting in the way of our finding it, yielding numerous valuable 'a-ha' moments about ourselves and our loved ones."

—**Shawn Achor**, *New York Times* bestselling author
of *Big Potential* and *The Happiness Advantage*

"Some books tell great stories but aren't grounded enough in research to be believable. Some books have great research but are too dry. This one is different. Captivating stories. Compelling research. I am in awe of how well-written, fascinating, and valuable *The Ten Worlds* is. A must read for all interested in finding the path to happiness and enlightenment."

—**Dave Kerpen**, *New York Times* bestselling author
of *The Art of People* and *Likeable Social Media*

"What a remarkable work! What obstacles, traps, or delusions get in the way of your happiness? *The Ten Worlds* will not give you easy answers to this question, but real ones. By reading this book—and following its wise advice—you may just find your path to happiness."

—**Tal Ben-Shahar**, *New York Times* bestselling author
of *Happier* and *Choose the Life You Want*

"In this highly informative and eminently readable book, Drs. Alex Lickerman and Ash ElDifrawi argue convincingly that happiness isn't determined by what happens to us, but rather by what we *believe* about what happens to us. Filled with compelling stories, backed up by up-to-date research, and sprinkled with timeless wisdom, *The Ten Worlds* is a book that provides both practical insights and actionable steps for finding happiness that can't be destroyed by anything."

—**Steven Julius, Ph.D.**, President and CEO, H
and former Director of Player Pro

"If you are on a path to seeking happiness, this is the book for you. The authors brilliantly and creatively mix the evidence of science and the narrative of story to uncover what we need to know to experience greater happiness in our lives. Many of my clients and students believe that 'happiness is out of reach,' but I shall recommend this book to them to let them know that it's within their reach. Ash and Alex are to be congratulated for guiding their readers to experience greater happiness in their lives and in the lives of others."

—**Marty Martin, Psy.D.**, associate professor, DePaul University, speaker, and author of *Taming Disruptive Behavior*

"In *The Ten Worlds*, Alex and Ash give you the tools to protect you from what can be your worst enemy: your own mind. They use everything from neuroscience to Buddhism to metacognition to guide you along the path toward happiness."

—**A.J. Jacobs**, *New York Times* bestselling author of *The Year of Living Biblically*

# The Ten Worlds

## The New Psychology of Happiness

Alex Lickerman, M.D., and Ash ElDifrawi, Psy.D.

Health Communications, Inc.
Deerfield Beach, Florida

*www.hcibooks.com*

**Library of Congress Cataloging-in-Publication Data
is available through the Library of Congress**

© 2018 Alex Lickerman and Ash ElDifrawi

ISBN-13: 978-07573-2041-5 (Paperback)
ISBN-10: 07573-2041-4 (Paperback)
ISBN-13: 978-07573-2043-9 (ePub)
ISBN-10: 07573-2043-0 (ePub)

HCI, its logos, and marks are trademarks of Health Communications, Inc.

Publisher: Health Communications, Inc.
          3201 S.W. 15th Street
          Deerfield Beach, FL 33442–8190

*Cover design by Heath Miller*
*Interior design and formatting by Lawna Patterson Oldfield*

**Ash**
*For my parents, Ahmed and Rafiah*


**Alex**
*For Rhea*

# CONTENTS

Acknowledgments • ix

Introduction • 1

**1** Hell • 21

**2** Hunger • 45

**3** Animality • 73

**4** Anger • 99

**5** Tranquility • 137

**6** Rapture • 173

**7** Learning • 211

**8** Realization • 235

**9** Compassion • 261

**10** Enlightenment • 289

Ten Worlds Diagram • 322

Afterword • 324

Notes • 326

About the Authors • 340

Index • 342

# ACKNOWLEDGMENTS

Thanks goes first to our agent, Stephany Evans, who was as excited about seeing *The Ten Worlds* make it out into the world as we were, and who found it a great home with HCI. Thanks also to our editors at HCI, Allison Janse and Candace Johnson, both of whom couldn't have been more supportive, collaborative, creative, and, above all, patient in helping us turn the manuscript into a published book. Thanks to Heath Miller for designing both the cover and the Ten Worlds diagram.

Thanks also to the following people who read and provided feedback on early drafts: Dave Albert, Kate Brennan, Jerry Coyne, Sheri Davis, Cheryl Graeff, Mark Ingwer, Steve Julius, Michael Small, Janet Lickerman, and Michael Lickerman.

We're also grateful to the nine patients whose stories appear in the pages that follow for allowing us not only to learn from their stories but also to tell them—albeit in a deeply disguised form—to help others learn as well.

*From Ash:* I owe a special thanks to my wife, Amy, and my kids, Allison and Aidan, for all the nights and weekends they graciously allowed me to devote to writing. I owe an even greater debt of gratitude to my co-author and best friend, Alex. This book stands as a tribute to the power of our friendship, a friendship that's proven itself to be as enduring as the type of happiness we argue it's possible to achieve.

*From Alex:* Thanks goes to my co-author, Ash, who first suggested the idea to write *The Ten Worlds* some twenty years ago and without whom this book would never have existed. Thinking about, debating, and refining its principles with

him over the last two decades has been one of the most challenging and gratifying experiences of my life. I consider it a privilege to call him my best friend.

I also owe a great debt of gratitude to my son, Cruise. This time around he
was old enough to recognize how much time my writing stole from him. That
he was willing to sacrifice as much of it as he was to permit me to do something
I not only love but also consider important makes me prouder of him than I
know how to express.

I owe the greatest debt of gratitude, though, to my wife, Rhea. The sacrifices
she made for my first book were small in comparison to the ones she made for
this one. I'm more grateful for her love, support, and patience than I can say.

While the key events depicted in
each of the stories in this book are based in fact,
the names, identifying details, and histories
of the people involved have been altered to
preserve their privacy and protect
their confidentiality.

# INTRODUCTION

Not long after I first began working as a primary care physician, my best friend, a clinical psychologist named Ash ElDifrawi, told me about a patient of his named April, who'd recently let him know that she'd been thinking about killing herself.

During her first two years in therapy with him, she'd been moderately depressed but mostly functional. Then a year and a half ago, her husband announced he was leaving her for another woman. Devastated, she begged him to stay, vowing to do whatever it took to make their marriage work. He refused, saying it was too late, and then moved out. In the months that followed, she reached out to him multiple times but to no avail. When she finally worked up the courage to confront him in person, he greeted her not with anger or even dismay, but indifference. He seemed switched off, as if she'd become just one of a million faceless people whose existence he hardly noticed. He left her, in short, with the impression that their relationship hadn't merely ended but had never actually existed in the first place.

Soon after that, she began to eat uncontrollably. She would snack on anything she could find—candy bars, popcorn, cookies, chips—and within twelve months she gained nearly thirty pounds. The heavier she grew, the more exhausted she became. She tried taking naps during the day, but they made little difference. When she finally nodded off at the wheel of her car one day, she decided it was time to see her doctor.

Her doctor, in turn, ordered a sleep study, which showed she had severe obstructive sleep apnea (a condition in which the tongue falls back in the mouth

1

and obstructs the throat during sleep, depriving the brain of oxygen). This had been the reason for her crippling fatigue, he explained. If she didn't lose weight, there was a good chance she'd eventually develop congestive heart failure. He recommended a gastric bypass, arguing that her obesity was no longer just a cosmetic concern but now a potentially life-threatening medical condition.

But she refused to consider it. So he prescribed a continuous positive airway pressure (CPAP) machine, which functioned by delivering a blast of pressure down her throat through a mask applied over her mouth to prevent her tongue from obstructing her airway while she slept. The machine worked, but she found using it a torture. She would fall asleep feeling like she was choking and dream of being strangled. Yet her physical discomfort seemed only a minor irritation compared to the self-loathing that now filled her with each blast from the CPAP machine, the cycling of its pneumatic gears an inescapable reminder that she'd been brought to this place by nothing other than her own weakness.

So she began to gain even more weight, the self-disgust her bloated stomach induced paradoxically only intensifying the pleasure that eating brought her. Knowing she was overeating at least partially to punish herself, though, failed to equip her with the will to stop.

Not surprisingly, the more weight she gained, the more depressed she became. So Ash referred her to a psychiatrist, who, over the course of a year, tried her on no fewer than four antidepressant medications. But none of them worked. Following that, April told Ash she no longer believed she was ever going to get better, and that she wanted to be dead.

So he sent her to the ER to be admitted to the hospital. Because she'd failed antidepressant medication, the attending psychiatrist decided to treat her with electroconvulsive therapy, the most effective known treatment for depression.

"Has it been working?" I asked.

Ash shrugged. "She doesn't want to kill herself anymore."

"Well, that's something."

"That is something," he agreed. "But I still don't know why she wanted to kill herself in the first place."

"She's depressed," I said, thinking the answer obvious.

"Sure," Ash agreed. "But why?"

"Her husband left her for another woman. She's obese and can't lose weight—"

"No, no, no," he interrupted. "I get all that. That's not what I mean. What I mean is I have at least ten other patients who've been through even worse than she has who have no idea what depression even is. What I'm asking is why does *anyone* get depressed? Ever?"

൙

In my first book, *The Undefeated Mind*, I argue that the pursuit of happiness isn't "merely an inalienable right with which we're endowed or an activity we're capable of choosing; it's a psychological imperative we must obey."[1] The notion that nothing is more important to us than happiness—in fact, that nothing *can* be—doesn't come just from observations about the human condition throughout history by writers, philosophers, and poets, but also from a modern scientific understanding of the way the brains of animals evolved to promote survival. We know that animals don't fight to survive because they grasp the meaning of death; they fight to survive because their brains evolved pleasure and pain circuits that motivate them to do so. And though we humans *do* have the capacity to understand the meaning of death and are therefore capable of being motivated by more complex incentives than pleasure and pain, we remain incapable of shrugging off our evolutionary heritage. Pleasure and pain—or rather, their more recent evolutionary offspring, happiness and suffering—remain the core incentives our brains use to motivate us.[2]

But what exactly *is* happiness that we spend our lives pursuing it more fiercely than anything else? We would answer in part, as Daniel Gilbert did in his book *Stumbling on Happiness*, that happiness isn't just a good feeling but a *special* good feeling[3]—in fact, the *best* good feeling—we're capable of having: a feeling that's better than all our other positive emotions combined, including serenity, hope, pride, amusement, surprise, interest, gratitude, and love.

Happiness is something we all want. Yet it's also something many of us fail to achieve. Look around you. How many people do you know who exude joy on a daily basis, who would say they feel a powerful sense of satisfaction with their lives? How many people do you know who wouldn't find their ability to be happy significantly impaired by the loss of a loved one, financial ruin, or a terminal illness?

The problem we face, however, isn't that genuine, long-lasting happiness is impossible to attain. Rather, it's that we're confused about how to attain it. So in the pages that follow, we attempt to clear up this confusion by exploring all the ways we get the pursuit of happiness wrong—the incorrect assumptions we make about what we need to be happy and our erroneous beliefs about what happiness *is*. We'll argue that only by attending to and embracing a correct understanding of happiness can we free ourselves from the limits our erroneous beliefs about happiness place on us and enjoy the kind of happiness we all want, the kind of happiness that can't be taken away by anything.

This, it turns out, is both easier and harder than we think. Easier because, as we hope to convince you, the number of erroneous beliefs we have about happiness totals only nine at the most fundamental level—far fewer false paths on the journey to happiness than perhaps we have any right to expect. Harder, though, because even though ideas flit in and out of our heads like mosquitoes, we cling to ideas we *believe* with magnetic force. Once we decide an idea is true, we develop an emotional connection and commitment to it that often has little to do with the merit of the belief itself.[4] As a result, freeing ourselves from our erroneous beliefs may be one of the hardest things to do in life.

Unfortunately, as authors, we're no more immune to being overly attached to our ideas than anyone else. So we need to concede at the outset that no definitive proof exists that the nine erroneous beliefs we discuss in the pages that follow unequivocally represent the elemental roadblocks to happiness. But our intent in writing this book wasn't to present our ideas as well-established scientific facts. Rather, we offer them as a set of hypotheses whose truth and relevance we invite you to test yourself in the proving ground of your own life.

For even if we fail to convince you that these nine erroneous beliefs are *your* erroneous beliefs—or that they're even erroneous at all—if we can convince you that the key to achieving happiness lies in correcting whatever erroneous beliefs you do hold about happiness, then we'll count *ourselves* happy, for we will have achieved the real purpose for which we wrote this book.

# Life-Condition

Psychologists now use the term *core affect* to describe the most basic feelings we experience as human beings—that is, pleasure and pain.[5] Neurologist Antonio Damasio calls pleasure and pain *primordial feelings* and argues that they "occur spontaneously and continuously whenever one is awake . . . [and] reflect the current state of the body" at the most basic level.[6] Though specific emotions like anger and sadness may appear and disappear like good and bad weather, at no time are we ever without a core affect—much in the same way, to switch metaphors, at no time are we ever without a body temperature. At every moment we're experiencing a primordial feeling somewhere between the two extremes of agony and ecstasy. Universal and irreducible, core affect, research now argues, represents the most fundamental aspect of all subjective experience.[7]

Psychologists have also argued that the reason our core affect varies has less to do with what happens to us than with how we *think* about what happens to us—with our mindset, if you will.[8] Mindset explains, for example, why some people remain joyful and optimistic no matter how awful the tragedy that befalls them while others suffer and complain no matter how much good fortune comes their way. It also explains how two people can react to the same event in completely different—even opposite—ways, as well as how someone can feel differently about the same event at different times. How can a lottery winner be miserable? Mindset. How can a quadriplegic be happy? Mindset. Mindset is the reason one person's mountain is another person's molehill.

Though the science documenting the effect of mindset on our core affect is relatively new, the concept of mindset itself is old. Buddhist philosophers captured the same idea more than two and a half millennia ago with the term *life-condition*. Having carefully observed all the various forms in which the self might exist, they delineated ten foundational life-conditions—or worlds—describing, in essence, the ten basic mindsets through which we continuously cycle. From the lowest to the highest with respect to the desirability of core affect they produce they are: Hell, Hunger, Animality, Anger, Tranquility, Rapture, Learning, Realization, Compassion, and Enlightenment.

Life-condition is defined essentially as the character of one's inner life. As such, it influences the most basic aspects of our being—our emotions, our thoughts, our behaviors, and our life energy. Not that any particular emotion is unique to any one life-condition (for example, we don't only get angry in the life-condition of Anger), nor that particular emotions always do only one thing to our core affect (for example, sadness doesn't always make us feel pain).[9] Rather, our life-condition is the lens through which we view both the world and ourselves and is therefore what determines which emotions we feel.

In one sense, then, the experience of life is really the experience of life-condition. Depending on which life-condition we find ourselves inhabiting at any one moment our experience of life will be different.[10] When we're in the life-condition, or world, of Hell, for example, everything will be warped by our suffering. In such a state we could win the Nobel Prize and not feel an ounce of satisfaction from it. But while in the world of Enlightenment, simply watching a sunset could give rise to the greatest joy we've ever known. Nothing, in other words, is inherently a burden or a delight, an obstacle or an opportunity. How happy or unhappy we are is ultimately determined by our life-condition and our life-condition alone.

## The Power of Our Beliefs

If this is true—if our life-condition determines what we think and feel and how we behave in response to the events of our lives—what, we may ask, determines our life-condition?

Certainly a variety of things *influence* it. This includes both fixed things, like our genes and upbringing, and fleeting things, like drugs, diseases, hormonal states, and the slings and arrows of outrageous fortune, to name just a few. We'll argue in the pages that follow, however, that what influences it the most is something else entirely: our beliefs.

The degree to which our lives can be changed by the transformation of a mere idea into a belief is truly unparalleled. Belief can banish the most intense of fears, as belief in an afterlife often banishes the fear of death. It can strengthen the weakest of wills, as belief in the inability to drink safely can strengthen the will of an alcoholic attempting to become sober. And it can overpower the strongest of desires, as belief in the vileness of apostasy can overpower even the desire to live in suicide bombers. Belief can diminish physical pain,[11] cause the release of dopamine in the brains of patients with Parkinson's disease,[12] and even induce signs of pregnancy—the cessation of menstruation, abdominal swelling, and breast enlargement—when a woman isn't actually pregnant.[13]

How does a belief gain such power? It would seem merely by being *stirred up*, or activated. A Buddhist metaphor compares our life to a glass of water and a belief to sediment lying at the bottom. It may be an event that stirs the water (our life), but it's the sediment (our belief) that clouds the water with suffering or colors it with joy. Remove the sediment, and no matter how vigorously the water is stirred, it will remain clear. So how do events like the loss of a job, the breakup of a marriage, or even the fleeting thought that we're less attractive than we once were cause us to suffer? By stirring up a *belief*—perhaps, for example, that we've lost our worth. How could such events instead bring us joy? By stirring up a different belief—perhaps, for example, that we've gained our freedom (in the case of our declining attractiveness, from the tyranny of our own ego). When our life-condition shifts, events represent only the *external* cause. The *internal* cause is always some pre-existing belief that the event stirs up. It's our beliefs that stimulate our emotions, thoughts, and behaviors. It's our beliefs that mediate our reactions to events. This isn't to suggest that events are unimportant. Rather, it's to suggest that events impact our happiness only and always *through* the particular beliefs they stir up. If we want to understand why we're thinking certain thoughts or feeling certain feelings in response to an event—whether an external event, like a divorce, or an internal event, like the realization we're not as attractive as we once were—we only need to ask ourselves what beliefs that event has stirred up.

One important implication of this hypothesis is that we can't predict—and shouldn't judge—the severity of a person's suffering based on the event that caused it. We may, for instance, expect a husband to be more devastated by the loss of his wife than an athlete is by the loss of a game, but the reverse could just as easily occur depending on the beliefs such losses stir up. We forget, or don't realize, the depth of a person's suffering is less determined by the ghastliness of external events than by the beliefs such events activate.

Ash and I were struck by the truth of this not long after we first met at the start of our senior year in college. I was a resident assistant charged with providing support to the students in the dormitory where Ash resided. One afternoon he came to see me in a panic. For as long as he could remember, he said, he'd wanted to become a doctor. He'd followed the traditional path, majoring in biology, taking the required pre-med courses, and studying for and scoring well on the MCAT. That afternoon, he finally learned that he'd been accepted to medical school. Yet instead of being flooded with relief, he'd been surprised to find himself flooded with anxiety.

After an hour or so of working through his thoughts and feelings about it, we figured out what we thought was the reason: while all his life he believed he'd wanted to be a doctor, he hadn't, in fact, wanted to be a doctor at all. Applying to medical school had simply been a way for him to fulfill the unspoken wishes of his parents.

But realizing this only *increased* his anxiety, for he now felt stripped of direction and confused about what he was going do with the rest of his life. Yet almost as quickly as we discovered that he didn't want to become a doctor, we identified his real area of interest: clinical psychology. But upon recognizing that, Ash found himself feeling even *more* anxious. It didn't take us long to piece together the reason for this as well: he'd taken no college courses in psychology, had no practical experience in the field, and had been told that getting into a doctoral program in psychology was even harder than getting into medical school. In short, he didn't believe he could do it. We thought we'd finally arrived at the central reason why his reaction to getting into medical school had been so negative: it had triggered a belief that he couldn't accomplish what he'd harbored as his real ambition all along.

## Stirring Up Beliefs

Yet Ash's anxiety wasn't induced by the certainty with which he now believed his real dream was out of reach. It was induced by the amount of *attention* he was now giving the possibility. Even a brief examination of our experience suggests the power of our beliefs to influence what we think, feel, and do is related less to the confidence with which we harbor our beliefs than to the frequency and intensity with which external causes draw our attention to them, or stir them up.[14] For example, we all believe with unassailable certainty that we're one day going to die, but that belief seems to exert little influence over what we think, feel, and do until something comes along and draws our attention to it (a serious illness, the death of someone close to us, or even a flood of spontaneous rumination about our own mortality). On the other hand, even if we believe only slightly that the plane in which we're flying might crash, a strong bout of turbulence can still stir that belief up intensely enough to terrify us. It seems we can be powerfully affected by even the weakest belief if only it's stirred up strongly enough.

It is true that the greater the confidence we have in a belief, the more power it will have to affect us. But this seems to be only because the greater the confidence we have in a belief, *the more easily—and therefore the more frequently—it gets stirred up.* It's the extent to which our beliefs get stirred up, the extent to which we pay attention to them and to which we're engaged by them, that ultimately gives our beliefs their ability to affect us.

This is why even though a weak belief is harder to stir up—and is therefore less likely to be stirred up—once it *is* stirred up, it can have as much influence over us as a strong belief. For example, even though we know that the probability we'll win the lottery or be involved in a car accident is low—meaning we believe in those possibilities only slightly—we still buy lottery tickets and wear seat belts.

We do these things because what stirs up weak beliefs isn't the strength with which we believe them but *the potential consequences of ignoring them.* If the potential consequences of ignoring a belief are significant, that belief is more likely to draw our attention and affect us.[15] And *that's* the reason turbulence can terrify us even though we believe correctly that the probability of it causing a plane to crash is low—because the consequences of a crash would be catastrophic.

## The Shifting of Life-Condition

In 1911 the neurologist Édouard Claparède concealed a pin between his fingers while greeting one of his amnesic patients with a handshake, causing her to yelp in pain when he stuck her with it. Within a few minutes, however, she'd forgotten not only that she'd been stuck but also that she'd ever met him! When Claparède then came back in the room to introduce himself a second time, *she refused to shake his hand*. The reason? Some part of her—likely the orbitofrontal cortex, which is known to perform nonconscious appraisals of threats[16]—remembered being stuck with a pin. So when she saw his outstretched palm approaching, it stirred up in her a belief that to shake hands with him was dangerous—even as her conscious mind remained completely unaware that she believed it.[17]

Additional evidence that feelings can outlast our conscious awareness of their origins comes from a study conducted by Justin Feinstein at the University of Iowa in which emotion-inducing films were shown to patients who, because of damage to the area of the brain called the hippocampus, suffered significant impairment in their ability to form new memories. When he surveyed their feelings after the films were over and they'd forgotten they'd viewed them, he found that they continued to feel the emotions the films had induced. Not only that, but also they continued to feel them for an even longer time and with even greater intensity than a group of control subjects with normal brains who remembered viewing the films in their entirety.[18]

But we needn't have suffered damage to our short-term memory to be unaware of the reasons we feel, and therefore behave, the way we do. In fact, we *all* frequently forget what's caused us to feel what we feel, sometimes just moments after we start feeling it. Who among us, for example, hasn't at some point found himself feeling anxious for no apparent reason? It's not, of course, that no reason exists; it's often that we've simply forgotten it, sometimes so quickly that our conscious mind was able to register it for only a moment (or perhaps, as with Claparède's patient, not at all). Maybe, for instance, a co-worker frowns at us as we pass her in the hallway, stirring up a belief that she might be angry with us, or even that she may not like us, and our life-condition plummets. In the very next second, though, we lose track of that belief as other thoughts fill up our mind. But that belief has only gone dormant. If it were to be stirred up again even a little—say, by a chance phone call from that co-worker's supervisor—our life-condition would likely plummet again. Just as a body at rest will remain at rest until acted upon by an outside force, so too our life-condition will remain in one world until an event stirs up a belief that shifts it into another one. It doesn't matter if we're consciously aware of that belief or not.

## *Our Beliefs About Happiness*

This brings us to the central thesis of this book: while many different kinds of beliefs are able to influence our life-condition, we'll argue that the beliefs that influence it the most are *our beliefs about happiness itself.* In fact, we'll argue that our beliefs about happiness are what *create* the Ten Worlds.

A story from Greek mythology about Hercules, the son of Zeus, king of the gods, illustrates this point. One day Hercules fell into a mad rage and inadvertently killed his wife and two children. To atone for it, he was instructed by an oracle to complete twelve labors. For the eleventh of the twelve, he was told to bring back the golden apples of the Hesperides to King Eurystheus. Because he didn't know where the apples were, he sought the advice of Atlas, a Titan who was the father of the Hesperides and whose job it was to hold up the world on his shoulders. When Hercules asked him where he might find the apples, Atlas replied that if Hercules would only take the world onto his shoulders temporarily, Atlas would get the apples for him. Hercules readily agreed. Atlas did return with the apples, but when Hercules asked him to take the world back, Atlas refused. He told Hercules that he would deliver the apples to Eurystheus himself. He wanted to have a chance to enjoy his new freedom, he said. Maybe he'd come back in a few years and take the world back. Then again, maybe he wouldn't.

Thinking quickly, Hercules told Atlas he would be happy to continue holding up the world if only Atlas would take it back for just one moment so he could adjust himself into a more comfortable position. Not being the brightest of Titans, Atlas put the apples down and complied. Of course, as soon as Hercules was free, he thanked Atlas, picked up the apples, and went on his way. Atlas raged at Hercules as he sped off but remained powerless to stop him. By the time Hercules was gone from sight, Atlas had once again resigned himself to his fate.

Though what follows doesn't appear in any book of Greek mythology, we imagine that one day, years later, Hercules returned to see Atlas. "Doubtless you've come back to chide me for being so easily tricked into taking back the burden of the world," Atlas said. But to this Hercules only replied, "When I gave you back the world, why didn't you drop it and come after me?" Astonished, Atlas said, "That would have meant the end of every living thing upon it!" To which Hercules replied, "Then you have your answer, great Atlas, as to why I came back. Not to ridicule you but to praise you, for a lesser Titan wouldn't have cared." And with that, Hercules left. Alone again, Atlas pondered what Hercules said. And then slowly he began to smile. And forever more, whenever anyone, man or god, would come to see Atlas and ask him about his burden, he would seem to straighten and say only, "It is no burden at all."

How did Atlas find relief from carrying what was literally the weight of the world on his shoulders? Not just by realizing that he cared about other people. Nor just by realizing that he had a purpose in keeping others safe. Rather, we would argue that his task was transformed from a burden into a delight when Hercules stirred up in him another belief lying *underneath* the belief he had a purpose in keeping others safe—namely, the belief that he needed a purpose to be happy.

## Delusions Are the Obstacles to Happiness

If we accept that our ability to be happy is determined mostly by what we believe we *need* to be happy, then the reason so many people *aren't* happy becomes obvious. Quite simply, most of our beliefs about what we need to be happy are wrong.

Though the word "delusional" is usually used to indicate the presence of mental illness, even those of us who don't suffer from mental illness are, to a certain extent, delusional. What makes us so isn't just that we believe implausible ideas, meaning ideas that contradict a general understanding of reality (that the sun is intelligent, for example). Though delusional ideas are, for the most part, implausible, so are ideas that are eventually recognized as groundbreaking truths (for example, that the entire universe is made of atoms). Nor are we delusional because something we believe turns out to be wrong. We may simply lack the relevant facts, as was the case when most of the world's population believed Earth was flat.

Instead, what makes a person delusional is the refusal to abandon an idea when confronted with incontrovertible evidence that it's untrue.[19] A delusion isn't just a false idea. It's a *fixed* false idea. We're not delusional because of the *content* of our ideas; we're delusional because of the *thought process* that maintains our conviction in them. Certainly, some people are rightly considered delusional based solely on the content of their ideas (for example, people who suffer from the Cotard delusion, the bizarre belief that one is already dead). But we wouldn't automatically consider someone delusional for believing, say, that the FBI is spying on him solely on the basis of the content of that belief, as we know the FBI has, in fact, spied on private citizens. We *would* be more likely to consider that person delusional if when confronted with convincing evidence that the FBI wasn't spying on him, he continued to believe that it was. Refusing to abandon a belief in such a case and offering instead impossible-to-falsify justifications for why he believed it was true—and, further, refusing to consider that anything could prove it otherwise—might, in fact, point to a diagnosis of schizophrenia.[20]

Then again, schizophrenia isn't the only thing that causes people to cling to ideas in the face of contradictory evidence. Nearly everyone, in fact, demonstrates what's known as *belief perseverance* at one time or another, suggesting that when it comes to revising or abandoning beliefs, emotionally healthy people can be almost as delusional as people suffering from mental illness. The beliefs that vaccines cause autism, that the earth is less than 10,000 years old, and that human beings were created in their present form and not through evolution are just a few examples of beliefs that persevere even in the face of overwhelming evidence that they're false.

The cause of belief perseverance, however, differs drastically from that of schizophrenia. Belief perseverance occurs because we're not perfectly objective about what we believe. We cling to beliefs for reasons that have nothing to do with the strength of evidence that supports the beliefs themselves: to protect or enhance our self-image,[21] to appear to be, and actually be, consistent,[22] and to make ourselves feel good—or at least, less bad.[23] Quite simply, we believe things without sufficient evidence, or even in the face of contradictory evidence, because we *want* to believe them—because believing them serves us in some way. This is almost certainly why, for example, people believe in astrology despite a complete lack of evidence that its predictions are accurate.

But how exactly do we convince ourselves that an unproven idea is true? Or that an idea that's actually been *disproven* is true? One study by researcher Craig Anderson and colleagues suggests the answer is surprisingly straightforward: we convince ourselves that an idea is true by explaining to ourselves *why* it's true.[24] According to Anderson's study, we're more swayed by good stories than we are by credible evidence. In fact, we're so swayed by good stories that we'll continue to believe them even when evidence comes to light that proves they're wrong. The reason, according to Anderson, is that we remember stories better than evidence. It's stories, not evidence, that draw our attention the most and therefore command our first allegiance, becoming, in essence, the bedrock upon which our conviction rests. What's more, other studies suggest that the easier a time we have creating a story, the more likely we are to believe it.[25] That is, the ease with which we come up with a story is itself what makes us believe that our story is correct.

## The Core Delusions

It's this propensity we have to believe the stories we tell ourselves that becomes the true obstacle to happiness. For once we become attached to beliefs about how to attain happiness that are erroneous, freeing ourselves from them becomes nearly impossible. This was what I told Ash I thought had happened to April. Events were continually stirring up her delusional beliefs about what she needed to be happy, and she simply wouldn't—or couldn't—abandon them. I thought these were beliefs that, despite her great confidence in them, had trapped her in the lowest of the Ten Worlds, the world of Hell. They were likely beliefs she didn't realize she held—or that she held without ever questioning—but which nevertheless were the cause of all the emotional, cognitive, and even physical manifestations of her depression.

"That's actually the foundational principle of cognitive therapy," Ash remarked. "Stressful situations activate dysfunctional beliefs, which lead to negative thinking, which leads to depression.[26] Correct the dysfunctional beliefs and the depression goes away."

I nodded. "Except I'm also wondering if there's just *one* dysfunctional belief—one *core delusion*—that's driving all the other dysfunctional beliefs that are causing her depression."

"The end-all-be-all cause of her depression?"

"The end-all-be-all cause of depression *period*. Or at least of one *type* of depression."

Unlike Beck's view that dysfunctional beliefs arise from early childhood traumas, I suggested that this core delusion arises from foundational life experiences common to us all. Further, I speculated, if there is indeed one core delusion that lies at the heart of the world of Hell, other core delusions would undoubtedly lie at the hearts of the other worlds.

This might explain, I argued, why people tend to make the same mistakes over and over in their pursuit of happiness. Though any of the core delusions could be stirred up in any of us at any time, because of our genetics, the way we were raised, the way our lives had unfolded—or some combination of all three—in each of us, I speculated, one core delusion would tend to get stirred up more consistently than all the others. Thus, though everyone has the potential to live in any of the Ten Worlds at any moment, each of us has one life-condition—one world—from which we come and to which we invariably return. One *basic life tendency*: the life-condition in which we live most of the time.

"When you say core delusions, are you actually talking about *core beliefs*?" Ash asked. "Because I could easily name ten of those just off the top of my head."

"I'm not sure," I said. "Name one and I'll tell you."

"Here's three: 'I'm worthless.' 'I'm incompetent.' 'I'm unlovable.'" Core beliefs, Ash said, were defined as "fundamental, inflexible, and generalized beliefs that people hold about themselves, the world, or the future."[27]

"Then, no, we're not talking about core beliefs," I said. "We *are* talking about beliefs that are fundamental, inflexible, and generalized, but not beliefs that people hold about themselves, the world, or the future. They're beliefs people have about what they need to be happy."

"That are wrong . . ."

"Yes. Except for the belief that lies at the heart of the world of Enlightenment," I added.

Ash thought for a moment. "So there are only *nine* false beliefs about what we need to be happy?"

"Nine at the core, yes. I'm sure April has several beliefs that are contributing to her depression—maybe even, for example, that she's worthless, incompetent, and unlovable. But I'm thinking there's one delusion that sits at the innermost layer, underlying all her other beliefs—a belief that represents the true cause of depression itself, the core delusion of the world of Hell."

"Which is—?"

I shrugged. "It would have to be something really basic."

Ash was intrigued by the paradigm and promptly suggested one way we could identify the core delusions—one way we could figure out if the concept even made sense—was by finding them at work in actual people.

"Like April," he offered.

I understood immediately what he was proposing. We could start with any one of April's more superficial dysfunctional beliefs and follow it along a trail of other, more deeply embedded dysfunctional beliefs until inductive reasoning brought us to the answer we sought. In fact, he added, we could do the same thing with other patients who came from the other worlds to identify the core delusions that created those other worlds as well.

"Because if we could identify the core delusions actually living and breathing in the lives of real people," Ash said, "if we could verify them as the most influential determinants of happiness, wouldn't we be looking at a unique way to explain why people *aren't* happy? Or happi*er*?"

"I think we would," I answered.

⟨᳗᳘⟩

From that conversation was born the idea for this book. And now, after twenty years of research, we've become convinced that the concept of life-condition offers a valid way to understand and categorize all the various life states through which human beings cycle. Each chapter, therefore, opens with a description of one of the Ten Worlds. Following that, we meet a patient of Ash's whose basic life tendency centers on that world and who granted Ash permission to share the details of his or her therapy with me. The bulk of each chapter is then spent in recreating both the therapy sessions themselves and the behind-the-scenes conversations that Ash and I were having as we attempted to puzzle out each of the core delusions. To show rather than merely tell readers what it's like to live in each world, we present the sessions as they unfolded, in many cases fictionalizing some of the dialogue for purposes of clarity.

Though readers may not recognize in themselves the same degree of pathology on display in the stories that follow, we believe the core delusions we were able to identify—admittedly not through experimental design but through reflection, reason, and thought experiment—are in fact the same core delusions that trap us all.

So though the core delusion we propose as April's doesn't explain in every instance why people get depressed, it does, we believe, explain why people suffer. We discuss the difference—as well as the difference between suffering and pain—in Chapter 1 as we recount the rest of April's story in an exploration of what it means to be trapped in the life-condition of Hell.

In Chapter 2 we tell Patrick's story, beginning with his struggle to rid himself of the irrational fear that his girlfriend is cheating on him and ending with the discovery that, despite the obsessive nature of his desires, he doesn't in fact enjoy any of his attachments or find satisfaction in any of his accomplishments at all. We discover the explanation for this paradox when we uncover his firm conviction in the core delusion of the life-condition of Hunger.

In Chapter 3 we introduce Dominique, a woman who appears at first blissfully unconcerned with the pain she causes others. Only when we learn how consumed she is by a craving that impairs her better judgment do we discover the belief that drives her impulsive behavior, the core delusion of the life-condition of Animality.

In Chapter 4 we tell Roosevelt's story, beginning with the conflict he feels between his desire to keep his family together and his need to maintain absolute control. Only when we identify the part of him that's driven by the need for that control do we recognize the degree to which he believes in the core delusion of the life-condition of Anger.

In Chapter 5 we meet Frankie, a police detective so desperate to avoid conflict that he's afraid to become angry at all. In helping him learn to prioritize his own needs over the needs of others, we discover the core delusion of the life-condition of Tranquility, a world characterized by the futile desire to keep everything in one's life unchanged.

In Chapter 6 we reach a turning point in our thinking about happiness itself when we meet Nick, an architect whose mood changes so abruptly with the rise and fall of his good and bad fortune that at first he appears to suffer from bipolar disorder. In identifying the true cause of his rapidly changing emotions as his belief in the core delusion of the life-condition of Rapture, we articulate a crucial distinction between two different types of happiness, relative and absolute, and argue that the kind of happiness we all assume we want is in fact a pale version of the kind of happiness it's possible for us to have.

In Chapter 7 we introduce Ken, the CEO of a midsize healthcare software company whose difficult personality and arrogance cause several high-value executives to consider quitting. This prompts a board member to hire Ash as Ken's executive coach. In seeking to explain Ken's excessive attachment to his own views, we discover the core delusion of the life-condition of Learning.

In Chapter 8 we meet Anjali, a social worker who finds herself unable to control her anger at one of her patients. When achieving several important insights in supervision with Ash fails to alter her reaction to her patient, she discovers that what drives her is the core delusion of the life-condition of Realization.

In Chapter 9 we tell Louisa's story, beginning with the death of her daughter and ending with her struggle to forgive her daughter's murderers. In helping her to navigate her grief, we're led to the core delusion of the life-condition of Compassion.

We finish in Chapter 10 with thoughts about how we might find our way into the tenth world, the world of Enlightenment. For in that life-condition, we'll argue, lies a joy in which no harmful overindulgence is possible, one that resists diminution by any and all adverse life events, and which is therefore absolute and indestructible.

## Key Points

- The moment-to-moment degree of pleasure or pain we experience is referred to as our *core affect*. Unlike other emotions like anger or guilt that come and go, we experience our core affect continuously.
- *Life-condition* is defined as the character of one's inner life. It reveals itself in ten different states, or worlds, each of which engenders a particular set of thoughts, feelings, and behaviors as well as an accompanying core affect.
- Though we can find ourselves in any of the Ten Worlds at any moment, each of us tends to spend most of our time in just one of them. That world is considered our *basic life tendency*.
- It's not the things that happen to us but rather our *beliefs* about the things that happen to us—specifically, our beliefs about how they impact our happiness—that determine the life-condition in which we find ourselves from one moment to the next.
- Beliefs about how things impact our happiness arise out of nine *core delusions,* which themselves create the life-conditions, or worlds, through which we continuously cycle. It's therefore our beliefs about happiness itself that determine our core affect, or degree of happiness.
- The core delusions are defined as our most basic erroneous beliefs about what we need to be happy.

# 1

# Hell

*Although the world is full of suffering, it is also full of the overcoming of it.*

—Helen Keller

Hell is defined as the life-condition of suffering. When fully immersed in it, all we know is misery; our energy falls so low we become nearly incapable of taking any action to help ourselves feel better.

In such a state, we tend to view almost everything, even positive events, in a negative light. When our suffering is extreme and prolonged, we may become inconsolable, leading to one of the worst consequences of being trapped in the life-condition of Hell, social isolation.

The more isolated we become, the more we flatten out, eventually becoming mere two-dimensional versions of ourselves—lethargic, sometimes even paralyzed versions that we hardly recognize—as we lose our ability to think clearly and with good judgment. We begin clinging to reasons why we can't solve our problems and blame our unhappiness on the problems we can't solve.

Sometimes we even come to feel we're worthless or disgusting and try to numb ourselves with alcohol, drugs, food, sleep, and the like. Alternatively, sometimes feeling worthless causes us to lash out at others, the impulse to destroy ourselves expanding to include those around us as well.

Sometimes, on the other hand, we suffer in silence, living a life of such quiet desperation that no one, not even our closest friends and family, suspects how overwhelmed we've become. At other times our suffering is so awful, so intense, it leaks out of our every pore, preventing us from hiding its existence from anyone.

But whether expressed or concealed, mild or severe, lasting decades or only the briefest of moments, the one constant feature of the life-condition of Hell—of suffering—is that it prevents us from thinking about anything else. All we have room left to want—in fact, what we want sometimes even more than life itself—is to escape it.

Though she no longer wanted to kill herself, when April followed up with Ash in his office three days after being discharged from the hospital, she still felt worthless and hopeless and had difficulty finding pleasure in anything. She felt little motivation to take care of herself. "I have no reason to move on," she told Ash.

She was still convinced that her ex-husband was the reason she was depressed. For the year and a half since he'd left, she'd persisted in her attempts to reconcile with him but had succeeded in provoking only one response—a handwritten letter mailed in an envelope with no return address in which he explained that he'd moved out of state specifically to get away from her. Despite this, April still felt it was possible that their marriage could be saved.

"How exactly do you envision that happening?" Ash asked her.

"I'll move wherever he is. I'm sure I could get a job at the local hospital." When he pointed out that her answer failed to address the real issue—that her ex-husband no longer wanted to be married to her—she insisted she could make him see that they were still right for each other. Yet when she went on to describe what she hoped their reconstructed relationship would look like, she talked only in vague platitudes, her voice devoid of emotion. Even when Ash got her to admit just how angry she was about the way her ex-husband had left her, she didn't actually *sound* angry. In fact, to Ash she seemed switched off in the same way she'd described her ex-husband had been when she'd confronted him in person after he'd left. When Ash remarked on it, she said that this was the way she'd always sounded, which made him wonder just how long her depression had been going on prior to the dissolution of her marriage.

"What made you decide to marry him in the first place?" he asked her after a moment.

"He asked," she answered simply. Though they'd known each other for only two months, she'd said yes before he could change his mind. "He was just so generous."

But almost immediately after they were married, his generosity seemed to evaporate. He began to abuse her verbally, calling her fat and stupid. She'd completed her master's degree in education and worked with physically disabled children at a local children's hospital, a job she loved. But he'd tell her she worked with disabled kids because they were "at her level." He seemed to have no interest in her needs or in pleasing her. She wanted children. He wouldn't even consider it.

She'd been able to refuse him nothing, however, no matter how immoral or unethical his request. She'd been reluctant to act against her principles, she said, but she'd found herself able to bear her own disgust more easily than his.

This imperative to avoid all conflict with him soon bled into other areas of her life. She began to dread crowds—a problem that had plagued her mother—and became shy and nervous in social situations.

Intrigued to learn that her mother had been agoraphobic, Ash began questioning April about her childhood. How had she grown up? What had her relationship with her parents been like? She told Ash she'd been an only child and had felt anxious as long as she could remember. Her father had worked at the loading docks of their small New England town and had hardly spoken to her at all during her childhood. Her mother, in contrast, had demanded that April remain at her side constantly. April would have to come home from school immediately every day to be with her—to buy her food, to cook her meals, to clean up around the house. She used April, in sum, as a shield against the world.

A shield, April said, that she held close only so she could get a better view of the things she wished to criticize: Why did April bite her nails so incessantly? Why did she suck her thumb until she was nine? Why didn't she try harder to make friends? Why was she so fat? April hated that she couldn't stand up to her mother, that she couldn't answer these criticisms. But no one ever knew it.

Despite her mother's constant belittling, April remained incapable of becoming angry with her.

"Why, do you think?" Ash asked her.

"I didn't want to make her even more critical of me than she already was. I still don't. There's only so much disapproval I can take."

"And her criticisms don't make you angry?"

She shrugged.

"Seems hard to imagine they wouldn't," Ash said.

"What good would getting angry do me?"

"Feelings are rarely that rational. It's hard to just turn them off."

"I don't think I'm having any feelings I turn off."

"Maybe. Or maybe you're turning them off so quickly you don't realize you're having them."

One corner of her mouth curved in a half-smile. "How would I be doing that if it's as hard as you say?"

"Touché," he said. "So here's another thought: If you won't let yourself get angry at your mother but you are actually angry at your mother, what *can* you do? Get angry at someone else. Someone safer."

"Who?"

"Yourself."

He reminded her she'd said to him in their first session that she knew she was overeating at least partially to punish herself. But now he was wondering if there was more to it, if she was feeling so much rage that she was overeating to *transform* herself.

"Into what?"

"Into the ugly beast your mother spent so much time deriding," Ash said. "The ugly beast your husband ran so fast and so far from. The ugly beast you believe yourself to be."

⌀

"She *could* be depressed just because she's overweight," Ash told me. "But what would that make the core delusion of the world of Hell? That you can only be happy if you're thin?"

"No, I agree, not broad enough," I said. "I do wonder, though, if it's connected to her low self-esteem."

Ash shook his head. "That doesn't seem likely either. Poor self-esteem may increase your risk for depression,[1] but people with healthy self-esteem get depressed all the time."

"True."

There was a pause.

"Okay, what about this," I said. "What if she isn't just afraid of her mother's disapproval? What if she's afraid her mother is going to *abandon* her? Maybe that's why she's never been able to get angry with her. Maybe she figures having a terrible mother is better than having no mother at all. And maybe that's the same reason she became suicidal when her husband left. Maybe having even a jerk for a husband is better than having no husband at all—because maybe she believes she can only be happy if she's loved."

Ash thought for a moment, then shook his head again. "For one thing, it's probably true that she can't be happy if *nobody* loves her. It's probably true for all of us. But even if it weren't, the belief that you can only be happy if you're loved can't be what creates the life-condition of Hell."

"Why not?" I asked him.

"Because people who feel loved suffer all the time," Ash said.

# The Difference Between Pain and Suffering

Where pain is defined as an unpleasant physical or emotional sensation, we would argue that suffering is defined as a *response* to pain, a way of *experiencing* pain. Specifically, it's the experience of being overwhelmed, or defeated, by pain. Indeed, studies argue that at a neurological level, pain and suffering are separate experiences. This is because pain actually arises from activity in two separate areas of the brain, one called the posterior insula, which registers the *sensation* of pain (its quality, intensity, and so on) and the other the anterior cingulate cortex, which registers the *unpleasantness* of pain. We know this because patients who've sustained damage to their anterior cingulate cortex will feel the sensation of pain *but not its unpleasantness.*[2] That is, astoundingly, they feel pain but aren't bothered by it. Suffering, we could therefore say, occurs when the intensity of pain becomes *so* unpleasant—when the activity in the anterior cingulate cortex becomes so great—that it becomes intolerable.

"But when does pain ever *not* cause suffering?" Ash asked.

"All the time," I said. "Are you suffering when you exercise? Or when you have your blood drawn? Or when you have a headache?"

"I guess it depends on the headache."

"Exactly. Not all pain causes us to suffer because not all pain is intolerable. Unpleasant, yes, by definition, but not intolerable."

What mostly makes the unpleasantness of pain intolerable is its intensity. On the other hand, the point at which we can no longer tolerate pain—meaning the intensity at which it starts to make us suffer—varies so much from person to person that pain intensity can't be what causes pain to become intolerable alone. (When researchers plunge the hands of test subjects into freezing cold water, the length of time the subjects are able to keep their hands submerged differs in some cases by as many as four minutes).[3] In fact, pain tolerance even varies from moment to moment in the same person. Studies show, for example, it's increased not only by a good mood,[4] but also by anger[5] and even cursing.[6] We're also better able to tolerate pain that's harmless compared to pain that represents tissue damage,[7] and pain that's caused accidentally compared to pain caused with an intent to harm.[8]

Interestingly, this seems to be true not just for physical pain but also for emotional pain. Perhaps this isn't too surprising, however, as the regions of the brain that physical and emotional pain activate are mostly the same.[9] This is probably why, for example, Tylenol, a pain reliever that acts on the central nervous system, alleviates not only the pain of a smashed finger *but also the pain of hurt feelings.*[10] In a very real sense, physical pain is just emotional pain mapped to a body part.

"Meaning the core delusion of Hell should be a belief that makes *both* types of pain intolerable," Ash said.

"Exactly," I said.

At the end of their session, April noticed a book lying on Ash's coffee table titled *Love's Executioner* by Irvin Yalom. She asked him if it were a manual for therapists with lovesick clients like her. Ash told her the book contained ten case histories from the author's psychiatry practice, and that he'd written it as a guide to healing for both patients and practitioners alike. April went out and bought a copy the next day.

That weekend at 2:00 AM, Ash received a page to a number he didn't recognize. He dialed it immediately. "Hello, this is Dr. Ash."

"You hate me!" a voice yelled at him. "Why didn't you tell me that was how you felt?"

"April—?" He could hear the sound of pouring rain in the background, the howl of wind.

"I read your book! I can't believe you feel that way about me!"

"I don't understand what you're talking about. Slow down. Tell me why you're upset."

"I hate you, too!" She was sobbing. "I just can't believe it. You're just like all the rest!"

Before he could reply, she hung up.

The next morning Ash pieced together what had happened. In one of the early chapters in his book, Yalom describes how revolted he'd been by of one of his female patient's morbid obesity. He even goes so far as to express mock outrage that overweight people would dare to impose their bodies on the rest of society, confessing he hates everything about them, "their absurd sidewise waddle, their absence of body contour, their shapeless, baggy dresses."[11] Once having admitted his prejudice, however, he writes about becoming determined to challenge it. Ash reasoned that April must have projected herself into the role of Yalom's patient—and Yalom's abhorrence of obesity onto him.

He tried to reach her several days in a row but never heard back. When she then failed to show up for her next appointment on time, he became seriously concerned. She'd always arrived early, and he feared her tardiness now was a message, that she was trying to tell him in a way she thought would be hurtful that she wanted to terminate therapy.

Ten minutes after their session was supposed to have started, however, he heard a rustling in the waiting room. He opened his office door and looked out, and there she was, sitting in a corner next to a pile of magazines, arms crossed in front of her, fuming. She looked like a petulant child, waiting, presumably, for him to come out and notice her.

He spent the next fifteen minutes coaxing her into his office. Once inside, he found her sullen and edgy, and for the first time since he'd known her, visibly angry. She wasn't so much angry at him anymore, she said. She'd spent the week sorting that out, her intellect arguing with her emotions until her anger had at last relinquished him as its target. But once uncorked, it was sprouting like blood from a slashed artery, splashing against everything near, and she had lost all ability to stem it. She felt like she wanted to kill someone—anyone—she told him, and it bewildered her.

Then, staring away from him, in a voice seething with rage, she began to list the faults of all the people who had populated the inner circle of her life. Her ex-husband was an alcoholic. Her father was cold and indifferent. Her mother was too needy. She spoke without hesitation or apology. She confessed the true extent of her negative feelings for each one of them in detail, feelings that had been buried so deeply and for so long that their existence took her by surprise. When she finally concluded her diatribe, announcing that she was "sick of being so nice all the time," Ash knew he'd witnessed a remarkable change. She'd finally begun to turn her anger outward, away from herself.

They spent the next few weeks processing what had happened and identifying appropriate ways for her to express her anger. The work was difficult as her anger often reoriented on him. But it was also productive, and soon she was reporting she'd become able to express her anger to others outside the confines of his office. She began to feel more in control of herself. Her weight steadied, and at long last her depression began to lift.

Then several weeks later she called to tell him that her mother had died. In between hysterical sobs, she told him she was afraid she was going to kill herself and desperately needed his help. "I don't have any more tricks up my sleeve," she wailed. "I'm done. There's nothing left. I don't know what to do."

"Tricks?" Ash asked. "What kind of tricks? Tricks for what?"

"To make someone love me."

# The True Cause of Suffering

"Because she doesn't believe she can," Ash announced.

"What, you mean make someone love her?" I asked.

"Yes! I can't believe I didn't think of this before. It's learned helplessness. The core delusion of the world of Hell is that you're powerless."

"Powerless," I repeated. Then: "Over what?"

"Over your problems. The core delusion of the world of Hell is that you believe you're powerless to solve your problems."

"What problems?"

"*All* of them!" Ash said. "Any of them. Any problem that matters."

"Any problem that—" I stopped. "Obesity, poor self-esteem, a loveless existence! Any problem that causes you pain. That's it! It's not a belief we have about pain that makes it intolerable, like whether or not we think it represents tissue damage. It's a belief we have about *ourselves*—that we're powerless to end it."

## *Withstanding Pain*

Recent research supports this idea. Jeroen Swart found that making competitive cyclists aware at every point along a racecourse how far they had to go to the finish line (letting them know not only *that* their pain would end but also *when*) enabled them to make greater efforts (tolerate more pain) than when they were prevented from knowing when the race would end. According to Swart, the brain is constantly calculating how much effort to make—how much pain it can tolerate—based on the expected amount of exercise (meaning pain) that remains.[12] Apparently, believing we have the power to *end* pain engenders a belief that we have the power to *tolerate* it.

And *believing* we have the power to tolerate pain, studies suggest, is what enables us to do so, which is then what prevents pain from making us suffer. One such study, for example, found that female undergraduates who were made to believe they could tolerate having their hands submerged in cold water were, in fact, able to do so far longer than subjects who were made to believe they couldn't.[13]

"But don't you think there's such a thing as pain that can't be tolerated?" Ash asked. "Pain so bad it makes you want to die?"

I nodded. "There clearly is. But just because people *don't* tolerate that kind of pain doesn't mean that they *can't*. It's certainly possible—maybe even likely—that past a certain level of intensity pain will always cause suffering. But if that's true, I wonder if it's because past a certain level of intensity we don't *believe* we can tolerate it."

"Except maybe we don't believe we can tolerate it because we *discover* we can't," Ash suggested.

"Except in some cases, people *have* been found to tolerate the kind of pain we're talking about." In a study by anesthesiologist Henry Beecher conducted during World War II, 75 percent of soldiers with severe injuries—injuries that in a civilian population required significant doses of narcotics—declined morphine entirely. The reason? According to Beecher, it was because of what their injuries meant—namely, *that they were going home.*[14] "The intensity of suffering," Beecher writes, "is largely determined by what pain means."

"So maybe, depending on what we believe pain means, our capacity to tolerate pain can be even *greater* than our capacity to feel it," I said.

## Solving Every Problem

"So April is in pain because she has no one to love her," Ash said. "But what makes her suffer is her belief that she can't find anyone who will—her belief that she's powerless solve the problem of a loveless existence. Which then prevents her from believing she can tolerate the pain a loveless existence causes her."

I nodded. "In fact, take any problem—a painful breakup, the loss of a job, a diagnosis of cancer—and imagine stirring up the belief—the certain knowledge—that it's solvable. You'll still be in pain—even terrible pain—but will you suffer? I don't think so. Not as we've defined it. Your pain won't overwhelm you. It won't defeat you."

In fact, a number of studies support this hypothesis. In one, people with a pessimistic self-explanatory style, characterized by a belief in one's powerlessness, were more likely to become depressed in response to negative life events.[15] In another, a belief in a concerned God increased the likelihood that depressed patients would respond to treatment specifically because that belief reduced feelings of powerlessness.[16] A third showed that the more powerless we feel, the less likely we are to respond to antidepressant medication.[17]

"Okay, but how is believing you're powerless to solve a problem always a delusion?" Ash asked. "Some problems really *are* impossible—or nearly impossible—to solve. Some cancers can't be cured. A truly loveless existence *is* unendurable. And the statistics on achieving long-term weight loss are abysmal. What if April can't lose the weight?"

"Without a doubt she'd need to summon up a greater determination than you or I would need to. But *can* April lose weight? Is it *possible*? Clearly, yes. Other people have done it. It's just really, really hard. *Impossible* is jumping off a building and floating into the sky."

"You really think there's no such thing as a problem that can't be solved?" Ash asked.

I thought for a moment. "I think there's no such thing as suffering that can't be ended."

"Really? How about the suffering that comes from knowing you're going to die? How do you end that?"

"You don't think it's possible to face death without being afraid?"

Ash paused. "I think it is for some people."

"Well, doesn't that solve the real problem of death?"

"No. You solve the real problem of death by not dying."

I smirked but shook my head. "You solve the real problem of death when the idea of dying no longer makes you suffer."

"So your answer is . . . what? Acceptance?"

"There's a lot of power in acceptance," I said.

"So you're saying *everyone's* pain can *always* be tolerated in *all* circumstances? That there's *always* a way to avoid suffering?"

"I don't know how we'd ever be able to prove that. I guess I'm saying I agree that believing we don't have the power to solve a problem that's causing us pain is the fundamental cause of suffering. But being denied the power to solve a problem that's causing us pain doesn't *always* cause suffering because sometimes we figure out that we don't need to solve the problem at all. Think about what happened to me with Melissa."

Melissa had been my first girlfriend and first great love. When she ended our relationship at the end of my second year of medical school, I fell into a severe depression that lasted months. I was convinced that the only way I could end my suffering and become happy again was to get her back. But that's not what happened. Instead, I had the sudden insight that I didn't need her to love me to be happy at all—that the only person whose love I needed was my own. I solved my problem, in other words, not the way I thought I needed to solve it and wanted to solve it, but through the acquisition of wisdom.

"Meaning you don't have to be able to solve a problem the way you think you do to stop it from making you suffer," I said. "So I guess what I'm saying is that the core delusion of the world of Hell is *the belief that we're powerless to end our suffering.*"

"So if a problem is making me suffer," Ash said, "the only way I can be happy *without* solving it is by ceasing to believe I *need* to solve it? Or that I need to solve it in a particular way?"

"That's it. Once you realize—once you *accept*—that your problem can be solved in another way—even a way you hate—your suffering will stop. Think about a professional athlete who blows a championship game and becomes depressed. There's no way, of course, he can solve that problem the way he wants. He can't go back in time and win the game. But he can solve the problem another way. He can let go of his belief that to be happy he needed to have won the game in the first place."

"So we're saying there are two ways out of Hell. One, we figure out a way to solve the problem that's causing us pain. Two, we figure out how we don't need to solve the problem at all. As you did with Melissa, we figure out how to solve a *different* problem that makes solving the first problem unnecessary."

"Yes," I said.

"Well," Ash said, "that second one's the thing, isn't it?"

Ash met with April for an emergency session the day after she'd called him with the news about her mother and found, to his relief, that her desire to kill herself had been only fleeting. But she reported feeling more depressed and anxious than she'd been in weeks.

"Depressed I understand," Ash said. "But why anxious?"

Her right leg jackhammering, she answered, "I don't know."

"People feel anxious when they feel unsafe in some way. So why would your mother's death make you feel unsafe?"

April nodded. "That's exactly how I feel," she replied, her leg still bouncing. "Unsafe."

"Can you say why?" Ash asked her again.

"She loved me. In her own way, she did. And now she's gone."

"And without her here to love you . . . ?"

She dropped her gaze to the floor. "I don't think anyone else ever will."

Ash nodded. "Why not?"

She shrugged feebly. "Who would want to love this?"

Ash sensed they'd come to a turning point in April's therapy. Despite her newfound ability to express her anger, she had yet to acknowledge that her self-worth had been constructed almost entirely out of her belief that her mother had loved and needed her. Now, with no one left whose love and attention could validate that worth (she'd long ago stopped talking to her father), her self-esteem had crashed like a plane shorn of its wings. Ash didn't think she would ever be granted a better opportunity—or more motivation—to confront her insecurities head-on.

"April, do you see the irony here?" Ash asked. "Your mother's death has taken away your ability to value yourself, but it was the way your mother treated you while she was alive that prevented you from learning to value yourself in the first place."

"Everything she said about me was true."

"What, exactly? The way you always put the needs of others before yours? The way you've done your best to live up to every demand your mother placed on you without complaining, no matter how unreasonable those demands were, because you think it's good to try to help people when you can? The way you've spent your entire career working with handicapped children, trying to teach them things that make it easier for them to get along in the world? The way you tell me you want to give up all the time, but you never do?" He held her gaze firmly. "April, if I wasn't describing you but some other person instead, wouldn't you say she sounded like someone who deserved your admiration?"

It was a sham, marching out this list of her positive qualities to prove she was worthy of admiration—not because she wasn't all those good things, but because her value as a human being couldn't of course be calculated by subtracting the sum of her weaknesses from her strengths and classifying her as worthy of esteem only if the balance were positive. But because she was so entrenched in the distorted view that her failings were evidence of her worthlessness, he thought countering with examples of her successes seemed a reasonable means to start her down a path toward healthier thinking.

"I tried to please my mom because I wanted her approval, not because I thought it made me a good person. And I work with handicapped children because I like them, not because I'm helping them. And if I haven't given up it's because you're a really great therapist and much more important to me than you should be, and I don't want to disappoint *you*."

Ash sighed as he watched his strategy fail. An amateur mistake, he realized, thinking he could change her view of herself just by arguing her into it.

"I'm the last person in the world you have to worry about disappointing," he said.

April shrugged, her expression blank. Wrong, Ash thought to himself. Wrong, wrong, wrong. He needed to try something else. He knew at some point he needed to explore the significance of his own importance to her, but he also felt a sense of urgency to offer her practical advice about managing her acute crisis. He thought for a few moments while her gaze circled his office.

"April," he asked suddenly, "why do you think you can't lose weight?"

She glanced back at him with an irritated frown. "It's not like . . . like . . . quitting smoking," she said. "I can't *give up* eating. I have to control it. That's *so* much harder."

"Harder, yes. But not impossible. Other people have done it."

"Is this your way of trying to make me feel *better*?"

"I'm trying to suggest something. I know you're grieving over your mom. But I don't think the reason you're suffering is because you feel like there's no one left to love you. I think the reason you're suffering—the reason you're anxious and depressed—is because you feel powerless to do anything about it."

April snorted. "Gosh, why don't you tell me what you *really* think?"

Rather than feeling dismayed by her sarcasm, he was actually encouraged by her feistiness. Engaged was far better than indifferent. "What I really think, April, is that the reason you want someone to love you so badly is because you don't love yourself. And I wonder if you're depressed because you feel powerless to fix *that*."

April looked down at the ground, despondent. "I'm such a cliché."

"Look, if the reason you think no one will ever love you—the reason you don't love yourself—is at least partly because of the way you look, maybe it's time to take on that problem with everything you've got. You've already stopped trying to punish yourself by overeating—don't forget the progress you've made!—so now maybe you actually have a chance to succeed. I know losing weight is incredibly hard, but ask yourself: if you were really going to get serious about it, what exactly would you need to do?"

She looked back up at him. "Eat less. Exercise more."

Ash nodded. "Okay. Then let's figure out how we can get you to do that."

## Understanding with Your Life

"I was just thinking if she could only experience herself as capable of accomplishing *something*," Ash said. "Especially something so closely tied to her self-esteem."

"It's an intriguing idea," I said. "You can't just *decide* you have the power to solve your problems. You have to become convinced you do—and what better way to become convinced you do than by actually solving a problem that's causing you pain?"

"You know, she told me she looks in the mirror literally fifty times a day."

"Why?"

"She's trying to figure out what angle makes her look the thinnest."

"Wow."

"Yeah."

"Well," I said, "I think your strategy is a good one. She needs to be confronted with evidence that she's not powerless. She needs to believe it the way she believes the sun will rise in the East. With all her heart. With her life."

"With her *life*?" Ash asked.

"It's a Buddhist term. It means with total conviction. It means thinking and feeling and behaving in accordance with your understanding. For example, we don't just understand the law of gravity intellectually. We believe it in a way that prevents us from jumping off buildings. With our lives." To believe something intellectually, I said, was to have confidence that it was true. To believe something with your life, on the other hand, was to have an emotional and behavioral response to that confidence. "You might, for instance, believe that smoking is bad for you intellectually—meaning, you have confidence that it's true. But you can't be said to really understand it—to understand it with your life—unless that belief causes you to quit."

"So maybe this will work," Ash said. "Maybe if she starts to lose weight she'll begin to believe with her life that she can solve her other problems, too, and her depression will start to improve. Maybe she'll convince *us* that believing you can't end your suffering is the fundamental cause of depression."

"Well," I said, "at least the fundamental cause of *some* depression."

## The True Cause of Depression

Though all depression causes suffering, not all suffering causes depression. We can suffer, or feel overwhelmed by pain, without experiencing the classic symptoms of major depressive disorder. And though we're arguing that believing we can't end our suffring is *often* the fundamental cause of depression,[18] we're not arguing that it's *always* the fundamental cause of depression.

Two other things cause depression besides the belief that we can't end our suffering. Studies show that differences in the genes that build the parts of the brain responsible for generating our core affect—the brain's *machinery of mood generation* (principally, as we'll discuss, the hypothalamus and the hippocampus,[19] but also the anterior cingulate cortex,[20] the ventral pallidum,[21] and the amygdala,[22] to name a few others)—lead to differences in mood vulnerability. Thus, variations in genes lead to differences in the risk of becoming depressed in response to stressful life events,[23] and even to differences in the risk of suicide.[24] So just as some people are born with poor athletic ability, some people are born with a mood-generating machine that does a poor job of maintaining a good mood, or positive core affect. They have a mood-generating machine that's *malformed*. On the other hand, the performance of even the best mood-generating machine could deteriorate as a result of a disease (a brain tumor, a stroke, hypothyroidism), a medication (beta blockers, steroids), hormonal fluctuations (from premenstrual syndrome), inflammation,[25] changes in gut bacteria,[26] a poor diet,[27] or factors as yet unknown. In cases like these, depression is caused by a mood-generating machine that's experiencing a *malfunction*.

Unfortunately, we often can't distinguish between depression caused by the belief that we're powerless to end our suffering and depression caused by a malformed or malfunctioning mood-generating machine. This is because when the cause of our depression is that we feel powerless to end our suffering, we often don't know that's why we're depressed. We often discover the truth only in retrospect, after we resolve the problem that's making us suffer—or the problem resolves itself—and our depression lifts.

Even if we're blind to its cause, however, the severity of our suffering will correspond to the urgency with which we believe our problem *needs* to be solved. Meaning we don't suffer or become depressed when we face just *any* problem we believe we can't solve. It has to be a problem we believe we *need* to solve to be happy.

In the worst case, when we find ourselves trapped in what seems like suffering without limit—in severe major depression—because the problem we believe we can't solve is one upon which we believe our entire happiness depends, we may have a hard time even recognizing ourselves. We don't just come to view our future as bleak; we become incapable of seeing how it could ever be otherwise. In that life state the capacity to self-reflect vanishes, and our ability to consider evidence that belies our belief that the future is hopeless falters under the weight of our impaired thinking. We refuse to believe any evidence that contradicts our hopeless outlook in the same way a patient with schizophrenia might refuse to believe any evidence that contradicts his belief that the FBI is spying on him. We may be unable not only to stop feeling bad but also to imagine ever again feeling good.[28] Depressed mood, sadness, hopelessness, impaired self-esteem, mental and even physical sluggishness, a lack of interest in pleasure,[29] suicidal thinking, even anger—all symptoms that flare to life when we're trapped in the deepest parts of the life-condition of Hell.

"Anger is interesting," Ash said. "That's not one of the traditional features of major depression."

"I know of at least one study suggesting anger is far more common in major depression than we realize, especially in men."[30]

"At ourselves," Ash guessed, "for being powerless?"

I nodded. "If nothing else," I said, "the world of Hell is rage turned inward."

⟪⟫

"I can't fucking do it!"

Ash winced. He didn't think he'd ever seen April this angry. When he'd held his office door open for her at the beginning of the session, she'd marched past him without a word of greeting or even a sideways glance, sat down in her chair, folded her arms across her chest, and fixed her gaze to the floor. He'd taken his place across from her, and after a moment bent his face down toward hers at a questioning angle in an exaggerated attempt to make eye contact. "You seem upset," he'd said finally, at which point she'd taken him by surprise by cursing in front of him for the first time since he'd known her.

"What exactly can't you do?" Ash asked her.

"Anything!"

"Okay, catch me up-to-date. I take it our plan for you to walk to work every day didn't work?" They'd decided last time that was to have been her only objective for the week.

"No, I did it." Abruptly, the anger drained out of her voice, replaced by a dull resignation. "But so what? I didn't lose any weight." She sighed. "And even if I did . . . I mean, even if . . . even if I was already thin, why would anyone want to be with me? It doesn't matter. I'm still the most disgusting person on the planet."

"That's the depression talking," Ash insisted evenly. "You've been here before, April. You know not to believe every voice that's in your head."

"Well, the depression is right!" Tears appeared in the corners of her eyes.

Ash leaned toward her. "April, I know right now you can't imagine that your pain will ever stop, that you'll ever be able to solve any of your problems, or that you'll ever be happy. But those are all feelings *created* by your life-condition. You're in Hell. Your thinking is distorted by *definition*. You can't trust it." This, he knew, was how people could become utterly convinced that suicide was a good option, that their loved ones would actually be better off if they were dead. "Your judgment, your outlook, your feelings—they're all so completely different when you're depressed compared to when you're not that you might as well consider yourself an entirely different *person*. When you're depressed, it's like you were never happy at all. Like the memory of having been happy, of having had that happy person's thoughts and feelings, belongs to someone else. But April, that happy person is literally only one moment away from this one."

"I miss my mom," April suddenly burst out.

"I know."

"It's like my insides have been ripped out. I'm not sure I'm going to make it."

"I know," Ash repeated. "I know."

"I don't want to talk to anyone. I don't want to see anyone. I don't want anyone to see me. I didn't even want to come here. I just want to stop . . . being."

Ash paused to wonder if he'd too quickly discounted the likelihood that April's depression came from an inherited tendency toward mood vulnerability. She had, after all, been depressed for most of her life, suggesting that her depression was at least partly a result of a malformed mood-generating machine.

Being accurately able to identify the cause of a depression is, of course, often crucial. If a patient is depressed because she's floridly hypothyroid, that patient needs thyroid hormone, not increased confidence in her ability to solve problems. On the other hand, when Ash helped patients find the confidence they needed to solve problems that were, they believed, serious threats to their happiness, that confidence didn't just improve their depression—it resolved it. He'd also seen many patients through the years who did well until they encountered one problem too many—one problem they didn't feel they could solve—and who then found themselves feeling that they couldn't solve any. Sometimes, interestingly, that would then cause them to lose sight of exactly which problem had been responsible for making them feel overwhelmed by them all.

This made him realize that believing yourself capable of accomplishing only *one* of the tasks necessary to solve a problem you believed was an obstacle to your happiness would do little to alleviate your suffering. You needed to believe you could accomplish them all, which brought his thinking back to the unhappy fact that some problems probably couldn't be solved. What if April really didn't have the ability to lose weight, to find love, or to improve her self-esteem? Was he right, then, to encourage her to believe that she could? Should he instead have begun working with her on accepting herself as she was, on smashing through the delusion that she could only be happy if she solved the problems she thought she needed to solve in the way she wanted to solve them?

For even if she did lose weight, what guarantee did she have that it would bring her love? And even if it did bring her love, when had he ever seen that improve a patient's self-esteem? Then again, maybe losing weight alone would improve her self-esteem enough to resolve her depression. Alternatively, what if she both lost weight *and* found love but experienced no improvement in her self-esteem? Would her depression lift then? Or what if, he thought suddenly, she needed to solve an entirely different problem that they hadn't even identified?

"April, last time you seemed genuinely hopeful about getting control over your weight," he said. "I know you're disappointed that you haven't. But now I'm wondering—even if you lost all the weight you wanted, do you think it would make you happy?"

April opened her mouth to speak—almost certainly to say yes, Ash thought—but then shrugged instead. "I honestly don't know anymore."

"Me either. Which makes me wonder what *other* problems you feel you can't solve."

"What, you mean, like, what else don't I think I can do?"

Ash nodded.

"How about everything?"

"I think it might be useful if we made a list."

Tears appeared in the corners of her eyes again. "It feels like it *is* everything." She put up her fingers one by one. "I can't lose weight. I can't get my husband back. I can't find a new one. I can't stop feeling like I'm a worthless piece of shit no matter how much I keep telling myself that feeling worthless is stupid—which of course only makes me feel worthless *and* stupid."

"That *is* a lot. But is that really it? Is there anything else at all?"

"Isn't that enough?"

"More than enough," Ash agreed. "But I think it's important that we iden-tify everything that could possibly be causing you to feel depressed. You'd be surprised how often people don't realize the real reason."

April looked away for a moment. Then she looked back at him and said, "How about this: I can't convince my mom I'm not worthless. Because now she's dead."

"So I think she went into a tailspin when her mom died not just because, you know, her mom died," Ash said, "but because it made her feel like she'd lost her last chance to be anointed a lovable person."

"We always thought her mom's opinion of her was the lever that controlled her self-esteem," I pointed out.

"*We* knew it. Now *she* knows it. I don't know if that's why—but she's less depressed now than I've ever seen her."

"She's okay knowing her mom died thinking she was worthless?"

"I'm not sure her mom actually thought that. I'm not sure even *April* thinks her mom thought that. I think April just felt constantly criticized and wanted to hear her mom say something just once that made her feel good."

"So why would she be better now?" I asked.

"I'm only guessing, but I think fully realizing—you know, like you said, with her *life*—just how badly she wanted her mom to say she was worth something made April realize just how much control over her self-esteem she'd let her mom have. Which I think helped her to see that even if she didn't have the power to control her mom's opinion of her, she did have the power to control how much that opinion mattered to her."

"Not necessarily—"

"Not necessarily," Ash agreed, "but in her case, realizing it was at least pos-sible seems to have made it so. I don't think she'd say it's *easy* for her not to care what her mom thought of her, but she really does seem to care less. Or, at least, less often."

"So what you're really saying is that she solved one problem by solving another—the other being not only a problem she *could* solve but also the problem she really *needed* to solve to be happy. That she cared too much about what her mother thought of her."

"I guess I am."

"So is she feeling more confident now about losing weight?" I asked.

"In fact," Ash said, "she's lost ten pounds."

## Key Points

- Hell is defined as the life-condition of suffering.

- Pain is an unpleasant physical or emotional sensation and is considered to be wholly separate from suffering, which is defined as the experience of being overwhelmed, or defeated, by pain.

- When trapped in the life-condition of Hell we live in a constant state of despondency. Feelings of hopelessness and helplessness fuel an inwardly directed rage that's often projected outward toward others. Pessimism and negativity are the watchwords that define the way we view all experiences.

- The cause of suffering is believing that we're powerless to solve a problem we think is preventing us from being happy.

- To end suffering, we can either figure out a way to solve the problem we believe is preventing us from being happy or we can figure out how to be happy without solving the problem.

- The core delusion of the world of Hell is that we're powerless to end our suffering.

# 2

# Hunger

*There are two tragedies in life. One is to lose your heart's desire. The other is to gain it.*
—George Bernard Shaw

Hunger is defined as the life-condition of desire. Simply desiring something, however, isn't what traps us in the world of Hunger. What traps us in the world of Hunger is obsession.

Desire itself, we should be careful to note, is neither good nor bad. It's merely the engine that makes our lives move. Whether it does so in a positive or negative direction depends entirely on what we desire and how that desire causes us to behave. Few people would consider the desire to live a principled life, for example, to be a bad thing. But when even a virtuous desire intensifies to the point of obsession—whether for a person, a thing, a state of mind, or anything else—we're more likely to convince ourselves that the ends justify the means and act in a way that causes grievous harm. History is filled with examples of people so consumed by their desires that they disregarded all moral concerns and became monsters.

On the other hand, sometimes obsessing over our desires enables us to move beyond a devastating failure when we might otherwise have given up. To achieve greatness, some degree of obsessiveness may even be necessary.

45

Yet even when it leads us to greatness, obsession exacts a price: it drives all other concerns into the background, leaving us uninterested in, or even dissatisfied with, what we already have. This in turn only enhances our sense of desperation to achieve our desire, as if our failure to attain what we want is a mistake we can't afford to make.

Yet, ironically, when we're trapped in the world of Hunger, attaining our desires does little to satisfy us as the joy of acquisition or accomplishment fades almost as quickly as it appears. This in turn creates a sense of emptiness that pushes us on toward the next thing, the next obsession, which then captures our thinking entirely, leaving our previous desire, which consumed us only just moments before, nearly forgotten.

⤜⤏

Ash had been telling me about a patient he believed was from the world of Hunger named Patrick, who'd come to see him because of severe anxiety.

"If I could just get over this one thing, I'm sure I'd be fine," Patrick told Ash at their first meeting as he slumped down in his chair. "Everything else is great."

"Get over what?" Ash asked him.

Patrick stared at the scene outside Ash's window for a few moments. "I know she's going to leave me," he answered finally. "She's trying to be subtle, but I know what's really going on. She's cheating on me. I'm sure of it."

His expression grew sullen, and he began to rock back and forth in his chair, gnawing at what was left of his already-mangled nails.

"Maybe you should start from the beginning," Ash said.

Patrick said he'd come in because of his growing concern that his girlfriend was about break up with him. He'd been having trouble sleeping, sometimes for the entire night, and couldn't focus during the day. When he wasn't with her, he had to fight with himself constantly to avoid calling her to find out where she was and what she was doing.

"How long have you been dating?" Ash asked.

"A little over a week. But we've seen each other every day," he added quickly in response to Ash's surprised expression. "I've never felt this way about anyone else in my life. She's just so beautiful. She could be—and I don't want to jinx this—but she could be the one. That's what scares me so much."

That Patrick had developed such a powerful attachment to someone in so short a time made Ash wonder what was compelling him to seek love so obsessively. Fear of loneliness? Poor self-esteem? Fear of missing out? Before Ash made any suggestions about how to achieve long-lasting relief from anxiety, he preferred in general to pin down its root cause as definitively as he could. Did it rotate around a specific issue or set of issues, or was it more generalized, not connected to any one particular thing? Many therapists made symptom management their main focus, often recommending behavior modification or medication to reduce anxiety quickly regardless of its cause. But Ash had learned that helping patients control anxiety too well at the outset often reduced or even eliminated the main force driving them to investigate the reason they felt it. So while he never wanted to leave anyone incapacitated by worry, neither did he want to resolve his patients' worry too quickly.

Ash's first step, therefore, was to assess each patient's level of distress. Did Patrick possess sufficient coping skills to prevent his anxiety from overwhelming him? Patrick said he wasn't sure. But he agreed that seeking the central cause of his problem was a good idea. How else was he going to solve it once and for all? "Sometimes my anxiety is so intense," he said, "it nearly stops me from functioning."

"Are you feeling that way now?" Ash asked.

"No. It helps to talk about it. It's good for me to get it out in the open."

"Good," Ash said, and then suggested they start by exploring the context that was triggering his anxiety, promising to make himself available by phone if Patrick found himself suddenly unable to cope with it. If Patrick started experiencing full-blown panic, Ash told him he'd have one of his psychiatry colleagues prescribe an anti-anxiety medication. Patrick readily agreed.

"So what's her name?" Ash asked.

"Angie."

They'd met three weeks earlier at a painting class. Even as she started setting up her easel next to his, Patrick had felt the first stirrings of chemistry between them. To his eye, she looked far younger than her twenty-five years, which he found titillating. By the time the class ended, she'd agreed to go out to dinner with him. By the end of that first date, they were back in his apartment having sex. Patrick told Ash he knew then that he was in love.

Within a few days, however, he'd begun to suspect Angie was cheating on him. When Ash asked what had triggered his concern, Patrick told him she'd stopped answering his calls on the first ring. When Ash then asked how this amounted to evidence she was cheating, Patrick replied he was worried she wasn't able to answer immediately "because she was giving some guy a blow job."

"You think she can't answer you because she's performing oral sex on someone else every single time you call?"

Patrick sighed. "I'm just so bad at this."

"What?"

"Relationships. Trust." He waved his arm dismissively. "She swears nothing is going on. I yell at her and tell her I don't believe her. I make her cry. Then I cry." He seemed suddenly exhausted. "I don't know why I do it. I know I'm being totally ridiculous, but I can't stop myself."

Ash was encouraged to find Patrick had at least some insight into the inappropriateness of his behavior. "Can you imagine anything she could do to make you believe she's telling the truth?"

Patrick thought for a moment and then shook his head.

"Do you think she'd be willing to come in to therapy with you?"

Patrick's eyes widened. "Actually, yeah!" Angie was already "sick to death of his jealousy" and desperate for him to stop hounding her, he said, so she had good reason to agree. Also, Patrick added in a breaking voice, if Ash had a chance to get a read on Angie, he might then find a way to convince Patrick once and for all that his suspicion she was cheating on him was nothing more than a paranoid delusion, something he knew in his head but still couldn't quite convince his heart.

## Anxiety as an Event

Where Hell is considered the world of suffering, Hunger is considered the world of pain. It's painful, after all, to be separated from a desired attachment. The intensity of our desire may be so minor we don't realize it *is* pain, but desire, at its core, is an ache.

Desiring something also frequently creates the worry that we won't get it. But anxiety itself isn't generated by a core delusion. As Ash told April, it's generated (when not by a neurologic abnormality) by the perception that we're unsafe in some way[1]—whether because our mother just died leaving us alone in the world, or we think we're about to be abandoned by a girlfriend.

Though anxiety is, of course, a feeling, it could also be considered an event—like a car accident or a marriage proposal. This means that anxiety, like any event, will affect us in keeping with the core delusion it stirs up.

"So," I said, "if your anxiety draws your attention more to the belief that you can't solve the problem that's causing it, you won't believe you'll be able to end your anxiety, so you won't feel able to tolerate it. And if you don't feel able to tolerate it, your anxiety becomes a pain that makes you suffer, thrusting you into the life-condition of Hell. Which is why for people like April anxiety is paralyzing."

"But if you're Patrick," Ash said, "and you believe that you *can* solve the problem that's causing your anxiety, then your anxiety isn't paralyzing. It's motivating."

"Meaning it motivates you to solve the problem that's causing it," I agreed.

"So maybe *that's* the reason we become obsessed in Hunger with getting what we want," Ash said. "Because getting what we want *ends our worry that we won't get it.* Maybe the core delusion of the world of Hunger is that to be happy you need to be rid of anxiety."

"Except that would mean anxiety is what drives every desire anyone would ever have."

"Every *obsessive* desire—yes. Anxiety *is* incredibly common. It's not a bad guess."

"I'm not disagreeing that people go to incredible lengths to avoid anxiety," I said. "But just because you're obsessed with something doesn't mean you're worried about being denied it. Not everyone trapped in the world of Hunger is anxious. Not by a long shot."

"Name an obsession you think *isn't* driven by anxiety," Ash said.

I thought for a moment.

"Stamp collecting."

Angie was every bit as beautiful as Patrick had described, with shoulder-length light brown hair and the toned body of a dancer. As Patrick held Ash's office door open for her, he seemed to swell with pride. He chuckled with an awkward, giddy excitement as he introduced her, as if he'd accomplished something important by connecting himself to so attractive a woman. He evinced none of the anxiety that had been evident in their first session.

"I really appreciate your coming in, Angie," Ash said. "I know this is a bit unusual."

"Whatever I can do to help," Angie replied. She seemed confident and comfortable, as self-possessed as Patrick seemed sophomoric.

Patrick beamed and hugged her with one arm. "Isn't she great?"

After they were seated, Ash dug right in. "In the two weeks you've known each other, Angie, how often would you say Patrick has become jealous?"

"A lot," Patrick interjected.

"Dr. Ash, no joke," Angie said, "I probably spend at least two hours a day trying to convince Patrick I'm not cheating on him."

Patrick stroked Angie's hand awkwardly and then said, "Patrick's sorry, baby. He's such a little jerk. He trusts you. Yes, he does. Yes—he—does." He sounded like a parent cooing at an infant. He lifted her hand and rubbed the back of it over the tip of his nose playfully.

Even more startling was Angie's reply. In the same singsong voice, she said, "Angie wuvs her widdle Patrick. Yes, I *do*. Yes, I *do*."

"I wuv you so much," Patrick said.

"I wuv you more."

Ash held up his hand. "Hold up a minute, guys." They both looked at him. "Do you realize you're both talking like . . . uh . . ."

"Infants," Angie said, embarrassed, as if she'd just realized he was still in the room. "Yeah."

"It's a thing we do," Patrick explained. "Baby talk."

"Baby talk?"

"Yeah," said Patrick.

"Why?" Ash asked.

"We know it's weird," Patrick acknowledged. "But it makes us feel better."

"Feel better about what?"

"It just makes us relax," Angie offered. She looked at Patrick expectantly. "I don't know, not take things so . . . seriously?"

"When do you usually do this?"

Angie thought for a moment. "When we're making up after a fight."

"After sex," Patrick added.

Ash's first thought was that this represented a bizarre form of regression. He could readily imagine why it might happen after they fought, especially if Angie was as receptive to it in their personal lives as she appeared to be in his office. What better way to mitigate the potentially fearsome consequences of conflict than to collude in making their fights appear as if they were occurring between children?

It might also explain, Ash thought, why Patrick had sought professional help. Regression is one of the most primitive defense mechanisms and is therefore easily overwhelmed. Ash wondered if when Angie wasn't present in Patrick's immediate environment to regress with him, his fear of being abandoned was free to mushroom—and apparently often did—into nearly full-blown panic.

Ash thought he might learn something about Patrick's fear of abandonment if he could convince them to reenact an argument that Patrick's jealousy had triggered. But despite his prodding, neither of them felt comfortable enough to do so. So he spent the remainder of the session using direct questioning to tease out the thoughts and feelings Patrick experienced that would lead him to accuse Angie of cheating. But this approach proved fruitless. With Angie present, Patrick simply had no access to his jealous nature. By the end of the session, Ash felt stymied and frustrated.

Patrick, on the other hand, felt Angie's presence had been of tremendous benefit and told Ash he wanted her to attend all his therapy sessions. This brought Ash to the only insight he was to have in the session: Patrick had wanted Angie to come to therapy for the same reason he would pull her into acts of regression—namely, to provide him relief from his anxiety.

Ash countered by proposing that he continue to see Patrick alone while agreeing to remain open to inviting Angie back if it seemed purposeful. When Patrick started to protest, Angie herself began to question the value of her involvement.

She thought Patrick's usually incisive insight had been dulled by her presence and concluded that he would likely get more out of therapy without her there. Overwhelmed, Patrick expressed his love for her several more times and then agreed that she knew best.

Two days later, Patrick phoned Ash to tell him that Angie had broken up with him. "What am I going to do!" he sobbed.

"Take a deep breath," Ash said. "Tell me what happened."

In a trembling voice, Patrick told him that Angie had announced "she couldn't handle his jealousy anymore." Patrick was certain now that he'd driven her away for good. He loved her so much he was going out of his mind. This was a pain he couldn't bear one more minute, an ache he felt along every limb, a throbbing in every joint.

Ash offered to see him immediately. But to his surprise, Patrick declined. "I don't want to talk about it anymore," he said suddenly.

Ash was concerned that Patrick's refusal represented another primitive defense mechanism—denial—and pressed him to come anyway. But Patrick remained adamant. "I'll be okay. It's just par for the course for my sorry ass. Maybe I could come in next week after I've had a chance to chill out a little."

When further entreaties failed to change his mind, Ash made Patrick promise to call if he felt like doing anything impulsive, hoping he was hearing more fatigue in Patrick's sullen voice than a desire to end his pain by ending himself. Patrick agreed, and they scheduled their next session for the following week.

But at the appointed time, Patrick failed to appear. Ash called his home phone and cell phone several times but to no avail. The next morning, without a word from him still, Ash began to worry in earnest. Though a suicide contract was often effective at preventing patients who struggled with depression from killing themselves, it was far less effective with histrionic patients whose suicide attempts were more impulsive.

Later that day, however, when Ash walked into his waiting room in between patient appointments, he found Patrick sitting in a chair reading a magazine.

Ash stared at him. "What happened to you yesterday?"

"What do you mean?"

"We had an appointment at one o'clock."

"We did? Are you sure? I'm sorry." He sounded genuinely apologetic. "I thought it was for today."

Ash was completely nonplussed. "No, it was yesterday. I was actually pretty worried about you. You sounded pretty upset last time we spoke."

"I'm fine," Patrick replied dismissively. "I'm totally over that situation. Angie just wasn't the one, you know? But I've got something totally amazing to tell you that you won't believe! I've met the real woman of my dreams. She's engaged to another guy—but not for long. Her name is Lily."

## The Need for Validation

"You've got to be kidding," I said. "He gets over Angie—the love of his life —in one week?"

"He's looking for love," Ash replied. "It doesn't matter who he gets it from. It's the love he wants; the person is incidental."

"That *does* actually sound like the world of Hunger."

"I'm definitely beginning to see how it's not such a fun place to be."

"And the baby talk?" I asked. "You said you thought he was doing it to make their fights seem less serious?"

"Or to get her to see *him* as a baby."

"Why would he want to do that?"

"I'm not sure. To send the signal that he's dependent on her? To make her feel responsible for him? I mean, think about it. What woman would leave a helpless baby?"

"What kind of man wants a woman to think he's helpless?"

Ash shrugged. "Maybe he believes he can only be happy if he has someone to take care of him."

"Or someone to protect him?"

"Or maybe just someone to be with him. Maybe the core delusion of the world of Hunger is that to be happy you need to be in a relationship."

"But how would believing that to be happy you need to be in a relationship cause you to become obsessed with things that aren't related to relationships?" I asked.

Ash frowned. "Right. It wouldn't."

"On the other hand: looking for love and terrified to lose it. Sound like someone else we know?"

"April," Ash agreed.

I nodded. "So maybe *that's* the explanation for the baby talk. Keep things light and silly not to make her think he's helpless but to hide his insecurities." As we'd both observed in our respective practices, people with poor self-esteem typically derived their sense of worth from the value other people assigned them. I wondered if this was why even though Patrick had been terribly hurt by Angie's rejection, he felt compelled to place himself at risk for being rejected again by pursuing Lily. Perhaps his need to find someone to validate him was so strong that it overpowered his fear of being judged worthless, compelling him to form relationships that filled him with dread.

⚜

Less clear to us was the reason Patrick might be struggling with low self-esteem at all. Ash wondered if he was using his romantic relationships to rewrite the ending of some critical scene, or series of scenes, from his past, ones in which he'd been denied the regard he seemed to be so desperately seeking now. So at their next visit, he told Patrick he wanted to construct a genogram.

"What's that?" Patrick asked.

Ash explained that a genogram is a family tree that documents a comprehensive history of relevant facts about immediate and extended family members. It includes everything from mental illnesses, addictions, and divorces to abuses, feuds, and family secrets, as well as the patient's reactions to being asked about them all. When the patient talks about his family, what's his mood? When does he get angry? Bitter? Indifferent? What does he remember? What doesn't he remember? What's difficult to talk about? A well-constructed genogram could predict a patient's pathology much in the same way a nearly completed puzzle predicted the shape of its missing pieces.

Patrick thought it was an interesting idea and proceeded to share a number of his observations about *Lily's* family—whom he'd already met—before quickly turning to Lily herself. Ash pulled out a notepad and began jotting down some of the phrases Patrick used as he talked about her. Then he pulled out his notes from their first session and started reading some of the phrases Patrick had used in connection with Angie. They were almost identical.

Patrick looked down at the two notepads placed side by side as if he'd just found a piece of gum under his shoe. Then he looked up at Ash, a confused, worried look creeping onto his face. "What does *that* mean?"

"It means none of this is really about Angie *or* Lily."

Patrick agreed to begin constructing a genogram immediately.

At their next session, however, he reported several fires had flared up in his life in the intervening week that required dousing. First, he'd decided to quit his job as waiter to commit himself full-time to painting. Then only three days after that, he'd decided to go into advertising. He was tired of being poor, he told Ash. He put his resume together and scheduled interviews with several advertising agencies, thinking to get into copywriting. He expressed great concern that if he didn't get the job he wanted, he had no idea "how he was going to survive."

All of these changes required processing, which Ash felt duty-bound to provide, especially given the breakneck pace at which they were occurring. But at the following session, Ash told him that they could spend the next several years dealing with the various manifestations of Patrick's anxiety and never come close to identifying the underlying cause of it. To do that, he argued, they needed to focus at some point on creating the genogram.

Patrick replied that he could provide his family history "in a few minutes." He wasn't close to his parents and never had been. His father was a surgeon and his mother a stay-at-home mom.

"Well, that's a start," Ash said. He stood up, walked over to his whiteboard, and picked up a marker. "But think about a genogram as a tree with lots of branches and leaves. We'll start at the bottom and work our way up and out." He pulled the cap off the marker and touched it to the board. "Why don't you start by telling me about your grandparents?"

Patrick groaned, but then dutifully began answering each question Ash asked. He did so, however, in an uncharacteristically stolid manner—a stark contrast, Ash noted, to the hyperbole that was his usual fare. They recorded the basic structure of Patrick's extended family, but the process rendered Patrick almost mute. At the end of the session, Ash announced his intention to discuss Patrick's immediate family next time, more as a warning than anything else.

But at the beginning of the next session, Patrick seemed once again his usual theatrical self and displayed no interest in continuing to work on the genogram at all. "You're not going to believe what happened!" he announced as he sat down in his chair. "Lily postponed her engagement! Can you believe it? She won't say it's because of me, but give me a break! And I got a job at an ad agency! This has been an unbelievable week. There's so much I want to talk about."

This time Ash actually found Patrick's opposition to continuing with the genogram encouraging. Most therapists considered resistance to be a signal that an important truth was about to be exposed. So when Ash said he wanted to hold off on discussing the events of the week and instead continue with the genogram, he wasn't surprised to see the excitement drain from Patrick's face. Undaunted, Ash picked up the marker and stood next to the genogram on the easel.

"Let's talk about your parents," Ash said. "What kind of relationships did they have with *their* parents?"

Patrick sighed. Then in a subdued voice he told Ash that his father hadn't gotten along well with Patrick's grandfather at all. Apparently, his grandfather had lost all interest in Patrick's father soon after Patrick's father left for college. His grandmother had died when Patrick was a child. His father rarely, if ever, talked about her.

"What about your mother's side?" Ash asked.

His mother was the youngest of six children, Patrick told him. She was the baby of the family, and apparently everyone had taken a turn caring for her at some point. His mother's family was extremely close, Patrick said, which he found "really weird."

"Any siblings?"

"A brother and a sister."

"Are you close to either of them?"

"Not really. My sister is fifteen years older than me and my brother is two years older than her. They were practically out of the house by the time I was old enough to notice them."

"Do you know if your parents planned to have children so far apart in age?"

After a moment's pause, Patrick answered, "I was an accident. I pretty much ruined the plans they had for their golden years. At least that's how my dad always put it. He took it out on my mom all the time."

"On your mom?"

Patrick nodded and then stared down at the floor.

"And what about you? Did he make *you* feel like an accident while you were growing up?"

Without looking up, Patrick nodded again.

"Tell me a little about that," Ash said.

"There was this one day . . ."

Ash waited. Patrick opened his mouth, then shut it. Then finally he said, "He was just going to let me walk out the door. He didn't care at all." He gave a half shrug.

"Tell me what happened."

Patrick took in a breath and said he'd been ten. The second storm of the Blizzard of '79 had just struck the Chicago area over the first weekend in January. The city and surrounding suburbs had been completely unprepared for the onslaught of snow that piled up to twenty-seven inches, a new record. By Monday, the roads had become impassable, forcing Patrick to stay home from school and his father to stay home from work. Patrick had suggested they build a snowman or go sledding together, but his father hadn't been interested. Instead, he'd picked on Patrick the entire day. Why hadn't his room been cleaned? Why hadn't his homework been done? Why weren't his grades better? He'd been freeloading, his father had said, sucking all the fun out his father's life with his mother. His father hadn't yelled, but every criticism he'd levied had been like a stab wound, leaving Patrick weak and dizzy with pain. They'd been standing in Patrick's room, his father marching out one issue after another, when Patrick announced he couldn't take it anymore and started crying. When his father started disparaging him for that, too, Patrick had darted from his room and down the stairs. He ran to the front door, opened it, and turned around to look back up at his father, who'd followed him as far as the top of the stairway.

He'd told his father that he hated him and that he was going to run away and never come back, and he meant it. He saw that his father believed him, and he felt a thrilling sense of power in anticipation of the pain he was about to inflict.

"But that's not how it went," Patrick said.

"How did it?"

Patrick finally looked up at Ash, his eyes shining. "He told me to make sure I closed the door after I left so the snow wouldn't get in."

After a moment, Ash told him he thought it was one of the worst things he'd ever heard a father tell his son.

## The Desire for Love

"So what if we suppose for a minute that one of Patrick's primary drivers is his need to be loved and accepted by his father," I said. "What might that cause him to believe he needs to be happy?"

"You mean aside from being loved and accepted by his father?" Ash asked.

"Aside from that, yes," I replied dryly. "Something more general. More generalizable."

"How about just love and acceptance, period? From anyone."

"That could explain his obsession with women. . . ."

"But not all the jobs," Ash said.

"You don't think so?"

"Love and acceptance from a job?"

"Not love and acceptance," I said. "Validation."

"Maybe. . . ."

"The need for love *is* one of the most universal needs there is," I pointed out.

"So is the need to be free of anxiety."

"True."

Then Ash shook his head. "It doesn't make sense. Do people become obsessed with—I don't know—*eating* because they're looking for love?"

"Sometimes."

"I thought *sometimes* wasn't good enough."

"Yeah, no, it's not," I conceded. "We're looking for a belief that explains *all* obsessions."

"Are people obsessed with *money* because they're looking for love?"

"Yeah, okay—"

"Power?" Ash added. "Survival?"

"Right," I agreed.

At their next visit, Ash told Patrick about a book titled *Man Enough*. The author, Frank Pittman, a psychiatrist, argues that sons who failed to be "anointed" men by their fathers will spend their lives not only trying to prove themselves men but also trying to resolve their anger at their fathers for not providing them enough respect and admiration when they were little. How do fathers "anoint" their sons? Not in any one single act, but in consistent, small ways throughout their childhood and adolescence: by attending their baseball games, by showing up to their graduations and smiling with pride for their pictures, by listening to their fears without judgment, and by accepting them so completely that no chip could ever form on their shoulders.[2] Properly anointed men, Pittman argues, feel no need to prove anything in their adult lives because they've already proven everything they felt necessary to prove when they were children. Pittman argues that men whose fathers haven't anointed them struggle to anoint themselves in three ways: by philandering, by overachieving, and by competing. The best way for these men to break out of these destructive behavior patterns, Pittman says, is to focus their energies not on anointing themselves but rather on anointing sons of their own.[3]

Patrick devoured Pittman's book in one night and affirmed at their next session that it read like a case study of his life. He believed now that his obsessive desire to find the "perfect woman" hadn't arisen out of a need to shore up his self-esteem but from a need to demonstrate to his father that he was a man.

After that, Patrick's progress in therapy began to accelerate. He started to report recurrent, albeit brief moments in which he felt "more self-contained, more whole." These feelings were subtle, occurring at odd times and for no reason he could figure out. Yet it was undeniable. Coming to understand just how much he'd needed his father's approval as a child had improved his ability to approve of himself as an adult.

Soon Patrick found his anxiety had receded enough that he no longer felt the need to continue therapy. Though Ash thought he had more to uncover and said as much, he told Patrick he'd support whatever choice he wanted to make. So they shook hands and said their goodbyes.

## A Universal Anxiety

"Any final conclusions about what was causing his anxiety?" I asked Ash.

"I'm still not sure," Ash said. "Fear of not measuring up as a man? Fear of disappointing his father? Fear of failure? Fear of *being* a failure?" He shrugged.

"But now his anxiety is gone."

"Seems to be."

"You think he's still from the world of Hunger?"

"I think he *was*," Ash said. "I'm not sure if he still is."

"Because he's not anxious anymore?"

"No, because . . . well . . . I don't know." Ash paused. "Yeah, because he's not anxious anymore."

I considered this. "So maybe anxiety *is* the right answer." But then I shook my head. "Except I still don't see how it could be the universal driver of *every* obsession—"

"That's the problem with *everything* we've suggested," Ash said. "The need to be free of anxiety, the need to be in a relationship, the need to be loved and accepted—none of them are universal enough. We're trying to figure out why we want things obsessively, but instead we keep coming up with different things we all want."

"It's the *way* we want them that's the problem. Like our lives are at risk if we don't get them."

"So maybe we've been asking the wrong question," Ash said. "Maybe instead of asking why people trapped in the world of Hunger are obsessed with getting what they want, we should be asking what they believe will happen if they don't."

"I guess there could be a *deeper* anxiety at work here," I offered. "Not a specific anxiety about losing your girlfriend or disappointing your father or being a failure, but an existential anxiety. A universal anxiety."

"Yes! Maybe that's why Patrick doesn't seem like he's trapped in Hunger anymore. Maybe he's freed himself from *that* anxiety."

"But anxiety about what?"

"Being abandoned? A loveless existence? Death? I don't know," Ash said. "But something elemental. Something we haven't figured out yet. The thing that really trapped Patrick in the life-condition of Hunger. The thing that traps us all."

Three years later, Patrick called Ash again. He was doing well, he said, still mostly anxiety-free, but he had a new problem that he wanted to discuss. Did Ash have room in his schedule to see him? Ash did and arranged for them to meet the following week.

When Patrick arrived, Ash noticed he'd gained some weight—enough to round out the edges of his face—and wore his hair shorter and neater than he'd remembered, making him seem more meticulously groomed. "You look different," Ash told him.

With a self-deprecating laugh Patrick admitted he hadn't been exercising much or following as rigorous a diet. His obsession with fitness had waned. "Which I'm sure is why this chair feels so tight against my ass." His tone was light, innocently self-mocking. Charming, even.

Ash was intrigued. Patrick's demeanor had changed almost entirely. No trace of his previous awkwardness remained. The frenetic mannerisms, the dramatic rise and fall in the pitch of his voice, the worried expression that spoke of a persistently distracting anxiety—all had vanished and been replaced by a steadiness of bearing and a calmness of tone that struck Ash as polished and powerful. He found himself thinking that where before he'd been presented with an anxious boy, now he saw before him a full-grown man.

Patrick quickly summarized the intervening three years of his life since he'd last seen Ash. He'd learned to confront anxiety maturely and proactively. Rather than regress, now he would take definitive steps to solve whatever problem was causing it. He'd been involved in a serious relationship with a successful, intelligent woman until six months ago when he himself had ended it. He'd been dating her for a little over a year when vague but persistent feelings of dissatisfaction had led him to conclude she simply wasn't the woman for him. The breakup had been painful, but not inappropriately so. He hadn't dated anyone since.

But the reason he'd come back to see Ash had nothing to do with any of that. He'd come back, he said, because after he left therapy three years ago, he'd decided to write a book.

Pittman had inspired him. He'd wanted to write about the numerous ways father-and-son relationships failed and how devastating the consequences of such failures could be. However, several agents to whom he'd pitched the idea had all pointed out not only that he lacked the credentials to write such a book, but also that the book had already been written—and written well—by Pittman himself.

Refusing to be discouraged, Patrick decided he would turn his idea into a work of fiction. By that point he'd also started business school, so he told himself that sleep was for the weak and started writing immediately.

After two months, physically exhausted but mentally energized, he finished the first draft and showed it to a writer friend. His writer friend, however, shortly returned it with pencil slashes scrawled across nearly every page pronouncing the prose amateurish and the story predictable and uninspiring. Patrick accepted the feedback stoically but was terribly hurt. He paused for a week to let the sting fade and then arranged to audit some writing classes.

After honing his writing skills for six months, he decided to rewrite the book from beginning to end. Rather than risk being criticized by his friend again, he decided this time to query literary agents. In short order, though, each one sent him back a rejection letter. At that point, almost everyone he knew urged him to put his manuscript in a drawer and to focus on business school.

Instead, he decided to rewrite the book a second time. By the time he'd graduated and found a job as a management consultant, the rewrite was done. This time he decided to send out query letters to publishers who, according to *Writer's Market*, accepted unsolicited submissions. By then, he told Ash, his desire to become a published author had completely taken over his life, becoming an itch just beyond the reach of his fingers to scratch.

Over the next four months, even as the rejection letters began to accumulate, he continued to open each successive response with a sense of hope, quickly shrugging off the pain of each rebuff, one after another. He continued in this way until he received the final response from the last of the publishers—it, too, was a rejection—and then his hope had crumbled. He couldn't understand it. What had he been doing wrong? Could he have been that deluded about the quality of his work?

His mother had recognized his distress and pulled him aside to encourage him. She'd told him she thought the book was good but that it read as though someone else had written it. Where was his quirkiness? The book was too serious. It needed an edge.

Patrick felt instantly re-energized and decided to rewrite the entire thing from beginning to end a *third* time but with humor, sarcasm, and wit, allowing his personality to roam wildly over the pages. It took him five months. Then he sent out this new and improved version to the same publishers—only then to be quickly and summarily rejected by them all again.

He'd felt then that he simply couldn't continue, that as badly as he wanted to publish his book, as much as he believed in it, he couldn't take any more disappointment. So he'd busied himself with other interests, hoping his desire to become a published author would pass or perhaps diminish enough to cease hurting him. He'd been about to shred the entire manuscript and delete all the files from his computer in a final effort to free himself from his obsession when he received an unexpected call from his friend, the writer. Patrick had impulsively sent the fourth version to him when it was making the rounds with publishers the second time. His friend had just finished reading it, he'd called to say, and he wanted Patrick to know that it was now, in his opinion, a publishable book. When Patrick replied that every publishing house to whom he'd sent it had disagreed, his friend suggested that he publish it himself.

Instantly, Patrick's heartache vanished, replaced by a swell of excitement, which in the next moment was joined by a sense of urgency to implement his friend's suggestion as quickly as he possibly could. By this time, however, he'd left his consulting job to try his hand at real estate development with two of his management consultant friends, so he had little cash on hand. Nevertheless, he began a search for an on-demand printer he could afford and soon found one who agreed to charge him a thousand dollars to print five hundred copies. He could print as many more as he wanted as long as the orders were placed in minimum batches of five hundred. Marketing, distribution, and sales would be up to him. Elated, Patrick had written them a check, purchased an ISBN number, and then gone in search of someone to design the cover.

He'd turned then to the business of selling and promotion. He asked every independent bookstore in the city to stock it, but they all turned him down. Frustrated, he'd started selling the book himself, at first to family and friends, then soon also to friends of friends, and then eventually to their friends as well.

After three months of "shameless self-promotion," he'd finally managed to sell all five hundred copies. By then a small following had developed online. Encouraged, he sent the finished book in manuscript form to a few carefully selected agents, one of whom agreed to represent it. Within a month it had sold to a publisher. Contracts were signed, a marketing plan developed, and a new book cover approved.

And now, nine months after that, a first run of five hundred copies were poised—finally—to land on the shelves of bookstores across the country. Patrick was about to realize his dream of becoming a published author at long last. And that, he concluded to Ash, was the reason he'd come back to therapy.

"Because . . . ?" Ash asked.

Patrick spread his hands helplessly. "Because it feels completely empty."

## A Worthless Life

When we're trapped in the world of Hunger, no matter what we may have or what we may have achieved, we're continually dissatisfied. We're always turning to something *else*, to our *next* desire, something bigger, something better, perpetually hoping to find the one thing that will resolve the painful sense of emptiness that continuously permeates our life. The world of Hunger is indeed the world of pain.

The root cause of such dissatisfaction? Psychologists Timothy Wilson and Daniel Gilbert argue we routinely overestimate both the intensity and duration of the emotions we expect to feel in response to future events, and therefore the degree to which getting what we want will improve our well-being.[4] In other words, we're predisposed to want things out of proportion to the pleasure or satisfaction that they're likely to give us.

"But that doesn't mean we're all disappointed by the pleasure or satisfaction we get," Ash said.

"No," I agreed.

"So then why would Patrick be?"

I shrugged. "Maybe he's just sitting on the far right of the curve. Maybe his expectations are so unrealistic that he *never* gets as much pleasure or satisfaction as he thinks he will, so what pleasure or satisfaction he does get seems, in contrast to his expectations, insignificant."

"But why would he keep expecting so much? Especially if he keeps being disappointed. You think he'd figure it out."

"Maybe it's not about *expectation* so much as *desperation*," I said. "Maybe the wound his father inflicted hasn't mended. Maybe all the things he's been doing have actually been attempts to heal himself in some way."

"I'm not sure what that wound would be at this point. He's clearly not looking for love anymore. And these days his self-esteem almost looks healthier than mine."

"I agree it doesn't sound like he's still having trouble valuing *himself*. But I wonder if he's having trouble valuing his *life*."

"That sounds like a distinction without a difference," Ash said.

"It's not. You can value yourself but still feel that the things you're doing aren't meaningful or important." Maybe, I said, his skipping from relationship to relationship and from job to job hadn't been a search for validation but for *meaning*—an attempt to fill a void left by an indifferent father whose final legacy to his son was an inability to feel good about any of his accomplishments. Nothing Patrick did was ever good enough for his father, so nothing he did was ever good enough for Patrick himself. He may have freed himself from the belief that he needed his father's approval and in so doing from the belief that he was worthless. But I wondered if his inability to find satisfaction in nearly everything he had or did had stemmed all along from a persistent belief that no matter what he was doing there was something else more meaningful he should have been doing instead. That although he'd discovered worth in himself, he nevertheless felt he was living a worthless life.

〰️

Patrick jerked his head back and blinked several times. "You mean not even publishing a book—" He stopped and heaved out an angry breath. "So I'm still damaged goods."

"What do you mean?" Ash asked. "No you're not. Why are you saying that?"

"I spent my entire life trying to please my dad, and now I have no idea how to please myself!" He shook his head in disgust. "All those years I wasted trying to do what *he* wanted me to do."

"How do you figure you did what he wanted you to do?" Ash challenged him. "Maybe you've spent your entire life trying to please him, but not by doing what he wanted. You did it by trying to accomplish great things! You've always known exactly what you wanted and aimed to accomplish your goals with a determination that's been nothing short of amazing. How else could you have pushed through all those obstacles if you didn't know exactly what you wanted? You may believe you're living a worthless life because painting and copywriting and getting your MBA and real estate development and publishing a book have all left you feeling dissatisfied, but in no way were you ever uncertain that you wanted to pursue each and every one of them."

"Then why aren't I any happier? Why does everything I do always—*always*—seem so goddamn empty?"

"Maybe you just haven't found the right—" Then Ash stopped. "Or maybe . . ." He tapped his fingers together. "Hang on a second." Another moment passed. Then he asked, "Patrick, what exactly do you think you need to be happy?"

Patrick looked at him helplessly. "That's the problem. I don't know."

"Actually, I think you do. I think you always have. You just don't know you know it. Just give me the first answer that pops into your head. What do you think you need to be happy?"

"I don't know," Patrick repeated. "That's why I'm here."

"You're not getting it. What do you think you need to be happy? Your father's approval? A girlfriend? The right job? A published book? Which one?"

"Stop asking me! I don't know! Fuck! All of them! How about that? Every single goddamn one!"

"That," Ash said, "is exactly right."

# Miswanting

"The core delusion of the world of Hunger," Ash announced, "*is that to be happy we need to get what we want.*"

"Interesting . . . ," I said.

"Think about it. Why would Patrick be so obsessed with everything he wants and at the same time be so dissatisfied by everything he gets? Because he doesn't expect just to *enjoy* the things he gets. He expects them to turn him into a *happy person.*"

I blinked several times. "Right! It's the belief that fulfilling your desires will *change* you. What drives every obsession there ever was and ever will be? The fear that if you don't get what you want, you won't be able to be happy at all. *That's* the universal anxiety we've been looking for!"

Yet getting what we want doesn't improve our long-term happiness in the slightest. For one thing, the intensity with which we want something doesn't predict how happy we'll be when we get it. Neurologically, it turns out that *wanting* and *liking* are two entirely different processes created by entirely different circuits in the brain, involving entirely different neurotransmitters.[5] This is how it's possible not only to want something far more intensely than we like it, like a fourth piece of chocolate cake, but also to want something we don't like at all, like a ride on a rollercoaster. This is something Gilbert and Wilson call *miswanting.*[6]

A second reason that getting what we want doesn't turn us into permanently happy people is that what makes us happy *today* often make us *unhappy* tomorrow. Think of an alcoholic who wants to drink, a dieter who wants to overeat, or a student who wants to see a movie instead of studying for a test.

Finally, even if what makes us happy today *doesn't* make us unhappy tomorrow, it's unlikely to keep making us happy the day after that. The principle of *hedonic adaptation* is as straightforward as it is difficult to avoid. Simply stated, for most of us, most attachments have the power to make us happy—or happier —only temporarily.[7] Getting what we want, in other words, is like chewing a piece of gum. It tastes sweet at first, but eventually the flavor fades.

"Except for most people, it fades slowly," Ash said. "With Patrick, it fades the minute he pops it in his mouth. Why would that be?"

"I think it's just what we're saying: When he finds that getting what he wants doesn't turn him into a happier person, he thinks the problem is that he just hasn't found the *right* thing to want. He doesn't realize he's nursing this open wound, this inability to find *any* of his accomplishments meaningful. So he goes immediately back to the trough, trying to make himself happy by accomplishing something else. He never has a chance to feel joy because he turns his attention away from the things he accomplishes the moment he accomplishes them."

Feeling that we're not happy enough—or that we could be happier than we are—likely explains why we sometimes *all* fall into the world of Hunger and become convinced that the entirety of our happiness depends on getting something we want. I reminded Ash of my own reaction to the success we'd had in optioning a television pilot to DreamWorks Television a few years earlier. We'd both been stunned by the studio's interest in our script and by the possibility that we might—dared we imagine it?—have the opportunity to write and produce a television series. For a period of several months that was all I thought about, all I dreamed about, all I worried about being denied—so much so that I couldn't sleep. I constructed an entire herd of rationalizations to justify not only why I wanted it to happen but also the actions I took to make it happen. I even rationalized actions I knew had hurt others—more actions than I care to admit—convincing me that the power of the world of Hunger to obliterate moral concerns can't be overestimated.

"Because we don't enter the world of Hunger just by wanting something," I reminded Ash. "We enter the world of Hunger by becoming obsessed with what we want. When what we *want* becomes something we think we *need*."

☙❧

"So what are you saying I should do?" Patrick asked Ash. "Just . . . stop wanting things?"

"I'm not sure how you could do that even if you wanted to," Ash replied with a shake of his head. "Wanting things isn't the problem. Wanting things is what makes life interesting. Wanting things is why people raise children and take care of the sick and write books and paint paintings and do everything else in life that matters. Think about it. Life without desire wouldn't only be boring but also short—lacking, as you would, the desire to continue it."

"Hah!"

"The problem isn't that you want things. The problem is you believe each and every thing you want is the key to your happiness. That if you could only get this or that *one thing*, you'd live happily ever after. But there is no happily ever after. So you jump from obsession to obsession, disappointed by everything you get because nothing you get makes you feel as good as you think it should."

"But why?" Patrick asked. "Why doesn't it?"

"Because nothing you get will ever fill the hole you have in your heart. That's just not how you fix those kinds of things. We all dip in and out of the world of Hunger sometimes, but believing that getting what you want will heal whatever wound you're trying to heal—that it will finally enable you to love yourself or make something meaningful out of your life, or whatever—that just traps you in the same place. It just locks you into a perpetual state of *wanting*."

Patrick eyed him silently.

"Do you remember the first thing you ever said to me?" Ash asked. "'If I could just get over this *one thing* I'm sure I'd be fine.'"

"I was talking about getting over my belief that Angie was cheating on me."

"Because you were obsessed with hanging on to the *one thing* you thought you needed to be happy: Angie herself."

"I guess that's true. . . ."

"Obsession is like a tidal wave," Ash said. "It washes away every other concern you have in life. It fills you up. And what a relief that feeling is if you felt empty before. Especially when the object of your obsession is a person. But the problem with becoming obsessed with a person is that a person isn't a thing. A person has value independent of any thoughts you have about her. But when you objectify someone—whether you put her up on the highest pedestal or dehumanize her in the worst way—you start to think that she only has value in proportion to your desire for her. And when you idealize her—like you did Angie—it isn't just *her* you idealize. *You idealize what you expect her to make you feel.* And what you expect her to make you feel is rarely matched by what she actually does."

"So you're saying it's okay to want things as long as I don't want them too much."

Ash shook his head. "It's hard to accomplish anything if you don't want it badly. How else do you stop yourself from giving up when you run into a roadblock? You know that better than anyone. To accomplish anything that's difficult—to publish a book, to lose weight, to run a marathon—you *need* to be just a little bit obsessed. To achieve some goals—goals that are actually important and good—obsession might even be necessary. If you have high cholesterol, you probably need to be at least a little obsessed about avoiding saturated fat. If you have life-threatening allergies, you should definitely be obsessive about avoiding peanuts. The key is to become obsessed with something just enough that it fuels your endurance but not so much that you start to believe it holds the key to your happiness. Because the moment you start to believe that, your obsession ceases to be your servant and becomes your master."

Patrick closed his eyes and pinched the bridge of his nose with his fingers as if he were in pain. "This conversation is officially making me insane."

"You just need to learn to want things in the right way for the right reasons," Ash said. "Don't let yourself fall into the trap of thinking that only the specific things you want can make you happy and nothing else. Don't expect that getting anything will *make* you happy. Not in the long run, at least. It's the degree to which you're happy in the first place that determines how much you're able to enjoy whatever it is you get."[8]

"But how can I be happy in the first place if I feel like I'm—like I'm living a worthless life." He stopped suddenly. "You know what? That's actually true."

"*What's* actually true?" Ash asked. "That you *have* been living a worthless life? Or that you've always *believed* you've been living a worthless life?"

Patrick paused. "As long as I can remember, whenever I wanted something I went after it with everything I had. Just like you said, like my happiness depended on it. And I'll tell you, to endure the agony of wanting all those things I've told you about wanting—and it really was *agony*, man—to fight for them as hard as I did, to keep fighting no matter how discouraged I got, and then only to achieve *one* of them—well, you'd think it would feel like the greatest victory in the world. But it doesn't. It feels like absolutely nothing. So you tell me: why *else* would it feel that way? Yeah, I believe I'm living a worthless life. I always have."

Ash studied him. "And how does it make you feel to recognize that now?"

"I guess . . . I guess when I really look at it square in the face it's like . . . whatever." He shrugged. "I'm more surprised it's taken me all this time to figure it out. But it really is just completely true." He tilted his head curiously. "I guess I'm not sure why it's not bothering me more."

"Maybe because in realizing you've always believed you've been living a worthless life you've also realized that you haven't, in fact, been living a worthless life at all."

"Huh," Patrick said thoughtfully. "Maybe so . . . that could be . . ." Patrick's gaze drifted sideways. He seemed lost in thought.

Ash waited. "What are you thinking now?"

"I'm thinking . . ." His expression went slack for a moment. Then he blinked and his eyes came back into focus. "I'm thinking—shit, man, I published a book. That's what I'm thinking. I published a book." And all at once his face lit up in a dazzling smile.

Ash smiled back at him. "Yes, you did."

Thinking he was seeing in Patrick's smile a long-overdue recognition that his life was far more meaningful than Patrick had previously believed, Ash found himself marveling at how wisdom seemed to possess a sentience of its own, a sentience that itself appeared to choose when and how it arrived. Usually, Ash reflected sardonically, it was with an unpredictability that made therapists want to wring their hands.

"That *was* quite an accomplishment, don't you think?" Ash said.

Patrick stared past Ash out the window behind his desk. His pupils constricted as the sun came out from behind a cloud and the room brightened.

"You know what?" Patrick said in a voice that seemed filled with equal measures of surprise and pride. "That is goddamn right."

## Key Points

- Hunger is defined as the life-condition of desire.

- People trapped in the life-condition of Hunger typically experience persistent feelings of restlessness and yearning. They often feel a great sense of emptiness that they look to fill through the attainment of their desires.

- The life-condition of Hunger also fuels persistence, however, driving people to move past obstacles and disappointment when they might otherwise give up.

- The core delusion of the world of Hunger is that to be happy we need to get what we want.

# 3

# Animality

*I can think of nothing less pleasurable than a life devoted to pleasure.*

—John D. Rockefeller

Animality is defined as the life-condition of instinct. In contrast to the world of Hunger in which we find ourselves at the mercy of our desires, in the world of Animality, we find ourselves—like an animal—at the mercy of our basic drives. Concerned exclusively with food, sex, sleep, and the like, in the world of Animality, our lives center almost entirely on the present moment and the satisfaction of our biological needs.

Though obeying our basic drives is, of course, crucial for survival, when we become consumed by them as we do in the world of Animality, we often give little thought to the consequences of our actions or the harm they might cause others. We may even lose our interest in other people altogether in pursuit of whatever pleasure happens to hold our attention or in retreat of whatever pain we're trying to avoid.

When this happens, it becomes easy for others to manipulate us as our obsession with pleasure and aversion to pain make our behavior highly predictable. Ironically, though, this pliability does little to endear us to anyone as our focus on our own pleasure sometimes blinds us to the emotional needs of others. For

73

this reason, when we're trapped in the world of Animality, we sometimes have a hard time maintaining friendships.

Invariably, though, we cause the most harm to ourselves, for rarely does the risk of long-term pain stop us from pursuing short-term gain. Indeed, when we're trapped in the life-condition of Animality, nothing deserts us quite so much as our regard for reason; sadly, any interest we might have in listening to its voice often gives way to an impulsivity that makes it appear as if we hardly think at all.

Ash and I had been discussing Dominique, whom he described to me as "one of the most self-indulgent patients" he'd ever met. She'd come to see him after having visited the only doctor she saw on a regular basis, her gynecologist, because she'd been crying uncontrollably for no reason and had begun to find most of her daily routine too difficult to manage. Showering, dressing, even brushing her teeth—all seemed now somehow beyond her ability. Tearfully, she'd told her gynecologist that her life had become unmanageable. He, in turn, diagnosed her with major depression, started her on a low dose of Paxil, and referred her to Ash.

When Ash escorted her from his waiting room into his office at their first appointment, she lurched through the doorway so haltingly that she almost tripped on the threshold. Then she plopped down in the chair to which Ash directed her with such an intense expression of relief, gripping the chair's curved leather arms so fiercely, that Ash wondered if she'd hurt herself.

"Have you ever been in therapy before?" he asked as he sat down in the chair opposite her. He'd learned early in his training that the ability to step into the role of patient varied greatly and that, as with most things, previous experience tended to correlate with aptitude. He always tried to get a sense at the beginning of therapy how much help his patients might need with skills like identifying and expressing feelings, reflecting, and accepting feedback.

"Not by myself," Dominique answered. She sat in her chair like a skittish cat, her green eyes wide as they nervously searched the room. Her hands remained in continuous motion: smoothing out her pants, pulling lint off her arms, freeing her hair from her face.

"Couples therapy?" Ash prompted. "Family therapy?"

"Once."

"Which?"

"Couples."

"How'd it go?"

Dominique shrugged. "He thought it would help us find common ground."

"Did it?"

She snorted. "No."

Ash paused to wonder if her flippant tone reflected her dim view of her ex-boyfriend or of therapy. He girded himself and pressed on.

"So I hear you've been feeling depressed."

"Dr. Haug told you?"

He nodded. "Can you tell me what's been happening?"

"I really don't know." Abruptly, she started to cry. "Here I go again with the tears. Everything's just so hard. I just feel really *bad*. Like all the time. I just can't seem to get it together."

"Since when?"

She waved her hand distractedly. "I don't know. Maybe two, two-and-a-half months ago." She wiped the tears out of her eyes with the tips of her fingers.

"Anything especially significant happen two-and-a-half months ago?"

Dominique hesitated. "I guess. Sort of."

Ash waited. When he realized Dominique wasn't going to say more, he asked, "What?"

Dominique sighed. "I had a fight with my parents."

"What about?"

"They cut me off." She kicked off her heels, raised herself up on the arms of her chair like a gymnast balancing on a pommel horse, and then sat back down cross-legged. "Can you believe it? I lost my job, so *then* they decide to stop paying my rent."

Her change of affect from sad to appalled was so rapid that it took Ash a moment to figure out an appropriate response. "Isn't that when parents are supposed to *start* paying your rent?"

"I know! Can you believe it?" Her eyes lit up with sudden excitement. "Maybe *you* could talk to them. You know—tell them how selfish they're being."

Ash started to reply, but then she quickly cut him off: "Actually, that's a terrible idea. Forget I said that."

Ash studied her for a moment. "How did your parents come to be paying your rent in the first place?"

Dominique shrugged. "We had a deal."

"What kind of deal?"

She heaved out a dramatic breath and told him that after graduating from high school, she'd decided to pursue a career in acting instead of going to college. It had been a horrible blow to her parents, who'd tried to instill in her a love of learning and an appreciation for the value of higher education as far back as she could remember. They'd always assumed, as had Dominique herself, that she would go to college and then to graduate school. She was, in fact, an excellent student, and by the time she'd worked up the courage to tell her parents she'd decided not to continue with her "formal education," as she termed it, she'd already been accepted to Northwestern University.

Instead of "totally losing it," as Dominique had expected, her parents had proposed a compromise: they would pay her rent and her basic living expenses if she would agree to attend college part time. She didn't need to finish in the usual four years, they said. She just needed to finish. If she chose to live modestly, she wouldn't have to work at all. Then she'd be able to preserve some time to pursue her acting career even as she prepared to be able to "compete for a better paying job," as they put it, in case her interest in acting turned out to be short-lived.

Though stung by her parents' lack of enthusiasm for her career choice, secretly Dominique had been pleased. She'd always prided herself on her ability to multitask and thought she'd easily be able to make it all work—which, in fact, she did for three full years.

Then six months ago while on winter break, she'd taken a full-time job as the assistant to the national sales manager at a hotel in Chicago. The salary had been too good to turn down, she explained—and was, she soon discovered, commensurate with the workload. After four months of failing to meet her boss's expectations, she'd been fired. Unwilling at that point to relinquish the lifestyle to which she'd become accustomed on a full-time salary, she found another full-time job as a concierge at another Chicago hotel and quit school once and for all to devote what little free time she had left to her acting career. And that was when her parents had cut her off.

"So it wasn't so much because you lost your job," Ash pointed out, "as it was because you failed to hold up your end of the bargain."

"I should pursue their dream instead of mine?"

Though Ash certainly had to agree with the underlying sentiment, he couldn't consider it a legitimate reason for expecting continuing financial support from her parents. Suppressing an impulse to comment on her overdeveloped sense of entitlement, he said, "So you've been depressed basically since they cut you off."

"Yeah."

"Do you think that's the reason?"

She shrugged noncommittally.

"It can be hard to act against your parents' wishes even as an adult. Do you think you might be depressed because you feel caught between your dream and your desire to please them?"

Dominique shrugged again. "Not really."

"No?" He was surprised at her answer. He paused to collect his thoughts. "Maybe you're worried you won't be okay financially? That you won't have a place to live or enough to eat?"

"No, my concierge job pays the bills now." But her tone was hesitant.

Ash glanced at the questionnaire on the table between them that she'd brought in with her from the waiting room. "You're twenty-two?"

She nodded.

"Is this the first time in your life you've ever felt this down?"

"Pretty much. I'm really a happy person. Or so I thought."

That Dominique couldn't readily explain her mood raised the possibility that her depression was the result of a malfunctioning or malformed mood-generating machine. Yet, though she wouldn't confirm it, Ash had a hard time believing her parents' decision to cut her off didn't also have something to do with it.

On the other hand, maybe the cause was a *different* adverse event than her parents' decision to cut her off. Being fired, for example. Maybe she'd interpreted that as proof of her inability to perform at the level she believed she was capable.

"Let's back up a minute," Ash said, to himself as much as to her. "You said you were fired from your job at the first hotel because you couldn't keep up?"

"Well, not exactly. I did have a little trouble keeping up. But that's not the *real* reason I was fired."

"Why, then?"

Dominique sucked in a breath. "I sort of slept with my boss."

Ash's eyebrows rose slightly, then furrowed. "He fired you for sleeping with him?"

"For sleeping with him only *once*."

"So he wanted an ongoing relationship and you didn't? *That's* why he fired you?"

"Yeah."

"Then it wasn't because you couldn't handle the workload."

"That's what he said, but I wasn't doing that badly."

"Except a few minutes ago you implied you were."

She dropped her eyes to avoid his gaze. "It's a less embarrassing reason." She paused. "Sorry."

Ash found himself liking her for her honesty. "But wouldn't firing you only increase the likelihood that you'd sue him for sexual harassment?"

"I guess some men think with their egos even more than they do with their dicks." She smiled as she said it, but then added, again, "Sorry," for which Ash presumed she meant the profanity.

"How'd it happen?"

"After an office party. I knew I shouldn't have done it even while I was doing it." Then, by way of explanation, she added, "I have a boyfriend."

Ash couldn't keep his eyes from widening. "A serious boyfriend?"

"Serious enough. He's about to ask me to marry him." Her gaze moved to the floor.

"You say that like you're not sure you want him to." He wondered if she'd cheated on him because she was ambivalent about getting married.

She sighed. "I don't know. It's complicated."

"It's pretty normal to feel at least a little conflicted when you're deciding whether or not to marry someone."

"See, and I'm almost never conflicted about anything. I've just always been really decisive. It's one of my strengths."

"Well, it's pretty common when you're depressed that your decision-making apparatus gets a little out of whack," Ash said.

"Yeah? So maybe that's why."

Ash sat quietly for a moment, thinking. "I take it your boyfriend doesn't know about you and your boss?"

She shook her head. "And he's not going to. I don't want to hurt him. I'm not a bad person."

"And how do you know he's about to ask you to marry him?"

"He just took me ring shopping. He's going to get me this totally amazing princess cut from Tiffany's." Her face was suddenly alive with excitement. "You should see it. It's really expensive. It's really going to make him happy."

"Make *him* happy?" Ash asked.

"Yeah," Dominique said. "He loves buying me things."

## Self-Centeredness

"*He* loves buying *her* things?" I exclaimed.

"That's not even the worst part," Ash said. "It turns out the real reason she's not sure she wants to marry Todd—her boyfriend—is because she's waiting to see what happens with Carson."

"Carson? Who's Carson? Her boss?"

"No. A *third* guy. The one apparently she's *really* in love with."

"Wow. When you said she was self-indulgent, you weren't kidding."

"Yeah, no."

"She almost sounds like a sociopath," I said.

"I don't think she's quite that bad. She may be completely self-centered—pathologically self-centered—but she does seem to care about hurting Todd's feelings. At least a little."

"You're sure she's not fooling you there? She *is* an actress."

"If she'd tell me the truth about cheating on him, why would she lie about wanting to spare his feelings?"

"Maybe it's just what she said—so you don't think she's a bad person."

"If she were a sociopath, she wouldn't care what I think about her at all," Ash pointed out.

"Unless she wanted something from you," I said.

"Like what?"

"I'm not sure. For you to like her maybe?"

"If she wants me to like her, she's not a sociopath, she's an idiot. Which, now that I think about it, is entirely possible. You said people trapped in the world of Animality are impulsive, right?"

"Yeah. . . ."

"Isn't that just a nicer word for stupid?"

I shook my head. "People trapped in the world of Animality aren't stupid. It's more that they're *unwise*. Animality isn't about a lack of intellectual capacity so much as it is about a lack of judgment. It's about giving in to your basic drives without restraint or thought."

"See, that's why I was thinking more narcissistic personality disorder. Everything's about *her*, about what *she* wants. But that doesn't add up either. There's no grandiose sense of self-importance, no preoccupation with fantasies of power or beauty. . . ."

I felt sorry for her suddenly. "Why does she need to have a diagnosis at all? We all get stuck in the life-condition of Animality sometimes."

"Fine, forget about giving her a diagnosis. What else—what belief—would turn someone into an unrestrained id?"

"An unrestrained id," I repeated. "I like that. That's exactly what Animality is. Total self-centeredness. A complete lack of empathy."

"Then maybe that's the answer right there. Maybe the core delusion of Animality is that to be happy you have to be selfish."

I shook my head. "How would believing you need to be selfish prevent you from, say, thinking about and planning for the future?"

"Actually, it wouldn't. Right."

"Remember, whatever we come up with has to explain *all* the characteristics of Animality—the obsession with indulging basic appetites, the tendency to act impulsively, the indifference to the pain and suffering of others, the diminished capacity to look beyond the present—"

Ash grinned. "You know what that all sounds like?"

"You mean besides an animal?" I asked.

"A child," Ash answered.

⌒≈⌒

When Dominique returned for her second session, Ash was struck by the change in her appearance. Her make-up, previously expertly applied, was sloppy, and her eyes were puffy and swollen, as if she'd been crying. Rather than the fashionable blouse, pants, and high heels she appeared in at her first visit, she wore a baggy T-shirt, gray sweatpants, and running shoes. Ash started by asking how she was feeling. She told him she was sick and had almost canceled but that "things had escalated," and she desperately needed his guidance.

"Okay," Ash said. "Tell me what's happened."

She hesitated, saying she was afraid that once he'd heard what she had to say he'd hate her. Astonished that she had something to reveal that was potentially even worse than what she already had—and mildly annoyed by her childish attempt to manipulate his reaction in advance—he nevertheless tried to reassure her that he wouldn't hate her no matter what she told him. "It's not my job to judge you."

"Maybe I should just figure it out on my own."

Ash paused and then shrugged, feeling uncharacteristically impatient. "It's your hour, Dominique. We can talk about anything you want."

She took a deep breath to encourage herself. Then in a hesitant voice she told him that the real reason she was dating Todd instead of Carson was because Carson was married. She was waiting for him to get divorced, which he'd told her he was going to do in the next couple of months once he'd had a chance to prepare his two children, who were seven and nine. She'd been telling him that his kids would be much better off once he was in a healthy relationship, but he thought they were certain to be traumatized no matter what. When Ash asked if she was aware if Carson had conducted affairs in the past with other women, she admitted he had—but, she added, none with any he'd wanted to marry.

"But none of that is why you're going to hate me."

The reason he was going to hate her, she explained, her voice growing even quieter, was that Carson and Todd knew each other.

Ash's eyebrows rose. "How?"

"They're actually . . . uh . . . hmm . . ." She stopped. Then she took a deep breath. "They're actually best friends."

"Ah. And Todd has no idea you're seeing Carson . . ."

Dominique shook her head.

"But Carson knows you're seeing Todd because everyone knows you're seeing Todd. Todd's your boyfriend. That's the relationship that's public. You're cheating on Todd with Carson, not the other way around."

Dominique nodded.

"All right," Ash said, deliberately imbuing his voice with an accepting tone. "Is there anything else?"

"One more thing." Her lips smacked as her mouth went dry. "I'm going skiing with Todd this weekend, and I'm pretty sure he's going to do it."

"It?"

She rolled her eyes. "Propose. I've made up my mind that if he does, I'm going to tell him I need a week to decide and then go to Carson and tell him it's now or never. He has to divorce his wife right now. If Carson says yes, I'll turn Todd down. If not, I'll tell Todd yes. But if Todd *is* going to propose I have to make sure we get along well during the trip, which means sex is in the cards. Which is now a bit of a problem. . . ."

"Why?"

Dominique rolled her eyes again, this time nervously. "Because it turns out . . ." She stopped for a moment and then said, "I have herpes."

Because of the way it had presented, she explained, her gynecologist was fairly confident she'd been infected recently, which in her mind meant she'd almost certainly caught it from her former boss. If she told Todd, he'd refuse to marry her for sure—both because he'd then know she'd been unfaithful to him and because never in a million years would he be willing to risk becoming infected himself. But because she'd been on the pill as long as they'd been together, she could think of no other way to justify making him wear a condom except by telling him. On the other hand, she reasoned, she wasn't having an outbreak currently, so the risk of infecting him in the next few days was low even if he didn't wear a condom. So maybe she didn't need to say anything at all.

"So what do you think I should do?" she finished.

Ash had to stop himself from shaking his head. He paused to consider his response. "Have you thought about how your plan will affect Todd?"

"Yeah. But like I said I'm not flaring right now, so—"

"I'm not talking about that," Ash interrupted. "What about the fact that you're using him to get someone else to propose to you? How is that being respectful of his feelings? If you do get him to ask you to marry him and then you turn around and marry Carson instead, don't you think he'll eventually figure out you were seeing Carson the whole time? How do you think that'll make him feel? I mean, how do you figure that's okay?"

As soon as the words left his mouth he knew he'd made a mistake. Several moments passed in uncomfortable silence. When he asked her what she was feeling in response to his statement that had made her so quiet, she only shrugged. He tried to coax her into discussing her reaction but received only monosyllabic answers in response. After several more awkward and protracted silences, he finally commented that they'd seemed to have lost their momentum and suggested they stop for the day and pick up again next time. Dominique glanced at her watch at the same time Ash glanced at the clock on the wall behind her. Fifteen minutes remained in the session. Without saying a word, Dominique got up and left.

## The Freedom to Do What We Want

"What *I* think is that you need to go back to the possibility that you're dealing with a sociopath," I said.

Ash looked at me dubiously.

"A pervasive and persistent disregard for morals, social norms, and the feelings of others," I said. "Exploits others in harmful ways for her own pleasure. Lacks remorse for her actions. Irresponsible. Deceitful. Fails to maintain stable employment or fulfill social obligations. Impulsive, problems with interpersonal relationships, forms weak attachments to others. Should I go on?"

"Should Animality be an official DSM diagnosis, then?" Ash challenged. "Is everyone in the world of Animality a sociopath?"

"Actually, that's a good point. No. A predisposition to being swept away by your basic drives doesn't make you a sociopath. Though I can see where getting swept away by your basic drives could make you *seem* like a sociopath—"

"Or maybe you're right," Ash interrupted. "Maybe she *is* a sociopath, and maybe there's something about sociopathy that makes you more likely to be swept away by your basic drives."

"Sociopathy as the gateway to Animality?" I mused. "Let's think about that for a minute. If you felt no empathy—if you had no moral conscience—what might that make you believe you needed to be happy?"

"Well, one of the theories about sociopaths is that the way their brains are wired interferes with normal socialization.[1] They have trouble processing the pain and sadness of others. They lack guilt. So basically they never learn to avoid antisocial behavior. They just do what they want without worrying about how it affects other people."

"So imagine if you felt you could do that," I said, "if you felt you could just do whatever you wanted and damn the consequences. If you routinely *did* that. What might that teach you?"

"How about that what you need to be happy is the freedom to do whatever you want? It would certainly explain the impulsiveness, the focus on the present moment, and the obsession with satisfying basic drives," Ash said.

"It would. Except believing that to be happy you have to be able to do whatever you want is basically the same thing as believing you have to be able to *get* whatever you want, which is the core delusion of the world of Hunger."

"Well, how convinced are we that Animality and Hunger are different?"

I paused. "I certainly agree that in the broadest sense, desire lies at the heart of both. But in Hunger it's the desire for *attachment*, which requires—one—self-awareness and—two—conscious thought. There has to be an implicit recognition that you exist separately from the thing you desire as well as a conscious recognition of the steps you need to take to obtain it. In Animality, it's more the desire for *experience*—food, sex, sleep—basic pleasures. It's desire, but a different kind of desire. It's desire *without* thought. It's *craving*, which doesn't even require self-awareness, much less conscious deliberation, and which leads to an entirely different set of feelings and behaviors—an entirely different life-condition—than you see in Hunger. So to answer your question, no, I think to consider Hunger and Animality a single life-condition would be to ignore the fact that for all our intelligence, human beings frequently act without thinking at all."

❦

Ash didn't hear from Dominique again for seven months. When he finally did—in a hasty message left on his voicemail at three in the morning—she sounded genuinely contrite about having disappeared so abruptly. She also wanted to know if she could come back in for an appointment. Ash returned her call that afternoon and made arrangements to see her later that week.

She arrived exactly on time and sat down opposite him without a word. After a brief pause during which he found himself thinking she looked even worse than she had last time, her face even paler, her frame even thinner, he asked how she'd been.

In a trembling voice, she told him that the night she left his office seven months ago she'd gone out drinking and hadn't made it home until four in the morning. A few days later she flew to Denver with Todd as planned and had unprotected intercourse with him without telling him she had herpes. Todd had, in fact, proposed, but to her own surprise she abandoned her plan and turned him down. Then, in an impetuous attempt to follow Ash's admonition to be honest, she told *Carson* she had herpes. She thought that if honesty was to be her new policy, she should start with the person who mattered to her most.

But in response, Carson summarily ended their relationship and broke off all communication with her. Devastated, she called him every day for a week, but he refused to answer her calls. So she went to his home to confront him in person. She begged him to take her back, but he told her that there was no longer any point in their talking or continuing to have any contact at all. He warned her never to come to his home again and closed the door.

After that, she said, she'd spiraled down into a depression even more severe than her original one, and she was in his office now to tell him she'd finally figured out why.

"I'm an alcoholic."

Ash blinked in surprise. That alcoholism could have been the cause of her bizarre behavior hadn't even for a moment occurred to him. To his chagrin, he realized he'd never even taken a drug and alcohol history.

"You're an alcoholic?" he repeated.

She nodded.

"Since when?"

"Since I was twelve."

Bored and looking for something to do one Saturday afternoon when her parents were out, she'd snuck into their liquor cabinet and ended up consuming an entire bottle of red wine. Then she drank half a bottle of vodka. By the time her parents had come home, she'd become semi-comatose. They rushed her to the hospital where she was diagnosed with acute alcohol poisoning.

She remembered thinking soon afterward that she must have been built differently in some fundamental way from her friends, none of whom had ever experienced anything remotely like what she had, and none of whom, she knew even then, would have felt what she was feeling as a result: a strong desire to drink again.

To her amazement, her parents never made any accusations or imposed any punishments—in fact, never made any comments about what had happened at all. Left alone in bewildering silence, the episode receding farther and farther into the past, Dominique found her initial surprise at their silence turning into relief. Eventually then her relief turned into complacency—a complacency from which she ultimately derived, she realized in retrospect, tacit permission to continue drinking.

Over time she progressed from sneaking sips from her father's wine glass before serving it to him at dinner to staying out all night drinking with her friends. Only occasionally would she notice that the gap between her behavior and that of her friends was gradually widening. None of them ever seemed to want to party to the degree she did.

By the time she was a junior in high school, her behavior had become even more erratic. Sometimes she wouldn't make it to school at all after having stayed out drinking all night. More and more she found herself forced to devise elaborate stories, weaving lies inside of lies, all to explain to her teachers, parents, and friends why she sometimes completely failed to live up to their most basic expectations.

But because these lapses were only occasional and in every other way she seemed to be leading a normal life, neither her family nor her friends imagined anything was seriously amiss. Even her first DUI charge at the age of eighteen was viewed as a venal offense. Everyone thought it was an aberration, a mistake any eighteen-year-old might make.

By then, keeping straight all the lies she was telling to cover up the consequences of her drinking had become difficult enough that she began to worry she wouldn't be able to keep her drinking hidden. This, she now revealed to Ash, had been the real reason she hadn't wanted to go to college—not only so she could pursue an acting career but also so she could clear more space in her life for drinking. Fewer responsibilities meant fewer instances of failing to live up to them, which meant fewer lies told, which meant lower odds of being found out. In the end, she'd agreed to go to college part-time mainly to maintain the fiction, both to her parents and to herself, that she was normal.

During her first three years of college, she adopted an additional strategy to maintain the illusion that her life was proceeding normally. She would space out her drinking binges several weeks apart—"blowouts" she called them—rewarding herself with a night of drinking only after she'd pass an exam or finish a project at work. Though at first she'd try to limit the number of cocktails she consumed during these evenings, in the end she'd drink more than anyone else she was with and stay out until early in the morning, often unable to remember where she'd been or what she'd done. By the time she quit school to take the job as a concierge, she'd been getting picked up by the police occasionally and spending nights in jail for drunk and disorderly conduct. By the time she showed up in Ash's office feeling depressed, she was drinking every weekend to the point of blacking out and waking up feeling physically ill, sometimes in places she didn't recognize, engulfed in regret and swearing to herself she'd never drink again.

In desperation, she began clutching at the strategy of trigger avoidance and refused to go out on the weekends. But then friends started inviting her to dinner during the week and she'd feel obligated to go—would want to go—telling herself that she'd only have a few drinks and then come home early. A few times it even worked. But that success only lulled her into believing she'd gained control over her drinking, which led to her first blowout ever during the work week a few days after her second-to-last session with Ash.

Feeling utterly defeated, she decided that becoming sick after a night of drinking was simply her cross to bear in life and that there was nothing for her to do but rise up and meet her commitments as best she could. She would simply have to drag herself into work each morning after a night of drinking, bleary-eyed but business-suited. She was convinced that as long as she could maintain the *appearance* of normalcy—could hold on to her job and continue to act in plays, or at the very least make it to a few auditions a month—she could prevent her two worlds from colliding. That way, she reasoned, she could keep her addiction a secret no matter how sick she got after a blowout and no matter how much shame and remorse drinking now made her feel.

But after her last session with Ash, feeling discouraged after being "kicked out of his office fifteen minutes early" for telling him about her plan to have unprotected intercourse with Todd, the drinking binge she'd gone on, she now confessed, had been one of her worst ever. She'd awakened the next morning lying on the floor of her living room with no idea how she'd come to be there. A throbbing pain in her hands brought her attention down to her palms, where she discovered crusted blood from multiple razor-thin cuts. She glanced over at the mirror in her foyer, hanging now at an angle, and saw it was empty except for a few jagged remnants of glass stuck in its frame. The glass it had housed was now scattered in shards across her entryway rug. She looked beyond it to the front door of her apartment, which was hanging wide open, and at that moment decided it was "time to make some major changes" in her life.

So she'd embarked on her trip to Denver with Todd two days later, Dominique now revealed, not as a manipulative attempt to secure the future she thought she wanted as she'd originally told Ash, but rather as a desperate effort to rewrite her life into some semblance of normalcy. She'd been drunk, she now admitted, when she'd had unprotected intercourse with Todd in Denver and drunk when she'd impetuously confessed to Carson she had herpes. When as a result Carson had ended their relationship, the pain she'd felt, she said, was finally—finally, finally—enough to catalyze in her an unambiguous desire to stop drinking. For not until the moment she appeared at Carson's doorstep after his repeated refusals to talk with her and she heard the real reason he never wanted to see her again did she at last understand the truth about what was wrong with her. For she hadn't been driven to his door by a pathetic hope to resuscitate the rotting corpse of their relationship for fear of ending up alone; she'd gone there because she believed that her life was about to come undone and only he could save her. "You've got a problem with alcohol," he'd told her calmly, stunning her with his awareness of her addiction, "and if you don't stop drinking, you're going to die."

So that was why she'd come back to see Ash, she finished. Because she was done. Just why Ash was willing to see her again she didn't know. She knew she didn't deserve his kindness. But that he *was* willing to take her back was all that mattered, she said, her voice still trembling. Because now she was truly finished drinking. For good. She knew—really knew—she needed to stop. She had every intention of stopping.

"I just don't know how."

## How Nature Motivates Animals

"So it turns out her problem has nothing to do with a delusion at all," Ash said. "She's an alcoholic." After her confession, he'd taken her through the Michigan Alcoholism Screening Test and confirmed the diagnosis.

"Wow," I said. "That's just—"

"I know. I couldn't believe it either."

"No, I mean, that's it! *That's* the core delusion of the world of Animality."

"What is?"

"The reason she drinks," I said. "It's because she believes the core delusion of Animality."

"Hang on a minute. You're saying alcoholism is caused by a delusion?"

"No, not alcoholism—"

"Alcoholism is a disease," Ash interrupted. "Like asthma or diabetes. It doesn't matter what an alcoholic *believes*. It's genetic. . . ."

I readily agreed that alcoholism was a disease, one whose likelihood of occurring was significantly influenced, we now knew, by the presence of certain genes.[2]

"But unlike asthma or diabetes, all the adverse consequences of alcoholism can be avoided by making a simple choice—not to drink."

"Except for an alcoholic that choice is anything but simple," Ash said. "And if you're an alcoholic, you don't just have to make that choice once. You have to make it every day for the rest of your life."

"That doesn't mean it's not about making a choice," I countered. "It just means it's hard."

"Okay, sure, but—"

"How else do you figure some alcoholics manage to avoid dying from their alcoholism?"

"If you're asking why *this* alcoholic stops drinking and *that* one doesn't," Ash said, "I don't think anyone knows."

"But in one sense we do. The answer's been in front of us the whole time. All we had to do was ask ourselves how nature motivates animals."

"How nature motivates animals?" Ash asked. "How does nature motivate animals?"

"With threats to their survival. Except it only *looks* like nature motivates animals with threats to their survival. Because that would require animals to *think* about survival, which they don't. Nature actually motivates animals—at least, vertebrate animals—with pleasure and pain. There isn't anything an animal does that *isn't* a response to one or the other. That's why pleasure and pain evolved. To direct behavior."

"Okay. . . ."

"So you know what I think? I think choosing to drink has *everything* to do with a delusion. I think *all* alcoholics who stop drinking manage to do so, one way or another and whether they realize it or not, by freeing themselves from the core delusion of the world of Animality, a delusion that explains everything we've been talking about—Dominique's mind-boggling degree of self-centeredness, her impulsiveness, her thoughtless manipulation of the feelings of others, her complete lack of judgment, *and* why sociopaths are likely to have the life-condition of Animality as their basic life tendency. What does Dominique believe she needs to be happy? *Pleasure.* The core delusion of the world of Animality *is that pleasure and happiness are one and the same.*"

"You mean pleasure *isn't* the best good feeling we're capable of having?" Ash asked.

"Not even close," I said.

◦◦◦

"Wait a minute," Dominique said after Ash suggested the reason she drank was because of a delusional belief. "You're saying alcoholism is caused by a belief?"

"No," Ash said. "Alcoholism is a disease. We don't know what causes it. We don't know how to cure it. But we do know there's something that renders it irrelevant: the decision to stop drinking. Alcoholics Anonymous is chock-full of people who've done just that. It can be done."

"I can't even *imagine* going to an AA meeting."

"The path to abstinence is different for everyone," Ash said. "I'm only suggesting that the last step is always the same. You have to free yourself from the belief that the pleasure you get from drinking is making you happy."

"I've never believed drinking made me *happy*. I just like it. It feels good." Then she rolled her eyes. "Even though it's also making me miserable."

## A Basic Drive *and* a Delusion

"But not every alcoholic drinks to feel pleasure," Ash argued. "Or at least *only* to feel pleasure. A lot of them drink to avoid feeling pain. To numb themselves."

"In the world of Animality, we're after both," I said. "The belief that pleasure and happiness are one and the same is functionally identical to the belief that pain and happiness are mutually exclusive."

Indulging in pleasure *is* known to reduce stress.[3] Thus, even apart from its direct pain-numbing effects, the pleasure alcohol makes us feel reduces pain simply because *all* pleasure reduces pain. This is likely why people also eat, drink, use drugs, listen to music, and even shop for comfort. Pleasure is just incredibly distracting.[4]

"But that makes it seem even less likely that the desire for pleasure comes from a delusion," Ash said. "You said it yourself—and I agree—animals don't look for food because they *believe* they need to eat. They're not even really *aware* they need to eat. They look for food because they're hungry and eating feels good. It's brain chemistry. It's neurology. So why invoke a delusion to explain an addiction to alcohol? To explain an addiction to any kind of pleasure at all?"

"Because even though alcoholics are from the world of Animality, they aren't like other animals. They're human beings, which means they're constantly forming beliefs about everything they do—rationalizations to justify their actions. Everyone needs to believe that what they do is right and good. That's why rationalizations have so much power: they help us avoid cognitive dissonance. So I'm suggesting that our rationalizations about pleasure—our beliefs about pleasure—drive our pleasure-seeking behavior every bit as much as our brain chemistry. Think about it: We don't only have children because sex feels good. We also have children because we believe it's rewarding and important. It's not just our brain stem that governs our behavior. Our cerebral cortex does, too."[5]

"We may want to have children because we believe it's rewarding and important, but we want *sex* because it feels good," Ash said. "We don't need to believe it *is* good."

"Then why don't we have sex with our mothers? Or our sisters?"

"Uh . . ."

"We may not need to believe a pleasure is right and good to *desire* it—desire is just a feeling—but we do need to believe it's right and good to *pursue* it—"

"Actually—okay—that's maybe an important distinction—"

"Especially when we're talking about a pleasure that *isn't* good, or isn't good for us," I added.

"Like drinking, you're saying."

"Like drinking in the face of adverse consequences. Remember, pleasure itself isn't bad. It's *overindulging* in pleasure that's bad. Which, by the way, is something you *don't* see with other animals. Only with us—when our experience of pleasure stirs up the belief—the rationalization—that happiness and pleasure are one and the same."

"So just like you can desire an attachment without entering the world of Hunger, you can desire pleasure without entering the world of Animality?" Ash asked.

"That's right," I answered. "We enter the world of Animality when we become *obsessed* with pleasure, when we overindulge in it—meaning, essentially, partake in it when there's a good chance partaking in it will cause us some kind of harm. When we're willing, in short, to pay for short-term gain with long-term pain. I'm not saying pleasure doesn't contribute to happiness. But I'd argue that pleasure—by which I mean the good feeling we experience when we satisfy a bodily need—isn't happiness itself. It isn't the best good feeling we're capable of having. That's what Dominique doesn't get. Which is why she's continued to drink in the face of adverse consequences. And why smokers light up, and people have sex with their best friend's girlfriend or boyfriend, or don't use condoms when they have sex with strangers. Because their desire for pleasure is out of control. Because they're trapped in the world of Animality."

"*Now* I get it," Ash said.

⚬⚬⚬

"What's wrong with pleasure, anyway?" Dominique asked. "Pleasure is great!"

"Pleasure *is* great," Ash agreed. "There's absolutely nothing wrong it. Nothing wrong with *enjoying* pleasure. But if you keep expecting pleasure to make you happy, there are good reasons to think you're asking it to do something it can't."

"That seems so unfair," Dominique said.

"It may just be the way we're built. Pleasure is undoubtedly a *part* of happiness, but too much pleasure is often paradoxically *unpleasant*. And it can lead to consequences that make us decidedly *un*happy. For example, too many jelly beans not only can make us feel sick but also can lead us to gain weight. And of course some pleasures—like alcohol, cigarettes, and other drugs—can be harmful in even small amounts. And not just by compromising our health. The unrestrained pursuit of pleasure frequently leads to terrible decision-making."

"You don't have to tell to me about terrible decisions. . . ." She glanced away from him. "What a mess."

# Where Neurology and Psychology Meet

"Except why doesn't the desire to *over*indulge in pleasure come from brain chemistry, too?" Ash asked. "Say that Dominique *does* come to realize that pleasure and happiness aren't the same and that her drinking is the cause of her depression. Why couldn't her desire to drink just turn out to be stronger than her desire to stop suffering simply because of the way she's wired?"

Studies do suggest that alcohol stimulates the opioid system in the brains of alcoholics more intensely than it does in the brains of non-alcoholics.[6] Not only that, but the opioid system, which creates the *experience* of pleasure ("liking"), isn't the only thing that makes it harder for alcoholics to resist drinking. The dopamine system, which creates the *desire* for pleasure ("wanting"), also becomes sensitized to the effects of alcohol and other drugs, resulting in a greater release of dopamine and therefore more intense "wanting."[7] This enhanced release of dopamine occurs as a result of the release of another neurotransmitter, glutamate, whose release is itself enhanced when addicts encounter environmental cues that they associate with alcohol or drug use, like certain smells or places.[8] This then represents evidence that alcoholics may often be constitutionally—*neurologically*—less capable of resisting the temptation to drink than non-alcoholics. Alcoholics may indeed have a harder time achieving long-term abstinence because of the way they're wired.

And yet a number of alcoholics manage to become sober anyway. So how do they do it? Perhaps, in the end, only by coming to understand with their lives that the pleasure of drinking alcohol *isn't* happiness, and that in fact for them, alcohol is poison. For what else could turn an alcoholic away from an overpowering desire to drink other than a competing desire that's even stronger—the desire to live?

The key, again, is *how* we understand that pleasure and happiness aren't the same. "So right now," I said, "Dominique understands she needs to stop drinking intellectually, which is enough to make her *want* to stop. But it's not enough to arm her with the power to do it."

Whenever any of us is tempted to indulge in a particular pleasure, two forces immediately set themselves in opposition. On the one hand, the belief that pleasure represents happiness, bolstered by dopamine-induced cravings, begins pushing us *toward* the choice to indulge. On the other, a belief that indulging might make us more *un*happy in the long run begins pulling us *away* from it. Which force wins? It depends on which belief gets stirred up more intensely.

"So say you put a plate of cookies in front of someone who's trying to lose weight," Ash said. "They look at the cookies and start comparing how much happiness they expect to get from eating them to how much happiness they expect to get from losing weight? And if the belief that eating the cookies will make them happy gets stirred up more intensely than the belief that losing weight will make them happy, they'll eat the cookies?"

I nodded. "Rationalizing as they eat them, of course, why that's the better choice—even if the belief that eating the cookies will make them happy *stops* being stirred up the moment they swallow the last bite."

What determines which belief gets stirred up more intensely? It depends on the thing doing the stirring. Maybe it's our concern about keeping our diabetes under control. Maybe it's the thought that we want to look good in a bikini for the summer. Or the fact that we haven't eaten a dessert in a month. Or that we're depressed and want something to make us feel better.

Ash paused. "Now I'm wondering exactly what it means to understand something with your life."

"Why?"

"Well, we said before it meant to feel and behave in accord with your intellectual understanding. But we talked about it as if it was something that only had to happen once. That once you understood something with your life it would *always* govern your feelings and behavior. But that's not what we're saying now at all. What we're saying now is that even once you come to understand something with your life, that understanding can slip back into the theoretical realm at any time. All it takes is for a competing understanding to be stirred up more intensely. So, in fact, you can believe with your life that to be happy you need to both eat the cookie *and* lose weight. You just can't believe those things with your life at the same time."

"That's exactly right. When two opposing beliefs fight for control over your behavior, only one wins."

"Even though the next time it could easily be the other one. Even though in the next *minute* it could be the other one."

"Yes," I said.

"Which also means, by the way," Ash said, "that just because you believe something with your life doesn't automatically mean it's true."

"I wasn't drinking because I thought it was the key to my happiness," Dominique said. "I drank because I thought drinking was normal. Everyone in my life drinks. My parents still drink every night. When my friends and I go out, we *all* drink."

"But that can't be the whole story," Ash said. "If drinking was only something you liked—say, as much as you like getting a massage or eating sushi—why would quitting be so hard?"

She shrugged helplessly. "I don't know."

"Doesn't that tell you that drinking is more than just something you enjoy? Doesn't that tell you it holds a special place in your heart?"

"I'm not denying that drinking holds a special place in my heart. I just never thought about it as something that made me happy."

"You never thought about it as something that made you happy, but do you behave as if anything else makes you happier? Is there anything else you'd rather do more?"

"Actually," she admitted, "no."

"No," Ash agreed.

"Wow." Dominique's eyes widened. "I didn't . . . I didn't know I was going to say that. That's just . . . this is just . . ." Her eyes brimmed with tears. She shook her head. "I can't do this."

"Yes, you can. You can."

"How?"

"You've already figured out that drinking is what's been making you miserable," Ash said. "Now you just have to become convinced that happiness is possible without it."

"So I suggested that the most effective way to become convinced in her heart that it's possible to live a happy life without drinking would be to surround herself with other alcoholics who've done it," Ash said.

"So you suggested AA?" I asked.

"I did."

"And how's it been going?"

"Three months sober so far."

"And you think now she believes she can be happy without alcohol?" I asked.

"Too early to tell. She's still learning just how to *live* without alcohol. Being happy without alcohol comes later. One step at a time."

"Fair enough," I said. "Fair enough."

"I'll tell you one thing she has done, though. Step Nine: 'Made a list of all persons we'd harmed and made direct amends to them wherever possible, except when to do so would injure them or others.'"

"Amends?"

"She apologized," Ash explained. "To Todd and Carson, no less."

"No kidding. How'd *that* go?"

"They forgave her. She asked them to forgive her, and they did." Ash shook his head in amazement. "Both of them."

## Key Points

- Animality is defined as the life-condition of instinct.

- People trapped in the life-condition of Animality obsessively seek pleasure and avoid pain. As a result, they often behave impulsively and unwisely. Their personal relationships tend to be tumultuous and their lives chaotic.

- The life-condition of Animality also fuels the will to survive, however, enabling people to manifest a strength they often didn't know they had.

- The core delusion of the world of Animality is that happiness and pleasure are the same.

# 4

# Anger

*The task we must set for ourselves is not to feel secure, but to be able to tolerate insecurity.*

—Erich Fromm

Anger is defined as the life-condition of ego. Unlike the world of Hunger in which we're overly attached to our desires, and the world of Animality in which we're overly attached to pleasure, in the world of Anger, we're overly attached to the way we're viewed by others. Being overly attached to the way we're viewed by others then leads us to worry excessively about our own worth. As a result, when trapped in the world of Anger, we live in a state of constant anxiety.

We bury this anxiety so deeply, however, that we often don't recognize it's there. Our lack of awareness then serves only to magnify its influence on our behavior (obviously we can't guard against something we don't see). Thus, we conceal our true feelings out of fear of being scorned, cling to any advantage we have over others out of fear of being bested, and refuse to accept responsibility for our mistakes or take advice from others out of fear of being viewed as incompetent.

In fact, when trapped in the world of Anger, we're obsessively concerned about being viewed negatively in any way at all. Because of this, we work tirelessly to appear virtuous, accomplished, and strong. Often, to convince ourselves that we are in fact all these good things, we attempt to dominate those we perceive to be weaker than ourselves, even as we remain wary of and even fear those we perceive to be stronger.

At the same time, feeling contemptuous, competitive, and jealous toward everyone, we criticize others constantly, especially those whose faults we recognize in ourselves. Certainly, when well managed, this competitiveness can result in groundbreaking achievement. But when it isn't, as when it erupts out of the world of Anger, it results in the most vicious forms of discrimination—nationalism, racism, sexism, and so on.

This propensity to discriminate against others is further bolstered by our exaggerated belief in our own importance. When trapped in the world of Anger, we feel we deserve—and possess—the very best of everything: the highest salary, the best-looking spouse, the grandest home, the most accomplished life. What's more, we delight in broadcasting these achievements as loudly and as broadly as we can, for when trapped in the world of Anger there's nothing we desire more than universal acclaim. Indeed, nothing, we find, soothes the wound that lies at the heart of the world of Anger, the wound of insecurity, more effectively than the adulation that comes with fame. The great irony of the world of Anger then is that when we're trapped in it, we spend most of our time and energy working to convince others to view us in a way that's in direct opposition to the way we view ourselves.

When Roosevelt first came to see Ash with his wife, Kim, and their infant daughter, Heather, two things about him struck Ash immediately. The first was his complete lack of facial hair—whiskers, eyebrows, even eyelashes—which Ash would learn in a subsequent session was due to a condition affecting his entire body called atrichia, present since birth and the cause of merciless teasing throughout his childhood. The second was the painstaking attentiveness with which Roosevelt did everything—the way he delicately opened Ash's office door for Kim, as if it might fall off its hinges if he opened it too quickly; the way he rushed back out into the waiting room to retrieve a chair for himself after he'd gingerly deposited Kim and Heather on the leather one across from Ash; even the way he'd knotted his tie into a perfectly symmetrical triangle.

So when Roosevelt confessed he'd come to see Ash because he thought he might harm his daughter, Ash was puzzled. How had so terrible a possibility taken up residence in so gentle and meticulous a person?

"I'm not an angry person," Roosevelt told him, his voice as soothing as an aquarium's hum. As he shifted in his seat, Roosevelt's muscles bulged under his silk shirt from what Ash presumed had been years, if not decades, of weight lifting. "People treat me well. I treat them well. Customer service is my thing. I mean, I work at a men's clothing store. I've always prided myself on how well I get along with people. But lately I've been finding"—and here his voice faltered slightly—"there are times when"—he cleared his throat quietly—"there are times when I just get so *mad*, out of nowhere, that I can't stop it. I don't know where it's coming from."

"*Do* you stop it?" Ash asked.

"Just barely. But I've come really close to actually doing something to her."

"Your daughter," Ash clarified. "Hurting her, you mean."

"I don't want to. But I'm afraid I will."

"What does she do that makes you so mad?"

"She won't stop crying. No matter what I do. Feeding her doesn't work. Her diaper's clean. She doesn't want to be held. She's not too cold. She's not too hot." He turned to Kim. "I mean, what is it, you know?"

Kim looked at him helplessly.

"She's fussy?" Ash asked Kim.

"I keep telling him it's not her fault," Kim said. "She's just a baby. How can he blame her for crying? That's what babies do."

"I don't blame her," Roosevelt responded evenly. "I'm not mad at her because I think she's doing it deliberately."

"Then what's it because of?" Kim asked.

Roosevelt shrugged. Sweat had begun to gleam off his ebony skin. "I don't know."

"What do you do when she cries?" Ash asked Roosevelt.

"I imagine doing really bad things to her."

"Like what?"

"Like throwing her against the wall. Smashing her head in. I actually imagine doing it."

Kim was trying hard to mask the alarm she felt at hearing this. Her hand stroked Heather's head, twirling circles around her tiny black curls of hair that were just beginning to come in. Heather smiled.

"But you haven't," Ash said.

"You won't report us to anyone, will you?" Kim asked suddenly. "We're here to get help. That's got to count for something, right?"

"It counts for a lot," Ash said.

"See?" Kim said to Roosevelt.

"That's great," Roosevelt replied. "But how *much* does it count? Aren't you guys obligated to report child abuse?"

"Only if we think a child is imminent danger of being abused or already has been. You said nothing's happened, though, right?" Ash clarified.

"That's right."

"Look, you've come to a therapist," Ash emphasized. "You've been honest about having some pretty unpleasant thoughts. That sounds to me like someone who wants help avoiding doing something he knows is wrong and doesn't really want to do. So let's just get into it. Why do you think you're having such a hard time controlling your temper?"

"I don't know," Roosevelt replied. "Like I told you, I'm really not an angry person. Just this one thing gets me so unbelievably mad. It's like a storm blowing in out of nowhere—with hail the size of baseballs."

## A Reaction Formation

"Babies *are* notorious for provoking frustration," I said.

"All parents think about hurting their children at some point," Ash agreed. "The question is why is *he* so worried about it that he decided to come to therapy?"

"Especially when he's supposed to be such a tranquil person."

"Exactly. Makes me wonder if that's an act. Or a reaction formation of some kind."

"What's a reaction formation?" I asked him.

"A defense mechanism. Basically, when someone perceives their true feelings or desires to be unacceptable, they try to convince others—and themselves—that the opposite is true, often in an exaggerated way. Think about why gay men are sometimes the most homophobic people you meet."

"It is true that sometimes people who appear completely calm on the outside are the angriest underneath."

"Or it could be he *is* a generally calm person who's just reaching the end of his rope with the crying," Ash said.

"But then why would Kim be so worried about you reporting him to DCFS?"

"It seemed like she wanted to make sure he feels it's safe for him to get the help he needs," Ash said.

"Which would mean whether he's angry in general or just at the end of his rope with the crying," I said, "she feels the danger to her daughter is real."

When Ash next asked Roosevelt if anyone else besides Heather provoked such disproportionate anger in him, Roosevelt said no.

"No one at all?" Ash asked, glancing meaningfully at Kim.

"Well, sure," Roosevelt said, following Ash's gaze to his wife. "We fight just like any other couple. But mostly I'm pretty calm. Wouldn't you say, honey?"

Kim shrugged.

"No?" Roosevelt asked with a smile.

"You are calm. Except when you're not."

"Meaning what?" Ash asked.

"It's like he's two people," Kim said. "Like right now you probably think he's the nicest, most reasonable person in the world. Wouldn't hurt a fly. But other times . . ." She blew out a meaningful breath.

"Other times what?" Ash asked her.

"He gets *really* mad."

"Come on," Roosevelt protested gently. "That's only once in a while."

"How often would *you* say it is, Kim?" Ash asked.

"Until Heather was born, it wasn't even once in a while," Kim said. "It was actually bizarre. Nothing *ever* bothered him. Like he didn't have it in him. Now it seems like we fight all the time."

"Come on, now," Roosevelt prodded her with the same calm voice and easy smile. "It's not all the time."

"Since Heather was born . . . ," Ash mused.

Kim nodded.

"Which was . . . ?"

"A little over six months ago."

"So you," Ash continued, looking at Roosevelt, "think you only have an anger problem with your daughter, and you"—looking at Kim—"think he gets mad at *you* just as much as he does at her."

"At least fifty percent of the time when he's mad," Kim said, "he's mad at me."

"And you don't agree?" Ash asked Roosevelt.

"What husband doesn't get mad at his wife now and then?"

"Except Kim seems to think it's more often than that."

Roosevelt shrugged. "She's entitled to her opinion. I just disagree with it."

"That's how I experience it," Kim insisted.

"I understand," Roosevelt said, his voice relaxed and his expression composed, as if he were unconcerned or even unaware that he was the one Kim was accusing.

"It doesn't matter anyway," Kim said. "We're not here to talk about us. We're here to make sure he gets the help he needs so he doesn't hurt our daughter." She tightened her grip on Heather, whose face lit up with another smile.

Though Kim thought Roosevelt rarely felt anger before Heather was born, Ash wondered if what had changed since then was merely his ability to hide it. Perhaps he'd actually been angry with Kim as long as they'd been married, and the additional stress of caring for a baby had simply overwhelmed his ability to contain it.

"How would you characterize the quality of your marriage?" Ash asked them.

"Good," Roosevelt said.

"It's all right," Kim said.

Roosevelt looked at her in surprise.

"Have you ever hit her?" Ash asked Roosevelt.

Roosevelt jerked back in his chair. "No!"

"But you have shoved me," Kim said.

"Not hard. And only a few times in the heat of the moment. Never enough to hurt you. Tell the truth."

Kim remained silent.

"So he *hasn't* actually hit you?" Ash asked her.

"No."

"Yelled at you?"

She laughed ruefully. "Oh, yeah."

"Called you names?" Ash asked.

"Yeah."

"Deliberately tried to make you feel bad?"

She frowned, her chin quivering slightly. She nodded.

"Now that's not true!" Roosevelt protested. "How can she know what's in my mind unless I tell her?"

"She seems to think it is true, Roosevelt."

"She's wrong."

"Maybe it hasn't been your intention, but it sounds like that's how she's been taking it."

"I can't control how she feels."

"Funny then how you keep trying to," Kim muttered.

This remark reverberated in Ash's ears like a thunderclap, the clearest indication yet that Roosevelt's problem with anger neither began nor ended with Heather.

"Why did you shove her?" Ash asked Roosevelt. "I mean, what's provoked that kind of anger in you in the past?"

Roosevelt admitted that her tone often irritated him—certainly more than anything she actually said. "When we're having an argument, there's usually a point in the conversation, if it went another way, if she just backed down and gave me some space, I'd be okay. But it seems sometimes she deliberately tries to push my buttons. And when she does, it's like there's no going back for me. That's when I feel like I'm going to lose it."

"When she's intentionally trying to make you mad, you mean," Ash clarified. "When you perceive that."

"Yeah." He paused. "I think if she'd stop trying to push my buttons on purpose, I wouldn't get so mad when Heather cries."

"Why?"

"I think I'd just be less mad in general."

"Yet you don't consider yourself an angry person," Ash reminded him.

"I only get angry when she tries to make me angry on purpose," Roosevelt reiterated. "It's like she's trying to control me. *That's* what sets me off. Otherwise I'm cool."

❦

"Cool?" I exclaimed. "He's shoved her. He tries to control her. He thinks she's trying to make him mad on purpose. In what universe does any of that make him cool?"

"Although that last thing could actually be true," Ash cautioned. "We don't know yet."

"What's utterly bizarre is that he insists he's not an angry person even as he admits that he's an angry person!"

Ash shrugged. "Maybe that's why he's accusing her of trying to make him mad—or actually *believes* she's trying to make him mad—to absolve *himself* of responsibility for his own anger. If *she's* responsible for making him angry, he can get angry and still not be an angry person."

"So here's a question then," I said. "What's he got against being angry?"

❦

"But I'm *not* trying to make you angry on purpose," Kim insisted.

"It sure seems that way," Roosevelt replied.

"All I do is ask you to help around the house once in a while."

"Once in a while? Try nagging me the minute I walk through the door!"

"I just want a nice home. Is that so much to ask?"

"You have a nice home," Roosevelt answered sharply.

"Only because I make the effort to keep it that way. If I didn't, you'd see how nice our home would be."

"The only reason you have a home in the first place is because I bought it for you. If it wasn't for me you wouldn't have anything."

"If it wasn't for me we'd live in a pig sty. You never appreciate what I do. It's always about what you do."

"I *never* appreciate what you do?" Roosevelt shot Ash an amused look.

"Never spontaneously," Kim said. "No."

"I'll tell you what," Roosevelt said with a malicious grin. "How about I actually stop helping out around the house. Maybe *then* you'll see how much I do."

"Why wait?" Kim asked, her voice full of sarcasm. "Tell me now. Tell me exactly what it is that you do."

Flushing slightly, Roosevelt said, "How about all the hours I work to pay the mortgage so we can stay in our nice home?"

"How about wiping up the kitchen countertop after you make a sandwich? How about taking out the garbage more than twice a month? Hanging up a towel when you're done drying yourself after you shower in the morning instead of dropping it on the floor?"

"Man!" Turning to Ash, he said, "See what a nag she is?"

Ash felt like he was watching a train approaching a curve at too great a speed, able only to watch helplessly as it sped toward disaster.

"I'm not a nag," Kim insisted. "I just want a nice home. We both live there, remember?"

"How could I forget with you reminding me every time you open your mouth? Roosevelt, do this! Roosevelt, do that! You're driving me crazy!"

"If I didn't ask you to do things, they'd never get done."

"Maybe if you asked me at better times you'd get better responses."

"Better times?" Kim asked. "What better times?"

"Not when we're about to have sex, for one. Just when we're starting to get in the mood, you have a million things for me to do first."

"Why should you get sex from me when I don't get any help from you?"

"What, sex is my *reward* now? Like it's not important to you?"

"It's hard for me to enjoy it when I feel you don't care about my needs," Kim said.

"I do care about your needs! But I'm working twelve to thirteen hour days, I haven't had a vacation in months, and every time I come home you dump her on me before I can even get my shoes off! I mean, Jesus! Why can't you ever leave—me—the—fuck—*alone?*"

## The Importance of Autonomy

"That doesn't sound like someone who's just at the end of his tolerance for crying," I observed.

"Now you know why I'm thinking he's from the world of Anger," Ash said.

"Well, actually, just because you're angry doesn't mean you're from the world of Anger."

"No? Then why is it called that?"

"It's also called Belligerence, or sometimes even Arrogance. The world of Anger isn't about the *emotion* anger. Or I should say, it isn't *only* about the emotion of anger. It's about the ego; about an excessive belief in your own importance. The emotion of anger is just one of the ego's tools. Just one of the things it uses to protect itself."

"So if Roosevelt gets angry because someone tells him he looks funny without any eyebrows, he's using anger to protect his ego, which means he's coming from the world of Anger. But if he gets angry because he feels like his wife is trying to control him, he's just angry."

"Actually, if he gets angry when his wife tries to control him, he's probably coming from the world of Anger, too."

"Why do you say that?" Ash asked.

"Because the idea of being controlled probably also threatens his ego."

"Not necessarily. We all want to feel that we're in control of our own actions. Autonomy is a universal and innate psychological need.[1] We all want the freedom to make our own choices."

"Is that why you think he's getting mad at Kim then?" I asked. "Because he feels like she's trying to compromise his autonomy?"

"It's not a bad thought. In some people the desire for autonomy is so strong that they even resist doing things they *want* to do when someone—especially a spouse—tries to push them too hard to do it. Human beings just don't like to be controlled."

"To cheat yourself out of what you want to do just to maintain your sense of autonomy?" I said. "Talk about cutting off your nose to spite your face."

"Are you kidding? People sacrifice their *lives* to preserve their autonomy. We're talking about the psychological underpinnings of the desire for liberty. For some people, it's that important."

"I wasn't disagreeing. In fact, I might be one of those people myself." I confessed to having felt the need to defend my own autonomy beyond the point of rationality when my wife, Rhea, pushed me too hard also. I understood Roosevelt's anger all too well.

"So maybe *that's* the core delusion of the world of Anger," Ash suggested. "To be happy you have to maintain your autonomy."

I shook my head. "I don't think so. For one thing, I'm not sure the belief that you need to maintain your autonomy to be happy *is* a delusion."

"It *is* pretty hard to be happy when your autonomy is compromised," Ash reflected.

I nodded. "For another, how do you imagine the desire to maintain your autonomy would give rise to the other characteristics of Anger? How would it create, for example, an excessive belief in your own importance? Or lead you to discriminate against others?"

"That's a good point," Ash said. "Being excessively attached to your autonomy isn't at all the same thing as being excessively attached to your ego."

"And even if Roosevelt *is* getting mad at Kim because he thinks she's trying to control him—because he's trying to preserve his autonomy—that wouldn't explain why he's getting mad at Heather. She's not trying to control him at all."

Ash paused. "When patients have a hard time controlling their anger, I always wonder if they're using it to suppress another feeling they like even less."

"That was definitely true for me with Rhea."

"Yeah?" Ash asked.

I nodded. "It took me a long time to figure this out, but whenever she'd get on me about something I hadn't done—whenever she seemed disappointed in me— what really made me mad was that her criticisms made me feel incompetent."

⚭

At their next session, Kim began by looking away from Roosevelt and saying, "Maybe we just need to take a break from each other."

"Yeah, right," Roosevelt replied with a laugh.

"What, you think this marriage is actually working?"

Roosevelt fixed her with a skeptical look. "Just where are you going to go? How are you going to make money?"

"Don't worry about me. I'm a big girl. I'll manage."

Suddenly, Roosevelt leapt out of his chair.

"You—are—such—a—fucking—*bitch*!" he shrieked, and he glared down at Kim with an expression so murderous it sent fear knifing into Ash's stomach.

Heather started to cry, and Roosevelt threw up his hands. "Great!" he shouted, and he turned and began marching toward the door.

Here at last, Ash thought, was the anger for which Roosevelt had presented himself to therapy fully manifested, as real and vicious as he'd described it.

But rather than bursting into tears or yelling back at Roosevelt with even greater fury, Kim only repositioned Heather on her lap to comfort her and said to Ash in a composed voice, "See, this is what he does. Nothing makes him angrier than when I tell him I don't need him. Like I'm this totally helpless female who wouldn't survive a minute in the world without a big strong man like him to protect me."

Roosevelt froze on his way toward the door and spun around. "You wouldn't. You've been riding my coattails since the day we met."

"And you're not quite the cool customer you want us all to think, now are you?" Kim retorted, measuring the distance he'd walked from his chair to the door with her eyes.

"I'm cool," Roosevelt insisted, the angry creases between his eyes smoothing out and disappearing as if they'd never been. "I'm cool. I'm just trying to make a point."

Ash felt disoriented by the speed with which Roosevelt's anger had vanished. "Which is . . . ?"

Roosevelt sauntered back to his chair and sat down. He smoothed out some wrinkles in his pants. "She wouldn't be able to survive a week without me."

Though Roosevelt continued to insist he only became uncontrollably angry when he couldn't get his daughter to stop crying, clearly his wife had the power to shatter his self-control as well. Ash was confident that if he probed more deeply he'd find Roosevelt also had trouble controlling his temper at work and in social situations with friends—in short, in every major arena in his life. Though Ash was now convinced that Roosevelt's calm demeanor *was* a reaction formation to his anger, he still didn't know why Roosevelt was so angry, or why he found anger so objectionable.

So he decided to start their next session in deliberate denial of Roosevelt's denial, suggesting in a professorial tone that the best way for Roosevelt to learn to control his temper was to understand its origins. Kim and Roosevelt both agreed with this approach and expressed their frustration at having already failed to figure it out on their own. Ash suggested they only needed a little help, reasoning that the cause of any particular behavior, even a behavior that had its origins years or even decades in the past, always remained alive in the present. At every moment in which a behavior manifested, he told them, the original thought process and beliefs that created it remained persistently "stirred up," even if only subconsciously, and therefore were always available for examination.

The only thing they needed then, Ash said, was a context in which the behavior manifested, a situation in which Roosevelt found himself angry. Though they'd come to therapy to prevent Roosevelt from hurting Heather, Ash dismissed the idea of using Heather as too impractical. He suggested instead they explore how Roosevelt's anger came out in the context of his relationship with Kim. When Roosevelt reiterated that he rarely got angry at Kim, Ash pointed out he'd already become angry at her during their previous sessions several times and that any one of those instances would have provided them the conduit they needed.

Ash proposed they try a type of therapy called Internal Family Systems Therapy, or Parts Model, named for its reference to an individual's internal community, or "family" of parts. It had been created by a Family Systems therapist named Richard Schwartz.[2] Mostly, Ash explained, people tend to conceive of themselves as one indivisible whole, one cohesive identity. But Parts Model took the opposite view, defining each person as a system of separate parts, each with their own roles and agendas.

"So say you have a problem with procrastination," Ash said. "Parts Model would identify that tendency as one of your parts, as an actual member of your internal family—call him the Procrastinator. Whenever you're confronted with an important task, the Procrastinator might instead make you vegetate in front of the television. In most people who tend to procrastinate, though, there's usually another part—call him the Manager—that gets mad when the Procrastinator gets his way and nothing gets done. Internal Family Systems Therapy is interested in exploring the polarity between these kinds of parts that don't get along. What makes this type of therapy unique is that it approaches a person's parts as if they were literally separate individuals."

"How's all this supposed to stop me from hurting my daughter when she cries?" Roosevelt asked.

"By giving the part of you that wants to hurt her a voice to explain itself," Ash said. "No part ever behaves in a way it considers irrational. Every part always acts based on reasons it finds compelling. Internal Family Systems Therapy tries to uncover those reasons to understand how our different parts think. Because once we understand how a part thinks, we can negotiate with it to change the way it behaves."

"How *it* thinks," Roosevelt said. "Like it's not really me at all," he offered to Kim.

"Of course it's you," Kim said.

"No, this is starting to make sense," Roosevelt said, warming to the idea. "How do we figure out how this part of me thinks?" he asked Ash.

"By having a dialogue with it."

Roosevelt stared at him blankly. "What—we just . . . ask it?" He looked down at his own stomach. "Why do you get so mad when Heather cries?"

"Sometimes," Ash answered, smiling. "But it seems to me you've already asked yourself that question in more a serious way and haven't found the answer."

"Otherwise I wouldn't have had to come here," Roosevelt agreed.

"Fortunately—and unfortunately—a person's parts don't only come into conflict with one another internally," Ash explained. "They also come into conflict with the parts of others. In fact, if you really think about it, conflict between people really comes down to conflict between their parts. One person's lazy part frustrates another person's ambitious part, or someone's messy part irritates someone else's organized part. The idea is to get parts that are in conflict with one another *talking* instead of *reacting*. With Parts Model the most enlightening dialogue doesn't occur between the patient and the therapist but rather between the parts that are in conflict with each other."

Roosevelt said nothing for a few moments. "But what if the reasons I get angry at Kim are different from the reasons I get angry at Heather?"

"They may very well be," Ash said. "But I'm thinking those would only be the superficial reasons. What we're after is the common reason. The underlying reason."

Roosevelt let out a long breath. "So how do we make this happen?"

The first step, Ash explained, was for each of them to identify what they considered to be their most prominent parts. They needed to do this by relying on their internal sense of them, without thought or regard for how they came to be. He asked them to come next time ready to name them. Then they'd figure out which parts were "partnered" in conflict and start them talking. And from that dialogue, Ash assured them, change would come. By the end of the session, both Roosevelt and Kim agreed they both felt a hope for progress that neither had experienced in a long time.

However, when they arrived for their next session, their excitement had vanished and been replaced by a subdued acrimony. "Why so glum?" Ash asked them.

For a moment, neither of them spoke. Kim shifted Heather from her right arm to her left and then down onto her left leg. Roosevelt watched in silence as she pulled off Heather's small pink mittens, stuffed them under her thigh, and then removed Heather's coat. "We've been in a fight the entire week," she said finally. "He's still mad about it."

"What, and you're not?" Roosevelt bristled. "I'm the only one here with an anger problem?"

"Fine," Kim said, sounding more exhausted than angry. "We're both still mad about it."

"How did it start?" Ash asked.

"The way all our fights do," Roosevelt answered. "With her nagging me."

Before Kim could raise an objection, Ash asked quickly, "What was she nagging you about?"

"The same old thing," Roosevelt said. In a mocking voice he mimicked her: "Roosevelt, can you take out the garbage? Roosevelt, can you vacuum? Roosevelt, can you wipe down the kitchen countertop? Nag, nag, nag, nag, nag."

"While I'm taking care of our daughter, you asshole!" Kim snarled.

"And then when I do what she asks," Roosevelt added, "it's never good enough! Everything has to be absolutely perfect or forget it. If I fold the shirts in the wrong way, they have to be redone. If I leave the smallest drop of water on the kitchen countertop, I get a dirty look while she wipes it herself. Her standards are impossible." He turned to Kim. "You have no idea how hypercritical you are."

"If you're going to do a job," Kim said, "do it right."

Ash held up his hands to stop them. "Okay," he said. "Time out. Take a breather." They both became still. Ash allowed several moments to pass before speaking again. "This is actually just what we need."

"Us fighting?" Kim said.

"Your *parts* fighting," Ash replied. "Now we have a context in which we can get them *talking*, just like we planned. How did you guys do with your homework assignment?"

Roosevelt shook his head. "We never got to it."

"Okay, let's put names to them now," Ash said. He asked Roosevelt, "How do you feel when Kim nags you?"

"Like nothing I do is ever good enough. It doesn't matter that I make the money, that I bought the house, that even though I work and she doesn't, I'm still getting up in the middle of the night half the time to feed this damn kid and burp her and put her back to sleep. I'm a walking zombie at work, and still she wants me to clean up around the house when I get home."

Ash regarded Roosevelt intently. "So what I hear you saying is that when Kim nags you it makes you feel like you're not good enough. Like you're inadequate. Small, even."

"I guess so," Roosevelt admitted. "Yeah. Small."

"Could we even say," Ash asked, "you have a small *part*?"

Roosevelt shrugged. "Yeah. Sure." Then he added, "Doesn't everybody?"

Ash nodded charitably. "So let's call that part Little Boy." He turned to Kim. "And what do you think, Kim, when Roosevelt doesn't want to do his share of the work around the house?"

Kim paused. "Like he thinks it's not important to do. Like he thinks what *I* do isn't important."

"And that makes you feel—?"

She shrugged. "Unappreciated."

"Could we say then," Ash continued, "you have an unappreciated *part*?"

Kim nodded. "Sure."

"Why don't we call that part Tired Housewife?"

"More like Exhausted Housewife," she said with a grimace.

"Fine," Ash said, turning to Roosevelt. "So the fight started when Kim asked you to take out the garbage?"

Roosevelt nodded.

"And what did you say?"

Roosevelt looked uncomfortable. "Uh . . . something like: 'Do you mind if I take my shoes off first?'"

"Actually you said, 'Can I get my *fucking* shoes off first?'" Kim said.

"And then what did you say, Kim?" Ash asked.

"I said how can you take out the garbage without your shoes on?"

"Yeah," Roosevelt said, starting to get hot, "and then I said—"

"Hold it," Ash interrupted, his hand held up. "Before we retrace the rest of the conversation, let's ask each of the parts we just identified what was going on with them when these things were said. Kim, you asked him to take out the garbage, but what was Exhausted Housewife thinking?"

"I guess she was thinking she could really use some help around the house."

"I help around the house, goddammit—!"

Ash held up his hand for Roosevelt to be silent again without turning his gaze from Kim. "I understand that's what *you* were thinking, Kim, but what I'm asking is why did *Exhausted Housewife* want Roosevelt to take out the garbage?"

Kim was silent. Then she said, "Because that would be proof."

Ash raised his eyebrows. "Of what?" he asked.

"That he values what I do. My contribution."

"So if it had been Exhausted Housewife talking that day when Roosevelt refused to take out the garbage, what might she have said?" Before she could answer, he inclined his head toward Roosevelt. "To him."

Kim turned to Roosevelt and took a deep breath. "When you don't want to take out the garbage it makes me feel you think what I do isn't as important as what you do."

Roosevelt crossed his arms in front of his chest. "It's not. It's not even close."

## The Appearance of Competence

"What was it you said about people in the world of Anger?" Ash asked. "They have an overblown belief in their own importance . . . ? A need to dominate anyone they perceive as weaker than themselves out of fear of being viewed as incompetent . . . ?"

I nodded. "Being made to feel incompetent could definitely explain Roosevelt's anger at Kim, just like it explained my anger at Rhea. He pretty much admitted that when she nags him about doing things around the house, he feels like an incompetent husband."

"It could also explain his anger at Heather. When he can't stop her from crying, it makes him feel like an incompetent father. The need for competence is easily as important as the need for autonomy."[3]

"For some people, even more important," I said.

"So then maybe *that's* the core delusion of the world of Anger," Ash said. "To be happy, you have to be competent."

I paused. "No, I don't think that's right either. If the core delusion of the world of Anger is that to be happy you need to be competent—presumably to satisfy the innate need we all have for mastery—why would it feel even more important to *appear* competent? I ask that because even when I felt I hadn't made a mistake, if Rhea said, or even implied, that I hadn't done a good job—if she made me feel incompetent even when I knew I hadn't been—it still made me angry. It wasn't *being* incompetent that bothered me. I didn't get mad if I screwed up when I was by myself with no one watching me. It was the idea that she *thought* I was incompetent."

"It was her opinion of you, you mean," Ash clarified.

"Yeah. Somehow, if she even *seemed* disappointed, it felt like an accusation."

⟡

Kim turned to stare out the window, her chin quivering.

"You're doing great," Ash encouraged her. "Let's keep going. Why is Exhausted Housewife so upset to hear Roosevelt say that what you do isn't as important as what he does?"

Kim brought her gaze back to Ash, who tilted his head to indicate she should address her comments to Roosevelt.

"For as long as I can remember," Kim said, her lips smacking tackily, "I've been in awe of my mother. Watching her put everyone else first, never complaining. I grew up wanting to be just like her. So I decided from day one of our marriage I would do my best to always put your needs before mine because that's what a dutiful wife does. It made me happy. And when Heather was born, I found taking care of her made me even happier than taking care of you. Being a mother and a wife and a homemaker are who I am. But when you say what I do isn't—" She stopped. "I always thought before Heather was born that caring for a child and maintaining a home would bring us closer together. I'm just so sad that instead it's driven us farther apart."

Roosevelt stared at her in surprise. After a few awkward moments, he mumbled that he hadn't known she'd felt that way.

"Roosevelt, if it had been Little Boy talking that day when Kim asked you to take out the garbage," Ash said, "what might he have said?"

Roosevelt pushed out a skeptical breath. "Leave me alone."

"Why?"

"Because, Christ, isn't the fact I just worked a full day enough? I have to work at home, too?"

"Why doesn't Little Boy want to work at home?"

"He's tired."

"No," Ash said. "That's another part talking: your *tired* part. Why doesn't *Little Boy* want to work at home?"

"Oh," Roosevelt said. He thought for a moment. Then his gaze moved to the floor. "Because what I do at work should be enough."

"Enough for what?" Ash asked. "Tell Kim."

Roosevelt angled his head toward Kim without looking up at her. "For you to think I'm a good partner."

Ash nodded and suggested that they were both trying to find validation through one another in ways that simply wouldn't work. Exhausted Housewife wanted Roosevelt to validate the importance of Kim's caretaker and homemaker duties because those seemed to be the primary means through which she derived her sense of self-worth. But Roosevelt couldn't because Exhausted Housewife triggered feelings of inadequacy in Little Boy when she asked for help with household chores, which felt to Roosevelt like a criticism of his performance as a partner.

"How is asking for help criticizing?" Kim asked Roosevelt incredulously.

"To Little Boy, something you want him to do is something he should have already done," Ash explained. He glanced at Roosevelt, who nodded.

"I hate him," Roosevelt said. "I hate Little Boy."

"So much so," Ash agreed, "that you refuse to let his voice be heard. It's just too painful. So to avoid feeling inadequate when Kim proves unable or unwilling to recognize the importance of your role as your family's bread winner, Little Boy continuously turns to another one of your parts. Your angry part."

"My angry part?" Roosevelt said.

"The part that takes care of Little Boy," Ash explained. "Vicious Protector."

## The Power of Anger

Anger works. If we feel weak, it makes us feel strong. If we feel intimidated, it gives us confidence. When we feel bullied, it hands us back control. Unfortunately, the way it works is by casting illusions. It makes us feel big by making others feel small, not by actually making us bigger. And though it makes us feel like we're in control, it actually takes our control away. In using anger to gain control over others, we paradoxically lose control over ourselves.

"But *feeling* like you're in control is the whole point," I said. "When you're trapped in the world of Anger, losing control of yourself seems like a small price to pay for the power anger provides."

"So could *that* be the core delusion of Anger, then?" Ash asked. "To be happy you need to have power over others?"

"I do think people in the world of Anger want control over others," I said, "but I don't think control over others is what they believe they need to be happy. I think for them, controlling others is a means to an end, a way of protecting themselves. Think about it. How better to prevent yourself from feeling vulnerable to someone than to make *them* feel vulnerable to you?"

"I get that," Ash said, nodding. "But the problem with using anger to make you feel big is that it doesn't address the reasons you feel small. It doesn't address your insecurities. And here's the problem with not addressing your insecurities: getting angry doesn't make them go away; it just covers them up. And as long as anger *seems* to keep working, you won't address the *reason* you feel insecure, so you won't actually *stop* feeling insecure—which will require you to keep getting angry. Which is why, despite Roosevelt's repeated assertions to the contrary, he *is* an angry person. Which puts him at risk for doing all sorts of destructive things like abusing his daughter and alienating his wife. *That's* the problem with using anger to control others. In solving one problem it creates others that are far worse."

"I completely agree. It *is* a problem that anger works. It's just totally seductive. I much preferred feeling angry to feeling incompetent myself."

"Yeah, it's one of the main reasons people get angry—to prevent themselves from feeling something else," Ash said. "To manage any feeling that causes them distress."

"In fact, if I'm going to be completely honest," I said, "I didn't only get angry because Rhea's criticisms made me feel incompetent. I also got angry to avoid feeling something else I felt as a *result* of feeling incompetent. Something I liked even less and that caused me even more distress."

"Fear?"

"No," I said. "Shame."

༄

"I'm wondering if the reason you get so angry at Heather," Ash said to Roosevelt, "is that your inability to stop her from crying triggers Little Boy, too, who then triggers Vicious Protector."

"It feels like it just triggers Vicious Protector," Roosevelt said.

"We usually get angry in response to distressing emotions," Ash said. "So can you tell me what you feel *before* you feel angry?"

"There is no before angry," Roosevelt said.

Ash shook his head. "Think. When Heather cries and you can't calm her down, how does that make you feel *first*?"

Roosevelt shifted his shoulders under his shirt. Several moments passed in silence. Then, in a voice Ash had to strain to hear, Roosevelt said, "Impotent."

Kim stared at him in shock. "Impotent?"

Roosevelt nodded once quickly, embarrassed. "When I can't get her to stop, yeah." Then he shook his head in self-disgust. "Little Boy . . ."

"I had no idea," Kim said.

As if on cue, Heather abruptly burst into tears and began reaching toward Roosevelt imploringly from atop Kim's lap.

With an irritated glance at Kim, Roosevelt reached to take her. Once she was safely ensconced on his lap, he removed her hat and dropped it on the rug between his chair and Kim's. Then he bent down close to her ear and whispered in a calming voice, "It's okay. You don't need to cry. You're fine." Kim retrieved Heather's hat from the floor and held it on her lap.

"She's a baby, Roosevelt," Kim said. "I can't get her to stop crying either sometimes. Why would that make you feel impotent?"

Roosevelt shrugged again.

Ash wondered, too, why failing in such apparently insignificant ways triggered Little Boy so easily. Just how had his problem with low self-esteem started?

"How would you describe your relationship with your parents?" he asked Roosevelt.

Roosevelt snorted. "Nonexistent."

Ash inclined his head slightly, puzzled at his tone.

"They're dead," Roosevelt said.

"What happened?"

"Car accident."

"How old were you?"

"Six months."

"So you never knew them at all," Ash said.

Roosevelt shook his head.

"Who raised you?"

"My grandparents. My grandmother."

Kim rolled her eyes. "If you could call it that."

"She did fine," Roosevelt said, his voice rising, though whether in irritation or just so he could be heard over Heather's continued crying, Ash couldn't tell.

But Kim wouldn't be deterred. "She spent eighteen years telling you what a worthless piece of shit you were and beating you with everything she could get her hands on."

Roosevelt tried to soothe Heather with some gentle rocking, but she only started struggling against him and crying even harder. "My grandmother raised me," he emphasized between clenched teeth. He bent down to sniff at Heather's bottom. "She needs to be changed."

"Then change her," Kim said.

"Then give me the diaper bag."

Kim reached down beside her, unsnapped the Velcro strap of a medium-sized blue bag lying against her chair, and pulled out a diaper. But instead of handing it to Roosevelt, she spread it open and placed it on the coffee table in front of her.

"Why are you disrespecting my grandmother?" Roosevelt asked Kim. "She didn't *ask* to be the one to raise me."

"Because every time you come back from seeing her you feel like shit," Kim replied. She pulled out three wipes from the diaper bag.

"It's not every time," Roosevelt objected, but now his voice had grown thin, as if his lungs had lost the strength to push the words out.

"Yes, it is."

Roosevelt gripped Heather's arms tightly, trying to force her into quieting down. Ash watched with growing concern, distracted by Heather's distress. Kim held out her hands to take Heather back.

"How do you know?" Roosevelt demanded. "How do you know I feel like shit *every* time?"

She lowered her hands slightly. "Because every time you come back from seeing her you treat *me* like shit."

"Now *that's* a load of shit."

"I see your face," Kim said. "I don't care what you say. She makes you feel like shit."

"No, she doesn't."

"Yes, she does."

"I'm telling you she doesn't!"

"Why can't you just admit it?"

*"Because, you fucking bitch, she doesn't!"* Roosevelt screeched and then all at once tossed Heather at her as if heaving a heavy rock into the air.

Kim's body jerked backward even as her arms darted forward, flailing like the tentacles of a startled octopus as Heather sailed in a gentle arc into the space between their chairs. Kim's hands tracked her as if following the trajectory of a tossed egg and snagged her just before she hit the ground. In one continuous motion, Kim yanked her up roughly against her breasts and onto her lap.

Shuddering, Kim felt up and down Heather's limbs frenetically for signs of injury. "Oh, my God," she heaved. "Oh, my God. . . ." But Heather had stopped crying, as surprised as Kim to have landed back on her mother's lap.

Finding her daughter unhurt, Kim looked up and screeched at Roosevelt, "Are you out of your fucking mind, you fucking *freak!*" Hearing the panic in her mother's voice, Heather started crying again, which caused Kim to burst into tears herself. A vein throbbed up the center of Roosevelt's forehead, and his face seemed to swell as if a tourniquet had been tied around his neck.

"If you ever, *ever* do that again—" Kim said, tears flooding down her cheeks, "Oh, my God—"

"Roosevelt," Ash said falteringly. "Roosevelt . . ."

Roosevelt had broken out into a sweat, his eyes darting in panic. "What?" he asked Ash sharply.

"You need to . . . calm down," Ash said, trying to modulate the nervousness out of his voice. "You need to try to turn your anger into language—"

"Into *language* . . . ?" Roosevelt laughed. "What the hell are you talking about? She's fine. Nothing happened to her. She's fine."

Kim, meanwhile, had turned away from Roosevelt as if from a bloody wound that had made her stomach go weak. Quickly wiping away her tears, she placed Heather on the coffee table, removed her soiled diaper, and wiped her bottom several times. Heather instantly calmed. "You're fine, sweetheart," Kim soothed her. "You're just fine."

"What we just saw was Vicious Protector *reacting*," Ash told Roosevelt, wiping a sheen of sweat from his forehead. "We need to keep him *talking*. Why is he so upset?"

"Because—" Roosevelt sputtered. "Because—" A small bubble of saliva appeared on his bottom lip.

"Because why?"

"All she does is criticize me! Fuck!" He smacked himself on the side of his head with his palm so violently that both Ash and Kim flinched. "No matter how hard I try, they both . . ." His voice tapered off, as if completing the thought was too difficult.

"They both what?" Ash asked, noting, but for the moment deliberately ignoring, Roosevelt's move from the use of the singular "she" to the plural "they."

"Make me feel like shit!"

"You mean they make you feel bad."

"Yeah!"

"You mean angry?"

"Yeah!"

"How about depressed?"

"How would *you* feel if the two people closest to you in the world were always telling you that nothing you do is ever good enough?" Roosevelt asked.

"I think I'd feel like shit."

"See?"

"Even sometimes ashamed," Ash said.

Roosevelt looked at him in surprise. "Yeah!" he said after a moment. And with that final admission, his rage at last seemed to collapse. He looked down at his lap. "Yeah."

# Protecting the Ego

"So it really *was* his grandmother," Ash said. "She's the reason he's so ashamed to fail."

His grandparents, it turned out, hadn't just been the only parents he'd ever known. Until he was twelve, he'd thought they *were* his parents. "That's when his grandmother told him what had happened," Ash explained. "Apparently, though, she told him like it was nothing. They were sitting at lunch one day and she just blurted it out. Like, 'They died.' As if how it impacted him didn't matter. As if *he* didn't matter. That's apparently how she still makes him feel. Like he's nothing."

"So now that's what he believes he is," I guessed.

"What he's *reminded* he is whenever he thinks he's failed at something. When he feels he's failed as a husband because Kim criticizes him for not helping around the house, or when he feels he's failed as a father because Heather cries. He takes those failures as evidence that *he's a failure*. For him, failing is like pouring salt on a wound—the wound of his damaged self-concept."

"So he's constantly having to buoy his self-esteem by finding ways to feel powerful and capable and in control," I said. "Which of course anger does."

Ash nodded. "When failing makes you feel like a failure—makes you feel worthless—what other option do you have but to find ways not to fail? To avoid failure at all costs? To deny that you do fail?"

"So *that's* why he hates Little Boy. What else does it mean to be little but weak, powerless, and vulnerable? And what does being weak, powerless, and vulnerable mean except that you're worthless?"

"Which is why Little Boy keeps triggering Vicious Protector. To protect him from feeling worthless," Ash reasoned. "Like you said, the world of Anger isn't really about getting angry at all."

"No," I said. "It's about defending yourself against insecurity."

❧

Roosevelt charged into Ash's office, alone, sat down across from Ash, and fumed. After a few moments, he burst out, "She left me! Can you believe it?"

"When?" Ash asked. "What happened?"

Roosevelt told him that Kim announced her decision to file for divorce a few days after their last session. Convinced she'd never have the guts to go through with it, however, his only response at the time had been to look up from his dinner and reply, "Go ahead." But two days later a process server found him on his lunch break and presented him with divorce papers. He called Kim immediately.

"What the fuck are you doing?" he demanded. "What the fuck is this?"

"The beginning of the end," she said in a voice filled with a confidence that scared him, and then hung up.

Roosevelt rushed home, but by the time he'd arrived she and Heather were already gone, along with all their clothes and toiletries. Stunned that she'd managed to engineer her exit so quickly—suggesting she'd been planning it for far longer than she'd made it appear—he flew into a rage, smashing their dining room table and chairs to pieces.

"So she left," Ash said.

"Yeah, she left," Roosevelt repeated. "So I need you to talk to her."

Ash regarded him carefully. "What did you have in mind for me to say?"

"I want you to tell her the reason I'm so angry now is because of you."

Ash's eyebrows rose dubiously. "I doubt there's anything I could say that could convince her of that. She thinks you've been angry ever since Heather was born."

Roosevelt grimaced. "Then tell her—tell her the reason it's *worse* now is because of you. Because of what you had us do."

Ash considered. "Let's say I agreed. Let's say she even believed me. What are you hoping would come of it?"

Roosevelt rolled his eyes impatiently. "She'd come back."

"Let's say she did," Ash allowed after a moment's pause. "Then what?"

"Then what?" Roosevelt asked incredulously. "Well, we'd"—and here he paused, groping for the right words—"you know . . . figure out a way to move forward . . . to be happy . . . as a family. . . ." He cleared his throat uncertainly.

Since their last session, Ash had been wondering if he needed to report Roosevelt to the Department of Child and Family Services. The only thing that had stopped him was something he thought he'd seen in the split second after Roosevelt had thrown his daughter—a second intention in Roosevelt's body language, a straining of his arms into full extension, as if at the last moment he'd been trying to take back what he'd done or to somehow transform the throw into an extended handoff. So Ash decided that if he could leverage the fear he was now seeing written so plainly in Roosevelt's face to break through Roosevelt's denial that he was, in fact, dangerously out of control with anger, there might not be a need for him to report anything.

"Did Kim give you a specific reason why she left?"

"She said she had an epiphany," Roosevelt answered, and he laughed. "An *epiphany*. I didn't even know she knew that word. She said if I could endanger Heather's life like that how could she ever trust me to be alone with her? When I told her to stop being so dramatic, I certainly did not endanger Heather's life, she said that was why she was leaving, because I wouldn't even admit what I did. And if I wouldn't even admit it, how could I ever take responsibility for it? I told her I may have handed Heather to her a little aggressively, but I certainly didn't *throw* her, so there was nothing for me to take responsibility for. She said that was why she didn't think I was ever going to change, because how can you change when you don't even recognize you have a problem? And if there was no chance of my changing, why should she stick around? So I need you to tell her I didn't throw Heather." As he said this, he clutched the arms of his chair forcibly enough to make his knuckles whiten.

"But Roosevelt," Ash replied gently, "you did throw Heather."

"You're out of your mind!" Roosevelt exclaimed, his eyes widening as if he'd been jabbed. "How could either of you think I would ever do anything to hurt my little girl?"

"But, Roosevelt, isn't that exactly why you came to see me? Because you *were* afraid you might hurt her?"

"But I didn't! You were right here!"

"You didn't," Ash agreed, "because Kim caught her."

"I did not throw my daughter."

"Because what kind of man would do that?"

Roosevelt hesitated, caught off guard by the question. "A lunatic. A man who can't control himself. A loser."

"And you're not a loser."

"I'm the farthest thing from it," Roosevelt insisted.

"Even though both your grandmother and your wife make you feel like a loser all the time."

"They try. But I'm not."

"How do they try? You've told me how Kim tries. How does your grandmother try?"

Roosevelt's temples pulsed as he alternately clenched and relaxed his jaw. "She's always telling me what a burden it was for her to raise me. How much she didn't want to do it, and how ungrateful I always was to her." His voice cracked slightly. "I tried, man—I swear I tried—but nothing I did was ever good enough for her. Why didn't I get better grades? Why didn't I catch that pop-up ball? Why was I always the one the other kids beat up? Why didn't I have any hair?"

"You could never do anything right."

"No."

"You were a worthless piece of shit."

Roosevelt looked at him in surprise. "That's what she thought. What she thinks."

"That's what you *are*."

"W-what . . . ?"

"Everyone else is better than you."

"No, they're not."

"Yes, they are. *They* got good grades, didn't they? Better than yours, right?" Ash challenged.

"S-some of them."

"*They* caught the easy pop-ups—"

"What are you trying to—?"

"*They* beat *you* up—"

Roosevelt seemed to shrink back into his chair. "Jesus, what kind of therapy is this . . . ?"

"*They* have hair—"

"Okay, stop . . . just—"

"They're *all* better than you. Isn't that right? Isn't that what you really think?"

"No, I don't!"

"Yes, you do! Come on, Roosevelt! You want to know why you're so angry all the time? You really want to know?"

"Yeah, that's why I—"

"Because you're angry at yourself!"

"W-what? Why would I—for what?"

"For being a worthless failure!"

"That's not true."

"No, it's not. But that's what you *believe*! Why can't you just look at that honestly and own it?"

"Because I don't!" Roosevelt roared. "I don't think I'm a failure! I don't think I'm worthless! I don't know *anyone* who's better than me! I'm better than them! *I'm better than them*!"

## Arrogance Is a Reaction Formation

"Harsh," I said.

"Yeah," Ash admitted. "I was thinking that he's just so well defended—so puffed up with arrogance—he won't admit even to himself, much less anyone else, that he's suffering from a near-paralyzing level of insecurity."

"I guess in a way that's what arrogance is: a reaction formation to insecurity," I said. "Feeling insecure is totally unacceptable, so you pretend—even to yourself—that you're exactly the opposite: supremely confident."

"Right! Because if you can convince *other* people you're confident, you might start to believe it yourself."

"In fact, it occurs to me that the entire world of Anger is a reaction formation to insecurity," I said. "To be trapped in the world of Anger is to suffer from a damaged self-concept that's just too painful to acknowledge."

"So then is everyone who comes from the world of Anger arrogant?" Ash asked.

"It may not always seem that way, but I think so, yeah. To be from the world of Anger is to be constantly trying to convince everyone you're better than they are."

"Then why isn't *that* the core delusion of the world of Anger?" Ash asked. "To be happy you need to be better than everyone else. Isn't that what every fragile ego really wants?"

"You know . . . actually . . ."

"You said it yourself—the world of Anger is a reaction to the wound of inse-curity. What does someone with that kind of wound—someone who feels they're *less than* everyone else—want more than anything? To be *better* than everyone else. When Roosevelt told me he was better than everyone else, he wasn't telling me what he believed he *was*. He was telling me what he wanted to *be*."

"Better than everyone else!" I repeated. "Yes! *That's* why Roosevelt can't stand to be criticized. That's why failing makes him feel ashamed. Because the only way he can value himself is by feeling superior to others. I can't believe we didn't think of this before! That's what the world of Anger is really about—believing that you can only be big if someone else is small."

"If *everyone* else is small," Ash said.

"It actually explains everything—why people trapped in Anger go to such lengths to conceal their true feelings, why they cling to any advantage they have over others, why they try to dominate anyone they perceive as weak and fear anyone they perceive as strong. Why else would you work so hard to appear virtuous, powerful, and accomplished, and criticize anyone you secretly think is better than you are? Why else would you work so hard to convince yourself you're the best, that you have the best of everything, and that anyone connected to you, merely by virtue of *being* connected to you, is also the best? Because you believe *that to be happy you have to be better than everyone else*."

"*And* why Roosevelt doesn't want anyone to think he's an angry person," Ash added. "Because superior people don't get angry. They stay calm."

I nodded. "The world of Anger is always about trying to look like something you aren't. Which is why the insecurity is so easy to miss. I mean, look at me."

"You?"

I nodded again. "Anger isn't quite my basic life tendency, but I've spent a lot of time there. I'm not even talking about the way I'd get mad at Rhea when she made me feel incompetent. If I'm being completely honest, I do a lot of things to make myself look better than other people. I try to portray myself as uncommonly wise; as someone who has answers to questions that others don't; as someone who understands others better than everyone else. I lift weights so I can look better than other men. It's not about whether or not I *am* superior. It's about how much pleasure I get from *thinking* I am. It's kind of perverse, actually."

"Perverse?" Ash asked.

"Yeah. It's perverse to fuel your ego at the expense of others. It's perverse to conceal your need to display your superiority under a pretense of virtue and humility until circumstances lay your insecurity bare and you become openly belligerent and condescending. Like I did with Rhea when her criticisms would stir up my insecurity and Roosevelt does with Kim. What else would you call it when you remain utterly unconcerned about any damage you do in the name of gratifying your ego? If rage is the world of Hell, greed is the world of Hunger, and stupidity is the world of Animality, the world of Anger is perversity."

"Don't you think you're being a little hard on yourself? We all have insecurities. We're all susceptible to having our egos bruised."

"I'm just being honest. I definitely have a need to feel superior to others— to be special—just like Roosevelt. Maybe not in the same way or to the same degree, but for just the same reason—insecurity. I don't fully understand why I feel that way—maybe telling myself I was better than everyone else was how I soothed myself whenever I felt excluded as a child. I don't know. But I do feel that way, without question. The fact that you don't see it only proves my point. The world of Anger can manifest in ways that are so subtle you often don't realize that the world of Anger is what you're seeing."

"Aren't we *all* narcissists, then?" Ash asked. "I mean, who doesn't want to believe they're special?"

"We all do. Sure. But there's a difference between wanting to feel special and *needing* to feel special. Between feeling special because of what's inside you and feeling special because you've convinced yourself that what's inside you is so much better than what's inside everyone else. Between wanting to win, which can be a powerful driver of accomplishment, and *needing* to win, which can be a powerful driver of havoc and destruction. I'm thinking we need just enough ego to take pride in our accomplishments but not so much that safeguarding our pride becomes our primary goal."

"You know," Ash reflected, "there are CEOs, professional athletes, and artists whose success has been driven—even *created*—by their need to prove themselves.

They called them 'insecure overachievers' when I worked at McKinsey. It's the type of person they actually sought out. So maybe the world of Anger isn't all bad."

"Healthy competition is absolutely a good thing," I said, "as long as healthy is what it stays."

"So then maybe not everyone who's insecure lives in the world of Anger," Ash said.

"They don't," I agreed. "Only those whose insecurity has led them to conclude that they need to be better than everyone else to be happy."

Roosevelt and Ash stared at each other for several awkward moments in silence. Ash was dismayed, but not surprised, that his attempt to force Roosevelt into acknowledging his feelings of worthlessness had failed. A direct assault on any defense mechanism, he well knew, usually serves only to strengthen it. He should have tried to find a way to slip past Roosevelt's denial quietly, to make the crime to which he wanted Roosevelt to confess seem more like a misdemeanor than a felony. Now Ash feared he'd compromised the one thing that made such a confession possible: Roosevelt's sense that he was in a safe environment.

"I'm really not a mean person," Roosevelt said finally. "I always treat my customers and my coworkers with deference and respect, just like I've been trained. Customer service is a major part of my job. It's what I'm all about. The only type of person who makes me mad is someone who acts like he's better than everyone else. And even then I mostly keep it to myself." He paused and glanced down at his lap. "But . . ."

Ash despaired to see Roosevelt now even more deeply entrenched in his denial and returning to the original thinking with which he'd started therapy, refusing to accept that he was angry at all. "But—?" Ash prompted.

"But my wife and my daughter—man!" He exhaled, then shook his head. "Why is it the ones you love the most are always the best at bringing out your worst?"

Ash smiled tolerantly. "For the same reason we often treat the ones we love worse than we do people we don't know at all. Because we have the least tolerance for the irritating things we see every day."

"Do you think . . . do you think Heather . . ."

Ash waited. "Do I think Heather . . . ?"

Several moments passed in silence. Then Roosevelt said, "The one thing I'm scared of more than anything else is having my daughter grow up afraid of me."

Ash looked at him in surprise. "Why do you think she'd be afraid of you, Roosevelt?"

"Because—because I yell at her all the time, man. All the time." Tears sprang into his eyes suddenly. "Something's not right, man." He shook his head. "Something's not right with *me*."

Ash couldn't believe what he was hearing. Careful to keep his excitement in check, he asked, "What do you think it is?"

"I don't know." He shook his head. He stayed silent for several moments. "What kind of man needs to terrorize his little girl to feel like a man?"

"Is that what you've been doing?"

Roosevelt pressed his palms against his temples with his fingers splayed wide, pushing inward as if to squeeze his brains out. "Oh, my God," he said. His skull glistened with sudden sweat.

"What is it?" Ash asked, alarmed.

Roosevelt glanced up at him, blinking furiously, and then back down at the ground. "You're right, I—" he started to answer. "I threw my . . . I threw my daughter . . . my precious little girl . . . in the air. . . ."

Ash released a breath he hadn't realized he'd been holding as relief flooded through him. Somehow, instead of strengthening Roosevelt's resolve to bury his feelings of inadequacy as deeply as he could, Ash's assault on Roosevelt's denial had been as sharp and cutting as a surgeon's scalpel, and now the truth about what he'd done—about how he'd been feeling—was flowing out of him.

"It's okay," Ash said. "You didn't hurt her. She's fine."

"That's not the point . . . everything you said about me . . . it's true . . . everything."

"You're not the only one in the world with insecurities, Roosevelt. Or the only one who gets angry when they're pointed out. Believe me."

"Stop! You're only making it worse."

Ash opened his mouth to reply, but then said nothing.

"This . . . this is just . . . I'm the most miserable person on the planet!"

Ash couldn't help a tiny, crooked smile, thinking to himself that Roosevelt even needed to be the best at being unhappy. "Take a few breaths. You're okay."

"I don't *feel* okay. In fact, I feel pretty fucking far from okay!"

Ash nodded. "You're letting yourself feel something you've been working hard to avoid feeling for a long time. You've just seen something you haven't ever wanted to see."

"What? That I'm an asshole?"

Ash shook his head. "That you have a worthless *part*. Failing Man."

Roosevelt laughed. "Failing Man. Great . . . that's just great."

"Look, who we are isn't actually up to us. It's about which of our parts other people trigger. But if you can acknowledge the reason you get mad at Heather and Kim is that they *both* make you feel impotent, and that feeling impotent makes you feel worthless, you can actually do something about it."

"What?" Roosevelt asked. "How?"

"You can talk to Failing Man yourself! You can take care of him. You can explain to him he may have failed to anticipate your wife's wishes or to stop your daughter from crying or whatever, but that doesn't mean that he is—that you are—a failure! You can let yourself off the hook."

"Off the hook?"

"For being impotent. Roosevelt, you're going to make mistakes in life. Let that be okay. Forgive yourself for failing and move on. Failing at something doesn't make you a failure. If you can fully own this part of yourself, face it squarely without trying to silence its voice, you can dramatically reduce its influence on your behavior. Whenever you get mad, let that be a signal to you that Failing Man has been aroused. And then let Failing Man speak. Let him tell you he feels worthless. Let him tell you he feels ashamed. Let him tell Kim! Don't shut that feeling out. That's why you're getting angry—because you don't want to feel ashamed. You don't want to feel like a failure. But those are just feelings. They're not fun to feel, but they can't hurt you. Only when you refuse to acknowledge them, when you refuse to let yourself feel them because feeling them is so awful, do they gain the power to control your behavior. You might be surprised how the simple act of acknowledging unpleasant feelings and giving yourself permission to feel them actually gives you more—not less—control over them. Over yourself."

Roosevelt remained silent for a long time. Then finally he asked, "Do you think if I said all this to Kim—if I did what you said, and she saw me getting myself under control—that I could get her back?"

Ash paused, his heart breaking a little. "What I think, Roosevelt, is that you've made a real breakthrough here today. But I also think the honest answer is that it depends on you both."

Roosevelt sat quietly a few more moments.

Then all at once he lurched to his feet, grabbed his coat, and headed toward the door.

"Where are you going?" Ash called after him.

"To call my wife," Roosevelt called back, and then he was gone.

"That could easily have gone the other way," I said to Ash.

"Yeah," Ash acknowledged. "Trying to smash a defense mechanism to pieces isn't usually the best idea. But with Kim having just left him—with the stakes suddenly raised as high as they were—I thought it was a risk worth taking. The problem with people like Roosevelt is that they often don't believe *they're* the problem. They only come in to therapy when something that really matters to them is at risk. Like a job or a relationship."

"Actually, that's sort of what happened with me, too," I said. "Roosevelt and I really are a lot alike."

"How so?"

"There was this one point where Rhea and I really weren't getting along at all. I felt it was because she was doing things and saying things that kept making me angry. I mean, I was angry all the time. I really hated it—in fact, I hated it so much I was considering divorcing her. And then a friend of mine asked me what I thought I was feeling *underneath* my anger. And I'll tell you, not until he asked that question did it even occur to me that there might *be* anything underneath my anger. But that was when I realized I was getting angry at Rhea because she made me feel incompetent, which then triggered my shame, and that it was the shame I was really trying to stop myself from feeling. I don't know why I was able to see it just then, if it was because the stakes had become so high for me too—because I *was* genuinely contemplating ending my marriage—but that's when I figured it out."

"And when you get mad at her now, what happens?"

"I *don't* get mad at her now. At least, not as much—or for the same reason. Because now that I know she triggers my own Little Boy when she does something or says something that makes me feel incompetent, I recognize—just like you encouraged Roosevelt to do—that I'm actually feeling shame. And accepting that I feel shame and letting myself feel shame rather than trying to suppress my shame or deny my shame—rather than judging myself for feeling shame—most of the time stops me from becoming angry."

"That's exactly it!" Ash exclaimed. "It's accepting that you're feeling what you're feeling. It's completely counterintuitive, but once an unpleasant emotion is aroused, the best way to end it is to *let yourself feel it*. Resisting unpleasant emotions is often what prevents them from resolving—or at the very least, increases how much they stress you.[4] Resisting an unpleasant emotion, in fact, only tends to make it stronger.[5] But by tolerating an unpleasant emotion in the short term, by actually accepting and expressing it, you're much more likely to prevent it from persisting in the long-term.[6] It may not be the case for everyone stuck in the world of Anger, but for Roosevelt, acknowledging that failure makes him feel worthless, letting himself actually *feel* worthless, is the one thing that prevents him from believing that he *is* worthless. And the less often the belief that he's worthless gets stirred up, the less often the belief that he needs to be better than everyone gets stirred up. Allowing himself to acknowledge when he feels worthless prevents him from entering the world of Anger."

"He's been actually doing it? Interrupting his anger?"

"He has."

"With you?" I asked.

He nodded. "And with Kim," he said. "In couples therapy."

# Key Points

- Anger is defined as the life-condition of ego.

- The emotion of anger is only one tool among many that people trapped in the life-condition of Anger use to protect their egos. Often the life-condition of Anger disguises itself in a veneer of exaggerated benevolence and subtle arrogance.

- People trapped in the world of Anger are obsessively concerned about being viewed negatively in any way. Theirs is the wound of insecurity. For this reason, they often try to dominate those they perceive to be weaker than themselves and fawn over those they perceive to be stronger.

- The life-condition of Anger also fuels the spirit of competition, which, when well-managed, engenders innovation and advancement.

- The core delusion of the world of Anger is that to be happy we need to be better than everyone else.

# 5

# Tranquility

*Pain in this life is not avoidable, but the pain we create avoiding pain is avoidable.*

—R. D. Laing

Tranquility is defined as the life-condition of serenity. Whereas in the world of Animality we surrender our good judgment in the pursuit of pleasure, in the world of Tranquility we surrender our desires in the pursuit of peace of mind.

Entry into the world of Tranquility is often a passive process, occurring whenever our emotions settle down of their own accord. Yet when in the grip of the core delusion of Tranquility, we work to keep them settled down intentionally. Consequently, in contrast to the world of Anger in which our need to feel superior frequently causes us to antagonize others, in the world of Tranquility we avoid conflict whenever possible. We are in fact willing to tolerate almost anything, including serious problems, to prevent even minor disruption to our well-being.

Slow to anger, resistant to passion, in the world of Tranquility we embrace and find comfort in the status quo, sometimes resulting in an almost neurotic resistance to altering our life routines. As a result, we shun variety and stubbornly resist trying new things. When positively expressed, the static nature this lends

to our lives helps us remain imperturbable, keeping us calm in a crisis and functional under stress. When negatively expressed, it tends to make us idle—even,
in the most extreme cases, lazy, negligent, and apathetic.

Perhaps the most striking characteristic of the world of Tranquility, however,
is that it fixes our core affect exactly midway between the extremes of joy and
suffering. The life-condition of Tranquility is a fundamentally neutral state—a
break, so to speak, from other life-conditions and the emotions they produce.
Emotion and the world of Tranquility are, in fact, like two magnets of identical
polarity that refuse to touch, explaining why, given the difficulty of avoiding
emotion in general, the life-condition of Tranquility is so difficult to sustain.

Early in his career Ash went to work for large health system in Chicago
that had contracted with the city to provide counseling services to the Chicago
Police Department. Ash liked and admired most of the police officers he treated
but found most of them had little interest in exploring their inner workings.
(As one of his colleagues put it, "Cops tend to have long-distance relationships
with their feelings.") So when Frank, a thirty-five-year veteran, called and said
only that his sergeant had told him to make an appointment, Ash wasn't at all
surprised that he declined to give a more specific reason and accepted him into
treatment immediately.

The first thing Ash noticed when he opened his office door a week later to let
Frank into his office was the massive bloat of Frank's stomach. It was straining
against his shirt so fiercely that several buttons seemed about to pop off. Ash
found himself wondering how Frank could ever chase down anybody moving
at a pace faster than a trot.

"Frank Miles," Frankie said as he engulfed Ash's hand in a crushing grip.
"Everyone calls me Frankie." Then he brushed past and entered Ash's office.
Noting the moistness of Frankie's palm, Ash paused to turn the thermostat down
before trailing him inside.

As they settled down opposite one another, Ash took a moment to study
Frankie's rough-skinned face with its penetrating blue eyes—which he saw were
sizing him up just as intently.

"You talk to my sergeant yet?" Frankie asked.

Ash shook his head. "Was I supposed to?"

Frankie shrugged. Ash waited for him to say more. When he didn't, Ash finally offered, "You said on the phone he told you to come see me."

Frankie nodded.

"Why?"

Frankie sighed, his stomach seeming to deflate a little, then stared out Ash's window. "I sort of got into a fight at work."

"What kind of fight?"

"It wasn't really a fight," Frankie amended. "I just got a little more assertive than I should have with a fellow officer."

"How much more assertive?"

"I shoved him a little." He looked pained.

"Why?"

"He said something I didn't like."

Ash waited again. "Which was?" he finally prompted.

A few weeks ago, Frankie told him, he and his partner had been involved in a high-speed chase down Lake Shore Drive. The perpetrator had lost control of his vehicle and ended up wrapping it around a light pole. He managed to escape unhurt, though, through the driver's side window. Then he ran across the drive and into a small alley that their squad car couldn't fit through. So Frankie and his partner had to chase him down on foot.

"And I got a little short of breath," Frankie finished. "Had a dizzy spell or something."

"So your fellow officer gave you a hard time about the guy getting away?"

"No, my partner got him."

"Then what?"

Frankie heaved out another sigh. "Me and this officer, we have sort of a sarcastic relationship. He's always razzing me about something."

"And what was it this time?"

Frankie's eyebrows flickered once dismissively. "He asked me if I thought the perp was pretty." One corner of his mouth curled in an embarrassed half-smile.

"Pretty?"

Frankie nodded. "You know—pretty enough to make me dizzy. It was stupid. I don't know why I let it get to me."

"Why do you think you did?"

Frankie shrugged. "It really wasn't like me, doc. And it's definitely not going to happen again, I can guarantee you that."

Though this certainly wasn't the first time Ash had encountered a police officer who seemed to have a problem with anger management, he paused to consider Frankie's claim that aggressiveness was unusual for him. Had his fellow officer inadvertently—or even purposely—pressed on an area that needed attention, perhaps related to Frankie's declining vitality and fitness for his job? After all, if this had been only a minor police-house squabble, why had his sergeant ordered Frankie into therapy?

"Your conflict with this guy ever get physical before?"

"I wouldn't exactly call it a *conflict.* . . ."

"So that's a no then?" Ash clarified.

"No. I mean, yeah, that's a no. I'm the one who took it there. Which I can't really explain. I'm usually the guy trying to keep everybody calm."

"Does it make you uncomfortable? Conflict, I mean."

Frankie shrugged. "That's what police work is. Conflict resolution."

"That doesn't answer my question."

"I don't mind it."

Ash sighed inwardly. The only thing that was clear to him so far was that Frankie wasn't going to reveal anything substantive about himself without it being yanked out of him. So, thinking that Frankie would only trust him if he nurtured that trust slowly enough that Frankie hardly noticed it was being nurtured at all, Ash decided for the time being to focus on the more superficial—and, he hoped, nonthreatening—aspects of Frankie's life.

For his part, Frankie seemed eager, if not relieved, to talk about his background. Irish Catholic, born and raised in Chicago, he'd left to join the Marine Corps at the age of twenty-two, just two months after his wife, Sharon, had given birth to their son, Conrad. After being discharged he moved his family back to the city to join the Chicago Police Department. Thirty-five years later, he and Sharon were still married. Conrad was now a law professor at the University of Chicago—though, he added, they hardly spoke.

"Any particular reason for that?" Ash asked, unable to help himself.

Frankie shrugged dismissively. "You know how it goes, doc. Sometimes kids and their parents just don't see eye to eye."

Ash glanced at the clock above his door, noting to his surprise that they'd almost reached the end of the hour. Frustrated by how little information he'd managed to gather, he paused and then said, "Frankie, we're just about out of time and I don't feel I've learned nearly enough to be helpful to you yet. I wonder if it might in fact be a good idea for me to talk to your sergeant as you suggested. Get his take on what happened."

"Fine by me, doc."

So Ash called his sergeant the next day. Like Ash, his sergeant worried that the incident with Frankie's fellow officer suggested the presence of an underlying problem. "You know what we call him around here, doc?" his sergeant asked him. "The Ref. He's always interceding somewhere, trying to keep the peace. The guys all look up to him as an example. He's never been involved in anything like this before. I don't know if it's from stress at home with his wife or what, but I thought I'd better try to nip it in the bud."

When Ash asked him why he thought Frankie's outburst might be related to problems he was having with his wife, his sergeant became as reticent as Frankie. "Just little things he says."

## The Fear of Conflict

"It's like Kabuki theater," I said.

Ash nodded. "I actually considered it a victory every time he answered me in a complete sentence."

"Is that why you think he's from the world of Tranquility?"

"No. I think he's from the world of Tranquility because he's the most self-contained, emotionally flattened patient I've ever met."

"Maybe he's just really private," I said.

"There's no doubt he's *that*. But it was more the way he minimized everything. Like he was determined not to be affected by *anything*. Except being taunted by that other cop, which he said was unusual for him. Which I completely believe."

"I'm not saying he's *not* from the world of Tranquility," I clarified. But there was a difference, I argued, between *feeling* tranquil and actually being from the world of Tranquility.

To feel tranquil doesn't take much, I suggested. It happens every time our emotions quiet down. But that can happen for two entirely different reasons: either our environment temporarily stops triggering our emotions—an entirely passive process that happens more often than we might think—or we deliberately stop *allowing* our environment to trigger our emotions. "So we're only *from* the world of Tranquility," I said, "when the core delusion of Tranquility is the delusion that gets stirred up the most for us, which then impels us to actively *suppress* our emotions."

"So what if Frankie really *isn't* comfortable with conflict?" Ash asked. "What if he believes the key to happiness is avoiding it? Maybe that's the core delusion of Tranquility—to be happy you have to avoid conflict."

"I'm sure he's *not* comfortable with conflict if he's from the world of Tranquility. But that's an *effect* of Tranquility, not the cause."

"But why couldn't it be the cause? There aren't too many things that disrupt your peace of mind like conflict," Ash pointed out.

"Actually, there are. Getting fired from your job. Failing out of school. Getting divorced. Also, how would wanting to avoid conflict produce the other characteristics of Tranquility, like being resistant to change or the aversion to variety and trying new things?"

"I guess it wouldn't, directly," Ash said.

"Also, just because you don't like conflict doesn't mean you're from the world of Tranquility. You could just as easily dislike it because you're from the world of Hell and feel powerless to advocate for yourself. Besides, Frankie told you conflict doesn't bother him. Like he said, cops deal with conflict all the time."

"Having to deal with conflict isn't the same as being comfortable with it," Ash said. "And cops deal with *other* people's conflicts—conflicts between people they don't know concerning things that don't involve them personally. He could have no problem intervening in other people's conflicts and still be uncomfortable with conflict in his own life."

Frankie shuffled into Ash's office at his second visit in the same awkward way as before, skirting sideways through Ash's office door without a word of greeting, his gaze pointed down at the floor.

"I talked to your sergeant," Ash said as they sat down.

Frankie watched him with a neutral expression.

"He's concerned you may have snapped at your fellow officer because you're stressed about your wife."

"My wife?" Frankie's eyes widened slightly against the heavy flesh of his eyebrows. "Where'd he get that?"

"From things you've said."

"Things *I've* said? Like what?"

Ash couldn't hold back an ironic smile. "He wouldn't say."

"I don't know what he's talking about."

"So things between you and your wife are good?" Ash asked him.

"Sure."

Ash paused, hoping his silence would spur Frankie to say more. In Ash's experience, most patients couldn't withstand more than about thirty seconds of a conversational lull before rushing to fill it, usually with something about themselves.

Frankie, however, seemed impervious. After a full minute, Ash finally asked, "What can you tell me about your relationship with her?"

Frankie shrugged. "Not much to tell."

"How'd you meet?"

"High school."

"So you've been together . . . how long?"

Frankie paused to add it up. "Thirty-eight years? Something like that."

"What's your secret?"

"I don't know. Not letting things get to you, I guess."

"Easier said than done."

Frankie shrugged again, a gesture Ash was beginning to think was his most salient form of expression.

"What kinds of things does she do that *would* upset you if you weren't good at not letting them?"

"She's pretty easy to get along with, doc."

"How often do you have sex?" Ash asked, his impatience causing him to abandon his previous resolution to move at a slow pace.

Frankie's head jerked back. "Getting a little personal there, aren't you, doc?"

Ash almost laughed. "Frankie, I know you're uncomfortable being here, but I have the sense that you're more troubled than you're letting on—maybe even more than you realize yourself. I may be wrong about that, but there's no way for me to help you unless you're willing to share things that are personal." With a crooked smile, Ash added, "You do know this is therapy, right?"

Frankie smiled bashfully. "Yeah."

"I'm just trying to do my job here, Frankie. Help me out a little."

Frankie's expression softened. He passed a few moments in thoughtful silence.

"Maybe once a month," he finally answered. "How often we have sex," he clarified.

"Would you like it to be more?"

"I don't mind things the way they are."

"Does she?"

"Don't think that means I don't love her, though," Frankie added.

"*Do* you?"

"Love her? Sure."

"And you think she's satisfied with having sex only once a month?"

Frankie looked uncomfortable. "We've never really talked about it. It just sort of . . . evolved. We're both pretty busy."

"Does she work?"

Frankie nodded. "She's a real estate broker. A lot of her showings are at night and on the weekends, so . . ."

"When do you find time to spend together?"

"It's not *every* night she shows places."

"What do you guys like to do when you *are* together?"

Frankie grinned sheepishly. "Whatever she wants."

"What about what you want?"

"Not so much." He seemed more embarrassed than resentful.

"Why not?"

"Not much I want, really. Honestly, it's just easier, doc. I get my needs met. There just aren't that many of them. A few things."

"Don't you ever take *any* time for yourself?"

"I do," Frankie replied. "Once a year I go hunting for a week in Wisconsin with some of the guys."

"There's nothing else you do just for you?" Ash asked.

Frankie paused. "Maybe one thing. If you want to count it."

Ash gave him a mildly exasperated look. "Come on, Frankie. Give."

"When I go to the bathroom," he confessed, "I read."

## Denial of Desire

I burst out laughing.

Ash smiled. "Yeah."

"No, I totally get it," I said. "I do the same thing. How else are you going to get away, right? I just have a hard time believing that all he wants in life is to go hunting—only once a year, at that—and read in the bathroom."

"I'm not sure he *knows* what he wants in life. When you consistently ignore or suppress your desires, you tend to lose track of what they are."

"You think that's what he's been doing?"

"Oh, yeah," Ash said.

"Why?"

"That's the question, isn't it? It may not be the core delusion of the world of Tranquility, but it's seeming more and more to me that he *is* uncomfortable with conflict. He's not comfortable, for example, choosing *his* desires over his wife's. So how does he deal with that? Maybe by convincing himself he doesn't have any desires at all. Or at least that he doesn't have any desires that conflict with hers."

"Or maybe it's even more basic than that," I said. "Maybe he's suppressing his needs to solve the problem of attachment."

"You mean to prevent himself from feeling the pain of losing something he cares about?" Ash asked.

"Or to prevent himself from feeling the pain of longing for something he wants. Don't you see this all the time? People who tell themselves they don't have desires so they don't have to experience disappointment? Or so they can save face when they fail at something?"

"Sure. But it only works sort of and then only until they fail at something they *really* want, which is when they come to see me."

"Maybe that *is* why he came to see you," I suggested.

"Actually, you know what? Why couldn't that be the core delusion we're looking for? That you can only be happy if you don't want things?"

"Interesting," I said. "Sort of the opposite of the core delusion of Hunger."

"Isn't that also one of the key principles of Zen Buddhism—that desire is the root of all suffering?"

I nodded. "One of the four noble truths—which figure more prominently in Theravada Buddhism than Nichiren Buddhism—is that suffering arises from attachment. Eliminate your desire for your attachments—rise *above* your desire for your attachments—and you eliminate suffering. On one level, it actually makes sense. In fact, there was a period back in high school when I tried it. I thought being imperturbable was akin to being enlightened. I thought it made me superior."

"You mean you wanted to live in the world of Tranquility because you believed the core delusion of the world of Anger?"

"Actually, that's right," I said, smiling. "The only problem is, just like you told Patrick when he was struggling in the world of Hunger, you *can't* eliminate your desires. You can only try to suppress them. But suppressing my desires didn't make me feel tranquil; it made me feel numb."

"How are those different?"

"Tranquil is what you feel when you're not feeling any emotion at all. Numb, on the other hand, is what you feel when you're overwhelmed by so many emotions you don't know which one you're feeling. It may *seem* like you're not feeling anything when you're feeling numb, but you're actually just not allowing yourself to acknowledge what you're feeling."

"Interesting," Ash said. "So what emotions weren't you acknowledging you felt when you tried to deny your desires?"

"Frustration. Resentment. Loneliness. Sadness."

"Why those, do you think?"

"Because forcing myself not to care about anything cut me off from other people.[1] When you force yourself to deny your desires, you feel like you're not participating in life. Like everyone else is swimming in the stream and you're just watching from the bank. Like you don't *deserve* to have any desires. I may have *looked* tranquil from the outside—which I suppose was my real goal because, of course, appearances are what you're really concerned about when you're from the world of Anger—but I didn't *feel* tranquil. So, no, I don't think the core delusion of the world of Tranquility is that you can only be happy if you don't want things. Denying my desires didn't land me in the world of Tranquility. It landed me in the world of Hell."

❦

Ash decided to spend their next session trying to get at the reason why Frankie felt unable to express his own needs whenever they came into conflict with his wife's. Thinking Frankie might be more willing to open up about things that had happened in his past, Ash began asking him about the early days of his marriage, before its rules of engagement had been cemented into their lifelong shape. "You told me last time you and Sharon only have sex about once a month. How often was it when you first got married?"

"Aw, jeez, doc," Frankie groaned.

"*Frankie . . . ,*" Ash admonished in a comically exaggerated tone.

Frankie sighed. "I know a lot of guys get married because they want regular sex, but that wasn't me."

"So what was *your* reason?"

"It was just time."

Ash regarded him dubiously. "You were *how* old again?"

"Nineteen."

"Most people aren't thinking about getting married at nineteen," Ash reflected.

Frankie shrugged. "I've always liked things to be in their right place at the right time."

"How do you mean?"

"I'd just finished high school. I was ready for the next stage of life." Frankie told him that putting his life in order—even temporarily—had always felt enormously satisfying to him. His favorite time of the month, for example, was at the beginning because that was when he was able to pay all his bills.

"So you like your life neat and tidy."

Frankie grew quiet, his expression intent. "I guess I just thought getting married at that point made sense. That it meant my life was progressing in the right order. Something like that, anyway. . . ."

Ash chuckled. "You actually expected marriage to make your life more orderly?"

Frankie laughed with him. "Like I said, I was nineteen."

"What was being married like for you early on?"

Like he was riding a wild horse, Frankie answered, "just barely hanging on." He never knew which way Sharon might turn next, what she might want to do or what choice she might make that would send them both galloping toward disaster. "Go there, do this, buy this, sell that," Frankie said. She was always accusing him of "trying to rein her in" and control her, but he felt like he was just trying to keep them from crashing into something.

Ash was startled by the image and the depth to which Frankie had suddenly ventured. "Was she really that dangerous?" Ash asked.

"You have no idea," Frankie said earnestly. "At least," he added evenhandedly, "that's how it felt to me." And yet, he had to admit, when she'd ask him why he didn't want to do what she wanted he usually found himself unable to provide a good enough answer to satisfy her. Then she'd get hurt or mad, and he'd feel guilty and march off somewhere to sulk.

Ash wondered how much of Frankie's impulse to resist following Sharon's lead was an automatic reflex borne out of a compulsion to balance her in a way that kept their lives—that kept *him*—feeling tranquil. "What kinds of things did she want to do that were so risky?" he asked.

"It was always something different. Scuba diving. Skydiving. Travel to third-world countries." Eventually, though, she seemed to lose interest in doing those kinds of things, and their marriage settled down.

"Sounds like she was a real adventurer—" Ash began.

"Never mind we couldn't afford any of it—" Frankie added.

"And you're not."

Frankie sighed. "Let's just say we approach life a little differently."

"Sounds like a lot differently."

Frankie shrugged.

"You ever think about leaving her?" Ash asked. "Back then, I mean?"

Frankie stared at Ash silently. "I thought about it," he answered after a moment. "But then I'd think about how the pain of leaving would be worse than the pain of staying. So I stayed."

## Feeling Safe

"He wants to divorce her?" I exclaimed.

"Sounds like he *did*," Ash said.

"Sounds like he's even angrier than we thought."

"I think I'm beginning to understand why," Ash said. "He's afraid of conflict—uncomfortable with conflict, nervous about conflict, whatever—so he suppresses his own desires whenever they come into conflict with his wife's. But suppressing his desires makes him resentful and angry. Of course, he's really only angry at himself for being so uncomfortable with conflict that he can't choose his desires over hers. Which means that every once in a while, something—often something small—is going to trigger him.[2] Like taunting from a fellow officer."

"That all makes perfect sense—except for one thing," I said. "If he's so afraid of conflict, how did he manage to stand in the way of his wife's desire for adventure?"

"That's . . . actually a good question."

"I'm not saying he's *not* afraid of conflict," I said. "I'm just wondering if he's more afraid of something else."

"Like what?"

"Like scuba diving. And skydiving. And travel to third-world countries. All dangerous pursuits, according to him."

"Some of them *are* dangerous," Ash pointed out.

"Skydiving, sure," I agreed. "Maybe even scuba diving. But travel to third-world countries?"

"Not everybody is going to be as comfortable with that as you are."

"I'm not saying *I'm* comfortable with it. I'm just making an observation: he's afraid of the unfamiliar. For him, unfamiliar means *unsafe*."

"Actually, that's a great observation," Ash said.

"Could it be, then, that what he's really afraid of is being hurt?" I asked. "That he *is* uncomfortable with conflict—and not just with his wife—because conflict makes him feel unsafe? That he fears doing the things his wife wants him to do more than he fears her anger and disappointment, so he's willing to endure the second to avoid the first? Could it be, in fact, that the core delusion of the world of Tranquility is that to be happy you have to be safe?"

We both paused to consider it.

Ash shook his head. "The drive to be safe *is* one of the strongest drives we have. And I can see how actually *being* safe could make you feel tranquil. But how does *wanting* to be safe, focusing all your energy and attention on it—which, by the way, I agree Frankie is doing—create the characteristics of the life-condition of Tranquility?"

"Well, it could make you less emotional, for one thing," I answered. "It's much easier to monitor for threats when you're thinking calmly and rationally. Also it would motivate you to maintain the status quo."

"Why?"

"Because the status quo is safe."

"No, the status quo is *comfortable*, which creates the *illusion* that it's safe. Just because you're comfortable with the status quo doesn't mean it's good for you. People cling to the familiar to their detriment all the time."

"That's true."

"And here's another thing," Ash said. "Didn't you say that people in the world of Tranquility are willing to tolerate almost anything to avoid change, including serious problems?"

"That's right."

"But if the core delusion of the world of Tranquility is that to be happy you need to be safe, why would anyone living in the world of Tranquility ignore a serious problem? Don't serious problems make you unsafe by definition?"

"I guess they do," I said.

"So wouldn't their inclination to tolerate serious problems suggest that being safe is the *last* thing people living in the world of Tranquility think about? That they're being driven by something that feels even more important than being safe?"

"Or maybe," I added, conceding the point with a reluctant nod, "something that makes them *feel* safer than does *actually being safe*."

⟊⟊⟊

At the end of the session when Frankie rushed to clarify that he hadn't thought about divorcing his wife in years, Ash believed him, not because he thought Frankie had become happier in his marriage over time but because Ash thought he'd made peace with the idea that he needed to abdicate his desires to keep his marriage intact.

But why he'd chosen to abdicate his desires to keep his marriage intact remained unclear. Fear of conflict still seemed like a good explanation, but Ash wondered now if it was also a way to expiate his guilt for denying Sharon the life of adventure she'd wanted. But if *that* were true, why did he feel so strongly about denying Sharon the life of adventure she'd wanted? Because adventure scared him? Why might adventure scare him? That, Ash decided, was the question he wanted to explore next.

The day before their next session, however, Frankie called to cancel. Sharon was sick, he said, so he needed to stay with her. He ended up canceling three more sessions in a row before he finally reappeared a month later, looking haggard, unshaven, and sleep-deprived. "You look like hell, Frankie," Ash remarked as they sat down.

At first, Frankie seemed not to hear him. He glanced down at the arm of his chair and picked at a stud holding the leather in place.

"The thing is . . ." He cleared his throat. "The thing is, doc, I didn't tell you . . . when I said Sharon was sick . . . well . . . she died."

"What!" Ash's mouth fell open in shock. "What happened?"

"Breast cancer," Frankie said.

"Breast cancer? How long had she been sick?"

"A year and a half."

"Frankie . . . I'm so sorry." How, Ash wondered, could Frankie have withheld from him the fact that his wife had been terminally ill?

"I didn't actually believe it was going to happen," Frankie said as if in answer to Ash's question. "I still can't believe she's gone. I mean, I knew it wasn't good. Her doctor said it had spread and the chemo wasn't working but somehow . . . well, you know."

Ash studied him as he spoke, searching for some telltale sign of distress—a cracking of his voice, a tensing of his mouth, a sudden shining of his eyes to suggest impending tears. He was saying things Ash would have expected him to say, but his tone, his facial expression, his entire demeanor seemed completely devoid of emotion. Where, Ash wondered, was his grief? Had he somehow managed to compress it down into such a small space that he'd hidden it even from himself?

"Frankie, I can only imagine how devastated you are by this loss," Ash said after a moment, "but I'm trying to understand something. Why haven't you mentioned before this that Sharon was sick?"

Frankie shrugged. "I was dealing with it. I didn't think it was relevant."

"Your wife of almost forty years was dying and you didn't think that was important?" Ash couldn't keep the incredulity out of his voice.

"I didn't say it wasn't important. I said it wasn't relevant. I came here because I got into a fight at work, not because I needed help dealing with my wife's cancer. I had it under control. It wasn't affecting me."

To which Ash said, "Why not?"

Frankie shook his head quickly. "I didn't mean it wasn't affecting me. I meant . . . I didn't need any help dealing with it. It was what it was."

Was Frankie holding his emotions back because he wanted to process his grief in stages, Ash wondered, or was he engaging in full-blown suppression to avoid processing his grief at all? Ash worried that the latter possibility was more likely. And indeed, when Ash asked Frankie to tell him what it had been like to learn that Sharon had cancer, to watch her go through treatment, and finally to be with her at the very end, Frankie spoke dutifully but dispassionately, as if it he were recounting a story he'd read about rather than one he'd experienced himself. The rest of the session was spent mostly in silence, punctuated only by an occasional springing forth of a memory of his life with Sharon, a brief reminiscence, followed by a return to a brooding quiet.

# Freedom from Problems

"His relationship with his wife becomes the focus of his therapy," Ash said, "and he never mentions she's dying of cancer?"

I shrugged. "That's what people in the world of Tranquility do. Ignore their problems."

"Being in denial about how you're feeling—about the pain something is causing you—I can understand. That's a common defense mechanism. But being in denial that a painful *event* is actually happening is denial at an entirely different level."

"Just because he didn't want to talk about it doesn't mean he was in denial about it."

"If his marriage had never come up," Ash said, "I'd completely agree. But to deliberately exclude the fact that his wife is terminally ill from a conversation *about* his wife? It's totally bizarre. And also, frankly, clarifying."

"Clarifying?"

Ash nodded. "Like Yalom says in *Love's Executioner*, 'If something big in a relationship isn't being talked about (by either patient or therapist), then nothing else of importance will be discussed either.'"[3] Ash now believed the reason Frankie hadn't been discussing much of significance with him was because he hadn't been talking about the most significant thing he had to discuss. "So the question is, why wouldn't he want to talk about the most significant thing he had to discuss?"

"When you live in the world of Tranquility, you don't want to have any problems," I repeated. "So why would he talk to you about his wife's cancer if he wanted to pretend it wasn't a problem?"

"Okay, then why isn't *that* the core delusion of Tranquility—that to be happy you can't have any problems?"

I thought for a moment, then shook my head. "I can certainly understand the allure of the belief that happiness is the freedom from problems. But I'll ask you what you asked me when I suggested the core delusion was about staying safe: If you believe to be happy you have to be free of problems, why would your strategy be to deny that you have them? Why not try to solve them instead?"

"Maybe that's what people living in the world of Tranquility do with problems they think they *can't* solve," Ash said. "Maybe the desire to maintain the status quo—the willingness to tolerate problems—is really just a willingness to tolerate problems they think are unsolvable."

"Maybe. But if you really believe your happiness rests on being free from problems, I don't see how you ever stop trying to solve the problems you have—even the ones you believe you can't. Because how can you ever be *certain* you can't?" I paused and then shook my head. "I just don't see it. If you believe your happiness rests on being free from problems, I don't see how you *ever* turn to denial. I mean, don't you think if Frankie believed he needed to be free of problems—rather than just pretend he didn't have any—that he would have tried harder to help his wife?"

"What do you mean?"

"I mean, did he take her to every cancer specialist in the country? Did he research every drug trial in existence? I don't mean to pass judgment, but did he make sure anything and everything that *could* have been done for her was?"

"I don't know," Ash said. "I doubt it."

I nodded. "Wanting to be free from problems is definitely a *characteristic* of Tranquility. Just like wanting to be safe. But I just don't see it as the *cause*."

⁂

Ash tried to get Frankie to process his grief over the next several sessions but met with little success. Frankie would admit to feeling sad but in the same intellectual way he'd talked about all of his feelings—as if they were being felt by someone else. Stymied, Ash resigned himself to chipping away at Frankie's denial piece by piece, slowly over time, keeping alert for any sign of clinical depression.

Then, a few days after his fifth session, Frankie called Ash to ask if he could bring his son, Conrad, with him to his next appointment. "I'll pay extra," he said. Intrigued, Ash agreed, but told him the charge would be the same.

Conrad introduced himself to Ash at the start of the session with a direct gaze and a firm handshake. After they'd taken their seats, Conrad told Ash that he'd been arguing with Frankie about his mood for some time, trying to get him to talk to Ash about it, but that Frankie kept saying he didn't feel the need. Conrad had continued to press the issue, however, until Frankie had finally blurted out that if Conrad would come with him to a therapy session, he'd agree to talk with Ash about how he was feeling. And that, Conrad concluded, was the reason he'd come.

Ash turned to Frankie. "So how *are* you feeling?"

"I'm okay."

Conrad glared at him. "You're not okay at all, Dad! You're depressed." He paused as if groping for an observation that would prove it and then began listing off the evidence: "He's sleeping a lot during the day. He's lost his appetite. He seems really down all the time."

Frankie shook his head, closing his eyes briefly. "I haven't lost my appetite. I'm a bachelor now. You think I'm going to eat as well as when your mother cooked for me?"

Ash watched him for a moment. Then, thinking Frankie might be more forthcoming with Conrad present to keep him honest, asked, "How's it been these last few weeks, being without her?"

"Talking about it just makes it worse," Frankie said. "It just makes me think about her being gone when I wasn't."

Ash deflated. Clearly, Frankie was still as resistant to experiencing—or even acknowledging—his grief as he'd been during their last several visits. And yet here he was back in Ash's office accompanied by his estranged son having promised him to do just that in exchange for—what?

Surely not to have Conrad attend the session merely as an observer. Maybe, Ash reflected, Frankie's pain tolerance had finally been surpassed when the new pain of losing his wife had been added to the old pain of being alienated from his son. And maybe the pain of that alienation was the pain he was willing to address because it was the only pain he felt he could. Maybe Conrad was here so Frankie could work on the only relationship whose loss he still had a chance to prevent.

"Why *did* you want Conrad to join us today, Frankie?" Ash asked.

"Now that it's just us," Frankie said, "I figured it's time we started getting along better."

"What's been stopping you?" Ash asked them both.

Frankie continued to stare ahead blankly. Ash was about to turn to Conrad for the answer when Frankie blurted out, "I think it's because I took him hunting."

They both looked at him in surprise.

"You mean, when I was a kid?" Conrad asked.

Frankie nodded.

Conrad had been thirteen. He hadn't wanted to go, but Frankie had insisted, thinking it would be a good way for them to spend quality time together doing something Frankie enjoyed. Frankie had been the one who spotted the deer, but he'd wanted Conrad to be the one to shoot it. Conrad had looked at his father, then back at the deer. Wordlessly, he'd raised his rifle, aimed, and squeezed the trigger. A thunderous crack had split the air, and the deer had collapsed. They'd hurried over to it, Frankie beaming with pride. When they'd reached it they saw blood spurting from the ragged gash Conrad's bullet had torn in its neck. It was shivering violently as if it were freezing, all four of its limbs splayed out in agonizing extension. Conrad had been transfixed. His breathing had started to come in shallow pants, and he swayed. Frankie had worried he'd been about to faint. But then finally the deer became still and Conrad, seeing that its suffering had ceased, became calm. Then he'd turn to look at his father with an expression of misery that chilled Frankie's blood. They'd driven home in silence, the deer tied to the front of their truck. Conrad refused to talk about the experience. They never went hunting again.

"That was when things started to go downhill," Frankie said.

Conrad was staring at his father in shock.

"You remember this?" Ash asked him.

Conrad nodded. "How long have you known how that affected me?" he asked his father.

Frankie said, "I knew it then."

"And you never said anything?"

Frankie shook his head. "I never felt more inadequate as a father in all my life," he told Ash.

"Why are you saying that to *him*?" Conrad demanded. "Look at *me*. Are you telling me you never said anything because taking me hunting made *you* feel inadequate?"

Frankie nodded.

"How in the world was I supposed to know that?" Conrad asked.

"I kept thinking we'd get past it . . . forget about it."

"Forget about it?" Conrad said. "When I knew how important it was to you that I go? You think I didn't know how much you wanted me to enjoy it?" His eyes glazed over as he thought back. "That deer was—God, I haven't thought about this in years. I kept waiting for you to come to my room, to tell me it was okay, that your hobby didn't need to be mine, that it was okay I got upset. And now you're telling me the reason you didn't is because *you* felt like a failure. That's almost funny."

"Why funny?" Ash asked him.

"Because that's how his silence made *me* feel," Conrad said.

"I thought you were just pissed off at me," Frankie said.

"I *was* pissed off at you. How could you not know I didn't want to murder a deer?"

Frankie opened his mouth to reply, but then shut it. Then quietly he said, "I knew afterward."

"Then you're not a failure because you took me hunting." Conrad fixed him with a cold gaze. "You're a failure because you didn't let me know it was okay that it made me sick."

To this, again, Frankie said nothing.

Ash paused to consider how he might help them repair their relationship. A family systems approach that focused on their relationship as an ailing third party, an entity living an existence separate from them both, seemed likely to be the most helpful. They'd already shown him its main breakages—Conrad's anger and Frankie's guilt—and he felt confident he could help Frankie get past his failings as a father and Conrad forgive Frankie his mistakes.

But if Conrad was right that Frankie was depressed, that would need to be addressed first. Luckily, with Conrad present, it seemed that Frankie was, in fact, more predisposed to express his emotions.

"Frankie, to be honest, I'm not yet clear if what you're experiencing is normal grief, or if you really are edging into depression," Ash began. "So let me just ask you: do you *feel* depressed?"

Frankie paused. "I wouldn't exactly say I'm happy. But depressed . . . ?" He shrugged.

"How *do* you feel then?" Conrad asked him.

"When I'm not thinking about her, I'm fine."

"What the hell does 'fine' mean?" Conrad pressed.

"Even," Frankie clarified. "Not too good, not too bad. Right in the middle. You know, normal."

"Then why have you started drinking?" Conrad asked.

Ash looked at Frankie, eyebrows raised.

"I'm having trouble sleeping," Frankie said.

"Is it helping?" Ash asked.

Frankie shrugged. "Sometimes."

"Except this isn't the first time in your life you've had trouble sleeping," Conrad said, "but it is the first time you've started using alcohol to fix it."

Frankie was staring down at the floor. "When I try to go to sleep is when I end up thinking about her."

"You know what that sounds like to me, Dad?" Conrad said. "Like someone trying to numb himself. Remind you of anybody else we know?"

Frankie spat out a clipped, bitter laugh but then went silent.

"What was your alcohol intake like before this?" Ash asked.

"I didn't drink at all," Frankie answered.

"Not even socially?" Ash asked.

Frankie shook his head.

"Why not?"

Frankie sighed. He opened his mouth to speak, but then shut it. Then finally he said, "My dad was an alcoholic."

Ash looked over at Conrad in surprise. Conrad nodded knowingly.

Ash turned back to Frankie. "What was that like?"

"Not fun," Frankie replied.

"He ever hit you?" Ash asked.

Frankie shook his head. "He yelled a lot, though." Then, almost as an after-thought, he added, "Mostly at my mother."

"What would you do then?"

"Leave. If I could."

"And when you couldn't?" Ash asked.

"Try to make peace."

Ash thought about how commonly the children of alcoholics struggled with anxiety, how hard they'd work to avoid feeling it. Was that the driving force behind Frankie's discomfort with conflict, his inability to articulate and defend his desires to his wife, his attempt to maintain perfect order in his personal life?

"Now you know why they call him the Ref," Conrad said.

## A Life Without Pain

"Wait a minute," I said. "*Now* I understand what he's been doing! He hasn't just been suppressing his desires. He's been suppressing his *feelings*. He actually wants to be numb. *That's* the core delusion of the world of Tranquility—*to be happy you can't let yourself feel pain.*"

"Aha!" Ash said.

"It explains everything we've been talking about. Why he avoids conflict, why he suppresses his desires, why he's so willing to tolerate problems instead of confronting them. His attraction to the status quo. He doesn't want to feel pain of any kind. *That's* the thing he's been after that looks like safety, that feels like safety, that's a proxy for safety, but that *isn't* safety. Freedom from pain."

"But he's not just trying to avoid pain," Ash pointed out. "He's also trying to avoid pleasure. Except for reading and hunting, he doesn't seem to want to do *anything*. He doesn't seem to want to *feel* anything. I understand why he might come to believe that to be happy you have to avoid *negative* feelings. But why would he believe he has to avoid *positive* ones as well?"

I thought for a moment. "Maybe because positive feelings *risk* negative feelings. Think about it. All you have to do is lose something you really care about, and the source of your joy instantly becomes the source of your misery. If you *fear* negative feelings, it's actually logical to *mistrust* positive ones. Which leaves only the complete *absence* of feeling to offer true happiness—to offer the only kind of happiness you can sustain. Negative feelings hurt. Positive feelings don't last. But the lack of feeling? It doesn't feel like a problem. It doesn't feel like a weakness. It feels like strength. It feels—transcendent."

"Sounds like you've had some experience with this yourself," Ash remarked.

"I have. When I was growing up I often felt anxious when my parents would fight, especially when my dad would get angry. He wasn't an alcoholic. He didn't even drink. He was just never good at controlling his frustration. Maybe having four boys just wore him out. Or maybe he just wasn't self-aware enough. But I had the same experience—and internalized the same lesson—that Frankie did. When you're young, if you're the victim of—or even witness to—frequent and unpredictable rages from someone who has near-complete control over your world, you can't help but grow up a little anxious. And when you're a child and you can't get away from your anxiety, what do you do?"

"You try not to feel it," Ash said. "You suppress it."

I nodded. "So maybe *there's* the explanation for why Frankie shoved his fellow officer. Because suppression doesn't stop you from experiencing feelings.[4] It does just the opposite. It makes them stronger.[5] So the more he suppressed his anger, the more he actually felt it, until just for a moment—and in response to the most offhand comment—it rose to a level he couldn't control."[6]

Not that suppressing our feelings is always bad, I was careful to point out. Often we *need* to suppress our feelings temporarily to be able to reason or to accomplish an important task. If a doctor allowed himself to express or even feel sadness or fear while treating a patient in the middle of an acute medical crisis, for example, he wouldn't be able to function. The problem comes when we try to suppress negative feelings chronically—when we think to be happy we need to be numb.

"Like when we try to numb ourselves with drugs and alcohol," Ash said. "So, in fact, when you're an alcoholic you might not be from the world of Animality at all. You might be from the world of Tranquility instead."

"That's right," I said. "It depends on whether you're drinking to feel pleasure or drinking to avoid pain. If you're drinking primarily to avoid pain, you're probably from the world of Tranquility. Or at least you're trying to get into it."

"But didn't you also say that believing pleasure and happiness are one and the same is functionally identical to believing that pain and happiness are mutually exclusive?"

"I did. But functionally identical doesn't mean literally identical. Think about it like a math equation. When you're in Animality you're focused on the pleasure side of the equation, and when you're in Tranquility you're focused on the pain side. For people trapped in the world of Animality, the primary goal is pleasure. They try to avoid pain but don't actively suppress it. For people living in the world of Tranquility, on the other hand, the primary goal is to avoid pain—which they accomplish by refusing to feel anything at all."

"So for people living in the world of Tranquility—for Frankie—the inability to feel pleasure is collateral damage."[7]

I nodded. "However you accomplish it, by drugs or force of will, the biggest problem with chronically suppressing painful feelings is that you get good at it. And when you get good at it, it can be hard not to lose touch with *all* your feelings.[8] And when you lose touch with all your feelings, you lose touch with yourself."[9]

Ash now believed the problems Frankie had brought to therapy—his outburst at work, his refusal to prioritize his own needs over the needs of others, the cloddish way he related to his son—all stemmed from his reluctance to feel his emotions. He also thought the best way to help Frankie recognize this was by exploring why he'd started suppressing his emotions in the first place. So Ash began the next session by asking Frankie to describe in detail how he'd learned as a child to manage his father's anger.

With an uncomfortable glance at Conrad, who'd once again accompanied him, Frankie answered that he'd taken on the role of peacemaker. He'd learned early on that the best way to function as a stabilizing force was through negotiation. So when his parents would fight, he'd leap in to try to resolve their conflict himself. He also learned how to prevent the fights from occurring in the first place by avoiding his father's triggers. So if the house was messy, he'd clean it. He'd go with his mother to shop for food to make sure she remembered to buy his father's favorite snacks. He often refused to let his mother spend money on him for fear of bringing down his father's wrath on them both. And when his father did get angry, he'd simply agree with every mean thing he said, imagining himself the punching bag against which his father needed to work his anger out.

"So you learned to keep a cool head," Ash said, "even in the face of what sounds like some pretty frightening rage."

Frankie paused. "I don't know that I found it all that frightening once I figured out how to manage it."

Ash looked at him curiously. "I wonder, Frankie, if that's more true than you realize. That you literally didn't know how much his anger scared you. I wonder if the strategy you used actually *prevented* you from knowing just how scared you were."

"I don't know what you mean," Frankie said.

"Well, how does a little boy figure out how to handle the anger of his alcoholic father so expertly? First, you have to figure out how to handle your own fear, how to prevent it from paralyzing you or from making you angry yourself. Because how else but by controlling your own fear could you have maintained the presence of mind required to deflect your father's anger until he wore himself out with it? A father's rage can be a pretty overwhelming thing to a little boy. So how did you manage not to be overwhelmed? I wonder if it was by taking all the fear he made you feel and simply squashing it out of existence—by simply refusing to let yourself feel it."

"Well, sure," Frankie acknowledged. "How else can you think straight when someone's two inches from your face yelling so loud he's spitting on you? I guess I could have taken a poke at him, but then he would have mopped up the floor with me."

"Exactly. That's my point. You had to take all your fear and bottle it up. It was unbearable to feel, so you simply made the decision not to feel it. What other choice did you have?"

"I guess I never thought about it."

Ash nodded. "You didn't need to. It just worked. In fact, it worked really well—when you were a child. But the problem, Frankie, is that as an adult you're still doing it. You're still refusing to feel. And not just fear. You're refusing to feel almost every emotion you have."

"I don't think I—"

"No, he's right," Conrad interrupted. "That's exactly what you do. It's just what he said. You never let yourself feel things. It actually explains a lot."

"Like what, Conrad?" Ash asked.

"Like why I've never been able to figure out what he's feeling," Conrad answered. "Why I've never *felt* anything from him. Because he doesn't feel anything himself."

Ash said, "But he does feel, Conrad. Suppressing your emotions doesn't get rid of them. It actually makes the negative ones even more intense. The guilt. The sadness. The anxiety. The anger." He turned to Frankie. "You think suppressing your emotions protects you from pain. But it doesn't. All you're doing is refusing to acknowledge the pain you feel. Only in identifying, accepting, and allowing yourself to fully experience your emotions without judgment can you ever finish with them. As long as you resist them, you're not blocking yourself from feeling them. *You're blocking their exit*. It's completely counterintuitive, but the only way to end an unpleasant emotion is to *let yourself feel it*."

"I don't think I'm suppressing my emotions," Frankie said.

"You're doing it with your feelings about Mom's death," Conrad said.

"How do you mean?" Frankie asked him.

"I *know* you're sad about it," Conrad said. "I know you miss her. But you won't talk about it. You won't even admit it."

"Of course I miss her. I miss her a lot."

"What about other feelings you have about her?" Ash interjected. "Less comfortable feelings."

"Like what?" Frankie asked.

"Like guilt," Ash said. "You talked last time about the guilt you have about the way you treated Conrad in the past. Do you also have guilt about the way you treated Sharon?"

"How do you mean?" Frankie asked.

Ash shrugged. "It's common after a loved one dies that their caregivers have regrets about things they did or didn't do."

"Well, sure. Yeah. There are always going to be things you wish you'd done better."

"Like what?" Conrad asked.

"Little things," Frankie said.

"Like what?" Ash asked.

"Okay—" Frankie said and paused. "I feel guilty that I watched television sometimes instead of spending time with her."

Ash nodded appreciatively. "What else?"

Frankie glanced uncertainly at Conrad. "I feel guilty that I wasn't more upbeat around her."

"Sure," Ash said. "What else?"

"I feel guilty that I—that I sometimes got angry when she asked for more of my time than I wanted to give." His voice had started to crack.

"What else?" Ash asked.

"I feel guilty that caring for her totally exhausted me and made me want to run away. Because I did. I wanted to run away all the time."

"It's okay, Dad," Conrad said.

"And that—that I ever refused her anything she wanted just because I didn't want it myself."

Frankie stared into a space a moment, and then all at once tears sprang to his eyes. Conrad and Ash glanced at each other, and then at Frankie, in surprise.

"What are these tears saying, Frankie?" Ash asked. "Give them a voice. Let them speak."

"I just can't believe . . . she's gone," Frankie wept.

"It's okay, Dad," Conrad said, his voice cracking, too. "It's okay to cry."

"I just feel so *dumb* that I was so surprised that—I'm just so fucking dumb!"

"It *is* a surprise," Ash said. "Even when you know it's coming."

Conrad was wiping at his own eyes. "It is."

"God, I miss her," Frankie said. "What a thing. What a thing this is." He reached for a tissue on the table between them and wiped his eyes and face, which seemed somehow craggier and even more swollen than usual, his blue eyes made somehow brighter by his tears.

# Feeling What We Feel

"There's no way to end an emotion except to feel it," I repeated. "That is exactly right."

"It's an easy thing to forget even when you know it," Ash said. "No one wants to feel pain. It may sound strange, but a lot of people need practice letting themselves feel what they feel."

"It's so funny you'd say that. That's the reason I joined a Men's Group."

"What's that?" Ash asked.

"It's organized around the idea that in our society men in particular often suppress their emotions.[10] Basically, a bunch of us get together each week to practice identifying and expressing our feelings in a safe, confidential environment. We literally go around the room and tell each other what we're feeling. The goal is to practice actually feeling our emotions without judging ourselves or each other. That's actually how I figured out I was getting angry at Rhea to avoid feeling shame. It's really been helping me to be my authentic self. Not that I'm always so great at it. But I'm learning."

"I've never heard of anything like it," Ash said. "It sounds great."

"It's actually been extraordinary."

"And what exactly does it mean to be your authentic self?"

"Well," I replied, "I'll tell you what it *doesn't* mean. It doesn't mean speaking out loud every thought, belief, or judgment you have to anyone who'll listen. Or being rude in the name of being honest. It means speaking the core truth about what you're *feeling*—no matter if what you're feeling is ugly, or you're afraid that you'll be judged harshly for feeling it, or you're afraid that revealing it might damage a relationship. And as scary as it's been sometimes, I'll tell you this: never once, even when it felt like a risk, have I regretted speaking the truth about what I was feeling."

"Sounds like something that would be good for Frankie. For a number of my patients, actually."

"Not that by any means are the men in the group all from the world of Tranquility," I added. "Just because you sometimes suppress painful emotions doesn't mean you believe that suppressing painful emotions is the key to becoming happy."

"What if you avoid the creation of painful emotions in the first place?" Ash asked. "Are you from the world of Tranquility then?"

"How would you avoid the creation of painful emotions?"

"It's called *cognitive reappraisal*. It's where you interpret the meaning of an event in a way that alters its emotional impact *before* you have an emotional reaction. So instead of suppressing unpleasant emotions once they occur, you prevent them from occurring in the first place by changing the way you think about what's happening to you. You tell yourself a different story. So, for example, if you're about to go out on a date, you choose to view it as an opportunity to meet someone interesting rather than, say, as a test of your attractiveness. So you end up feeling excited to learn what your date is like instead of dreading the possibility that she won't like you. Cognitive reappraisal ends up being a much more effective way to manage unpleasant emotions than suppression.[11] So I'm wondering if it's avoiding feelings itself or avoiding feelings in an unhealthy way that traps you in the world of Tranquility."

I shook my head. "It's not the *strategy* you use to regulate your emotions that determines whether or not you're from the world of Tranquility," I said. "It's the *reason* you're using a strategy at all. If you believe you need to avoid painful emotions to be happy, whether you use emotional suppression or cognitive reappraisal, you're coming from the world of Tranquility. If you use either strategy for any other reason—for example, to stay cool in a crisis—you may find yourself *feeling* tranquil—or numb, as the case may be—but you wouldn't technically speaking be in the world of Tranquility."

Gradually, Frankie slowed his breathing down and stopped crying. Ash waited to give Frankie a chance to let his emotions settle and then asked, "How do you feel now, Frankie?"

"I feel . . . a little better." He sounded surprised.

Ash nodded. "How long has it been since you let yourself experience that kind of sadness?"

Frankie looked at Ash helplessly. "I really don't know."

"Emotional maturity—emotional health—doesn't lie in pretending you don't feel painful emotions or in rejecting emotions you judge to be unmanly or shameful. It lies in allowing yourself to feel what you feel and in expressing what you feel in appropriate ways until whatever emotion you're feeling is finished. None of us can control how we feel, so some of us aim for what we think is the next best thing: trying to not let ourselves feel at all. Or at least, to not feel anything painful. But the idea that we can be happy that way is a delusion."

"Why?" Frankie asked. "Why is that so bad?"

"It's not all bad. Or always bad. We often need to suppress what we're feeling to stay rational and calm. That's why you did it when you were a kid. To stay in control of yourself. But when you do it all the time as a way to stay happy, you develop a divide between what you're willing to *admit* you feel and what you actually *do* feel. And that prevents you from feeling authentic, which creates a whole other level of pain."

"Sometimes what I feel—saying what I feel—is just plain embarrassing," Frankie said.

"Then admit you feel embarrassed!" Ash told him. "I know this sounds paradoxical, but only when you allow yourself to feel painful emotions do you gain the ability to withstand them, to feel them without being controlled by them. There's just an incredible power—a freeing power—in learning how to speak the core truth about what you're feeling. But if you keep suppressing your feelings, not only won't they go away, they also tend to escape when you don't want them to, somewhere else or in some other way. Disguised. Maybe as physical symptoms, like headaches or dizziness. Or as a sudden angry outburst. We have this idea in our society that we're only supposed to feel good. We judge the so-called negative emotions so harshly. We think there's something wrong with us if we ever feel badly. It's not just you, Frankie. We're *all* taught from an early age not to feel what we feel.[12] When we fall on the playground our parents rush to us and say, 'It's okay! Don't cry! You're okay!' But all that teaches us is that it's not all right to be sad. Or mad. Or anything we judge as bad. To one degree or another, we all grow up emotionally constipated."

Frankie turned to Conrad. "Is that what you learned from *me?*"

"I don't know if I learned it from you," Conrad replied, "but if I'm being honest, it's definitely a lesson I learned. I don't think I'm nearly as bad as you are, but . . ."

"If not from me, then who else?" Frankie asked in a self-accusatory tone.

"I'm sure you had something to do with it," Conrad said. "What son doesn't want to be like his dad?"

Frankie looked down, a mixture of emotions playing across his face.

"So am I way off base here, Frankie?" Ash asked. "Or does what I've been saying make sense? Does this sound like you, or not?"

"Yeah, it makes sense," Frankie said. "Yeah, it sounds like me."

"So what can we do about it?" Conrad asked Ash.

"Practice," Ash answered, turning to him. "Practice identifying *that* you feel an emotion and then *what* that emotion is. Then speak the feeling, no matter how painful, no matter how embarrassing, no matter how shameful. No matter if you think it's going to destroy the relationship you have with the person you're speaking it to."

"That sounds hard even to me," Conrad said.

"It is," Ash agreed. "It's really hard. Which is why it's best to practice with someone in your life who makes it okay for you to do it. Someone who has your back no matter what. Who cares more about your long-term happiness than their own short-term feelings. Who's willing to create a safe space for you to be vulnerable. Who won't judge your feelings, or you, for having them. Someone like"—and here Ash smiled—"a father or a son."

After a moment, Frankie said, "I'm willing to try it if he is."

Ash glanced at Conrad, who nodded.

"So what do we do?" Conrad asked. "How do we do this?"

Ash said, "When one of you sees the other suppressing an emotion, call him on it. Or if you find yourself on the receiving end of an inappropriately expressed emotion, use *language* to express how it makes you feel. So if one of you yells at the other, the other might say, 'When you yell at me like that, I feel afraid.' Or, 'When you yell at me like that, I feel angry myself.' It sounds really hard, I know. But try. Because this is what it means to conduct yourself as an emotionally mature adult."

"Okay," Frankie said.

"What you *don't* do," Ash told Frankie, "is *dismiss* Conrad's emotions, or"—and here Ash turned to Conrad—"try to make a case for why Frankie *shouldn't* feel an emotion, or judge him for feeling it, or try to fix the problem that's causing him to feel it. All you do is tell him that you understand he's feeling it."

"That's it?" Conrad asked.

"I know," Ash said, nodding his head slowly. "It seems like just the most insignificant thing. Something that wouldn't have any effect at all. But just try it. Don't worry about empathizing with each other or telling each other you've felt what the other is feeling. Because whether we realize it or not, what we really want when we feel an emotion—especially a difficult emotion that we judge ourselves for feeling—is simply to have that emotion *acknowledged*."

"Actually, they're doing surprisingly well," Ash told me a few weeks later when I asked after them. He'd continued to see them together; Frankie's individual therapy had transformed at their mutual request into Frankie and Conrad's family therapy. Conrad was now helping Frankie feel not only emotions he'd buried for years, but also more recent emotions, most notably the guilt he felt over his failures with Sharon. Frankie, in turn, had been helping Conrad grieve himself, both the recent loss of his mother and what had apparently felt to him like the bygone loss of his father.

"Heady stuff," I said.

"The things they've been confessing to each other have been incredible," Ash continued. "Just really brave. Conrad tells Frankie he feels like he's never even had a father, and Frankie replies that he feels like he's always been a coward. Then Frankie tells Conrad he's always felt intimidated by Conrad's intelligence, and Conrad tells Frankie he never felt he was good enough or smart enough to earn Frankie's praise."

"Wow."

"You know what's really interesting, though?" Ash said. "There was this one offhand comment Frankie made. He was talking about recognizing how hard he worked to avoid feeling his emotions while Sharon was alive. Especially the constant feeling of tension from her wanting him to do things that he didn't want to do, from his wanting to avoid conflict with her, and from all the anxiety and regret and guilt he felt about denying her the life of adventure she wanted. He was saying just how hard it was to be always looking for a path through life that yielded the least amount of disruption. All that. And then he said, 'You know what I think I've really been after all this time?' And I said I thought he'd been looking for happiness. And then he said, 'No. I've been looking for *relief*.'"

"And what did you say to that?" I asked.

"I said that's exactly what avoiding painful emotions feels like—relief. Which *masquerades* as happiness. I told him that the absence of suffering isn't the same thing as the presence of happiness. Just like antidepressants don't actually make anyone happy. They just make you feel less depressed."

"That's right."

"Then he asked me what I thought happiness was. He said if he wasn't going to be suppressing his feelings anymore, he wanted to know what he should be doing instead."

"What did you say to that?"

"I said I wasn't sure. And I'm still not. I mean, up till now we've been figuring out all the things that happiness *isn't*: The power to solve important problems. Getting what you want. Pleasure. Being better than everyone else. The absence of pain. But if we're saying those things don't have the power to make us happy, what does?"

"It's not that those things don't have the power to make us happy," I said. "The question is, what kind of happiness do those things have the power to make?"

## Key Points

- Tranquility is defined as the life-condition of serenity.

- The life-condition of Tranquility represents a fundamentally neutral state in which our core affect lies exactly midway between the extremes of joy and suffering.

- People living in the world of Tranquility continually suppress both their emotions and their desires. As a result, they often don't know what they're feeling or what they want.

- The life-condition of Tranquility results in an excessive attachment to the status quo, a reluctance to change, and in extreme cases a passivity that engenders an unhealthy tolerance for adverse circumstances.

- People living in the world of Tranquility value stability. They're typically calm in a crisis and remain functional under stress.

- The core delusion of the world of Tranquility is that to be happy we need to avoid pain.

# 6

# Rapture

*We get attached to temporary things, then wonder why our happiness never lasts.*

—Unknown

Rapture is defined as the life-condition of joy. In stark contrast to the world of Hell in which we know only misery, in the world of Rapture, we at last achieve the ultimate aim of all our endeavors: happiness. The world of Rapture, in other words, is the world we're seeking in every world that lies beneath it.

In the world of Rapture our energy seems limitless. Life itself feels exhilarating and full. Even our senses seem sharper and more acute. We view almost everything—events, other people, even our own failings and mistakes—in a positive light. We're so consumed and enlivened by everyday experiences, which feel charged with meaning, that time rushes past us.

Our confidence soars when we're in the world of Rapture, and with it our ability to achieve goals whose outcome primarily depends on our own effort and skill.[1] Problems seem like challenges and obstacles like opportunities. We radiate optimism, frequently becoming the person to whom others look for leadership, inspiration, and encouragement.

In Rapture our thinking becomes broader, more creative, and more flexible, enhancing our resilience.[2] Setbacks and even outright failure discourage us less, if at all. In fact, the joy of Rapture diminishes the unpleasantness of all negative experiences, including even the unpleasantness of physical pain.[3]

Sadly, though, our stay in Rapture is only temporary, for inevitably we become accustomed to every good thing that happens to us, and the joy that each new attachment brings inexorably fades as we attend to it less and less over time.[4] What's more, whenever we lose an attachment, as inevitably happens from time to time, our attachment itself then becomes the very thing that places us into the life-condition of Hell.[5]

⚖

"I have a patient I'm seeing now who I think *was* in the world of Rapture for a long time but then fell out of it," Ash said. "I'm not sure it had anything to do with losing an attachment, though."

Nick was a forty-two-year-old commercial architect who came to see Ash after he'd been laid off as a result of a downturn in the real estate market. He told Ash he had a good reputation in his industry and a resume with some prestigious projects on it, and had already interviewed at several high-profile architectural firms. But despite all that he'd been feeling anxious about his prospects. At first his anxiety had been minor. But more recently it had begun to interfere with his ability to concentrate. He wasn't yet having trouble functioning, he said, but his anxiety seemed to be getting worse.

"Some days I don't feel anxious at all," he said. "I get to the end of the day and realize, hey, I didn't feel anxious today. But other days I wake up with this low-grade anxiety . . . this uneasiness . . . that I don't seem to be able to shake. And some days it really gets in the way."

"How else is it affecting you?" Ash asked him. "How's your appetite, for example? Your sleep?"

"I think I'm sleeping and eating pretty well. But like I said, it's definitely affecting my ability to concentrate. When it's bad I really need to focus to get it under control."

"Can you get it under control?"

"Mostly, yeah. But it's getting harder."

"How do you do it?"

"I take myself through a journey. I basically talk myself through a bunch of 'what if' scenarios. You know, what if I could never work again? What if no one hires me, or I get some terrible disease? I ask myself, what would happen to me? And usually the answer is I'd figure it out. I'd be okay. Then I say, well, if I could survive even the worst, most unlikely thing, then what am I worried about? That usually gets me feeling better."

"That's actually a technique we use in therapy."

"Is it? Cool."

"So your anxiety centers mostly around finding another job?" Ash asked.

"I think so. I mean, I should be able to find something good. But who knows?"

"Seems like a reasonable thing to be worried about," Ash reflected. "And a reasonable amount of worry."

"Is it? I keep thinking there's something wrong with me. I've never been worried this much before."

"About finding work?" Ash asked.

"About anything."

"Really?"

Nick nodded.

Until he'd lost his job, Nick's life had been surprisingly free of trauma. He came from a loving, "highly functional" family and had no history of drug or alcohol abuse (in fact, he didn't smoke or drink at all). He'd always been a good student, which had gained him entry to an Ivy League college and then a top architecture school. He'd been hired by a commercial development company immediately after earning his graduate degree. There he'd been well-liked, well-respected, and well-treated right up until the day he'd been laid off. He was gay but had accepted it early on and "without any drama." When he came out in high school he'd been embraced by both his family and friends. He was currently involved in a long-term relationship and was deeply in love.

"I've just always been really happy," Nick said.

"And now you're not?"

"No! Which really surprises me. I never thought my happiness depended on my job. I always thought I was happy because of me."

"A lot of us define ourselves by what we do," Ash said.

"Maybe. But . . . I don't know . . . I just keep thinking there's something more to it."

"Like what?"

"I don't know. I guess that's what I'm here to figure out."

"It is hard to be happy when you're anxious."

"Except I'm not so sure I'm *that* anxious. At least, not about finding another job."

Ash found that a strange remark given that he presented with exactly that complaint. "Anxious enough to come to therapy," Ash pointed out. "Anxious enough that it's interfering with your ability to focus."

"True," Nick acknowledged hesitantly.

"You don't sound convinced," Ash said.

Nick held out his hands and shrugged.

"Would you say you're depressed?" Ash asked.

"I'm not sure. How would I know?"

"One of the main characteristics of depression is that it decreases your ability to find pleasure in activities that normally you'd find enjoyable. So do you think that's going on for you?"

Nick thought for a moment. "If you mean do I still like listening to music and spending time with my boyfriend? Yeah. I'm just not . . . happy."

## Positive Emotion

"So he's anxious because he lost his job, which meant more to him than he realized?" I asked.

"That's what he came in saying," Ash said. "It's just not what he said when he left."

"So maybe he's worried about something else. Something he doesn't realize he's worried about at all."

"He does seem fairly confident he can find a new job," Ash mused. Then: "I guess I really don't know why he's anxious. Or unhappy."

"Maybe he's unhappy *because* he's anxious, like you said."

"Except here's the other thing," Ash said. "He says his boyfriend has been unbelievably supportive since he lost his job. So supportive, in fact, that their relationship has been totally rejuvenated. They're getting along better than they ever have. They feel closer than they've ever been. They have a completely new appreciation for what's really important in life. So even though he says he came to therapy because he's anxious and unhappy, when you really pin him down, it sounds like most of the time he's actually been feeling good."

"So . . . ?"

"So some researchers argue that happiness is defined by the amount of time we spend feeling positive emotion—that happiness *is* the experience of positive emotion.[6] So if most of the time he's feeling positive emotion—despite losing his job—why is he saying he's *un*happy?"

"I'd agree that positive emotion *tracks* with happiness," I said carefully, "but I don't think positive emotion *is* happiness. Which, if you think about it, is exactly what Nick is telling you. Even as he agrees that most of the time he's feeling positive emotion, he's also saying he's not happy. Which, if you think about it, makes sense. For example, we may not be able to feel an emotion like gratitude *without* feeling happy, but that doesn't mean gratitude and happiness are the same thing. And we can feel as positive an emotion as love and still be miserable—for example, if the love we feel is unrequited. Certainly, positive emotion stimulates happiness—gratitude and love can make us happy—but they don't represent happiness itself. Happiness is its own feeling; it isn't reducible to any other."

## Hedonic Happiness
## versus Eudaimonic Happiness

How can we define happiness other than as "the best good feeling we're capable of experiencing"? Psychologists have attempted to answer this question by first drawing a distinction between *hedonic happiness* and *eudaimonic happiness*. While the definitions aren't entirely uniform from researcher to researcher or even from study to study, hedonic happiness is generally considered to be comprised of three things: the frequent feeling of positive emotion, the infrequent feeling of negative emotion, and a sense of satisfaction with, or a positive assessment of, one's life as a whole.[7] Eudaimonic happiness, on the other hand, focuses on the expression of one's values, the fulfillment of one's potential, and the finding of one's purpose in life.[8] Thus, hedonic happiness is about feeling good, while eudaimonic happiness is about feeling that one's life has meaning.

Ash agreed with me that the concept of hedonic happiness needed to be refined, that it didn't make sense to say it involved the frequent feeling of *any* positive emotion, but rather the frequent feeling of a *specific* positive emotion—namely, joy. "But then it gets confusing," he said. "When we were talking about the world of Animality we said that pleasure and happiness aren't the same. But we were talking about physical pleasure. What about psychological pleasure, like the pleasure you get from listening to music, which Nick says he still feels? Is that what joy is?"

"I agree, it *is* confusing," I said, "but I think we can sort it out if we look at what we now know about how, why, and where the experiences of pleasure and joy get created in the brain."

## Pleasure versus Joy

To begin with, the type of pleasure that people in the world of Animality mistake for happiness isn't so much physical as it is *homeostatic*. Homeostasis refers to the processes by which our bodies keep their systems operating in the narrowly defined ranges necessary for life—the process of regulating the acidity of the blood, for example. The need to maintain homeostasis is the reason we have basic drives at all. Our brains reward us with pleasure when we drink water, for instance, so we'll act to maintain our water content in the normal range when we become dehydrated. Pleasure evolved to motivate us to maintain homeostasis so we can survive long enough to reproduce (another behavior pleasure evolved to motivate). For that reason, we prefer the term *basic pleasure* for the kind of pleasure that motivates our basic drives.

Perhaps not surprisingly, basic pleasure is generated in one of the earliest parts of the brain to evolve, the *reward circuit*, which is made up of the hypothalamus and other related structures.[9] This reward circuit is also the part of the brain that drugs and alcohol hijack to produce far more intense pleasure than basic pleasure ever could.[10]

Joy, on the other hand, according to researcher Stefan Koelsch, arises from an entirely different part of the brain, one that evolved later than the hypothalamus, called the hippocampus.[11] What causes the hippocampus to produce joy—in contrast to what causes the hypothalamus to produce pleasure—is attachment.[12] Whenever we think about and attend to a valued possession—a car, a career, a relationship, an ability, an idea, and so on—our hippocampus generates the feeling of joy. This explains why we experience joy, as opposed to pleasure, when we fulfill a desire or realize an unexpected benefit—because they represent the gain of some attachment.

Thus, pleasure and joy are generated in two different parts of the brain as a result of two different causes. As a result, the experiences of pleasure and joy are quite distinct. For one thing, pleasure has a physical dimension that joy doesn't. Joy doesn't localize to a limb or to one of the senses. Nor does joy link to a physical activity like drinking or eating. For another, as we mentioned in Chapter 3 during our discussion of the world of Animality, neither the desire for pleasure nor the experience of pleasure requires higher-order thought. This is because the hypothalamus, where the brain generates pleasure, isn't involved in cognition. From an evolutionary perspective, this makes complete sense. We shouldn't need to *understand* we're dehydrated to enjoy drinking water when we're thirsty. This isn't to say we can't have thoughts about pleasure that influence our experience of it. (Just try drinking milk when you *think* you're about to drink orange juice.) It's just that cognition isn't necessary for pleasure.

On the other hand, the hippocampus, which produces joy, *is* involved in cognition—specifically, in learning and long-term memory—sending and receiving connections to and from the cerebral cortex.[13] This is consistent with the observation that, in contrast to pleasure, joy *requires* cognition. We don't feel joy about having an attachment without first understanding, at some level, that the thing to which we're attached is good. *This is all to say that joy comes from thinking about an attachment, while pleasure comes from having an experience.* This distinction offers a simple litmus test for distinguishing between them: if we can explain why we're feeling good, we're feeling joy. If we can't, we're feeling pleasure.

"That's it?" Ash asked.

I nodded. "Think about it. Why do you like chocolate cake?"

"Because I like the way it tastes."

"Yeah, but *why* do you like the way it tastes?" I asked him. "As opposed to, say, broccoli?"

"Because it's sweet and moist and . . . I don't know . . . I like the frosting."

"But why do you like things that are sweet and moist?"

"Because I . . . well, because . . . hmm . . . okay, I don't know. I just do."

"That's right," I said. "You just do. Pleasure isn't a cognitive experience. On the other hand, you can always explain why you're feeling joy—why you consider an attachment good. Your job is good, for example, because you find it interesting and lucrative. Your house is good because you have a big backyard. Your spouse is good because she's kind and smart."

Of course, to make things even more complicated, nothing prevents us from feeling pleasure and joy at the same time. For one thing, joy *itself* is pleasurable.[14] When the hippocampus generates joy, it also stimulates the reward circuit to generate pleasure. Thus, the reason we *like* joy is because joy triggers pleasure. In fact, we can't feel joy *unless* we feel pleasure, as demonstrated by the case of a man who suffered damage to his reward circuit and could no longer feel pleasure *or* joy.[15] Pleasure and joy are perhaps best imagined as two Russian nesting dolls, one (pleasure) sitting inside the other (joy). Thus, we can feel pleasure without joy, but without pleasure, joy remains empty.

Additionally, pleasure can also *trigger* joy. Presuming we have a healthy marriage, why do we feel joy when we think about our spouse? Because he or she brings us so much pleasure.

And not just pleasure from sex. We also get the pleasure of looking at him. And the pleasure of hearing her laugh. The reward circuit, it turns out, also produces pleasure in response to the so-called *higher-order pleasures*—pleasures unrelated to maintaining homeostasis or to motivating reproduction.[16] Pleasures like art and music, beautiful vistas—and the face of our spouse. Higher-order pleasure involves the senses just like basic pleasure but also activates additional areas of the brain beyond the reward circuit, most notably the orbitofrontal cortex.[17] This explains how eating chocolate cake and listening to a good song, for example, can be equally pleasurable but in entirely different ways. Not that higher-order pleasure requires cognition either. We can enjoy a song, for example, without paying attention to—or even understanding—its lyrics, or a painting simply because of its colors, textures, and forms. We can like those things, in other words, without having any thoughts about them whatsoever.

Thus, like basic pleasure, higher-order pleasure is different from joy. In fact, just like basic pleasure, we can experience higher-order pleasure that actually makes us feel sad or depressed. We could experience higher-order pleasure, for example, while looking at someone we found attractive yet feel both sad *and* depressed knowing that we weren't attractive to him or her.

The last way we can tell the difference between pleasure and joy is that pleasure *satiates*.[18] Said another way, the pleasure we experience from behaviors that maintain homeostasis—from eating and drinking, for example—decreases as we continue those behaviors until at a certain point they actually become *un*pleasant. This is because once a behavior satisfies a homeostatic need, there's no advantage—and often a disadvantage—to continuing it. So, for example, we find eating past the point of being full unpleasant. Interestingly, higher-order pleasure also seems to satiate, though perhaps not in the same way and not to the same degree (not to the point of becoming unpleasant). Why else would we eventually tire of hearing the same song or looking at the same view? The length of time different higher-order pleasures take to satiate seems to vary, however. So we might stop feeling higher-order pleasure, or at the very least see it diminish, after hearing a song a hundred times, yet still experience higher-order pleasure after looking at the face of our spouse a thousand times. But the higher-order pleasure we feel from looking at our spouse's face will also diminish eventually, even as the joy that our spouse brings us does not.[19]

## Hedonic Adaptation

But what about the principle of hedonic adaptation, the tendency over time for our attachments to lose their power to bring us joy? Doesn't joy, in fact, satiate, too? In point of fact, no. Hedonic adaptation happens, yes, but not because over time our attachments lose their power to make us feel joy. It happens because over time our attachments *stop commanding our attention*.

As Daniel Kahneman writes in his book *Thinking, Fast and Slow*, "Adaptation to a new situation, whether good or bad, consists in large part of thinking less and less about it. In that sense, most long-term circumstances of life, including paraplegia and marriage, are part-time states that one inhabits only when one attends to them."[20] This is why when we take the time to pause and ask ourselves if a particular attachment—even one we've possessed for years—still brings us joy, we usually find that it does. And if for some reason we can't tell or don't think that it does, we only need to be threatened with its loss to discover the truth. For nothing brings our attention back to an attachment and teaches us how much we still value it more than the possibility of losing it.

It also seems as if our attachments bring us less joy with the passage of time because our attachments don't only bring us joy. They can also bring us pain and suffering. For example, a mother may not immediately be able to access the joy she gets from her children if they're misbehaving at the moment she's asked to focus on it. (It may be easier to recognize that joy doesn't satiate when we examine the joy we get from our pets, which tend not to frustrate us nearly as much as our children do.)

Finally, because hedonic adaptation doesn't occur as a result of feeling joy itself but rather as a result of our tendency to think less about our attachments over time, it occurs for different attachments at different rates for different people. For example, though studies show that *on average* people return to their baseline level of hedonic happiness within two years of getting married, there exists a large variation among individuals. After getting married, some people come to a *higher* level of hedonic happiness that never returns to its premarital baseline.[21]

## Pleasure, Joy, and Hedonic Happiness

How then do pleasure and joy relate to hedonic happiness? The answer can be found once again in the metaphor of the nested Russian doll: the same way pleasure sits inside joy, joy sits inside hedonic happiness. In the same way pleasure is necessary but not sufficient for joy, joy is necessary but not sufficient for hedonic happiness.

We could, for example, feel joy about winning the lottery but still experience a low level of hedonic happiness if we were simultaneously grieving over the death of our mother. Recall that hedonic happiness doesn't just require the frequent feeling of joy. It also requires the *in*frequent feeling of pain and suffering. Or more accurately, the feeling of *less* pain and suffering than joy. In fact, research suggests that if the amount of joy we're experiencing is greater than the amount of pain or suffering we're experiencing even by only a small amount—even if our core affect is only slightly positive—we'll count ourselves hedonically happy.[22]

That is, as long as we also feel a sense of satisfaction with our life as a whole. Unlike assessing the current balance between our joy and suffering, however, to assess our satisfaction with our life as a whole involves a look back over some period of time. What determines whether we feel our life has been satisfying? Though to some extent it's how meaningful our life has felt to us,[23] to a greater extent it's the degree to which we feel our life has been joyful.[24] If it seems as we look back that we've experienced an abundance of joy, we'll feel a high level of life satisfaction even if we've also experienced an abundance of pain and suffering.[25] On the other hand, if it seems as we look back that we've experienced a paucity of joy, we'll likely feel a low level of life satisfaction even if we've also experienced a paucity of pain and suffering. This is all to say that we feel satisfied with our lives in proportion to our remembered joy, not our remembered pain and suffering.[26]

The only problem with this is that the way we remember joy isn't the way we actually experience it. It turns out, bizarrely, that we consistently misremember the way we experience our emotions. Studies show that our remembering selves judge the quality of an experience not based on the *duration* of the joy or suffering it causes us, but rather on the *peak* intensity and *final* intensity of the joy or suffering it causes us.[27] As a result, a period filled with consistent but only modest joy that ends with intense suffering can be remembered as relatively unsatisfying, while a period filled with mostly suffering interspersed with occasional periods of intense joy can be remembered as satisfying. This is how, for example, we can remember enjoying a vacation far more than we actually did. Or dislike a good movie that had a disappointing ending. On the other hand, while the remembering self may get it wrong, it's the only self that has the power to evaluate life satisfaction at all.

# Relative Happiness

In Buddhism, another name for hedonic happiness—the happiness found in the life-condition of Rapture—is *relative happiness*. It's called this for three reasons. First, because the degree to which an attachment has the power to make us happy varies from person to person. A car might be a source of great joy for one person while for another it's just a way to get from one place to another. Second, it's called relative happiness because the degree to which an attachment has the power to make us happy also varies by the degree to which we're attached to what *other* people have. So we might become extremely happy to learn we're getting a raise until we learn a colleague got an even higher one. And three, it's called relative happiness because the happiness we get from an attachment is entirely dependent on our actually having the attachment. Meaning, to state the obvious, that if we lose an attachment, we also lose the joy it brings us.

Relative happiness is, in fact, what most of us think happiness *is*. And we're not wrong. The world of Rapture is a genuinely desirable state. Hedonic happiness—relative happiness—is a completely legitimate form of happiness. For this reason, unlike the lower worlds, we aren't *trapped* in the world of Rapture so much as we're continually trying to enter it. And in fact, we try to enter it by pursuing exactly the kinds of attachments we've been arguing *won't* make us happy: the power to solve our problems, the achievement of our desires, the experience of basic pleasure, a sense of superiority, and a life free of pain.

"So wait, are we saying then that those attachments *don't* make us hedonically happy?" Ash asked.

"Actually, no," I answered, "they do."

"Yeah," Ash agreed. "So why have we been calling them the core *delusions*?"

I nodded. "They're not core delusions because we're wrong to believe they have the power to make us happy. They're core delusions because we're wrong about the nature of the happiness they have the power to make. Because we're wrong about the nature of relative happiness itself."

"How so?"

"It doesn't represent the kind of happiness we believe it does," I answered. "It doesn't give us the kind of happiness we really want."

"What kind of happiness do we think it represents? What kind of happiness do we really want?"

"*Absolute* happiness," I said. "Happiness that isn't dependent on attachment at all."

Ash paused. "Why would we think that's even possible?"

"Because when we feel joy from thinking about our attachments, it makes us feel as if we've been made happy permanently—as if once they've made us happy, our attachments are no longer necessary. If the core delusion of Hunger is that *getting* what we want will make us happy permanently, the core delusion of Rapture is that *having* what we want will make us happy permanently. We forget, or don't let ourselves recognize, that we're only happy as long as we have the attachment that made us happy in the first place."

"But why posit a core delusion that creates the world of Rapture at all if we know joy is created by a neurological circuit in the brain?" Ash asked.

"Because I think there's more to it, just like there's more to the reason we pursue pleasure. It's not only because our neurology impels us but also because of what our neurology leads us to believe. We said the experience of pleasure gives rise to the delusional belief that pleasure and happiness are one and the same, which then creates the life-condition of Animality. So I'm suggesting that the experience of joy gives rise to the delusional belief that our attachments have the power to make us happy permanently, which then creates the life-condition of Rapture."

"I don't think the analogy holds up," Ash said, shaking his head. "Believing that relative happiness lasts isn't what creates the world of Rapture. What creates the world of Rapture is the *feeling of joy itself.* Think about it. It's the feeling of joy that gives us increased energy, not believing that joy from attachment lasts. It's the feeling of joy that casts everything that happens to us in a positive light. It's the feeling of joy that makes our thinking more flexible and creative."

"Hmm." I paused. "It *is* joy that's doing those things, isn't it?"

"Right?"

I paused again. Then I said, "Right. I'm wrong."

"So maybe there *isn't* a core delusion of Rapture at all."

"Or maybe even though the life-condition of Rapture isn't *created by* a core delusion, it *creates* one—the delusion that our attachments have the power to make us happy permanently. Which *then* compounds our desire to acquire attachments the way the core delusion of Animality compounds our desire to experience pleasure."

"Even if joy does create a core delusion," Ash said, "I don't see how the core delusion it creates is that our attachments have the power to make us happy permanently. I get that we *want* our attachments to make us happy permanently, that when we express our ambition to be happy we don't just mean happy temporarily. We mean happy all the time, right up until the day we die. But I can't think of a single reason why the experience of being happy itself—why simply being in the life-condition of Rapture—would lead us to believe that our attachments have the power to do that."

"Then what would?" I asked. "Because don't you think we *do* believe our attachments have the power to make us happy permanently?"

"I think *some* of us believe it, yes," Ash said. "But I think many of us understand that they don't, that they only have the power to make us happy—or happier—for a little while."

⤜⤚

"Look, I'm not naive," Nick said at the start of their second session. "I know bad stuff happens to people all the time. I know I've just been lucky. But I guess *because* I've been lucky I've never really believed bad stuff would happen to me. It feels kind of dumb to say this, but I've always felt I was special in that way. Not special in the sense that I'm better than other people. Just . . . luckier. Maybe even—I don't know—protected somehow? That sounds really stupid, I know. But . . . like bad stuff was always going to be something that happened to someone else." He sighed. "But now . . ."

"Now—what?"

"I don't know." He was silent for a moment. "Nothing is safe."

"What do you mean?"

"The way I lost my job. It was totally random. I was doing good work, but that didn't matter. So if I could lose my job like that, why couldn't I lose something else? Why couldn't I lose everything else?"

Ash nodded. "It's not a happy moment when we recognize the degree to which our happiness depends on luck."

"Yes! That's exactly it!" Nick's eyes had gone wide. "*That's* why I'm feeling anxious. I did everything right and I still got laid off. I've just had blinders on, thinking nothing bad was ever going to happen to me. I've been an idiot. What was I thinking? This idea that any of us have control over what happens to us, that if we're happy it's because of the efforts we've made—it's total crap!"

"It's not *total* crap," Ash consoled. "You may not have *control* over what happens to you, but you do have *influence*. Your efforts do matter. Just maybe not quite as much as you think."[28]

"The thing is, if I never got hired again, I know I'd survive because what choice would I have? But I just realized that surviving isn't what I'm worried about. What I'm worried about is being happy. *That's* the reason I'm anxious. It's not just about finding another job. It's about how do I hang onto *anything* that makes me happy? How do I hang onto what I *need* to make me happy?"

"That's a pretty significant insight," Ash noted. "In fact, I actually think it might explain why you're *not* happy right now."

"How do you mean?"

"Being happy isn't just a matter of feeling joy. You also have to avoid suffering. Basically, we're happy to the extent that we feel a greater degree of joy than suffering, and unhappy to the extent that we feel a greater degree of suffering than joy. So you may not be feeling too much anxiety about finding another job, but it sounds as if now that you've realized how easy it is to lose things that make you happy, you've started to feel anxiety about your ability to be happy at all."

"That's right—" Nick started to say.

"And it sounds like the amount of suffering you're experiencing at the hands of *that* anxiety has become greater than the amount of joy you're experiencing in being enveloped by the love and support of your boyfriend."

"I think that's exactly what's going on with me!"

Ash nodded.

"So how do I fix this?" Nick asked. "What do I do?"

"First, you can try to recognize that we all typically judge the events that happen to us way too quickly. Whether a loss is good or bad often depends on the context in which it occurs, which can and does change. There's actually a great Chinese parable about this.

"One day a farmer's horse broke through a section of fence and ran away," Ash told him. "When his neighbors heard about it, they said, 'What bad luck! Now you have no horse to help you plant your crops.' But to this the farmer only replied, 'Good luck, bad luck. Who knows?' Then a few days later, the horse returned with a second horse in tow. When his neighbors heard about it, they said, 'What good luck! Now you have two horses to help you plant your crops.' To this the farmer only replied, 'Good luck, bad luck. Who knows?' The next day, the farmer's only son was thrown from one of the horses and broke his leg. When his neighbors heard about it, they said, 'What bad luck! Now you have no one to help you ride the other horse to plant your crops.' To this the farmer only replied, 'Good luck, bad luck. Who knows?' Then the next day the emperor's army rode into town and conscripted the eldest son of every family, except for the farmer's son whose leg was broken. When his neighbors heard about this, they said, 'What good luck! Your son was the only one not taken from his family.' To this the farmer only replied, 'Good luck, bad luck. Who knows?'"

Nick looked at Ash skeptically. "I agree that how you look at anything impacts your experience of it," he said. "But some things are just bad, period."

"Like what?" Ash asked.

"Like if I suddenly went blind and *couldn't* work—or read or write or watch movies or look at beautiful sunsets or do anything that requires seeing—there's no perspective that would make that anything except bad."

"And yet there are blind people all over the world right now who've learned to carve out happy and fulfilling lives for themselves," Ash said. "Or do you think every blind person on the planet is living in a state of interminable suffering?"

"I know I would."

"Actually, there's good evidence you wouldn't." Ash pointed out that studies show adverse events don't affect us nearly as much or as long as we assume they will.[29] For instance, when we imagine how we'd feel if we lost our job or our romantic partner, we consistently overestimate how negatively and how long such losses will impact us.[30] This is because when we imagine how we'll feel in response to negative events, we fail to imagine other, more positive events that will also occur, and therefore fail to take into account the fact that the negative event we imagine won't be the *only* thing that impacts our happiness.[31] What's more, Ash added, there exists a *psychological immune system* that, according to psychologist Daniel Gilbert, "defends the mind against unhappiness in much the same way the physical immune system defends the body against illness."[32] Once we arrive in a future in which an event we'd dreaded has actually come to pass, our minds will unconsciously pick a perspective that minimizes the impact of that event on our happiness. "Which is how paraplegics can end up saying getting paralyzed was the best thing that ever happened to them and mean it," Ash finished.

"So some people are really good at lying to themselves," Nick said dismissively. "I'm not. I'm completely clear that losing my job has totally sucked. I'm not rationalizing it at all. There *is* no good perspective to have about it."

"What if it leads to an even better job? More money? Better projects? More prestige?"

"That would all be great, sure. But what if it leads to years of unemployment? Look at the economy right now. I mean, what if I really never do work again?" he added suddenly with real fear in his voice.

"How likely is that? Realistically?"

"Not very. But being an architect is what I am. I just don't see myself being happy doing anything else."

"I understand," Ash said. "That's what it means to be attached to something. But if you can't be happy one way, you can be happy another. If you're blocked from finding joy in *this*, you can find joy in *that*." As Ash said this, though, he began to feel uneasy. He thought he was beginning to sound more interested in defending a position than in helping Nick manage his anxiety.

"But what if there is no *that*?" Nick demanded. "What if I *did* lose my sight? That really could happen. People do go blind. Why couldn't it happen to me? I understand you're saying I could learn to be happy doing something else. But what if I was prevented from doing *anything* else?"

"I suppose, yes, that could happen. But realistically—"

"I know it's not likely," Nick interrupted. "That's not the point. The point is I could lose everything that matters to me the most in a moment. Everything that makes me happy."

"I understand. But what I'm saying is that you don't need *everything* that makes you happy to stay happy."

"But what if there isn't *anything* to make me happy? What if I'm blind, paralyzed, lying in a hospital bed, and can't feed myself or even wipe my own ass?"

"Being happy doesn't only come from enjoying good circumstances or having the things you want—"

"Are you kidding me?" Nick interrupted him. "What else *could* it come from? How can you be happy if you have nothing to be happy *about*?"

## Experience Stretching

Part of the difficulty in maintaining hedonic happiness is that once we have something, we can no longer know what it's like *not* to have it. Daniel Gilbert calls this the process of *experience stretching*,[33] arguing that the more our experience is stretched—the more experiences we have and the more attachments we accumulate—the harder it becomes to derive joy from previously acquired experiences and attachments. Proof that experience stretching actually happens comes from a study that looked at the effect of money on the ability to savor experiences. According to the study's authors:

> A simple reminder of wealth produces the same deleterious effects as actual wealth on the ability to savor, suggesting that perceived access to pleasurable experiences may be sufficient to impair everyday savoring. In other words, one need not actually visit the pyramids of Egypt or spend a week at the legendary Banff spas in Canada for one's savoring ability to be impaired—simply knowing that these peak experiences are readily available may increase one's tendency to take the small pleasures of daily life for granted. This perspective is consistent with the intriguing theoretical notion that hedonic adaptation may occur not only in response to past experience, but also in response to anticipated future experiences.[34]

The implication here, unfortunately, is that the more ambitious we become in our quest to attain more and better attachments in hopes of increasing our hedonic happiness, the *less* hedonic happiness we'll experience from the attachments we already have.[35] What's more, whenever we lose an attachment, getting ourselves to avoid thinking about all the experiences in life we'll never have—or have again—becomes extremely challenging. So our attachments don't just put us at risk for suffering over their loss. They put us at risk, as Gilbert writes, for "ruin[ing] all future experiences that don't include them."[36]

What can we do then to combat the deleterious effect of experience stretching when we lose a precious attachment? The answer may lie in controlling where we place our attention. Will it be on the attachment we've lost or on what we still have and can still do? After the actor Christopher Reeve had the accident that turned him into a quadriplegic, he wrote about his struggles with this very thing at the end of his memoir, *Still Me:*

> Every time I think about all I took for granted in the past—making love, sailing, acting onstage, or simply giving a friend a hug—I am conflicted between the desire to revisit these memories and to keep them alive, or to try to let them go now that they are receding further into the distance.[37]

## An Even More Distant Focus

The way Reeve concludes his memoir, however, points to an additional option. He says, "My mind and spirit refuse to let the injury define who I am now. And when I look to the future, I see more possibilities than limitations."[38] While this statement might only have been a reflection of his belief that he would eventually walk again, it might also have reflected his recognition that hedonic happiness wasn't the only kind of happiness he could experience. The fact that he could "see more possibilities than limitations" from a wheelchair might have meant that he'd become determined not just to avoid dwelling on what he'd lost, but also to focus deliberately on creating as much value as he could—to focus, in short, on eudaimonic happiness, the kind of happiness that comes from creating meaning. (In point of fact, he directed his first movie *after* he became paralyzed, a project his wife, Dana, described as a "godsend," saying at the time that "there's such a difference in his outlook, his health, his overall sense of well-being when he's working at what he loves.")[39] Indeed, research shows that paraplegics and quadriplegics are in fact almost as happy as everyone else if they have high levels of social support, friends they enjoy, and feel in control of their lives,[40] all of which, interestingly, are linked to eudaimonic happiness.[41]

"Could *that* be the core delusion of the world of Rapture, then?" Ash asked. "That the only kind of happiness available to us is hedonic happiness?"

"That would certainly help explain our obsession with it, if we thought hedonic happiness was the only kind of happiness we could achieve," I answered. "And I do think many people believe it is. In fact, we probably all believe it is at one point or another. On the other hand, many people don't believe it is at all. In fact, many people *forego* hedonic happiness to achieve eudaimonic happiness. Think about an Olympic athlete or an oppressed political activist like Nelson Mandala. So I'm thinking—no."

❧

At the end of Nick's second session, Ash found himself feeling as if he'd been engaged more in a philosophical dialogue than a psychotherapy session. He wasn't sure if Nick was argumentative by nature or if his newly developed anxiety about being able to remain happy had simply made him difficult to console.

Thinking the latter to be the more pressing—and treatable—problem, Ash spent the next few sessions introducing Nick to a number of anxiety-reducing cognitive and behavioral strategies. He taught him how to proactively identify and reject negative thoughts. He encouraged him to avoid suppressing his anxiety, to approach it instead with an attitude of acceptance, the idea being to allow himself to feel it while also distracting himself from it by participating in engaging activities whenever it flared. He taught him several muscle relaxation techniques. He also encouraged him to take every step possible to increase his chances of being hired, including sending out his resume to as many companies as possible.

Within a few weeks, Nick reported that his anxiety had become much more manageable. Then a month later he was offered a job at a start-up and reported that his anxiety had completely resolved, at which point he thanked Ash for his help and terminated therapy.

Six months later, however, Nick reached back out to Ash to schedule another session. When he arrived for his appointment, Ash thought he looked tired and flat. When Ash asked why he'd come back, Nick told him it was because he'd broken up with his boyfriend.

"What happened?" Ash asked. "Why?"

"I don't know."

A month before, he said, his boyfriend had come home and announced that the relationship wasn't working for him and that he was ending it. Despite Nick's attempts to engage him in dialogue, to try to understand how things that he thought had been going right had instead been going horribly wrong, his boyfriend never fully explained why he was leaving. Nick still didn't know what he'd done wrong.

"Sometimes it's nothing *you* did at all," Ash consoled him.

Nick shook his head. "So where does that leave me? What do I do now?"

"Grieve," Ash said gently. "Find a way to move on. Find someone else."

"I don't want someone else. I want him."

Ash nodded sympathetically. Concerned Nick might be depressed, Ash took him through the PHQ-9, a screening questionnaire for depression, which suggested he was depressed, but only mildly. Nick said he still felt excited about working at the start-up he'd joined after leaving Ash's practice six months ago, still felt motivated to get up every morning to work, and still felt optimistic about his future.

Given Nick's resistance to cognitive interventions, Ash decided this time to try behavioral activation therapy, aiming to improve Nick's mood through action. Whenever Nick found himself getting lost in rumination, thinking about the loss of his boyfriend over and over again and as a result becoming more and more depressed, he was to take a specific action to expose himself to enjoyable activities, like taking a walk, playing volleyball at the beach, or working in his garden.

Ash also convinced him to join an online dating site. At first only a reluctant participant, within a few days Nick's profile began attracting significant attention, and he began throwing himself into the process with abandon. At the same time, he began remarking on his ex-boyfriend's many flaws, abruptly convinced he should have ended the relationship himself.

Over the next few months, Ash discovered a pattern to Nick's approach to dating. He'd go through a series of dates that disappointed and dejected him. Then he'd meet someone he was excited about, reveal too much about himself too quickly, and scare his date away. When Ash suggested he slow down and let these dating relationships unfold at a natural pace, Nick argued that anyone who couldn't handle his "complete honesty" was, by definition, someone he didn't want to date.

Cautiously, Ash responded that this sounded like a rationalization. And while rationalization could be used in a healthy way—say, to get over a breakup—he thought Nick was using it in a way that interfered with, rather than assisted, helping him recover from his loss.

"How do you figure?" Nick challenged.

"Because you're right: nothing heals a broken heart like a new love. But the oversharing isn't weeding out people who can't handle honesty. It's making people who might be a good match for you uncomfortable and driving them away. It seems like your desire to share too much about yourself upfront is more driven by your desperation to find someone new as quickly as possible than by a desire to find someone who can handle honesty."

Nick shook his head. "I don't buy it." He wasn't *that* desperate to find a new love, he insisted. As proof, he offered the fact that he himself had broken off several relationships with men who, in response to his self-revelatory statements, became too clingy and desperate themselves. He thought his oversharing represented a carefully considered—even brilliant—tactic. "It's the perfect screening test for someone who wants emotional intimacy without emotional dependency."

"But why the sense of urgency?" Ash said. "What's the rush?"

"I just . . . want to find someone. I'm happier when I'm in a relationship."

"It just seems like so much is riding on this," Ash said. "Even when *you've* been the one to break things off, you've become dejected." And when there came the occasional lull in Nick's dating life, Ash pointed out, he'd begin to doubt his attractiveness and become almost inconsolable—until someone else appeared on the scene who attracted his interest. Then his mood would rebound with a speed and to a degree that almost made Ash wonder if he was bipolar. Nick scoffed at the idea, arguing that his reaction was merely evidence that he was a basically happy person who only needed a little hope that his love life might improve to snap back to his normal self.

# Rapture as a Basic Life Tendency

"Do you think he *is* bipolar?" I asked.

"No," Ash answered. "He doesn't meet the criteria. There's no flight of ideas, no grandiosity, no decreased need for sleep, no increase in risky behaviors. He's not really even *hypo*manic. It's more like his mood is just at the complete mercy of the last thing that happened to him."

I nodded. "Sure."

"He may *want* to make Rapture his basic life tend—" He stopped. "Actually, does that even happen? Is anyone ever *from* the world of Rapture?"

"Sure. It might not be that common,[42] but you know who I think is from the world of Rapture?"

"Who?"

"Rhea."

Ash considered this for a moment. "Actually, I can see that," he said. "So how does she manage it?"

"Not the way you might think. First, she's more attached to having *experiences* than she is to *things*. Second, and perhaps counterintuitively, she doesn't hold on loosely to the things she *is* attached to, thinking to protect herself from loss or disappointment. She does exactly the opposite. She fully invests in everything she cares about, enjoys her attachments to the fullest extent, and then grieves hard when she loses them. But then she moves on. Interestingly, she doesn't focus as much on getting what she wants as she does on finding something to want in everything she gets. She's just one of those people who finds everything interesting and engaging. She's really good at paying attention to and appreciating what she has."[43]

"Highlighting the point that we *stay* in the world of Rapture more by noticing and appreciating the attachments we have rather than by acquiring *more* attachments."

"I think a lot of people do try to stay in the world of Rapture by continually trying to acquire more attachments. But which strategy sounds better: constantly setting your sights on new attachments, hoping for the luck you need to acquire and keep them, or regularly paying attention to the joy your current attachments bring you?"

"Not that you can't do both," Ash said. "But, yeah, hope isn't a plan."

"Not only isn't hope a plan, but hanging on to all the attachments that bring us joy is impossible. *All* attachments are temporary."

"Well, most of them anyway," Ash agreed.

I shook my head. "Whether because *they* go away or *we* do, all attachments are temporary."

"That's a cheery thought."

I nodded. "Which is why I think appreciation is the superior strategy."

"So that's all there is to it? Appreciate what you have and Rapture becomes your basic life tendency?"

"Not quite." Our ability to be hedonically happy, I said, is at least partially determined by the quality of the mood-generating machinery our genes build for us.[44] In fact, according to research, a full 50 percent of the variation in hedonic happiness among individuals is accounted for by differences in heredity,[45] which, in the words of happiness researcher Sonja Lyubomirksy, "probably reflects relatively immutable . . . personality traits . . . that are rooted in neurobiology."[46]

"So if you don't have the luck to be born with a good mood-generating machine," Ash said, "you're starting from a lower happiness baseline, so it's harder to make Rapture your basic life tendency."

I nodded. "But not impossible. Research also suggests that forty percent of the variation in hedonic, or relative, happiness among individuals is attributable to what those individuals do. To the actions we take—actions, for instance, like appreciating what we have.[47] Heredity may create our happiness baseline, but heredity isn't destiny."

Despite Nick's assertion that he was "basically a happy person," after six months of failing to find a boyfriend, he seemed to Ash to have become mostly sad. And what was sad about *that*, Ash reflected, was that he'd brought it on himself. He'd repeatedly sabotaged his efforts to find a new boyfriend by finding the flimsiest of reasons to reject one promising choice after another. *This* one wasn't smart enough, *that* one wasn't attractive enough, *another* didn't get Nick's sense of humor. Though on the surface these objections all seemed reasonable, as they continued to pile up, Ash began to suspect that none of the reasons Nick offered constituted the real reason he dismissed them all.

"Because he doesn't *recycle*?" Ash had a hard time keeping the disbelief out of his voice.

"If you don't care about the environment, you're not the person I want to be with."

"Don't you think you're being just a little bit too picky?"

"I'd rather be alone than with someone who's not right."

Ash had already noted how quickly Nick became defensive when he thought Ash was viewing him as anything other than self-aware and wise, and how resistant Nick was to self-examination when he wasn't feeling good or good about himself. So he decided to focus his efforts not on breaking down Nick's defenses but on getting Nick to a better place emotionally. But any encouragement he gave Nick about appreciating what he had was met only with skepticism. Where before Ash felt like he'd been conducting a philosophical dialogue more than a therapy session, now he felt like he'd been participating in a series of arguments.

Then Nick called Ash between appointments to see if he could come in for an unscheduled session. Disaster had struck. The start-up he'd joined was collapsing, its investors pulling out their money, and Nick was not only once again unemployed, but now also broke.

Ash worked diligently over the next few weeks to stabilize Nick's mood, but couldn't seem to stop him from slipping into severe major depression. He lost his appetite and with it some weight. He began having frequent early morning awakenings. He was no longer interested in dating or much of anything that had previously given him pleasure. And his anxiety had returned full force.

Ash tried the same technique Nick had used on himself when he'd lost his job the first time, encouraging him to imagine the worst possible future that he could, one in which the only job he could find was as a draftsman or a cartoonist. He challenged Nick to imagine what such a life would really be like, to recognize that it almost certainly wouldn't be as bad as he worried it would be, and to believe that he could not only survive his current circumstances but also find a way to thrive in them. But it didn't work.

"It's just too much all at once," Nick said. "Less than a year ago I was in love with a great guy, had a great job, and had the beginnings of a nice little nest egg. Now I'm alone, unemployed, and broke."

Ash realized he needed to do more than help Nick imagine how he could still enjoy a safe and happy future. He needed to help him find a way to secure it. If Nick's depression had robbed him of his sense of power as depression so often did, then Ash would simply substitute his own. He hoped that if Nick could only enjoy a few small successes, he'd become convinced that all was not lost.

So he became uncharacteristically directive. He told Nick to revise his resume and send it out to all the larger development firms. "It doesn't matter if you want to work for them or not," Ash said. "You just need to garner some interest. Get some options on the table." Nick agreed and said he'd get to work on it right away.

A week later when Ash asked him how the revisions were going Nick told him, "They're going." But when his answer remained the same after two weeks, and then after three and even four, Ash finally blurted out, "This is the longest revision in the history of resumes. What's taking so long?"

"Actually, it's done."

"When?"

"It's been done."

"Why didn't you say so?"

Nick shrugged. "I've been sitting with it. Letting it sit. . . ."

Ash eyed him skeptically. "You know the sooner you send it out—" A thought stopped him. "Or are you afraid you won't garner interest from any of them?"

"No. It's not that."

"So what's been stopping you?"

Nick's expression abruptly became despondent. "I'm not sure I want to be an architect at all."

"What! You said being an architect is what you *are*. That you couldn't see yourself being happy doing anything else!"

"I know."

"It wasn't true?"

"Maybe it's just not true anymore." He sighed. "Or maybe it never was. I don't know. . . ."

"Maybe it never—!" Ash stopped, thinking this was the depression talking. He'd seen depression turn despair about the future into regret about the past many times. When hopelessness took root, *everything* seemed wrong, especially choices made in the past that had led, however inadvertently, to the unhappy present.

So Ash referred Nick to a psychiatrist, who agreed that Nick's depression was severe and put him on an antidepressant. Ash was glad to have the help, hoping the antidepressant would treat Nick's depression well enough to improve his energy, which he thought might then rekindle his interest in design and make clear to him that he still wanted to be an architect.

But after four weeks, Nick's energy level seemed unchanged. When Ash asked if he'd begun to experience any improvement in his mood, Nick replied that he hadn't—but, he added sheepishly, that was probably because he'd never started the antidepressant.

Ash's eyebrows rose. "Why not?"

Nick looked suddenly overwhelmed. "It's just . . . it's just another decision I'm not . . ." Then he shook his head and waved his hand.

"Nick, depression is renowned for robbing people of the energy and motivation to help themselves. It's part and parcel of being depressed. It's totally expected. But if you don't—"

"No, you don't understand," Nick interrupted. "It's not the depression. I'm all for helping myself. I want to help myself. I'm just not sure taking an antidepressant is the right thing."

"I've got to say, in your case, I think it is. You need to get to a place where you have hope again."

Nick looked at him uncertainly. "What if the reason I don't have hope is because there's no real hope to have?"

"Think about that for a minute. I know you *feel* hopeless, but intellectually, does it make sense for you to *be* hopeless? We talked about this the last time you lost your job. What's the real likelihood that you'll never find another job as an architect?"

"I'm still not sure I even want one."

"I've got to tell you, Nick, I'm pretty sure that's the depression talking, too—"

"No!" Nick said with uncharacteristic heat. "You don't get it! Not knowing whether or not I want to be an architect isn't because I'm depressed! I was questioning whether I should be an architect the first time I lost my job. I've always been like this!"

Ash looked at him, confused. "Like what? What are you like?"

"Like I—I don't . . . I don't trust myself."

"You don't trust yourself," Ash asked carefully, "to do what?"

"To make decisions."

"What decisions?"

"*Any* decisions!" Nick moaned. "Any decision at all. I don't trust that my decisions will make me happy. That's why I haven't done anything to help myself. I can't tell which decisions I should make."

## The True Cause of Joy Is Pleasure

"Sound like anyone else we know?" Ash asked.

"You?" I asked. "Still?"

He nodded. "I'm better than I used to be, but, yeah, still."

"Why, do you think?"

He shrugged. "I guess I've just always felt that if I make a wrong decision, I've got a lot to lose."

"You mean because what you have makes you happy, so if you make a wrong decision, you might lose something you need to stay that way? Like if you changed careers, or your house, or your wife."

"Not that I'm thinking of changing any of those things," Ash said, "but yeah."

"Although Nick sounds more like he's afraid of not getting something he needs to *become* happy."

"I think what's emerging here is that he's not sure what he wants at all."

I nodded. "Because he's afraid that whatever he wants won't make him happy. That he doesn't want what he *should* want. He's afraid of wanting the wrong thing. Of miswanting."

"That's exactly right," Ash said. "He's afraid of wanting the wrong thing."

"So here's a question," I said. "What if there's *no such thing* as wanting the wrong thing?"

"You mean could more than one thing make him happy?"

"No, I mean what if what he wants doesn't matter at all?"

Ash paused. "How could what he wants not matter at all?"

"Because maybe the feeling of being attached to something *itself* is what makes us feel joy. Maybe the specific things we're attached *to* are irrelevant."

"So we could be equally happy with *any* job? Any house? Any spouse? Our personal preferences don't matter at all?"

"I don't think they do. Just because we're attached to a particular job, a particular house, or a particular spouse doesn't mean only those specific attachments have the power to make us happy. Which means the specificity of our attachments isn't as crucial as we think."

"Not as crucial as we think, I get," Ash said. "But doesn't matter at all?"

"I think the only reason our personal preferences matter is because we tell ourselves they do. We just think we can only be happy if we have *this* job, or *that* house, or *that* spouse. But the idea that we can only be happy with what we already have is just as much a delusion as the idea that we can only be happy if we get what we want."

"But the only reason the idea that we can only be happy if we get what we want is a delusion is because other things besides what we want can and do make us happy. But only because we think those other things are good as well. Which means our personal preferences matter a lot."

"So let's think about this," I said. "What about your wife, Amy? What, in your mind, makes her good?"

"You said it yourself. She's kind and smart."

"So those are the reasons you wanted to be with her?"

"Yeah."

"Okay, you discovered she was kind and smart, so you decided she was good. Fast forward half a year or so, you were thinking she was *so* good you wanted to marry her, so you did. So then you were together, which made you happy. And when you ask yourself now why she still makes you happy, your answer is because she's kind and smart."

"Among other things, yeah."

"And what are those other things? What are *all* the reasons she makes you happy?"

"I don't know if I can name them all. She's fun. She's caring. She's a good mother. We share the same values. She's pretty. I love her."

"And how many of those things does she need to be for you to remain attached to her? *Which* of those things does she need to be for you to remain attached to her?"

"That's a good question," Ash said. "I don't know."

"Well, eventually she won't be as pretty. Do you think you'll still be attached to her then?"

"Yeah."

"What if she stopped being fun?"

"I guess it depends on the reason. If it was because she was depressed, I'd want her to get treatment. If it was because we just evolved in different directions and stopped liking the same things, I'd have to see."

"Let's say it was because she developed dementia."

"Ah. Then, yeah, I'd still be attached."

"Let's say because of the dementia she stopped being kind and living her life according to your shared values. In fact, let's say she got to the point where she couldn't talk to you or even recognize you. Would you still be attached to her?"

"Yeah," Ash said. "Still."

"And what would it be that kept you attached after all the things that attached you in the first place were gone?"

"I'd still love her."

I shook my head. "Love is a *response* to attachment, not a cause of it."[48]

"Then who knows why anyone feels attached to anyone? Why do you feel attached to Rhea? At a certain level it's just chemistry. Biology."

"It's *neurology*," I said. "Which is exactly the point I'm trying to make. The reason you'd still be attached to her isn't because of any of the reasons you gave. Think about it: if you still loved her even after all the reasons you gave for loving her were gone, why would you think those were the reasons that made you love her in the first place?"

"Because maybe the reasons I *fell* in love with her are different from the reasons I've *stayed* in love with her. Reasons evolve."

"You think? Then what are the reasons you love her now?"

"Because . . . we created a life together. Because of our shared experiences."

I shook my head again. "Now you're describing your attachment to your memories. What we're after is what would keep you attached to *her*."

"I guess—I guess then I really don't know. Maybe it's what you said. Maybe it's just neurology. Or maybe it's momentum. Maybe attachment just breeds more attachment. Maybe attachment takes on a life of its own."

"*That*, in fact, is exactly what I think happens," I said. "Attachment takes on a life of its own. The longer it exists, the deeper it becomes. We could even imagine a neurological explanation: having more experiences with an attachment over time creates additional layers of joy that then strengthen your feelings of attachment. I think the real reason you'd remain attached to Amy even if she became demented and stopped being everything you say made you fall in love with her is simply because you were *already* attached to her. Attachments don't break on their own. It takes force."

"But there still had to be *something* that made me want to attach to her in the first place," Ash said.

"There was. But I'd like to suggest it wasn't because of *any* of the specific things you said. It wasn't that you found her smart in a unique way, pretty in a unique way, fun in a unique way, or that you found *her* unique. What made you want her in the first place was simply that she pleased you. That's the reason we attach to things. Because they please us."

"Meaning, like you said before, she could have been anyone."

I nodded. "Anyone who pleased you enough. And who didn't displease you too much."

"So what makes us feel that an attachment is good is that it makes us feel *pleasure*?"

"Or helps us avoid pain. Yes."

"But that can't be the whole story," Ash protested. "Not everything that makes us feel pleasure also makes us feel joy. Think about Dominique."

I nodded. "What prevents pleasure from bringing us joy—which it otherwise always would—is our knowledge that it's also causing us harm. I'd argue, for example, that before Dominique recognized she was an alcoholic, drinking gave her both pleasure *and* joy. After she recognized she was an alcoholic and realized her drinking was causing her harm, it only gave her pleasure. Because it was no longer good."

"So what makes an attachment good—what gives an attachment its value—is that it makes us feel pleasure *without harm*," Ash said.

I nodded.

"So then all the reasons I gave for why I'm attached to Amy are really just rationalizations."

"Not rationalizations," I said. "More like superficial explanations. The real explanation is that they're all things about her that give you pleasure."

"So now we're saying attachment is really about pleasure?"

"No, joy is still the reason we covet attachments that we think are good. It's just that the reason we think attachments are good is they give us pleasure."

## Attachments Are Incidental

It is, in fact, only to feel joy that we attach at all. When we suffer over the loss of an attachment, we aren't so much mourning the loss of our attachment as we are the loss of our joy. It may not feel that way, but that's only because our brains fool us into believing that the joy our attachments bring is contained in our attachments themselves (in the same way it fools us into believing that the pain of a cut finger is located in our finger).

For this reason, we constantly conflate the attachments that bring us joy with the feeling of joy they bring us—so much so that when we're threatened with the loss of an attachment, or actually lose an attachment, we become convinced it's the attachment itself that we'd wanted all along.

But that's like thinking money has value in and of itself. But money is just paper. What we want isn't money. Money is merely a means to an end. What we really want are the things money can buy us. Similarly, what we want isn't any one particular attachment. Every attachment we might ever want is merely a means to a single end: joy. To say that we can only find joy with one particular attachment is like saying we can only buy a candy bar with one particular dollar. We can't buy a candy bar (joy) *without* a dollar (an attachment), but we can buy a candy bar with *any* dollar we happen to have. Similarly, we can't feel joy without thinking about our attachments, but any attachment we think about will do.

Not that all attachments produce equal amounts of joy. Just how much joy an attachment yields depends entirely on how much we value it, which depends on how much pleasure it gives us. But no matter how much joy an attachment does yield, all attachments are merely the conduits through which that joy flows. For this reason, no loss, no matter how horrific, has the power to destroy our ability to experience joy.[49] The proof of this can be found in the experience of anyone and everyone who's ever suffered a devastating loss and found their way back to happiness.[50]

On the other hand, when the loss is horrific enough, some people *don't* seem to recover. A car or a house, for example, are attachments most people feel can be replaced. But most of us believe some of our attachments are crucial to our joy—attachments, for example, like our children, without which we believe our ability to be happy can't survive.

Indeed, research shows that most parents who lose their children don't stop grieving—ever.[51] But that same research also shows that after enough time has passed the majority of bereaved parents also begin to describe themselves as happy.[52] *The two conditions aren't mutually exclusive.* The pain of being separated from a beloved attachment doesn't need to go away for us to be able to feel joy again. It *is* possible to sustain an unimaginable loss, to continue to miss a beloved attachment and grieve over it, and still find our way back to happiness—even if we're initially so devastated we become convinced that without our attachment happiness is impossible. But just because we can no longer be made happy in the way we *want* to be made happy, by *what* we want to make us happy, doesn't mean we can't be happy at all.

Not that the process of becoming happy again after a devastating loss is simple. But we can enlist a number of psychological principles to help. For one thing, as Kahneman reminds us, we only feel pain when we're actively thinking about our losses, the same way we only feel joy when we're actively thinking about our attachments. And just as we tend to think about our gains less and less once we attain them, so too do we think about our losses less and less once we lose them.[53] Also, we can combat experience stretching by summoning up and focusing on gratitude for what we still have. We can also find ways to remain connected to our lost attachment in a way that's healthy, that yields joy instead of continued suffering.[54] And we can find ways—as Christopher Reeve did—to make the loss of an attachment meaningful, to turn it into a catalyst for personal growth.[55]

Whichever strategy we use, recovery seems to begin in the moment we embrace the idea—whether consciously or not—that our hedonic happiness doesn't depend solely on the particular attachment we've lost. This is no easy task, though, given how our brains fool us into believing joy is contained in our attachments. In point of fact, evolution specifically selected the capacity to feel joy—as well as the capacity to feel love, the second emotion of attachment—to make us attach to things that increase our likelihood of surviving and reproducing.[56] Think of things like shelter, or our parents. Though from *our* perspective joy is an end, from an evolutionary perspective, it's merely a means.

This is likely why when we lose an attachment we consider necessary for our happiness, the pain we feel is overwhelming, and the loss of joy we experience seems permanent. Because losing an attachment might mean, from an evolutionary perspective, losing a survival advantage. Thus, evolution would have wanted to employ the most powerful force possible to motivate us to recover such an attachment. And what force could be more motivating than pain? Than believing that without our attachment we'll never be happy again?

"The thing of it is, though, the loss of joy *isn't* permanent," I said. "You have to grieve—and may never stop grieving over the loss of some attachments—to be able to feel joy again. But no matter how devastating the loss, we can recover from it. We think it matters what attachments we have, but it doesn't. When it comes to feeling joy, any attachment will do. Because what our brains use to manufacture joy isn't *what* attachments we have but the feeling of *having* itself. If Hunger is wanting and Animality is liking, then Rapture is having. So I think the core delusion of the world of Rapture *is the belief that our happiness depends on the specific attachments we have*."

"That's the most ridiculous thing I've ever heard!" Nick said. "You're saying it doesn't matter what I want to do for a living? I only think it does? My ex-boyfriend didn't matter to me? My parents don't matter to me?"

"No, no," Ash said, "of course they do—"

"Like I could just give up being an architect and not give it a second thought? Like I could just love anybody?" He scowled. "Just because I'm not with my ex-boyfriend anymore doesn't mean he didn't matter to me, that we didn't have something beautiful and special. Something I'll never have again with anyone else no matter how fabulous they might turn out to be." His eyes narrowed. "And you're telling me it doesn't matter if your child dies because you have other things to make you happy instead? Sorry, Dr. Ash, but that's just offensive."

Ash shook his head. "Just because you can find happiness in another job or in another relationship—or in your remaining children or even from having another child—doesn't mean you're *replacing* a relationship you lost or a child that died. And I'd certainly never *start out* by telling a parent who's lost a child that they'll eventually be happy again."

"You're saying the things we care about have no real value. That we're just fooling ourselves into thinking that it matters what—or who—we care about."

"No," Ash said carefully. "I'm saying that we become attached to things because of what makes them valuable to *us*, which is their ability to make us feel joy. Your ex-boyfriend has value whether you're attached to him or not."

"But you're making caring about things sound selfish, which I don't think it is. Like the people we care about only matter to us to the extent that they make us happy."

"Just because we only care about our attachments to the extent that they make us happy doesn't mean we can't act selflessly toward the attachments we care about, or that we can't or won't sacrifice for them. But if we *are* willing to sacrifice for them, it's only because of the intensity of our attachment to them, which is ultimately determined by the intensity of the joy they make us feel. And if we're willing to put someone else's happiness before our own—which, by the way, is the *definition* of selflessness—that's only because it would make us *un*happy not to. We can't get away from the fact that everything we do is ultimately motivated by our own pleasure and pain, our own happiness and suffering. But that doesn't mean everything we do is selfish."

"You're making connection sound so . . . clinical. Like we're all just robots running a program."

"I'm just trying to suggest we're far more resilient in the face of loss than we think. That *you* are."

Nick blew out a consternated breath. "So it doesn't matter *what* we're attached to because we only really care about feeling happy, not the actual things that make us happy?"

"I'm not saying the actual things don't matter, or that we can't and don't care about the happiness of the people to whom we're attached. I'm saying the joy our attachments bring us comes from the *experience of being attached itself.* So that even when we lose our most precious attachments, we don't lose our ability to feel joy. After we're done grieving, it comes back. If we believe we can only be happy if we keep the things we've decided are absolutely critical for our happiness, we're being fooled by our own brains."

Nick was silent for several more moments. Then he said, "You know what? I don't care. I don't care if my brain is fooling me. I want to be an architect. Design is my passion. I won't be happy doing anything else. And I need to be in a relationship. If I could just have those two things back, I know I'd be fine. I'd be back to normal. Like I was before."

⁂

"So he still doesn't get it," I said.

"To be honest, I didn't expect he would," Ash replied. "It's a hard thing to get."

"Truth be told, I often don't get it myself."

Ash nodded. "It's especially hard to get it right when you're grieving over a loss."

"I wonder if that's what grieving is for," I said. "Getting you to the discovery that you *can* go on, that you *can* still be happy. Maybe we have to actually *experience* the return of joy, even if only in small amounts and for brief periods, before we can actually believe with our lives that we can be happy again."

"Maybe so."

"Which might explain why it's even harder to believe we'll ever be happy again right *before* a loss. In anticipation of a loss."

"Actually, that's a good point," Ash said. "There was one good thing—practically the *only* good thing—that came out of Nick's therapy: when I told him his happiness didn't depend on being an architect, he felt like his ability to be an architect was being threatened, and he realized he still wanted to be one after all.

It turns out the thing he didn't trust himself to decide wasn't what he should do but where he should do it. He was afraid he was going to accept the wrong offer."

"He got another one?"

"Three of them, actually."

"So now he knows what will make him happy—but also thinks he can't be happy without it."

"The double-edged sword of attachment," Ash said.

I nodded. "It raises us up to the highest highs—and drops us to the lowest lows."

"That pretty much describes Nick himself. He's up, he's down, he's up again, he's down again. And now he's up again. It took a month for him to figure out which offer he wanted to take, but he finally decided. And then he quit therapy. Again."

I shrugged. "'Worthy persons deserve to be called so because they aren't carried away by the eight winds: prosperity, decline, disgrace, honor, praise, censure, suffering, and pleasure. They are neither elated by prosperity nor grieved by decline.'"[57]

"I'm not so sure Nick would qualify as a worthy person," Ash said. "Then again, I'm not sure *I* would either."

"Nor would I."

"Is that the best we can hope for then?" Ash asked. "Find things that please us and hang on to them as tightly as we can—appreciate them as much as we can—until we lose them?"

"That's not a half-bad answer, actually," I said. "But luckily, no. Rapture is only the sixth of the Ten Worlds. Though we have a hard time believing it, hedonic happiness—relative happiness—isn't the best good feeling we're capable of having either."

# Key Points

- Rapture is defined as the life-condition of joy.

- Pleasure and joy are different experiences created by different parts of the brain in response to different causes.

- Basic pleasure is the pleasure we feel in response to satisfying basic drives (thirst, hunger, fatigue, sex, and so on). Higher-order pleasure is the pleasure we feel in response to sensory experiences unrelated to satisfying basic drives (viewing a beautiful vista, listening to a beautiful song, and so on).

- Pleasure also serves as the basic building block of joy, which is what we feel when we think about our attachments that we consider good. Joy is synonymous with a positive core affect.

- Hedonic happiness arises when we feel more joy than suffering as well as a sense that life is satisfying. Hedonic happiness is considered *relative* happiness because it depends entirely on attachment.

- In the world of Rapture, the relative happiness we feel from contemplating our attachments turns us into our most confident, energetic, optimistic selves.

- The core delusion of the world of Rapture is that our happiness is dependent on specific attachments.

# 7

# Learning

*If one wanted to crush and destroy a man entirely, to mete out to him the most terrible punishment, all one would have to do would be to make him do work that was completely and utterly devoid of usefulness and meaning.*

—Fydor Dostoevsky

Learning is defined as the life-condition of mastery. That is, we enter the world of Learning in the act of desiring and acquiring knowledge and proficiency.

In the life-condition of Learning, we touch the world through our intellect. This isn't to say that in the life-condition of Learning we don't feel emotion. Nor is it to say that everyone who lives in the life-condition of Learning is smart. Rather, it's to say that when we're in the life-condition of Learning, we're more interested in understanding the world than we are in participating in it.

Nothing excites us more in the world of Learning than exploring new knowledge and breaking new ground. We are, therefore, relentless in our quest to develop expertise and seek to learn from any source available: from our own observations, from formal scientific research, and from anyone who knows more about a subject than we do. We consider no information too trivial that helps us satisfy our urge to create, build, and accomplish.

211

Yet sometimes the urge to accomplish becomes obsessive. When positively expressed, this obsessiveness can be and has been responsible for nearly every advance humankind has seen in science, technology, medicine, psychology, engineering, and more. When negatively expressed, it can produce such single-minded focus, concentration, and commitment that other important concerns—for example, relationships with family and friends—fade perilously into the background.

The most negative characteristic of the world of Learning, however, is arrogance. Though we may often feel humbled in the moments we glimpse how little we know in comparison to all there *is* to know, the certainty with which we believe our ideas are true often causes us to become excessively attached to our own views. Though not caused by feelings of inferiority as in the world of Anger, this arrogance then often causes us to dismiss or even disdain not just the opinions of other people, but other people themselves.

Ash had been telling me about someone who he suspected came from the world of Learning, the CEO of a medical software company named Ken. He'd been sent to Ash by a mutual friend of theirs named Nathaniel.

"Sent?" I asked.

"I'm not actually his therapist," Ash explained. "I'm his executive coach."

Nathaniel was a senior partner in a private equity firm that had acquired the software company with the intent to take it public. After being installed as chairman of the software company, Nathaniel had looked to replace the CEO with someone who had the experience and vision to scale the company quickly. Ken had been an internal candidate, having led three different divisions of the company in the last seven years, each time to great success. By all accounts, he knew the industry—and the company—better than anyone. Though the board had considered Ken too junior for the CEO position, Nathaniel had convinced them to hire him by promising to mentor Ken himself. He also brought in a seasoned CFO from one of their other companies to lend support. Ken, in turn, had welcomed both the challenge and the help.

At first, things went well. Ken was confident and poised both in front of his employees and the board. He created compelling strategic and financial plans for the company's growth, convinced some clinical trial investigators to use the company's software, secured contracts with some large healthcare providers, and established three pilot programs with the second-largest pharmaceutical company in the world—all of which, the board believed, made a successful IPO a virtual certainty.

A year into his tenure, however, Ken's executive team began showing signs of strain. They started complaining that Ken didn't respect them, that he expected them to follow his orders blindly, and that he didn't care about their professional development. The larger the company grew, they complained, the less he trusted them to do their jobs. He was obsessively focused on detail, refusing to allow anyone to make even minor decisions without his approval.

The team brought their concerns directly to Ken, but he brushed them off. So they turned to Nathaniel. Nathaniel himself then brought their concerns back to Ken, several times. "But each time he's convinced me he's right and they're wrong," Nathaniel told Ash. "He doesn't frame it like that, but that's essentially what he says."

Recently, some key executives had told Nathaniel that if Ken's behavior didn't change, they were going to leave the company. So Nathaniel gave Ken formal feedback about his behavior during his performance review. He thought by letting Ken know he believed the executive team's concerns were valid, he'd get Ken to make some changes. He also asked Ken to read the book *Good to Great* by Jim Collins, hoping he'd absorb the book's central thesis, that the defining characteristic of a great CEO is humility, and that a CEO is only as good as the people who surround him.

But after receiving Nathaniel's feedback and reading the book, Ken instead drew Nathaniel's attention to research that argued many companies were successful specifically because their CEOs *failed* to demonstrate humility. And from that point forward Ken's behavior actually worsened. He became even more arrogant, even more convinced that his was the only opinion that mattered.

So Nathaniel brought in an executive coach. After three months, however, the executive coach reported he'd been unable to make any progress. Though he was an expert at breaking through obstacles to behavioral change, he was typically successful, he said, only when the executives with whom he worked were interested in changing. Ken seemed to view their time together more as an opportunity to debate the merits of executive coaching itself. No matter how hard he tried, he could never get Ken to engage in the process—only to argue about it.

Finally, a key senior executive made good on his threat to leave, citing Ken as the reason. A day later, the CFO told Nathaniel he was thinking about leaving, too. So the reason Nathaniel was now reaching out to Ash was to see if Ash was willing to work with Ken as his new executive coach.

Ash pointed out to Nathaniel that he wasn't an executive coach but a therapist, and that trying to force anyone into therapy was a fool's errand. Nathaniel replied that he didn't expect Ash to do therapy with Ken but that he was thinking—hoping—someone with a clinical background might succeed where a traditional executive coach had failed. He hoped Ash might develop an insight into Ken that could be leveraged to spark Ken's interest in the process of self-evaluation and self-improvement.

"It sounds like he's pretty dug in," Ash said. "But I'll tell you what: I'll meet with him once. If I think I can get him to engage with me—and not just in a debate—I'll make a go at it. I have an idea that should help me figure out whether it'll be worth my while to even try."

So a week later, Ash went to see Ken in his office. Ash found Ken energetic, courteous, and poised, every bit the charismatic CEO he'd expected. What surprised him, though, given what he knew about Ken's apparent disdain for his previous executive coach, was that Ken was open to working with him. "I'm fully committed to the process," Ken assured him.

"Well, I know you aren't meeting with me exactly by choice," Ash said.

"I'm actually curious to see where it's going to lead."

Ash studied him carefully. "I'll confess I've been wondering where you're hoping it might."

Ken shrugged. "To me being a better CEO."

"Do you have any idea how you could be?"

"Honestly, my focus has been on making this company successful. For better or worse, I haven't had much time to spend on self-reflection."

"Fair enough. I know you're incredibly busy. So let me suggest something that might accelerate things. Have you ever done a 360-degree feedback evaluation exercise?"

Ken shook his head. Ash told him that a 360-degree feedback evaluation gathered anonymous feedback from everyone around an employee—from his subordinates, colleagues, and supervisors—about that employee's behavior. As a result, it was particularly effective in helping people recognize their blind spots. "It's meant to be used as a personal development tool," Ash was careful to emphasize, "not as part of a performance review—"

"I know what it's used for," Ken interrupted.

"Oh. Great," Ash said. "So what would you think about doing one?"

Ken shrugged. "Sure."

"Terrific." This was what Ash had to needed hear. With a 360-degree feedback evaluation, he'd have a road map with which to structure their sessions, and, he strongly suspected, data with which to attack Ken's refusal to acknowledge that he needed to change.

He also got Ken to agree to let Nathaniel pick the evaluators as well as to let Ash talk with them. Ash thought it would be instructive to see what differences there might be between what they told him in person and what they wrote in the 360-degree feedback evaluation. He suspected the gaps would be large and that confronting Ken with them would also prove useful.

The senior leaderships' direct feedback to Ash turned out to be remarkably consistent. They all thought Ken had a brilliant mind and an indefatigable work ethic. They thought he was particularly gifted at distilling complex problems into their simpler component parts and crafting strategies to solve them. They also saw him as obsessive about understanding the details of every aspect of the company's business. When it came to analytics and number crunching, he was, as more than one executive put it, "a machine." When forced to identify an area in which he could improve, most advised having him spend more time developing his people. He could also be a bit stubborn with his opinions once he formed them, they said. No one thought either of these issues represented a significant problem, however.

Ash was intrigued, but not entirely surprised, by the way they downplayed their criticisms. When he told Nathaniel about it, he only responded, "Let's see what the 360 shows."

And indeed the 360-degree feedback evaluation painted an entirely different picture. The comments about his ability to think strategically, analyze information, and solve problems were consistent with what Ash had heard. But the comments regarding his leadership skills, his interest in the well-being of his employees, the company's culture, managing people, collaboration, inclusion, and respecting alternative viewpoints were damning. "*Fire him. He's dangerous. In the long term, no matter how brilliant he is, leadership this bad will destroy the company,*" one evaluator wrote. "*Apparently, he's never been wrong,*" wrote another. "*He never lets anyone feel good. He takes credit for everything that goes well and distances himself from whatever doesn't,*" said a third.

"*He's an arrogant asshole.*"

## The Sense of Mastery

"Harsh," I said.

"And those weren't even the worst ones," Ash said.

"So what do you think his problem is?"

"I think he's from the world of Learning."

"Being from the world of Learning doesn't make you an asshole," I said. "Far from it."

"But sometimes it does, right? If you're convinced you're right about everything."

"You think that's his issue?"

"Everyone who works with him seems to think so," Ash said.

"It is true that relationships tend not to be the focus of people living in the world of Learning," I reflected.

"You said they're more focused on achieving mastery."

"That's right."

"Well, that focus seems to have made Ken insufferably opinionated and close-minded."

I nodded. "That would be the dark side of pursuing mastery."

"Maybe that's also what explains his resistance to feedback. If he admits he has deficiencies, it means he's not the master CEO he wants to be."

"Does he want to *look* like a master CEO, or does he already feel he *is* a master CEO?"

"Good question. I'd actually guess it's more the latter. I don't get the sense he cares what people think about him."

I nodded. "The latter would be more consistent with the life-condition of Learning."

"So what do you think drives the desire for mastery in general?"

I paused. "I think it's the need to accomplish something meaningful."

"So now we're talking about eudaimonic happiness."

"Are we?"

"I think so," Ash said. "A form of it anyway."

## Happiness from Knowing

Aristotle first introduced the concept of eudaimonia in his most famous work, *Nicomachean Ethics*. The word *eudaimonia* itself is derived from the Greek *eu* meaning "good" and *daimon* meaning "spirit." According to Aristotle, eudaimonia represents the greatest good to which human beings can aspire. In contrast to hedonic happiness, which Aristotle considered "a vulgar ideal [that made] humans slavish followers of [their] desires,"[1] eudaimonia comes from living well, by which Aristotle meant from living in accord with virtue and reason. And by *that* he meant taking action whose aim was to achieve "some final realization of [our] true and best nature."[2]

From those philosophical roots, modern-day psychology has defined eudaimonia more broadly *as the feeling that results from creating value*.[3] As the feeling that comes from taking meaningful action. Action that makes our lives feel important.

"But the world of Learning is also about acquiring knowledge," I pointed out.

"Yes, but you also said that was for the sake of accomplishing something meaningful."

"Or for the sake of knowledge itself."

"Which is also meaningful," Ash said.

I paused. "I suppose."

"You don't sound convinced."

"I'm just not sure when I learn something that I'm actually creating value. That I've done something important."

"Learning something new about the world doesn't strike you as important?"

"It strikes me as *enjoyable*. I like satisfying my curiosity. But important?" I shrugged.

"You don't think that in the act of learning something you're expanding your potential? That learning changes you in an important and fundamental way?" Ash thought for a moment. "And by learning, by the way, I don't just mean facts and figures. I mean learning how to reason. How to construct an argument. How to develop a testable hypothesis from experimental evidence. Think about it—when you develop and enlarge your understanding of the world, in a very real way, aren't you developing and enlarging *yourself?*"

"Actually, you are! I take it back. Acquiring knowledge does feel meaningful when you put it that way. You are creating value—for yourself."

Ash nodded. "Why do you think we evolved to be curious in the first place? Not to acquire knowledge for its own sake. To acquire knowledge that improves our chances of survival, one of the most meaningful activities there is."

"You're absolutely right," I said. "The world of Learning really is about doing something meaningful."

"Whether that meaningful something is ensuring basic survival," Ash said, "or helping to grow a company."

⟋⟍

Thinking now that Ken might be obsessed not so much with being right as with creating something of value—in this case, growing a great company—Ash began to worry in earnest about how he was going to respond to the results of the 360-degree feedback evaluation. While he'd hoped Ken would find them distressing, he now suspected he'd see them more as a threat to the value he meant to create—to the success of the company—and would simply reject them out of hand.

When he and Ken met next, however, Ken told him he hadn't even yet looked at the feedback. He'd just been too busy. Ash found this indifference concerning.

If Ken was that uninterested in how others viewed his performance, Ash had no idea how he was going to get Ken interested in examining his performance himself.

When they met again the following week, however, Ken reported that he had at last read through the feedback. He went on to tell Ash that he'd spent the rest of the week reading up on the research around the 360-degree feedback evaluation itself and felt the tool was riddled with flaws. Chief among them, he argued, was that evaluators frequently used it to further their own agendas and often lied. He thought, in sum, it offered data that was little better than that found in negative reviews on Amazon, Yelp, and other websites that were anonymous and unverified.

Ash held out a slim hope that Ken's attempt to divert the conversation away from the evaluation results and more toward the evaluation tool itself indicated his discomfort with the results rather than his indifference to the opinions of his evaluators. "Are you saying you don't believe their feedback is legitimate?"

"I believe it's what they believe."

"Every survey generates outlier responses that should be ignored," Ash acknowledged, "responses that speak more about the evaluators themselves than the person being evaluated. But recurrent themes are always worth thinking about. I mean, just how likely is it that all your people are biased in the exact same way? Why not consider the feedback on its merits?"

"I don't actually disagree with a lot of it," Ken said.

"You don't?"

"No. What I disagree with is that the issues they raise are actual problems. Look, it's clear that a lot of what I do gets misinterpreted. I understand that people here have a certain view of me. That I'm a control freak, that I have a low emotional IQ—whatever that means—and that I always think I'm right—"

"Wait," Ash interrupted, "you're saying you agree those things are all true—but that none of them are actually problems?"

"I'm saying I think their description of my *behavior* is accurate—I am extremely demanding—but the reasons I'm demanding have nothing to do with being a control freak, having a low emotional IQ, or whatever else."

"What do they have to do with then?"

Ken paused. "To achieve great things, you have to work hard. People say that all the time as if they know what it means, thinking they do work hard. But if you're comfortable, if your life feels balanced, if you aren't stressed in some way, then by definition you *aren't* working hard. Or hard enough. This company could easily fail. Its success hinges on people working harder than they actually want to. But that's how hard *I* work, and that's what I demand. My ultimate responsibility—my only responsibility—is to ensure the success of this company. I'm not saying culture isn't important. I'm not saying the people aren't important. But, look, Steve Jobs wasn't for everyone. Working at Amazon isn't for everyone. And working here isn't for everyone. They think I work them hard because I'm a control freak, that I have a low emotional IQ, and that I don't care about their stress or the culture. But that's not it. I work them hard because I care more about the success of the company than I care about the comfort of its employees."

Ash marveled at Ken's blatant misinterpretation of the feedback. Not one of his employees had complained that he was working them too hard; they'd complained that he didn't value their opinions or care about them as people. Was this deliberate obfuscation on his part, a subversive attempt to make *them* look like the problem, or was he unwilling—or even unable—to acknowledge the true nature of their complaints?

"But why does it have to be one or the other?" Ash challenged. "Why can't you care about and nurture the success of the company *and* its employees?"

Ken shook his head sadly. "They both pull from the same resource bucket. To change the culture the way they seem to want would necessitate pulling back the throttle on their effort, and we just can't afford to do that. I understand that many of these people are unhappy. And I'm sorry for that. I just disagree that they're unhappy because of me. I think they're unhappy because of the demands I've placed on them. Which only means this may not be the place for them."

"What if your demands are unreasonable?" Apart from his refusal to recognize what his employees were actually complaining about, just how well defended, Ash wondered, was Ken's belief that his behavior in general toward them was justified?

"That question presumes there exists an objective standard of reasonableness when it comes to working hard. Who's to say what that is? Them? You?" He shook his head. "I'm not obsessed with getting my employees to work hard. I'm obsessed with getting them to produce the results the company needs."

"So even though it seems to be a consistent reaction from most, if not all, of your evaluators," Ash said carefully, "in your mind their reaction to you is *their* problem. It speaks to *their* flaws, not yours."

"I don't think this is about our respective flaws. I think it's more about whether we're a good fit for each other. Whether they're a good fit for what this company needs."

Dismayed by Ken's apparent lack of willingness to entertain the possibility that his inferior leadership was the explanation for his poor reviews—or that the reviews were, in fact, about his leadership at all—Ash decided to press the issue. "You think they're all lodging the same, specific complaints about you because they're just unhappy about how hard you're working them? None of their complaints have merit?"

"Which specific complaints do you mean?"

Ash pulled out his notes and read from the feedback: "'The worst listener I've encountered in my professional career . . .' 'Disrespectful of anyone's time except his own . . .' 'Always convinced he's right . . .' 'Has to win every argument . . .'"

"Absolutely untrue," Ken protested. "The best *argument* wins with me, not the best person."

"And the best argument just mostly ends up being yours?"

"Yes."

Ash raised a skeptical eyebrow.

"Look, I know how that sounds. But I make it my job to know the data better than anyone," Ken explained. "The reason my arguments usually carry the day is because I'm usually the most informed. Look at our results. We've surpassed our revenue targets by ten percent every quarter since I've been CEO! We're expanding into markets no one else thought we could. What I've been asking everyone to do has been *working*. So you tell me: am I right, or are they?"

## The Importance of Creating Value

"You're sure he's not from the world of Anger?" I asked Ash.

"No, I think it's more what you said," Ash replied. "He's not arrogant because he's insecure. He's arrogant because he thinks he's right. He genuinely believes he's the smartest guy in the room. And he may be. But he's utterly incompetent when it comes to relationships and leadership. And he's even more incompetent when it comes to assessing his own competence. I have no idea how I'm going to get through to him."

"You may not."

"I appreciate the vote of confidence."

"It's not you. According to early Buddhist philosophers, people who live in the worlds of Learning and Realization are so attached to their own views that they can't attain enlightenment at all. Even people in the world of Hell are thought to have a better chance."

"So maybe that actually points us to the core delusion of Learning," Ash said. "Maybe it's the belief that to be happy you have to be right."

I shook my head. "That's just another way of saying that to be happy you need to be better than other people, which is the core delusion of the world of Anger. Think about it: isn't wanting to be right mostly about your ego?"

"That is true, yeah."

"Also, I don't get the sense from you that Ken thinks *he's* superior—just that his *ideas* are."

"That's probably accurate, too," Ash conceded.

"I actually think the core delusion of Learning is fairly straightforward," I said. "I think it's just what we've been saying, *that to be happy we need to accomplish something meaningful.*"

Ash considered this. "That probably makes the most sense. On the other hand, we've also been saying that accomplishing meaningful things *does* make us happy. So maybe it's not even a delusion. Maybe we're wrong to suppose there's a core delusion of Learning at all."

"No, it's a delusion for the same reason the core delusions of the lower worlds are delusions: because eudaimonic happiness isn't any more permanent than hedonic happiness. We still expect the joy that comes from value creation to last. But it doesn't. The joy of doing something meaningful doesn't turn you into a happy person any more than does the joy of possessing an attachment you consider good. Eudaimonic happiness is a type of relative happiness, too."

# Eudaimonic Happiness Defined

"The joy of doing something meaningful . . . ," Ash considered. "You know, I'm not sure that's actually what eudaimonic happiness is."

"No?"

"We said that eudaimonia was the feeling we get from taking meaningful action, right? From creating something of value."

"Right," I said.

"So why are we presuming that feeling is joy?"

"Well, because—"

"Because if it *is* joy," Ash interrupted, "aren't we then saying eudaimonic happiness is actually *hedonic* happiness? Isn't joy in the absence of suffering what we said hedonic happiness was?"

"Joy with *less* suffering, yeah."

"I'll tell you what I think," Ash said. "I think eudaimonic happiness isn't the feeling of joy at all. I think eudaimonic happiness is the feeling of meaningfulness *itself.*"

"The feeling of meaningfulness?"

"The feeling of having done something important," Ash said.

"So you're saying that meaningfulness is its own feeling. Like happiness, it's not reducible to any other."

"Yes. And that's how eudaimonic happiness *is*, in fact, different from hedonic happiness."

"Well, if you're right, that's not the only way they're different," I said. "Eudaimonic happiness also then requires us to *do* something, to take action, where hedonic happiness requires us only to *think* about something, an attachment we value—"

"Right."

"What's more, eudaimonic happiness requires that the action we take is *meaningful,* by which we mean important to us, where hedonic happiness requires only that our attachment is *good,* by which we mean pleasing to us."

"Exactly," Ash agreed.

## Eudaimonic Happiness Is a Type of Hedonic Happiness

"So all that makes sense to me," I said. "But wouldn't you also agree that doing something meaningful—taking action that creates value—*also brings joy*? Not that you can't do something meaningful that also makes you suffer, like throw yourself in the path of a bullet to shield someone else from being shot, or give up a job you love to care for a sick parent. But isn't doing something meaningful—the feeling of meaningfulness itself—*inherently* joyful? In the same way that joy is inherently pleasurable? Didn't we agree, in fact, that acquiring knowledge is enjoyable?"

"Well, you said it was for *you.*"

"You don't agree?"

"Actually—yeah, I do. It is."

"So then maybe eudaimonic happiness is really a *type* of hedonic happiness,"[4] I said, "where the attachment that brings us joy is meaning itself."

Just as the parts of the brain that create joy evolved later than and on top of the parts of the brain that create pleasure, so too did the parts of the brain that show increased activity in association with eudaimonic happiness evolve later than and on top of those that create hedonic happiness. These include the anterior cingulate cortex,[5] the right posterior superior temporal cortex,[6] the prefrontal cortex,[7] the inferior frontal cortex,[8] the lateral prefrontal cortex,[9] the insular cortex,[10] and the orbitofrontal cortex.[11] And indeed studies also show that acts that promote eudaimonic happiness (including the act of satisfying our curiosity)[12] activate the reward circuit as well.[13] This suggests that just as the experience of joy relies on the brain structures that create pleasure, so too does the experience of eudaimonic happiness rely on the brain structures that create joy[14]—that eudaimonic happiness is, in fact, joy in response to meaningfulness.

"You mean in response to doing something meaningful," Ash clarified. "Like saving someone's life."

"Or in response to experiencing something meaningful, like watching your son graduate college. It's not the activity itself. It's how meaningful the activity feels to you. So, for example, earning money could bring you hedonic happiness if you think about all the things you can buy with it. But it could also bring you eudaimonic happiness if you think about it as a measure of the value you've created with your business."

Ash paused. "What about the fact that studies show high levels of eudaimonic happiness also correlate with high levels of *negative* emotion?"[15]

"That makes sense, too," I answered. "Like I said before, many people *forego* hedonic happiness—attachment to things besides meaning—to *achieve* eudaimonic happiness. To achieve something meaningful—to feel the joy of meaningfulness—you often have to experience pain."

"Now you sound like Ken," Ash said, "trying to justify why he treats his employees like shit."

Nathaniel told Ash he'd met again with a number of people on Ken's executive team and that the news was bad. Five of the remaining seven were actively looking for jobs elsewhere. The company's general counsel had also told Nathaniel that none of them had noncompete clauses in their contracts, so they were all free to go to the company's competitors. The board had responded by requiring them to sign noncompetes to receive their bonuses and option grants. Unfortunately, only one of the five had done so. As a result, Nathaniel had decided that if Ash couldn't get Ken to commit to making some significant changes in his leadership style within the month, he was going to let Ken go.

Thinking that Ken was too well defended and that nothing Ash did was likely to get him to change, Ash was on the verge of telling Nathaniel he had nothing more to offer. Then he had a sudden, inspired idea: he'd bring the problem the company was having with Ken . . . to Ken himself.

"Your company has a major problem that needs solving," Ash began at their next meeting. "So I'm going to lay it out for you as objectively as I can and ask you how you'd solve it *if you weren't part of the problem yourself.*" He hoped to provoke Ken's interest in problem solving, thinking it could be the one thing that might break the attachment he felt to his ideas about how to lead the company.

"I want you to look at the data as if you were an outside consultant hired to identify the risk the current CEO poses to the company's future success and tell me what the company should do about it," Ash said. Then he disclosed that the majority of CEO's executive team were searching for other jobs because they were unhappy with the CEO's leadership. They felt that while they were achieving great success in meeting the CEO's expectations, it was at the cost of their personal and professional fulfillment. Nathaniel had brought Ash on to address the problem, he confessed to Ken, thinking an executive coach with a background in psychology might succeed in getting the CEO to recognize his failings as a leader where a traditional executive coach had failed.

On the other hand, Ash said, the CEO himself had made a compelling case for *not* changing. The company was doing extraordinarily well, growing even faster than the board had hoped it would. The question that Ash wanted Ken to answer, therefore, was this: was the CEO an obstacle to the company's success or a necessary part of it? He asked Ken to review all the data, the company's strategic plan, its past growth, its future growth projections, the 360-degree feedback evaluation results—everything, in short, he needed to make his assessment. And then, Ash told Ken, he wanted him to come back with a recommendation.

Ken listened to all this in silence. Then he gave Ash an appraising look. "That's a very interesting idea."

"So you'll do it?"

After a moment, Ken nodded. "Yeah."

Four days later, Nathaniel told Ash that Ken had requested some personal time off, something he hadn't done in almost a year. He'd asked for a week, Nathaniel said, and Nathaniel had given it to him.

A week and a day later, Ken reached out to Ash and asked for a meeting.

"So you've read back over the feedback?" Ash began after they sat down together in Ken's office.

"I have," Ken replied.

"And how successful do you think you were in viewing it this time from the perspective of an outside consultant?"

"Once you made that suggestion, I found it effortless. It was an inspired idea, actually. Which is why I agreed to give it a try."

Ash nodded appreciatively. "So what do you think? Does this company have a problem?"

"It does."

Ash nodded. "And how would you describe it?"

Ken paused. "The CEO is brilliant, effective, and gets the results the board wants. But his weaknesses are sowing the seeds of the company's destruction. He's overly attached to his own views, insisting on doing everything his own way, despite being surrounded by an incredibly talented executive team, which he micromanages and undercuts constantly, preventing them from doing even better work than they are—the work they're *really* capable of doing. He's created an unsustainable dichotomy: everyone agrees he's the driving force behind the company's success, but nobody wants to work with him. An alarming number of key executives are threatening to quit because of his leadership style. If they do, the remaining employees will become even more demoralized. The company will find it hard, if not impossible, to attract the talent it needs when the word spreads about why so many executives quit all at once. If things continue as they are, the company will fail."

Ash was stunned. "That's . . . quite an assessment."

"I think it's accurate," Ken said, both his expression and his tone flat.

"I have to say I agree. So what do you recommend?"

"The CEO should resign. Immediately."

Ash blanched. "What—?"

Ken nodded. "Which is exactly what I've decided to do."

## The Benefits of Eudaimonic Happiness

I was flabbergasted. "Why would he do that?"

"I can only tell you what he told me," Ash said. "It matters more to him that the company succeeds than he does. To him the company's success *is* his success."

"Wow."

"I know."

"I guess for some people, hedonic happiness *isn't* enough. Or isn't even important. But—seriously? He intends to fire himself?"

Ash nodded.

"And you think he's being honest about the reason?"

"What else would it be? You think he took another look at the feedback and suddenly realized, 'Oh, my God, they really don't like me here, so I better leave?' No. I think it's what he said. I think for him creating something of value is more important than anything else.[16] I think for some people, the desire to live a meaningful life is more than just a drive. It's a compulsion."

"For some people," I agreed.

Studies do suggest, for example, that people with high emotional intelligence are the most prone to engage in meaningful activity as a way to increase their happiness.[17] On the other hand, that might be because, being more emotionally intelligent, such people *require* more meaningful activity to be happy. In fact, that may be part of what being emotional intelligent *means*: being more in touch with the part of ourselves that craves meaning. Other people with less emotional intelligence may in fact be able to be just as happy—as hedonically happy—with *less* meaning in their lives.

"And then there's Ken," Ash said, "who despite being one of the most emotionally *un*intelligent people I've ever met, seems to care so much about creating something of value that he's willing to sacrifice his hedonic happiness entirely."

I shook my head. "Why not try to become the CEO his company needs so he can have both?"

"I know, right?" Ash could only shake his head.

"On the other hand—and possibly to Ken's credit—eudaimonic happiness may actually be superior to hedonic happiness in some ways," I said.

For one thing, a focus on meaning—on eudaimonic happiness—may actually protect people against certain kinds of mental illness, like depression.[18] Studies also suggest that a focus on meaning makes people more resilient, helping them recover more quickly from adverse events.[19] Research also shows that eudaimonic happiness is associated with better physical health. For example, engagement in meaningful activity tracks with a decreased risk for developing Alzheimer's disease, a decreased risk for heart attacks, a decreased risk for stroke, and even longer life.[20]

Also, when hedonic happiness dips or is lost due to the loss of an important attachment—like one's health as in the case of a quadriplegic like Christopher Reeve, or one's freedom as in the case of prisoners like Viktor Frankl or Nelson

Mandela—eudaimonic happiness may be the only way we can be happy at all. This was, in fact, the hypothesis Frankl advanced in his book, *Man's Search for Meaning*—that "suffering ceases to be suffering at the moment it finds a meaning."[21]

And in fact that very hypothesis points out the most important advantage eudaimonic happiness has over hedonic happiness: it depends more on our own efforts, and less on luck, than hedonic happiness. As a result, it's arguably easier to achieve and harder to uproot.

"Harder to uproot, at least, I believe," Ash said. "Once you've done something that feels meaningful, it's hard to imagine how something else could take that feeling away from you. And that's worth a lot. But as you said yourself, eudaimonic happiness isn't any more permanent than hedonic happiness."

"No," I admitted, "it's not."

"Which, if you think about it, makes Ken's solution even dumber," Ash said with sudden heat. "Say he resigns and the company goes on to become everything he wants it to be. Whatever else he goes on to do next—and he'll have to do something—he'll always have to *think about* the success the company achieves after he leaves to experience the meaningfulness of his sacrifice. And though the eudaimonic happiness he feels from firing himself to save the company can't be taken from him easily—or maybe at all—it will only ever be a temporary state he gets to inhabit in the moments he brings his sacrifice to mind. In that sense, it's no better than the hedonic happiness he's giving up."

⁓

"So I completely agree with your assessment," Ash said to Ken. "But your recommendation is horseshit."

Ken raised a questioning eyebrow. "The CEO demonstrates little aptitude for—or frankly interest in—improving his leadership skills. I think he's wrong for the company, and the company is wrong for him."

"And I think that's a cop-out. He'll dedicate every personal resource he has to developing the company but won't even *think* about trying to develop himself? Does that make any sense to you? Isn't the CEO himself a part of the company he's trying to develop?"

"Mmm. True."

"The problem," Ash said, "is that your CEO is also *right* for the company. He's—" Ash stopped himself. "*You've* accomplished some amazing things here. Instead of firing yourself, why not challenge yourself to improve? Can you imagine what you could do here if you developed an ability to mentor people that was as advanced as your ability to assess problems and formulate solutions? Have you ever even *thought* about trying to do that?"

"To mentor people? No."

"Has anyone ever mentored *you?*"

"Not really. Though Nathaniel . . . has always been really encouraging," he added.

"You realize, by the way, what a terrible position you're putting him in if you resign. He was the one who put himself on the line for you with the board."

"That's true," Ken admitted.

There was a moment of silence.

"So *no one* has ever taught you how to be a leader?" Ash asked him.

Ken reflected a moment. "No."

"I mean, did you think it was something you could just pick up? Because you're smart?"

Ken allowed himself a small smile. "I guess I did, yeah."

"Well, if it was something you thought you could learn on your own, why would you also think it was something you couldn't be taught by someone else?"

Ken sighed. "I can't honestly say I've ever thought about it at all."

"Okay, then I have a proposition for you."

Ken sat back in his chair. "I'm listening."

"First, don't resign," Ash said.

"Okay. . . ."

Ash nodded. "Second, work with me to put together a training program for you that we can show to Nathaniel. Let him critique it. Let him finalize it. Let him participate in it. Be open to feedback. His *and* mine."

"Okay. . . ."

"Third—and last—come to see me as a patient."

Ken looked at Ash in surprise. "What do I have to gain from seeing you as a patient?"

"I'll tell you exactly what you have to gain from seeing me as a patient," Ash replied. "I think you have a remarkable ability to rationalize exceptionally egregious behavior. It's served you well in many ways—it's enabled you to work harder than anyone else, for instance—but it's also blinded you to some of your worst flaws. And now that blindness is threatening your continued success and the success of this company. So the question is, why do you allow yourself to remain so blind? I suspect it's a defense mechanism that's protecting you from seeing something about yourself that you don't want to see. I don't know if that's right—and even if it *is* right, I'm not sure that figuring it out will necessarily help you. But if you *don't* figure it out—well, I'm pretty sure this job won't be the only thing it's ever going to cost you."

"I guess I feel the need to point out that most people who live in the world of Learning aren't nearly as arrogant as Ken," I said to Ash. "In fact, they're often the opposite. Humble in the face of all they don't know, holding on to what they do know only loosely, knowing that all knowledge—even scientific knowledge—is provisional. People in the world of Learning are just really committed to—well—learning. And also—I agree—to creating value."

"Actually, it turns out that *Ken* isn't nearly as arrogant as Ken," Ash said. "He started coming to see me last month."

"As a patient?"

Ash nodded.

"Well, what do you know," I said. "How's that been going?"

"Slowly. He loves to argue."

I laughed. "I'll bet."

"I have figured out one thing, though."

"What's that?"

"He really is from the world of Learning. He's just utterly consumed with living a meaningful life, with eudaimonic happiness. In fact, he's so consumed with it that he rarely thinks about other people at all. It's not even malicious. Other people just don't draw his attention. For him, living a meaningful life specifically means learning things and creating things, so he's utterly focused on whatever he's working on—and he's always working on something. As far as he's concerned, eudaimonic happiness is the only happiness worth having. It's far superior to hedonic happiness, in his mind."

"Except eudaimonic happiness can't be superior to hedonic happiness because eudaimonic happiness is a *type* of hedonic happiness, remember? I think what you meant to say is that the particular attachment that brings him the most joy is meaning."

"Yeah, that. The real problem is that he's *too* attached to meaning. He still thinks creating things is so important that it's okay to sacrifice people to create them—including himself."

"Any idea why?" I asked.

"I think he's just happiest when he's creating things. I think his behavior is explained by the simple fact that he believes the core delusion of the world of Learning. To be happy you have to create something of value."

I nodded. "So not much hope to keep him in his role at the company, I guess."

"No, I think he's going to be okay," Ash said. "He doesn't have to change what he believes. He just has to change his behavior. It's not that he *can't* focus on other people. He just doesn't prioritize it. But the 360-degree feedback evaluation convinced him he needs to treat his people differently for the company to be successful. Now he just has to master different behaviors. So I started him on a behavior modification program."

"How's *that* been going?"

"Like training a five-year-old to say 'please' and 'thank you.' I've just had to be really specific with him. When one of his people disagrees with him, instead of saying 'that's wrong' I've had him practice saying 'that's interesting' and pausing to actually consider their perspective. When he's about to make a decision, I've had him practice asking his executive team for their views. He said he's actually been enjoying debating them—and listening to them debate each other."

"So Nathaniel's not going to fire him?" I asked.

Ash shook his head. "No. Apparently, the executive team has all decided to stay."

## Key Points

- Learning is defined as the life-condition of mastery.

- The life-condition of Learning brings us eudaimonic happiness, which is defined as joy in response to the feeling of meaningfulness. Eudaimonic happiness, therefore, is a type of hedonic happiness where the attachment that brings us joy is meaning.

- The feeling of meaningfulness that provides us the eudaimonic happiness we feel in the world of Learning is harder to lose than attachments that provide us hedonic happiness but is just as temporary.

- In the life-condition of Learning we live not just to learn but also to create. Fueled by curiosity, we derive our eudaimonic happiness from building things that express our values.

- The core delusion of the world of Learning is that to be happy we need to accomplish or experience something meaningful.

# 8

# Realization

*The problem with self-improvement is knowing when to quit.*

—David Lee Roth

Realization is defined as the life-condition of self-improvement. Though driven by curiosity to the same degree as we are in the world of Learning, in Realization our curiosity isn't so much about the world *around* us as it is about the world *inside* us. In the world of Realization, the subject we're most interested in mastering is ourselves.

Fully embracing Socrates' notion that the unexamined life isn't worth living, in the world of Realization we're constantly dissecting our thoughts, feelings, and actions in an effort to understand and explain them as parts of a coherent and consistent whole. Armed with this understanding, we continually try to better ourselves in an effort to become the best people we can be.

Though sometimes we acquire this self-knowledge through sudden and unexpected insight, often we acquire it through analytic problem solving using what Daniel Kahneman calls the slow-thinking, "conscious, reasoning" part of our minds.[1] And while this conscious, reasoning part is rightly described as one of evolution's greatest marvels, it's also, as Kahneman points out, vulnerable to numerous biases that limit the accuracy of its conclusions. For this reason, when we're in the world of Realization we often see what we want to see rather than what's actually there.

Yet so intent are we on seeing what *is* there that our interest in self-reflection occasionally devolves into self-absorption. And when we become self-absorbed and our goal to better ourselves becomes obsessive, becoming better versions of ourselves paradoxically becomes harder. For as admirable a goal as self-improvement is, self-absorption invariably disconnects us from, and even makes us indifferent to, the suffering of others.

⁓

Ash had been telling me about an intern he was supervising named Anjali who he thought came from the world of Realization. "She's more focused on personal development than anyone I've ever met," he explained.

Anjali had already been a practicing licensed clinical social worker for nearly ten years when she decided to go back to school to earn her doctorate. She'd decided to do her internship at Cook County Jail, she told Ash at their first meeting, because she thought it offered her the best opportunity to become a better therapist. She wanted to see everything—anxiety, depression, addiction, personality disorders, sociopathy, schizophrenia, and more. She also thought there was no better place to improve her ability to approach her patients without judgment. It was easy for her to do so with patients she liked, she said, but there was no challenge—no virtue—in that. She wanted to be able to do it with everybody.

"An ambitious goal," Ash said.

He quickly discovered that she was an exceptional therapist—insightful, committed, and, above all, eager to learn. She constantly asked for feedback, wanting him to review every session she conducted with every patient. She was hard on herself when he would point out therapeutic perspectives she'd missed, but always grateful to have his insights. She was, in short, a pleasure to supervise.

As a result, Ash wondered only briefly why she waited a full four weeks to mention her patient Trent after she started seeing him in therapy. Ash soon learned, though, that Trent wasn't a typical inmate. He'd been a graduate student at a top Midwestern business school. He was only one year away from graduating with a position at a large investment bank already secured when he and some friends decided to attend a fraternity party at a nearby college. There he was seen drinking and flirting with a number of undergraduate women. Two days later, one of them accused him of sexual assault, and he was arrested.

Trent's family was poor—he'd been paying for school with student loans—so he wasn't able to make bail. After only a week in general population, he lost his appetite, developed insomnia, and started verbalizing a desire to kill himself. So he was transferred to the psychiatric wing, started on an antidepressant, and placed on a suicide watch. It was then that Anjali was assigned to evaluate him.

She quickly confirmed that Trent was severely depressed, so she started seeing him once a week. Initially, she aimed merely to reassure him that he hadn't been abandoned, and slowly his depression began to improve. By the time she told Ash about him, he was no longer suicidal. According to Trent, in treating him like a human being she'd convinced him that he still was one.

The reason she'd finally brought him up with Ash, however, was that she was feeling anxious about continuing to work with him and wanted the jail to assign him to another intern. But even contemplating that made her feel like a failure. She was stuck and needed Ash's advice.

"You're uncomfortable with how attached he's become to you?" Ash speculated.

"No," Anjali replied. "I'm uncomfortable because he wants to tell me what happened at the fraternity party."

"Oh. Well, the good news is you're still bound by patient confidentiality. Even if he confesses to committing a crime, you can't disclose it. And whatever happened, it would probably be good for him to talk about it."

Anjali sighed. "I'm sure it would be for him. But not for me." She said she didn't feel she could maintain objectivity, much less view him without judgment, if Trent told her that story.

"Why?" Ash asked.

"Because my sister was raped once, too."

Her sister had been completely wrecked by the experience, Anjali told Ash—as had Anjali herself. She recognized now just how enmeshed with her sister she'd become during that time and how she'd overlooked—even suppressed—her own anger so she could focus entirely on supporting her sister. But now her anger was beginning to surface. So the reason she was anxious about continuing therapy with Trent, she confessed, wasn't because she was uncertain about how to handle the ethical implications of discovering he might be guilty. It was because if she heard his story and decided he *was* guilty, she wasn't sure she'd be able to control her rage.

# Self-Development

"Is this supervision you're doing with her," I asked, "or therapy?"

"Sometimes supervision *is* therapy," Ash replied. "Nothing blurs that line like a supervisee having a strong emotional reaction to a patient."

"When do you decide that the reaction is so strong it's time to find the patient another therapist?"

"That's always a judgment call. If she actually starts raining down righteous anger on him, that would obviously be bad. On the other hand, this could be a real learning opportunity for her. People don't grow unless something forces them to."

"Though maybe that something shouldn't be a patient she's responsible for helping."

"I get what you're saying," Ash acknowledged. "But how else can she learn to manage her emotions in therapy except by doing therapy that challenges her to manage her emotions? How do surgeons learn to operate except by operating on people who need surgery?"

"That's fair," I said. "But would you have a concentration camp survivor taking care of a neo-Nazi? Or an African American taking care of a white supremacist?"

"I don't think her issue goes quite that deep."

"Deep enough that she wants to stop being his therapist," I pointed out.

"Part of her does, yes. But another part wants to use this as an opportunity to become a *better* therapist."

I paused. "I take it that's why you think she's from the world of Realization? Because she's running toward the issue rather than away from it?"

"Isn't that what Realization is all about?" Ash asked. "The quest to better yourself? I actually admire her for it."

"It *is* what Realization is all about," I agreed. "As is the tendency to minimize or even ignore the pain and suffering of others as we do it."

᠗᠉

When Ash told Anjali that they could easily have Trent assigned to another intern, she told him she appreciated that he would be willing to do so. Then she expressed worry that Trent would be reluctant to talk to another intern about what had happened the night of the party. He had in fact told Anjali he'd never intended to talk about it with anyone (besides his lawyer) but that he'd come to trust her and now wanted to talk about it with her.

"It's your choice, Anjali," Ash said. "Let me just say that I'm willing to meet with you as often as you want to process any issues that come up for you if you decide to stick with him."

Anjali paused briefly, then nodded with obvious relief. "Okay, I'll stick with him."

The next time she and Ash met, however, she mentioned nothing about what had happened at the party. Instead, she focused entirely on Trent's emotional state. He was scared more than anything else, she said, and mostly in need of reassurance. He had questions no one was answering: Why wasn't his lawyer more forthcoming? Why was everyone assuming he was guilty? Why was the process taking so long? He felt unsafe and lonely and wanted to go home. Anjali listened, empathized, and tried to encourage him that there *would* be an end to his ordeal, that he just needed to be patient.

What struck Ash, however, was what Anjali *wasn't* doing. She wasn't making the effort to excavate down into the deeper layers of Trent's psyche. She wasn't asking any second or third questions, wasn't forcing any uncomfortable conversations or drawing Trent's attention to issues he was trying to avoid. Ash began wondering if she was eschewing the real work of therapy so as not to draw attention to the issue *she* wanted to avoid.

When Ash suggested this to her, she blinked several times in surprise. "I can't believe I—I didn't even realize I was doing that."

At their next session, though, Trent told Anjali that his hearing date had finally been set and that he wanted to talk to her about his plea. Flustered,

Anjali reminded him she wasn't a lawyer and therefore couldn't give him legal advice. Trent replied that he wasn't looking for legal advice but rather for help in processing what had happened. He was confused about how he *should* plead.

"How you *should* plead?" Anjali asked. "What are you saying? You don't know if what you did was wrong?"

Trent looked at her in astonishment. Then with narrowed eyes he reminded her that he was in jail, not prison, and that he hadn't yet been found guilty of anything. Further, she knew nothing about what had happened, and had in fact been deliberately avoiding the subject despite his repeated attempts to broach it with her.

Horrified that he'd recognized she'd been dodging his attempts to address what had happened, she tried to backpedal, saying she only meant that she was confused by his confusion, that every inmate she'd ever seen had insisted on his innocence. She hadn't pursued a conversation about the night of the party, she said, because it wasn't her place to judge him.

"But I want your judgment," Trent said. "I'm honestly *not* sure if I did anything wrong. I need your help to figure it out."

"How can he not know?" Anjali demanded of Ash.

"There's only one way to find out," Ash replied. "You have to talk to him about what happened. Hear the story from his perspective." He reminded her that her job *wasn't* to judge Trent's guilt or innocence. Here was a patient who wanted to process an experience, he told her, and if she wanted to be his therapist, she needed to help him do it. Ash reiterated he would help her work through the emotions that helping him aroused, but it was time for her either to engage Trent in real therapy or to step aside.

## Becoming Happier

"Why doesn't she just tell him the truth?" I asked. "She's mad about what happened to her sister. If she wasn't making such an effort to hide her anger, maybe she'd be able to control it better."

"In fact, telling him the truth is exactly what she's thinking about doing," Ash said. "But I told her that telling him about what happened to her sister would be a mistake."

"Why?"

"As a therapist you have to be really careful about sharing the emotions your patients arouse in you. More often than not it makes them feel responsible for taking care of *you*, which just makes them hold things back. Therapist confessionals usually serve the therapist more than the patient."

"What did Anjali say when you said that?" I asked.

"She kind of dismissed it, actually. She's more worried about losing his trust."

"As opposed to what's going to happen if she keeps lying to him?" I asked. "She wasn't confused by his confusion. She was mad that he wasn't taking responsibility for a crime she's presuming he committed!"

Ash nodded. "Which is why, despite her concern about losing his trust, she's leaning toward telling him the real reason she's angry. She thinks he already has to know she wasn't being completely honest with him."

I paused. "She's pretty committed to this guy, isn't she?"

"She is," Ash agreed. "Though I'm beginning to worry she might be committed to her own development more."

"What do you mean? I thought you admired her for that."

"I do," Ash said. "But I'm starting to worry about what you said, that the dedication people have to their own growth in the world of Realization sometimes makes it easy for them to overlook the pain of others. I'm wondering if Anjali might be a little too focused on helping herself and not focused enough on helping her patient."

"Let's say for a minute you're right," I said. "Can you think of a belief that might be driving that kind of zeal?"

Ash considered. "Maybe that you can only be happy if you're perfect? Perfectionism *is* a pretty common issue, especially among professionals."

"But don't you think the need to be perfect is usually driven by some kind of wound, like a damaged self-esteem or a pathological need for approval?"

"Yeah," Ash said. "And that's certainly not Anjali."

I nodded. "The world of Realization isn't about self-perfection. It's about self-reformation. Taking responsibility for your own unhappiness and looking to yourself for the cause of it. People living in the world of Realization don't want to be perfect. Just better."

⟋⟋⟋⟋

At the start of their next session, Anjali apologized to Trent for her reluctance to "go where he'd repeatedly asked her to go." She confessed that she'd been judging him without knowing the facts, which she acknowledged was unfair. She reiterated that she was committed to helping him in any way she could, and she now very much wanted to hear about what had happened at the party and help him process it. She mentioned nothing about her sister's rape.

Visibly relieved, Trent proceeded to tell her how he'd walked into the party, spotted Rachel almost immediately, and started talking to her. He didn't remember the exact sequence of events after that—they both had quite a lot to drink over the course of the night—but eventually they found themselves alone in one of the fraternity bedrooms, kissing. One thing led to another, and they started having sex. Then Trent estimated after about five or ten minutes into it, "out of nowhere" Rachel started yelling for him to stop. But he found he couldn't. Despite all the alcohol he'd consumed, he was already starting to climax. "From the moment she said stop to the moment I finished, it literally couldn't have been more than five seconds," Trent said. Then he collapsed on top of her. When he sat up, he immediately began apologizing, explaining he'd already passed the point of no return when she'd told him to stop. Her only response to this, however, was to shrug. They got dressed in an awkward silence and went back to the party. He tried to talk to her, asking her multiple times if she was okay, but she just kept shrugging and saying nothing. He offered to take her home, but she declined. Finally, sensing she wanted nothing more to do with him and feeling hurt, he left.

"It was even worse than I expected," Anjali told Ash. "He was totally unaware that he did anything wrong. I kept trying to find some sympathy for him, to view what happened from his point of view, but all I felt—all I feel—is rage."

Ash knew he had to be careful. If he let Anjali know that Trent's story had actually stirred his empathy, she might very well become angry with *him*. On the other hand, he thought, how else but by provoking her anger in supervision could he create an opportunity to examine it, understand it, and ultimately help her learn to manage it?

"There's a lot to unpack here," Ash said. "A lot of nuance, both with what's going on with Trent and with what's going on with you."

"What do you mean with what's going on with Trent?" Anjali asked suspiciously.

"Well, for one thing, it sounds like the sex started consensually but then Rachel changed her mind at the very end."

"What does it matter how it started?" Anjali bristled. "When a woman says no—*whenever* a woman says no—that decision needs to be respected."

"I'm not suggesting otherwise. I'm just trying to point out there's some ambiguity here. It doesn't sound like Trent's intention was to force himself on her."

"But that's exactly what he did!"

Ash paused. "Did he?"

"Are you kidding me?" Anjali exclaimed. "Are you telling me you think what he did *doesn't* constitute sexual assault?"

"I'm saying that from a therapist's perspective it doesn't matter. Whether or not what he did constitutes a sexual assault is a question for the courts. Our job—your job—is to help him process his trauma—"

"*His* trauma?" Anjali interrupted. "*His* trauma? Who cares about his trauma! He *deserves* to be traumatized! He's not the victim here! He's the perpetrator! What about *her* trauma? How can you say it doesn't matter if she was sexually assaulted?"

## Predicting Change

"Do you really think it doesn't matter if she was sexually assaulted?" I asked Ash.

"Of course not," Ash said. "What I meant was—and I know you agree with this—no matter what a person may or may not have done, as healthcare providers we do what we can to help them. It doesn't matter if we don't like them. It doesn't matter if we think they're reprehensible. If we only treated people we liked, half the people in the world wouldn't get treated at all."

"Are you still thinking Anjali will be able to achieve some professional distance with this guy? Because I'm not seeing it."

Ash sighed. "At this point, I honestly don't know. I'm really struggling with this. Do I keep working with her on her anger, or do I tell her it's time to find Trent another therapist?"

"I don't know either," I said. "Helping someone to change is hard enough. Predicting *who* will change, *when* they'll change, and *how* they'll change is even harder."

"Well, that's helpful."

"Well, look, aren't there certain things that make change more likely?" I asked. "Leading indicators that help you predict it?"

"Sure. You're more likely to change—to state the obvious—if you *want* to change.[2] And you're more likely to change if you believe you're the one responsible for changing.[3] Both of which, by the way, are true for Anjali."

"Which only suggests that wanting to change and feeling that you're responsible for changing aren't enough to actually *cause* change."

Ash shrugged. "Maybe you have to want to change with your life."

I looked at him. "What exactly do you take that to mean?"

"That you have to be convinced you *need* to change. That you believe the problem you're having, whatever it is, is caused by—or partially caused by—something in *you*, even if you have no idea what it is. That every time the problem manifests in some way, it stirs up the belief that you can best solve it—maybe even only solve it—by changing yourself."

"Do you think Anjali feels that way about the problem she's having with her anger?" I asked.

Ash paused. "I guess I'm worried she doesn't."

❧

Abruptly the anger drained from Anjali's face, and she covered her mouth with her hand. "Oh, my God. . . ," she said. She looked as if she were about to cry.

"Take it easy," Ash said. "It's okay."

"I can't . . . I can't believe I just . . . I didn't mean—I mean, I'm totally out of control . . . what's wrong with me?"

"Nothing's wrong with you. You're just angry—*and* trying really hard not to be. So it's going to come out when you're least expecting it. And more strongly than you want. It's okay. It's good. It needs to come out if we're going to figure out what's causing it and help you figure out how to manage it."

"Okay," she said, shaken. "Okay."

"Anjali, you may be angry at Trent, but I know you also care about what happens to him, right?"

Anjali closed her eyes. "Yes, I do."

"Okay. So being mad at him doesn't mean you're a bad person. Let's just get that out of the way right now. We all get mad at people we care about sometimes, right?"

"Sure."

"So look—you're safe here. You know that, too, right?"

Anjali nodded.

"Okay. So I want you to let it all out. Tell me exactly how mad you are at him. Tell me *why* you're mad at him."

"I'm not mad at *him*. I'm mad at the man who raped my sister. I'm just projecting my anger onto Trent. I'm being totally unfair."

Ash shook his head. "Stop intellectualizing. You're mad at Trent. It's okay. Tell me about it. Give your anger a voice."

Anjali paused. Then all at once she burst out: "I just can't believe what he did! I get that he was worked up. I get that he was right in the middle of the act. But he made a *deliberate* decision to ignore her! She said *stop*. I don't care that he was about to climax! A woman says stop, you stop! Right then! Pull out! Back off in *some* way. Let her know you heard her. That's what he did wrong. He wanted to *get* off before he got off, so he ignored her. That's why it was sexual assault."

"He didn't listen to her," Ash said. "That's what makes you angry."

"Yes!"

"Okay, let's talk about that. I'm not trying to be deliberately obtuse here, but why does the fact that he didn't listen to her make you angry? I understand why being ignored in general would make someone angry, but—"

Anjali interrupted him with a shake of her head. "You don't get it. It's not like he just refused to take her opinion into account. He nullified her autonomy. He took away her right to decide what she wanted to do, which was to say no."

"So you're angry because he failed to respect her," Ash said.

"Respect her? Are you kidding me? I'm angry because he overpowered her! Because he victimized her!"

"Because he rendered her powerless."

"Yes!"

"Because *you* don't like being powerless."

"Me?" Anjali asked, slightly taken aback. "No."

"So let's pause for a second. Can you think back to a time in your life when *you* felt powerless?"

"What—like—ever?"

"Sure."

Anjali thought for a moment. "When I couldn't help my sister."

Ash nodded. "And did feeling powerless to help your sister make you angry?"

"I guess . . . I guess it did," she said. "I guess . . . I mean, I thought I was angry at the man who raped her . . . and I *was* . . . but now that you ask that question, I wonder—"

"What?"

"If maybe some of that anger was directed at myself."

"For feeling powerless?" Ash prompted.

"For *being* powerless."

Ash nodded. "And getting angry does help to reverse that, to make us feel power*ful*."

"It does," Anjali agreed.

"So what does it mean to you to be powerless?"

"I don't know. Helpless . . . useless . . ."

"Unsafe?" Ash prompted.

Anjali's eyes widened. "Yes! Unsafe. Not being able to help my sister made me feel unsafe."

"Because it just as easily could have happened to you?" Ash asked.

"No, that wasn't it at all. It was seeing her fall apart. As long as she wasn't okay, *I* wasn't okay. I don't know why, but seeing her like that really unnerved me."

"It made you feel afraid?"

"Yeah."

"Interesting," Ash said. "Could that be another reason you got angry when your sister fell apart? To prevent yourself from feeling afraid?"

Anjali inclined her head thoughtfully. "You know, maybe so. Maybe I wasn't just trying to find a way to regain a sense of power. Maybe I was trying not to feel afraid. That could be right."

## Gradual versus Sudden Change

"So let's say you *do* want to change with your life, *and* you believe you're the one responsible for changing," I said. "In your experience, what else needs to happen for change to actually occur? What is it that enables someone who feels they *have* to change to actually succeed in changing?"

"You mean everything else being equal, why does one person change and another not?" Ash said.

"Exactly. What's the key ingredient required for change?"

"I guess I'd say it depends on whether the change you're talking about is gradual or sudden."

Change that happens gradually, Ash argued, is mostly unintentional. It's caused by small, incremental advances in our thinking that we don't even notice, but that over years or even decades can turn us from pot-smoking slackers into visionary CEOs, or from angry, insecure narcissists to mature, thoughtful parents.

The cause of sudden change, on the other hand, is more complicated. Though sudden change *is* intentional, it's not usually driven by an intent to change ourselves, but rather by an intent to change a situation that's causing us pain. In fact, it's typically only because we *can't* change a situation that's causing us pain that we even think about trying to change ourselves.[4]

Yet even then change remains unlikely. For while we're usually able to identify the external cause of our pain quite easily (a stressful job, a controlling spouse, an inoperable tumor), we often fail to identify, or even recognize there exists, an internal cause—a belief that the external cause stirs up.

Ironically, though, it's often awakening to the existence of such a belief that itself causes the belief to change and therefore our pain to remit. This, we'd argue, is what happened to Patrick when, in the act of realizing he'd always believed he'd been living a worthless life, he abruptly realized he hadn't been. It's as if the act of observing ourselves believing an idea grants us a more objective perspective on the idea itself, much like suddenly being made aware we're watching a movie bounces us out of it and reminds us that the images on the screen aren't real.

So we don't change by recognizing intellectually that we have a flaw and trying to bend our thoughts, feelings, and behaviors by force of will to conform to the vision we have of ourselves without it. Even when we aim to change our thoughts, feelings, and behaviors by changing our environment in some way—by avoiding the external causes of the thoughts, feelings, and behaviors—we'll only have effected the outward *appearance* of change. To accomplish real change—what's known in Buddhism as *human revolution*—we have to free ourselves from our beliefs. Only then will we find ourselves thinking, feeling, and behaving differently without conscious effort or force of will, without having to summon up any emotional or intellectual energy to be different. Only then will we have genuinely changed ourselves.

"So real change isn't Anjali learning to *control* her anger at Trent, though that would certainly be a good thing," I said. "Real change is her not getting angry at him in the first place."

Ash thought for a moment. "At this point, I'd be happy if she could just learn to control it."

❧

"So now let's come back to Trent," Ash said.

"Okay," Anjali said.

"Does *he* make you feel afraid?"

Anjali opened her mouth, then closed it. Then she laughed. "It's silly, isn't it? He's in jail. How can he hurt me?" She paused. "But, yeah, he makes me feel afraid. I don't trust him."

"In what way?"

"I don't trust him not to abuse his power. Even though I know he can't. No, I don't trust him."

"You don't trust that *he* won't abuse his power, or that men in general won't?"

Anjali paused. "Not men in general," she answered finally. "*People* in general."

"*People* in general," Ash repeated. "Why don't you trust that people in general won't abuse their power?"

"I'm not saying I *expect* people in general to abuse their power. I'm just afraid they might."

"Why are you afraid they might?"

She shrugged. "I don't want to get hurt."

"So you're walking around thinking anyone at any moment might hurt you?"

There was a pause, and then all at once tears sprang into Anjali's eyes. "Yeah," she whispered.

"Why?"

"Because I don't think I'm . . . I'm not—"

"What?" Ash prompted.

"Strong."

Ash's head moved back in surprise. "You mean physically?"

"Not just physically. Psychologically. Emotionally."

"So the reason you're afraid of Trent is because he makes you feel . . . vulnerable?"

"He does," she said, looking down. "He makes me feel vulnerable."

"So when Trent describes overpowering Rachel, even for just a minute, even in the heat of the moment—"

"It's not that I'm afraid he's going to do the same thing to me. It's just—like you said—it makes me feel unsafe." She took in a small, shuddering breath. "It makes me feel weak."

"It makes you feel weak," Ash repeated. "I wonder: could *that* be the reason your sister's emotional distress made you afraid? Because being powerless to help her made you feel weak?"

"Yes."

"Because it stirred up the *belief* that you're weak?"

Anjali stared at him. "That's exactly what it did. It stirred up my belief that I'm weak."

# Acquiring Wisdom

"So is *that* the internal cause of her anger?" I asked. "The belief that she's weak?"

"*She* thinks it is," Ash replied.

"It does make sense," I reflected. "We've already talked about how getting angry prevents us from feeling things we don't want to feel—like afraid or powerless. I wonder, though, if she's getting angry to prevent herself from feeling powerless—if she feels powerless—why isn't she depressed?"

"Well because, one, believing you're weak isn't the same thing as believing you're powerless. Anjali actually has a fair amount of confidence when it comes to problem solving. And two, because she's been avoiding anything and everything that triggers the belief that she's weak, so she's been able to avoid *feeling* weak almost entirely. Why do you think she worked so hard to avoid talking to Trent about what happened the night of the party?"

"Right," I said. "I guess even people living in the world of Realization only change when they're forced to."

"Which is a bit strange given they presumably believe self-development is the key to being happy."

"They *may* believe self-development is the key to being happy, but that doesn't mean self-development is easy or fun. Lots of people believe they should exercise but don't do that either," I noted.

"True."

"The real irony here is that the pain associated with self-development doesn't come from trying to change yourself. It comes from *avoiding* trying to change yourself while trying to change your circumstances instead."

Ash nodded. "On the other hand—as we said—without that pain we probably wouldn't think about changing ourselves at all."

"The problem is some people never figure out when they're facing circumstances they can't change that changing themselves is the only way they can make their pain go away."

"It raises an interesting question," Ash said. "Why is it when people suffer that only some of them—in fact, only a rare few—are willing to entertain the notion that they're suffering not only because of their external circumstance but also because of something inside of *them*?"

"I don't know," I said. "But that has to be considered a crucial first step. After all, how can you begin to fix a problem if you don't recognize that it's a problem? Plus, when you open your mind to the possibility that one of your own beliefs might be the cause of your misery, you start looking at all your beliefs more skeptically. And then when you identify the belief that *is* causing your misery, that skepticism predisposes you to stop believing it."

"Which might explain why—as we also said—sometimes all you need to do to free yourself from a delusional belief is recognize it exists," Ash said.

"Except we can't say it's just recognizing the existence of a delusional belief that frees you from it," I said. "It's recognizing the existence of a delusional belief in a particular way—a way that changes how you *feel* about that delusional belief. I actually have no idea why in the act of recognizing that he believed he was living a worthless life Patrick suddenly stopped believing it was true. Do you?"

Ash shook his head. "So the question isn't just how do we get ourselves to recognize our delusional beliefs? It's how do we get ourselves to recognize them in such a way that we stop believing them?"

I nodded. "What is it," I asked, "that creates wisdom?"

## Conscious versus Unconscious Problem Solving

We would define wisdom as knowledge that propels us toward happiness. In a practical sense, then, wisdom is most properly regarded as the ultimate solution to the problem of suffering. We need wisdom both to change painful life circumstances and, when we can't, to change ourselves instead so that those life circumstances cease to cause us pain. As I write in *The Undefeated Mind*:

Wisdom is so powerful . . . it can even put a halt to suffering without changing the circumstances that cause it (as when I freed myself from suffering not when I resumed my relationship with my girlfriend but when I realized I didn't need to). Most of us deem a problem solved when it no longer confronts us, but from a Nichiren Buddhist perspective, a problem is solved when it *no longer makes us suffer*, our escaping or overcoming oppressive circumstances representing only one particular means to that end. Certainly it may be the means we most prefer, and in many cases what we need to do to be able to declare true victory. But it's not the only means at our disposal. As Viktor Frankl wrote, "When we are no longer able to change a situation—just think of an incurable disease such as inoperable cancer—we are challenged to change ourselves."[5]

If wisdom is most accurately viewed as a solution to a painful life problem, we should be able to find wisdom the same way we find solutions to problems in general. That is, by means of two distinct but complementary processes: analytic problem solving and problem solving through insight.[6]

Analytic problem solving involves the consciously directed search for solutions by trial and error. It requires an intense focus on the problem itself, which, when combined with the challenge of analyzing large amounts of complex information simultaneously, tends to restrict the type of solutions it yields to the more conventional.[7] Though the path to such solutions is always traceable, such solutions must always be tested to see if they're correct.

Problem solving through insight, in contrast, is characterized by the sudden appearance of solutions that seem to come out of nowhere, typically resulting in an intense feeling of pleasure (the so-called "ecstasy of discovery"). Insight only *appears* to come out of nowhere, however. It's actually the product of extensive unconscious deliberation. Unlike our conscious minds that can focus on only one thing at a time, our unconscious minds are capable of processing copious amounts of complex information simultaneously.[8] This is also perhaps why studies have found that answers arrived at through insight are, intriguingly, more likely to be correct than those arrived at through conscious analysis.[9] Indeed, our unconscious minds might be the smartest part of us. Evidence suggests that in addition to having superior processing power, our unconscious minds aren't influenced by the same misleading biases as are our conscious minds.[10] This may be why, for example, one study showed that our unconscious minds are far better at detecting lies than our conscious minds.[11]

Unfortunately, it also turns out that we can't accurately distinguish correct insights from incorrect insights simply according to the degree of confidence we have in them.[12] That is, we can't distinguish correct insights from incorrect insights when we're trying to figure out the answer to an external-world problem, like the secret to a magic trick.

Yet when we're trying to figure out something about ourselves—for example, why we get angry when criticized—we're actually able to verify the truth of our insights with unerring accuracy. The reason for this is simple: we have immediate access to our own feelings and can therefore judge quite easily how well our insights explain them.

So after I had the insight that I believed I needed my girlfriend to love me to be happy, I was immediately struck by the degree to which that belief had been the primary driver of my feelings and behavior throughout our entire relationship. As a result, I recognized not only that I *did* believe that to be happy I needed my girlfriend to love me (and in fact the admiration of others in general), but also that this belief was without question the internal cause of my pain when we broke up.

## Transient Hypofrontality

What can we do, then, to increase the frequency with which we gain wisdom through insight? Studies suggest both that being in a positive mood and doing things that help turn our attention inward, like shutting our eyes, increase the likelihood that we'll be able to solve a problem through insight.[13] The key, however, may lie in trying *not* to solve a problem analytically. Research suggests that taking a break from analytic problem solving actually increases the likelihood that we'll solve a problem through insight if during the break we occupy ourselves with a cognitively undemanding task.[14] Cognitively undemanding tasks, it turns out, promote mind wandering. Mind wandering, in turn, seems to promote unconscious associative processing, which is what then produces insight.[15] Further, deliberately turning our conscious attention away from the problem we're trying to solve may also protect "the processing of weak associations and interconnections" and help us avoid "focusing on the strong—but misleading—associations elicited by the problem" itself.[16]

The neurological mechanism by which cognitively undemanding tasks promote mind wandering and insight appears to involve a phenomenon known as *transient hypofrontality.* The transient hypofrontality hypothesis argues that the brain has limited resources for which its different systems are constantly competing.[17] Put another way, when we use one part of our brain, the other energy-intensive parts of our brain become idle. To accomplish a cognitively *un*demanding task, therefore, the brain reduces activity in the frontal cortex, the part of the brain that enables us to perform cognitively demanding tasks. This decreases our ability to maintain focused attention and thereby enhances unconscious associative processing.[18]

While presumably any cognitively undemanding activity will induce transient hypofrontality, physical activity seems to induce it the most, especially physical activity that doesn't require our conscious attention to perform.[19] Thus, not only repetitive high-intensity movement like running but also low-intensity movement like walking,[20] swinging a baseball bat, and even showering all induce transient hypofrontality, increase mind wandering, and promote insight. In fact, any type of automatic, repetitive movement should. Indeed, studies show that even chanting a mantra like the Nichiren Buddhist mantra *Nam-myoho-renge-kyo* causes transient hypofrontality,[21] suggesting that transient hypofrontality is the mechanism by which chanting produces insight.[22] There isn't, it turns out, anything mystic about the effects of chanting at all.

Finally, as to how any and all of these cognitively undemanding activities produce insights that pertain to our specific problems—how they produce wisdom—studies suggest that the generation of insight is a goal-driven process. This means, in essence, that we can direct our unconscious mind to focus its deliberations where we want.[23] Thus, engaging in a cognitively undemanding activity while at the same time focusing on solving a specific problem will tend to yield insights that address the problem we're trying to solve. This seems to hold true whether the problem involves figuring out how to get over a failed relationship, how to get a new business started, or what to say next in a book.

⚭

At their next session, Anjali reported to Ash that Trent's anxiety had significantly increased—so much so, in fact, that he was started on clonazepam. Despite this, he was a wreck.

"The government's finally offered him a deal," Anjali explained. "They're willing to drop the charge from criminal sexual assault down to misdemeanor criminal sexual abuse. He only does a year in prison, but he gets placed on the sex offender list."

"That'll follow him the rest of his life," Ash said. "And he can kiss his job at the investment bank goodbye."

"Except if he doesn't take it and he's convicted of criminal sexual assault, he's looking at anywhere from four to fifteen years."

"Hence the increased anxiety," Ash said.

"Part of the problem is that no one is offering him any advice. His lawyer is leaning toward the deal but won't tell him what he thinks his chances would be if he goes to trial. His parents are paralyzed with fear. He has absolutely no idea what to do."

"What a mess," Ash said.

To Ash's surprise, Anjali nodded with a pained expression. "It *is* a mess. He's really suffering."

Ash paused. "So when Trent told you all this, and you saw how anxious he was, what was your reaction?"

"I felt sorry for him. I felt sympathy for him."

"Not anger?"

"No," she said.

"That's really interesting. Any idea why?"

She shrugged. "For whatever reason, I've suddenly started seeing him as a scared little boy who's just totally in over his head."

"So you're not afraid of him anymore?"

"I think I'm less afraid in general. When you helped me see just how afraid I—well, I'm not entirely sure why, but I feel less afraid than I have in a long time. It's been remarkably relieving actually."

"That's really great to hear," Ash said.

"It's even better to feel, let me tell you. Trent and I have been talking about what happened the night of the party, and all I've been feeling is sad. Sad for her, and sad for him. The whole thing is just really sad."

"So your anger really was about fear then?" Ash asked.

"I guess it was. Though it's also helped that he's been so earnest in trying to figure out the reason he did what he did. He's been exploring what he was feeling right before and after Rachel told him to stop and asking himself if he *couldn't* stop or if he didn't *want* to stop. It's kind of hard to condemn someone who's willing to admit the possibility that he might have done something wrong and take full responsibility for it."

"You know what's interesting?" Ash asked.

"What?"

"I'm not hearing you passing any judgment."

Anjali gave a small smile. "Maybe not."

"You changed *something*, Anjali," Ash said.

"It does feel that way. The whole thing is just really odd. Wonderful—but odd. It's not just that I feel different about Trent. I feel different about everybody."

"Because maybe what you really feel different about is yourself."

Anjali flushed. "I suppose I do. I guess we'll see."

"So what do you think Trent is going to do? Take the deal or take his chances?"

Anjali's expression once more grew pained. "It depends on what he figures out about the reason he did what he did."

"What do you mean?" Ash asked.

"If he decides he just didn't *want* to stop, he's going to take the deal," she said. "If he decides he *couldn't* stop, he's going to take his chances with a trial."

"Are you saying that if he decides what he did amounted to sexual assault, he's going to *let himself be punished*," I said, "but if he decides it wasn't, he's going to fight to prove his innocence even if it means risking a longer sentence?"

"It's not what *I'm* saying," Ash said. "It's what Anjali says Trent is saying."

"That's absolutely . . . I've never heard of . . ." I shook my head in amazement.

Ash nodded. "I guess Trent turns out to be made of sterner stuff than we knew."

"Well, I can't tell what Trent's basic life tendency is from listening to all this, but right now I'd say he's every bit as much in the world of Realization as Anjali is."

"What makes you say that?" Ash asked.

"If there's anything that defines the world of Realization it's an intense interest in discovering the truth about yourself. Even an ugly truth."

"Well, if Anjali is any indication, I'd say it's defined by quite a bit more than that," Ash said. "She didn't just want to *understand* why she couldn't control her anger. She wanted to stop feeling it. She wanted to change herself into someone who could approach everyone without judgment."

"I think that's right. I think if the core delusion of the world of Learning is that to be happy we need to do something meaningful, the core delusion of the world of Realization is *that to be happy the meaningful thing we need to do is change ourselves.*"

Ash considered this for a moment. "So the happiness we feel in Realization is the same as the happiness we feel in Learning? It's eudaimonic happiness—joy from meaning? From value creation?"

"Yes."

"So what lands you in the world of Realization is the belief that to be happy you need to grow," Ash said.

"I think so, yes."

"So let's think about this," Ash said. "Even though the eudaimonic happiness that growth brings may only be temporary, growth itself is usually permanent. When people really change, they tend not to go back to the way they were. In fact, growth that isn't permanent can't really be said to be growth at all, can it?"

"I suppose not," I agreed.

"And haven't we also been saying that the only way you *can* become a happier person is by changing yourself? That the path to becoming a happier person is in fact exactly what people living in the world of Realization think it is—personal growth? It's certainly the foundational premise of therapy."

"That's right."

"Then how is the belief that personal growth will make you happy a delusion?" Ash asked.

"No, no, you're right. Without a doubt, personal growth *will* turn you into a happier person—"

"That's a relief," Ash said. "For a minute there I thought I was going to have to find another job."

"You just have to understand *how* it turns you into a happier person."

"I do understand it. You become a happier person when you free yourself from a dysfunctional belief. Which is basically what we've been saying personal growth *is*: The abandonment of dysfunctional beliefs. The acquisition of wisdom."

"Exactly," I said. "And when you free yourself from a dysfunctional belief, or you change the propensity of a dysfunctional belief to get stirred up, you stop experiencing pain and suffering in response to events that previously caused you pain and suffering. And—or—you start feeling joy in response to other events that previously failed to cause you joy. So just by freeing yourself from a belief you spend less time feeling pain and suffering and more time feeling joy—or more time feeling more intense joy."

"So—again—how is the belief that personal growth will make you happy a delusion?" Ash asked.

"Because—again—no matter how many dysfunctional beliefs you leave behind and no matter how much happier it makes you feel—or how much more *often* you feel happy—the happiness you gain is still relative happiness, *happiness that's dependent on attachment.* Increasing the frequency with which we feel relative happiness definitely makes us happier people, but it doesn't give us the kind of happiness we really want. It doesn't give us happiness that's independent of attachment. Happiness that's indestructible. Happiness that's absolute."

"I guess not," Ash said after a few moments. "Though I'm not so sure absolute happiness is the kind of happiness Anjali expects to get."

"Maybe not."

"And what Trent wants right now has nothing to do with absolute happiness at all."

"Agreed."

"And I'll tell you one more thing," Ash said. "I honestly don't know if Trent sexually assaulted that girl or not. But I hope both of them get the justice they deserve."

"Me, too," I said.

A month later, Anjali told Ash that Trent had decided to go to trial. Two months after that, he was acquitted.

## Key Points

- Realization is defined as the life-condition of self-improvement.

- Self-improvement begins with a recognition that there exists a belief we hold that's serving as the internal cause of our pain.

- As with the life-condition of Learning, the life-condition of Realization brings us eudaimonic happiness. In the life-condition of Realization, however, freeing ourselves from delusional beliefs is what feels like the most meaningful thing we can do.

- We solve some problems best through insight, which is more likely to occur when we engage in any activity that promotes transient hypofrontality and mind wandering.

- In the life-condition of Realization, we live not just to learn about ourselves but also to improve ourselves. Fueled by the desire to live up to our potential, we derive our eudaimonic happiness from turning ourselves into better people.

- The core delusion of the world of Realization is that to be happy we need to grow.

# 9

# Compassion

*The sole meaning of life is to serve humanity.*

—Leo Tolstoy

Compassion is defined as the life-condition of love. It's not a romantic love, however, that seeks to possess another person selfishly. Rather, it's a benevolent love that places the suffering of others at the center of our attention. As a result, in the world of Compassion we not only feel empathy, the understanding and sharing of another's emotions, but also—not surprisingly—compassion, a concern for the happiness of others that rivals the concern we have for our own.[1]

In Buddhism, a person who comes from the world of Compassion is known as a *bodhisattva*, someone who dedicates himself to helping others become happy. A bodhisattva, therefore, doesn't so much wonder how it's possible to be happy when so many terrible things are destined to happen to him; he wonders how it's possible to be happy when so many people around him are suffering.

This isn't to say that in the world of Compassion we like everyone. We all have personal preferences. It is to say, though, that we worry about even the suffering of people we dislike, viewing all people with much the same concern as we have for our own children. In fact, that's how we look at everyone when

261

we're in the world of Compassion: as precious children in need of love, protection, and guidance.

As a result of this, in the world of Compassion we often place the happiness of others *before* our own. Unfortunately, this sometimes leads us to neglect ourselves. When this self-neglect becomes chronic and pervasive, we may begin to resent others and come to consider our desire to alleviate their suffering a burden.

Yet even then we find ourselves unable to ignore suffering when we see it. For in the world of Compassion to see suffering is to feel compelled to take action to relieve it. Because in the world of Compassion to see someone else suffering is to suffer ourselves.

Ash was telling me about a patient of his named Louisa who he was convinced came from the world of Compassion. He'd met her after members of a Chicago street gang had murdered her daughter, Annabelle.

On the night she was killed, Annabelle had been walking home with her ten-year-old son, Ben. Earlier that evening, the father of one of Ben's friends had gone to confront some members of the gang who'd been trying to recruit his son. What began as an attempt at an earnest dialogue quickly deteriorated into shouting and threats. Then one of the gang members brandished his gun. A local resident heard the yelling, recognized the gang members, and called the police.

The father fled, running down the street and into an alley, three of the gang members close behind him. The police pulled up to the other end of the alley just as the father ran out of it in front of Annabelle and Ben. Suddenly a hail of gunfire erupted from the alley, striking the father multiple times in the back, killing him instantly. From behind their squad car, the police officers returned fire. Annabelle, caught between the officers and the gang members, jumped on top of Ben, shielding him with her body as five bullets fired by the gang members—and one fired by one of the officers—tore into her. She died at the scene, her body draped limply over her son. Miraculously, Ben survived unhurt.

Because of the police officers' involvement in the shooting, the city offered Ben and his entire family free medical and psychological care for a year. Louisa asked that Ben see a therapist. Around that time, Ash had been seeing Frankie, who knew the detective who'd been assigned to Annabelle's case. At Frankie's urging, the detective reached out to Ash to ask him if he might be interested in seeing Ben.

Ash readily agreed. He was comfortable working with families who'd suffered violent losses. He also knew how important it is to recognize that children aren't just miniature adults when it comes to processing trauma. Depending on their age and maturity level, their ability to analyze, reflect on, and express their feelings ranges from modest to nonexistent. Ash's strategy with children who'd suffered a trauma, therefore, was to focus first and foremost on establishing a connection with them. How he did that depended on the child. Sometimes, especially with very young children, he did it through play. With slightly older children, he would try to bond over their mutual interests. Once he'd secured the child's trust, he'd start looking for opportunities to ask about the child's feelings.

Ash decided to hold his sessions with Ben at Louisa's home, where Ben now lived, to help him feel more comfortable. He found Ben serious, earnest, and pensive. Ash liked him immediately. He discovered they had a mutual love of football, and they spent their first few sessions talking about the Miami Dolphins. (At first, Ben didn't believe they had the same favorite team until Ash withstood a grilling that only a true fan could have survived.)

After three sessions, Ash brought in the entire family—Louisa, her second husband Carlos, who had been Annabelle's stepfather, and Ben's two sisters, Maria and Lisa—to get a sense of the family dynamic. Over the course of the session, it became clear that Ben's family couldn't have been more loving and supportive. So at the end of the hour, Ash decided it was time to broach the subject of Annabelle's death directly, thinking he wanted Ben to have his family with him when he did.

"I just want to say," Ash began, "that I think Ben's therapy is going well. He's a terrific kid. We haven't discussed anything about what happened to his mother yet, but I think he's ready to do that now, and that it would be helpful to him—and to all of you—to start talking about the feelings you're each having about losing Annabelle."

There was silence.

"It's been hard," Carlos said finally. "We all loved her. We all miss her."

Ash nodded, thinking he'd need to be even more direct if he was going to help the family—and especially Ben—grieve. So he began asking more specific questions. What did they miss about Annabelle the most? What had been the hardest part about losing her? What did they feel when they thought about her? Did they ever talk about her with each other?

Not surprisingly, the children returned only monosyllabic answers. So Ash decided to try a more oblique approach. Turning to Ben, he asked, "Would you say you think about your mom a lot or a little?"

But Ben only shrugged. So Ash turned to Louisa and Carlos and asked how well they thought the family was helping Ben deal with the aftermath of Annabelle's death.

"We're all chipping in to help him in different ways," Carlos said. "His sisters help him with his homework and play with him more. They even watch a little football with him," he added with a smile. "Louisa and I make sure he practices his piano and eats." No one, they all agreed, had noticed a difference in the way he engaged with his friends, his schoolwork, or them. "But he hasn't cried," Carlos said, "and that does concern us."

When Ash finally turned to Louisa, who up to that point had remained silent, and asked her how *she* thought Ben was doing, she paused a long time before answering. "My son—and he is my son now—is being pulled into the darkness," she said. "The only way I know to prevent that is to make sure he doesn't miss out on even one ounce of love his mother would have given him if she were here. The love a mother gives a son is boundless. So I'm determined to love this boy to death."

Everyone sat stunned. Then Louisa turned to Ben and held him with a gentle but unwavering gaze. "Please tell Dr. Ash what is in your heart, Benjamin."

Ben stared at his grandmother for several moments. Then he burst into tears. He flung himself at Louisa, who threw her arms around him. "There, there," she said as he sobbed against her. "There, there." Louisa was crying too, as were Ben's sisters. Carlos looked stricken.

Whether Ben perceived that Louisa had merely given him permission to express his grief or commanded to do so, Ash never discovered, but from that point forward Ben began discussing Annabelle with him at every visit. Over the next several sessions, Ben dutifully reported every emotion that thinking about her made him feel, from sadness to anger to loneliness to fear. Ash reassured him that allowing himself to feel these emotions was a good thing, that they would fade with time and that eventually thinking about his mother would bring other, happier emotions as well.

Gradually, Ben began to brighten, and four weeks later, Louisa took Ash aside to tell him she felt Ben had been pulled out of the darkness and would now be okay.

"I wonder, though, Dr. Ash," Louisa said, "if I could talk to you about Carlos." She told Ash that Carlos wanted to hire a lawyer to sue the city for the role the police had played in Annabelle's death. He thought they could get a quick settlement and set Ben up financially for life. They had, in fact, been hounded by attorneys who were anxious to hold the city accountable.

"I understand why Carlos wants to do this," Louisa said. "He wants to secure Benjamin's future. But he's angry. He wants someone to pay."

"I can understand why he'd feel that way, too," Ash said.

Louisa nodded. "He's been terribly hurt."

Ash looked at her compassionately. "You all have, Louisa."

Louisa nodded. "Yes, my heart is broken also." Tears abruptly sprang into her eyes. "But I'm not angry at the police. I don't feel they were at fault. It was a tragic accident."

"An accident?" Ash said, confused.

Louisa nodded.

"What about the men who killed her?" Ash asked.

"I'd hardly call them men. Boys with no future. Boys with no guidance."

Ash looked at her in astonishment. The perspective from which her words came seemed almost impossible to imagine. "What can I do to help, Louisa?"

"Carlos is just so angry. It's eating him up inside. He can't get past it. So I was hoping you could talk to him. Maybe do for him what you did for Benjamin."

Ash nodded. "I'd be happy to try." He narrowed his eyes. "But is there anything I can do for *you*?"

"No, no," Louisa said dismissively. "I'm fine. I'm not important. Just them. Just my family."

# The Nature of Compassion

"I have to admit I'm a little skeptical she actually feels that way," I said.

"Which way?" Ash asked. "That everyone else matters but her, or that the men who killed her daughter were just feeling hopeless as a result of poor mentoring?"

"Both."

Ash shrugged. "My sense is she really does. She's just . . . yeah."

"From the world of Compassion," I said.

"Yeah."

"Of course you don't have to sacrifice *your* needs—*your* happiness—to help other people become happy," I said.

Ash shrugged. "People who care about the happiness of others do that all the time," he said. "Don't you think that's what a lot of people think compassion *is*?"

## What Compassion Is

In *The Undefeated Mind*, I write about the Japanese term *jihi* (derived from the words *ji*, meaning to offer joy to others, and *hi*, meaning to alleviate pain):

*Jihi* is used to denote the profound mercy, or compassion, a Buddha is said to feel toward all living beings. Egoless and unconditional, *jihi* requires neither credit for its concern nor reward for its good deeds, the joy of feeling *jihi* itself representing a greater recompense than anything we might receive from the person toward whom we feel it. Though romantic love may provide the spark that gives birth to *jihi*, *jihi* and romantic love are not the same. If we feel *jihi* toward someone with whom we're also *in* love and at some point fall out of love with them, though our romantic feelings for them may disappear, the *jihi* we feel for them will not. If our children cease to speak to us, do we stop caring about their happiness—in effect, stop loving them? No. The love we bear our children, in fact, may represent the closest thing to *jihi* an unenlightened mind can feel. In one sense, then, to feel *jihi* is to feel the compassion we have for those we love above all others for everyone.[2]

When I suggested that Louisa sounded like someone who felt *jihi*, Ash remarked that *jihi* sounded a lot like unconditional positive regard. To feel unconditional positive regard, he said, is to accept and support a person no matter what that person says or does. According to Carl Rogers, who coined the term, the key to mustering unconditional positive regard is acceptance. Rogers believed that all people have the internal resources required for personal growth, and that it's the therapist's suspension of judgment and expectation that the patient *can* grow that made growth possible.

To approach people with unconditional positive regard, or *jihi*, is to embrace the idea that everyone possesses intrinsic worth. To view people with unconditional positive regard is to focus on the potential all people have to be good. This isn't to say that to feel compassion is to think all people *are* good. Rather, it's to recognize the capacity to *become* good can never be destroyed by even a thousand evil deeds, and that it will always exist beneath the morass of selfishness and greed under which it's often hidden.[3] It's our recognition of the existence of the capacity to become good that frees us both to sympathize with another person's misfortune and to empathize with their suffering, which then gives rise to the feeling of compassion, the desire to see the suffering of others end.

## What Compassion Isn't

The desire to see the suffering of others end, however, doesn't require us to adopt a gentle, passive demeanor or express only loving-kindness toward others at all times. Though compassionate people often do both of those things, to be effective at ending suffering, we must sometimes be "harsh, forceful, and even angry."[4] With the intent to increase another person's happiness as their constant thought, people from the world of Compassion may sometimes take action that on the surface seems to lack the very compassion that drives it.

This is because acting with compassion often means withholding from people what they want. Those who think otherwise are likely too easily incapacitated by the idea of disappointing others. Though giving people what they want will make them happy, it does so only temporarily and may in fact support behaviors that cause them more suffering in the long run. After all, people often want what isn't good for them, like the student who wants to watch television instead of doing homework, the compulsive gambler who wants to let it all ride on a single turn of the roulette wheel, and the alcoholic who wants to drink. If our aim is to relieve others of their suffering and help them become happy, we have to apply our own judgment to the actions we take toward that end.

Being compassionate doesn't mean we automatically like everyone, either. Indeed, being compassionate doesn't necessarily mean we like *anyone*. We don't need to have—or even want—a personal relationship with anyone for whom we feel compassion. In fact, we can actively dislike people for whom we feel great compassion. Though being compassionate may mean thinking benevolently about people despite their flaws, it doesn't mean pretending those flaws don't exist. It doesn't mean pretending that people don't annoy us. It only means that we care about their happiness and suffering.

Finally, and most importantly, caring about the happiness of others doesn't require us to sacrifice our own. Though our degree of compassion is often measured by what we're willing to give up, we shouldn't conclude that an act requires personal sacrifice to qualify as compassionate. Acting compassionately may often be, at the very least, inconvenient, but if we find ourselves willing to sacrifice our own happiness to secure someone else's, we've become confused about what compassion is. Being compassionate means caring about the happiness of others as if it were our own. It doesn't mean putting the happiness of others *before* our own. We're as deserving of our own compassion as anyone else—no more, *no less*. And as a practical matter, it's much harder to help others become happy if we're not happy ourselves.

"Maybe that's the core delusion of the world of Compassion then," Ash suggested. "That to be happy you need to put the happiness of others before your own. Louisa certainly seems to believe it."

I shook my head. "I don't think so. If you believe that to be happy you have to put the happiness of others before your own, you'll eventually start resenting the people whose happiness you care about. We're looking for a belief that *induces* compassion, not one that squashes it."

❦

Though occasionally still melancholy, Ben seemed more and more, as time passed, to resemble the boy he'd been before Annabelle had been killed, Louisa told Ash. Ash also began seeing Carlos, who was indeed angry—angry at the gang members, angry at the police, and even angry at Annabelle herself.

"I know that makes no sense," Carlos told Ash, "but I'm mad at her for getting killed! For covering Benjamin with her body, even though I'm so grateful she did."

Ash assured Carlos such feelings were common and normal. He listened, empathized, and helped Carlos process his anger, which, after several weeks, slowly began to recede. And then Carlos raised a concern about Louisa.

"She takes care of everyone but herself," he said. "And she's not doing so well. I wonder if you'd be willing to see her, too."

Ash told him that he'd be willing to see her if she were willing to see him. Carlos assured Ash she was. A week later, Ash found himself sitting down across from Louisa in his office for the first time.

After exchanging a few comments about how well Ben was doing and how pleased they both were about his progress, Ash asked, "So how are *you* doing with all of this?"

Louisa grew still. After a few moments, she answered, "I feel as if I, too, am now being pulled into the darkness, Dr. Ash. And I'm afraid I might succumb."

Thinking she must have finally reached the end of her strength, that the burden of taking care of everyone else while ignoring her own pain had at last become too much, Ash said, "Tell me what's been happening."

Louisa paused again. "Last week, I saw my daughter's murderers for the first time. In court."

Ash nodded for her to continue.

"I was afraid before I saw them that when I looked into their eyes, I wouldn't be able to forgive them," Louisa said.

Ash looked at her in surprise. "You *want* to forgive them?"

"Before I saw them that day in court, I already did."

Ash suppressed a frown. "How?"

Louisa shrugged. "I kept thinking how once they were little boys like my Benjamin who wanted only to be loved. Who wanted only to be safe. That's how I saw them in my mind. It made me so sad, to think of their circumstances. But then . . ."

"Then you saw them in court."

Louisa nodded.

"And what happened when you saw them?"

"They were . . . they were making gang signs and . . . their faces were so . . . Dr. Ash, I saw no repentance in them for taking my Annabelle away from me." Tears were running down her cheeks. "I wanted to forgive them. But I saw no remorse, and it made me so angry!"

"You have every right to be angry, Louisa," Ash said.

"I don't want to be angry," Louisa said, anguished. "What good does being angry do? It won't bring my Annabelle back to me. My anger is poison."

Ash sat back. He was surprised to discover he was feeling angry, too—at Louisa! Was it her rush to renunciate her anger? Her desire to forgive her daughter's murderers? Her insistence that they were merely misguided and her consequent refusal to condemn them as evil? He didn't know.

"Let's talk about the anger you *are* feeling for a second," Ash said.

Louisa rolled her eyes.

"Where do you feel it?" Ash asked her.

"I don't understand. What do you mean?"

"In your body. Where do you feel it in your body?"

She paused to consider. "I guess in my chest. Right here." She placed her hand over her heart.

"What does it feel like?"

"I don't know . . . heat? A burning? It's just anger."

Ash nodded. "If your anger could speak—if you could give it a voice—what would it say?"

Louisa's chin started to tremble, and her breathing came faster. "It would say, 'How dare you dismiss the life of the woman you killed! Do you care about no one but yourselves? How can you be so cruel? Is there no love left in your hearts?' Oh, but then, Dr. Ash, I feel so ashamed!"

"What makes you feel ashamed, Louisa?"

"I shouldn't be this angry. I should be able to forgive them."

"That's a lot to ask of yourself."

"I'm so disappointed in myself that I cannot."

Ash frowned. "Do they even *deserve* your forgiveness?"

"It's not for me to decide what they deserve. I just know that I *want* to forgive them. I don't want to keep carrying this anger in my heart."

"Wanting to forgive them so you can move on I completely understand," Ash said. "But I'm not sure how you do that without first thinking that they deserve to be forgiven."

Louisa wiped her eyes. "Doesn't everyone deserve to be forgiven, Dr. Ash? Don't you, a therapist, know this better than anybody?"

"No," he said, but just which of her questions he was answering he wasn't sure.

## The Value of Empathy

"The question isn't whether or not Annabelle's murderers deserve to be forgiven," I said. "The question is why does Louisa feel they deserve *her* forgiveness? What does she believe that causes her to care so much about their suffering?"

"Their suffering?" Ash shook his head. "I have absolutely no idea. It makes no sense to me at all."

"What, that she could still view her daughter's murderers as human beings?"

"I'm just surprised she feels they deserve her forgiveness at all. Can you imagine yourself feeling compassion for them if they'd killed *your* son?"

"I can *imagine* feeling it," I said. "Whether or not I actually would . . .?" I shrugged.

"I'm sure it's tempting to say you'd feel compassion, especially if you're invested in preserving your image as a compassionate person. But you're not imagining the pain, the sense of loss, and the anger you'd feel, too. I don't think you would feel it."

"Does that mean you don't think Louisa is, either? That she's just pretending? Or pretending to want to feel it?"

"I don't know." Ash paused. "I'll tell you what, though—when she said she wanted to forgive them, it really pissed me off."

"That's a pretty strong reaction to the idea of forgiveness," I said. "Any idea what's behind it?"

Ash paused. "If I'm being honest, I think it's because I don't like what her compassion says about me."

Early in his training, Ash said, he took a course on the therapeutic use of empathy. He was dismayed to discover, however, that his professor believed it was permissible—even important—for a therapist to fake empathy when he didn't feel it. Ash spent many hours in class arguing that expressions of empathy lacking the actual feeling of empathy behind them were not only useless but also dangerous. Manufactured empathy was what sociopaths used to swindle people, he said. He was offended by the idea that "pretending to care about patients" could be considered an acceptable therapeutic strategy.

Then during one of his externships, he was assigned to see a patient named Hilary. When Ash asked Hilary what had brought her to therapy, she replied in a quiet voice that while reading on a park bench near her home one day she'd heard a loud crack, followed by a heavy thud. When she looked up, she saw that a large tree branch had fallen on all three of her children, who had been playing nearby. Two of them were killed instantly. The third died in her arms.

Ash's mouth fell open. Then his chest constricted, and his breathing started coming in painful gasps. Realizing he was on the verge of a full-blown panic attack, he excused himself, walked out of the room, and spent the next several minutes trying to calm himself down. When he finally managed to do so, he re-entered the room determined to avoid any questions that might trigger Hilary's emotions in any way and to focus instead on the mundane details of her life leading up to the accident. Later, his supervisor suggested that the best thing he could do for her was simply be present. This meant, among other things, offering whatever expressions of empathy he could. And that was when Ash became a believer in the power of manufactured empathy. For the only thing he felt during his sessions with Hilary from that point forward was an intense fear that he would say the wrong thing and send her into a tailspin of grief, rage, and depression.

Yet after a few months of offering her expressions of empathy while she sobbed for entire sessions at a time, Hilary gradually began to improve. And when she eventually left therapy, it was specifically Ash's caring, she told him, that had given her the most comfort and had been the most helpful to her. She never suspected that all the while he'd been telling her how sad he felt about what had happened to her and how hopeful he was that she would recover, he hadn't been feeling anything of the sort at all.

"Meaning, basically, I was lying to her the entire time," Ash said.

"But, come on," I said, "you *did* care about her, didn't you? Just because you were feeling anxiety when you told her you were sad doesn't mean you were being dishonest. Weren't you feeling anxiety *because* you were worried about her?"

"I was worried about failing."

"Well, sure."

Ash shook his head impatiently. "The reason I told you that story was to make the point that a lot of the time I don't live up to my own expectations. It's not just that I lied to Hilary about what I was feeling. Sometimes I actually *don't* care about my patients. They never know it because I'm a professional. But sometimes they irritate me. Or frustrate me. Or bore me."

"Every provider feels that way about some of his patients," I said.

"Sure. Fine. But when I think about those gang members killing Annabelle right in front of Ben—when I think about how that could have been my own son, I—I—" Ash stopped, abruptly emotional himself. "I can't muster up any compassion for them at all."

"And that means what?"

"That I'm not who I want to be. That I'm not who I pretend to be."

"Ah," I said. "And then Louisa comes along—"

"Yeah, someone who's without a doubt the most genuinely compassionate person I've ever met—"

"And she makes you feel . . . ?" I asked.

"Like a fraud," Ash said.

"And what did *that* make you feel?"

"Ashamed," Ash said. "It made me feel ashamed."

I nodded. "And you didn't like feeling ashamed, so you got mad instead."

"So I got mad instead. Yeah."

"So you really do believe Louisa is as compassionate as she seems."

"I guess I do," Ash said. "Why else would her example have made me feel ashamed?"

"And the reason you feel ashamed is because you don't understand why she wants to forgive her daughter's murderers," I said.

"And I think I should. Yeah. I get that she's compassionate—but, I mean, come on. I can't even imagine what she believes that makes her feel that they deserve her forgiveness. I can't even guess."

"You can't even guess? Try."

Ash considered. "I don't know. . . maybe that all people are fundamentally good?"

"I'm sure she does believe that. But I don't think that's the core delusion we're looking for."

"Because it's not a delusion?" Ash asked.

"No," I said. "Because you don't have to believe someone is fundamentally good to care about their suffering."

Determined this time to keep his personal feelings firmly in check and to focus on the problem with which she'd come to him for help, Ash met with Louisa again.

"Louisa, last time you said you wanted to let go of your anger," he began. "So let me ask you something: why do you think you want to keep it?"

"Keep it?" Louisa's head jolted backward. "I don't!"

"I know a large part of you doesn't," Ash acknowledged. "But another part is angry for what it considers to be a good reason. I'm wondering what that reason might be."

Louisa's expression became despondent. "It's just every time I think about those boys making those signs . . ."

Ash nodded. "You said it was their lack of remorse."

"Yes."

"Why do you think it matters to you that they feel remorse?"

Louisa looked back at him in surprise. "Because that's what people are sup-posed to feel when they do something wrong! It means they *agree* they did something wrong. How can they not know what they did was wrong?"

Ash was nodding with her. "How can they not acknowledge your pain?"

"Yes! I'm a human being, too," Louisa said.

"So is this righteous anger you're feeling—anger at the injustice that was done to you and to Annabelle?"

"I—I don't know," Louisa said. "It's just anger."

"Well, to tell you the truth, Louisa, righteous anger is what I'm feeling right now myself," Ash confessed. "When I think about what those men did, it makes me furious."

"Thank you, Dr. Ash. It helps me to hear you say that."

"But I'm wondering if *you're* feeling angry for an entirely different reason. I'm wondering if you're feeling angry to stop yourself from feeling something else. Something even worse."

"Worse?" Louisa said, her expression worried. "What?"·

"Grief."

Louisa stared at him blankly. Then she looked down. After a moment, a tear fell from her face and landed on her lap. She cried silently for a few minutes, then let out a small gasp and started crying louder.

"Tell me what it's been like to be without her, Louisa," Ash prompted gently.

"It takes my breath away, how much I miss her."

"I know it does."

"I can't breathe when I think of her."

"I know."

"Which is why when I think of those—those—"

"Stay with the grief, Louisa. That's what you need to face to let go of your anger. As long as you refuse to feel the pain, all you'll feel is the anger. If you want to be able to forgive those boys, if you want to be able to move on, you need to let yourself grieve."

But Louisa was shaking her head, wiping at her eyes. "It's too much, Dr. Ash. It's too much."

Ash paused. Here at last was the wound that·Annabelle's death had left in her, and it was as deep and as jagged as any he'd ever seen. He noted a familiar fluttering in his stomach—a worry that he might say the wrong thing or presume too much and become the target of Louisa's anger himself. But he accepted that he was going to feel that anxiety and dismissed it as he renewed his determination to be fully present with her as she grieved.

"Why don't you just tell me about Annabelle then? What was she like? I'd like to hear about her."

Through her tears, Louisa managed a small smile. "What do you want to know?"

"Anything."

Louisa blew out a long breath. "She was a miracle." Louisa's doctor had declared her infertile after she'd failed to conceive for many years. So when she eventually did become pregnant, she was convinced Annabelle was a gift from God. Perhaps that was why, Louisa said, the moment Annabelle was born, Louisa loved her so fiercely. Though she tried hard not to play favorites among her family members, from early on she felt that she and Annabelle shared a special bond, one that was unusual even for a mother and daughter. "We never fought, Dr. Ash, even when she was a child. She was always exactly like me."

"Exactly like you?" Ash asked her.

"Loving. Caring. Someone who felt the pain of others as if it were her own."

## The Relationship between Empathy and Compassion

"Which got me thinking," Ash said. "What if the world of Compassion is actually about defending yourself against your own empathy?"

"How do you mean?" I asked.

"When we say we feel empathy for people, we're mostly saying we feel empathy for their pain, right? But to actually *feel* empathy—in contrast to merely making an empathetic statement—means to experience pain yourself in response to another person's pain. Feeling empathy is actually an *unpleasant* experience."[5]

"I guess that's true."

"So here's the thing," Ash said. "It turns out that compassion training has actually been found to counteract the unpleasantness of empathy.[6] In fact, compassion *transforms the pain of feeling someone else's pain into joy*."[7] It seemed to do this, the research suggested, by increasing activity in parts of the brain's reward circuit.[8]

"That's fascinating," I said. "It almost sounds as if you're saying empathy is the *cause* of compassion." Research does, in fact, suggest that empathy prevents aggressive and antisocial behavior.[9] It also shows that psychopaths, who demonstrate little in the way of compassion, have much lower levels of spontaneous empathy.[10]

Ash shrugged. "I don't know if empathy causes compassion or not. I'm just saying compassion may turn out to be the most adaptive response to the pain of empathizing with someone else's pain."

"It makes complete sense."

Ash nodded. "So then, what might someone like Louisa, who's incredibly empathetic, come to believe after she figured out the best way to alleviate the pain of feeling empathy is to take action to relieve other people of their pain? How about *that she can only be happy if she helps everyone around her to be happy, too.*"

I nodded. "Because for her—for anyone with a high level of empathy—it's literally true."

"So then why isn't *that* the core delusion of the world of Compassion?"

"I think it is," I said, nodding. "It's perfect. What could make us care more about the pain and suffering of others—what could make us more compassionate—than the belief that relieving other people of their pain and suffering is what we need to be happy ourselves?"

"Exactly," Ash said. "Which then leads me to the same question I asked when we were talking about the worlds of Learning and Realization: how is that a delusion?"

"Which then leads me to the same answer," I said. "It depends on the kind of happiness we think being compassionate brings."

## How Compassion Makes Us Happier

Research suggests that taking action to alleviate the suffering of others does indeed help us to alleviate our own:

In one study by researchers Carolyn Schwartz and Meir Sendor, patients with multiple sclerosis who were asked to call other patients with multiple sclerosis each month for a year to offer their support in any way they could reported significantly higher levels of adaptability, confidence, tolerance, and self-esteem than the patients they were calling.[11] Something about trying to help others, they said, made them feel better able to manage problems themselves. . . .

Not only that, but providing support to others also makes us feel *less bad*. In a study of 180 women and 25 men grieving the loss of their spouses, providing instrumental, if only minor, support to others by giving rides, running errands, doing housework, and so on was found to accelerate recovery from depression in subjects experiencing intense grief.[12] Interestingly, being on the *receiving* end of such support was not.[13]

In fact, taking action to help others become happy does more than just reduce our pain and suffering. It also helps us feel increased joy:

> According to one study that analyzed data from the German Socio-Economic Panel Survey, a collection of statistics representing the largest and longest-standing series of observations on happiness in the world, the characteristic most strongly associated with long-term increases in life satisfaction is nothing other than a persistent commitment to pursuing altruistic goals.[14]

But altruism doesn't just *correlate* with an increase in happiness; it actually *causes* it—at least in the short term, according to psychologist Sonja Lyubomirsky.[15] When she had students perform five acts of kindness of their choosing per week over the course of six weeks, they reported a significant increase in their levels of happiness relative to a control group of students who didn't.[16]

Other research even suggests a neurological mechanism: acts of generosity stimulate not only at least one area that's associated with eudaimonic happiness, the orbitofrontal cortex, but also, as when we feel compassion, the brain's reward circuit.[17]

"So helping to relieve someone of their suffering not only reduces our pain," I said, "but also increases our joy—and for the same reason that both personal accomplishment and personal growth do: because we're doing something that feels important. The only difference is that the important thing we're doing isn't for ourselves. It's for someone else."

"Sure," Ash said.

"So the happiness that comes from taking compassionate action is still dependent on attachment."

"On the attachment we have to meaning," Ash said. "I get it."

"Yes. Which implies that, just as with personal accomplishment and personal growth, you actually have to take compassionate action over and over again if you want to sustain the happiness it brings. Which is why we're saying it's delusional to believe that you need to help others to be happy. Not because helping others *won't* make you happy, but, again, because the happiness that helping others brings—eudaimonic happiness—is still relative, not absolute. What's delusional is expecting it to make you happy constantly and permanently. Indestructibly."

"So unlike personal growth in the world of Realization, altruistic action doesn't actually turn you into an intrinsically happier person. It just makes you happy whenever you do it."

"That's right," I said.

"Then why," Ash asked, "is the world of Compassion considered a higher world—one associated with a more positive core affect—than the world of Realization?"

"Ah, right," I said. "Because first, as we said, becoming an intrinsically happier person means changing your disposition, right? It means becoming someone who spends less time feeling pain and suffering and more time feeling joy."

"Or more time feeling more intense joy," Ash put in.

"Exactly. And the way personal development changes your disposition, as we also said, is by freeing you from dysfunctional beliefs. Which, if you think about it, is the same thing as saying it causes you to embrace more functional beliefs."

"Healthier beliefs, sure," Ash said. "Beliefs that are wiser. That's what we said acquiring wisdom means."

"Right," I said. "Wiser beliefs. Beliefs that *engender* happiness. *Like, for example, the belief that helping others will make you happy.* Because in fact that's where I'd argue the personal development we achieve in the world of Realization invariably leads—to the expansion of our compassion. The objective of the world of Realization *is* the world of Compassion. Because what action could be more meaningful—and therefore make us happier—than action aimed at helping a fellow human being suffer less?"

"Well, I think that's exactly the question," Ash said. "You're assuming that the eudaimonic happiness we get from altruistic action is greater than the eudaimonic happiness we get from anything else—greater than the eudaimonic happiness we get from personal accomplishment and greater than the eudaimonic happiness we get from personal growth. But how do we know that's true?"

❦

Over the next several weeks, with Ash's help, Louisa began to let herself grieve in earnest, and gradually her anger began to remit. What helped her the most, she found, was telling Ash stories about Annabelle. Ash listened and empathized, remaining fully present as she processed the feelings that the telling of them brought out of her. And gradually, in between her tears, there began to appear some laughter.

Gradually, too, Louisa began to talk more about herself. Ash learned that she'd been taking care of people all her life. The youngest of six children, she absorbed the lesson early on that life was best lived in the service of others. Even as a child she seemed to reserve a special warmth, a kind glance, and an encouraging word for everybody. As a result, she was often the first person to whom her family and friends would turn for comfort and support, knowing as they did that she would always give whatever she could. And whether remembering a nephew's birthday with a small gift, lending money to an uncle who was behind on his rent, or staying over at a friend's house to nurse her through the flu, Louisa never begrudged the giving.

"Why do you think it's so important for you to take care of people?" Ash asked her.

Louisa shrugged. "I think it is just how I was raised."

Ash eyed her suspiciously. "Would you say your brothers and sisters are as caring as you?"

Louisa hesitated. "If I am to be honest, Dr. Ash, no."

"Then it can't *only* be how you were raised, can it?"

She shrugged. "I can't take credit for how God made me."

"But there must be some *reason* you feel it's important to be caring. To take care of people."

"'Above all, love each other deeply, because love covers over a multitude of sins,'" Louisa said. "Peter 4:8."

"So you're caring because the Bible tells you to be?"

"You tell me, Dr. Ash—what more important thing is there for us to do on this earth than care for one another?" She sounded almost stern. "I've asked myself this over and over and over and have never found a better answer. Have you?"

Ash smiled. "Actually, no, I haven't."

"Maybe that is because God made you caring as well. Maybe that is your purpose also."

"Well, I think we make our own purpose."

"Do we? Then what have you decided is your purpose, Dr. Ash?"

Ash was surprised to find himself flushing at the question. "To help relieve suffering where I find it."

"And why is your purpose to help relieve suffering?"

"I guess because . . . well, I guess it's what you said—there really is nothing else I think is more important for me to do."

Louisa nodded approvingly. "Love is the most important thing in the world, don't you think? We must love everyone as much as we are able."

"Even people who've hurt us?"

"Those people most of all," Louise said.

"And why do you think *that*, Louisa?" Ash asked her.

"Because they are the most in need of it."

## The Power of Purpose

"It all sounds very noble," Ash said. "If everyone in the world were like her, we'd be living in a utopia. Unfortunately, she's one in a million."

"She may be," I acknowledged. "But she also answered your question. How can we say the world of Compassion is associated with a more positive core affect, or a greater feeling of joy, than are the worlds of Learning and Realization? Because the core of compassion is love. And giving and receiving love, studies show, enhances life satisfaction and brings more joy than any other emotion."[18]

Ash considered this. "So what we're saying is that meaning comes in three distinct flavors. First, there's the meaning that arises out of the world of Learning, from our urge to create, build, and accomplish. This kind of meaning feels important to us apart from any effect it has on anyone else. It just matters to us to express our values, our autonomy, and our creativity. Second, there's the meaning that arises out of the world of Realization, from our urge to learn about ourselves and grow. This kind of meaning also feels important to us apart from any effect it has on anyone else. It just matters to us to try to fulfill our potential. And third, there's the meaning that arises out of the world of Compassion, from our desire to create value for others. This kind of meaning feels important to us because . . . because . . . why?"

"Because it matters to us to feel like we have a purpose," I answered. "And it's meaningless to talk about having a purpose that doesn't involve creating value for other people."

"We can't find a purpose in creating value just for ourselves? From growing a company? Or becoming a great tennis player?"

"We can certainly find meaning in those activities, as we've said," I answered carefully. "But we won't necessarily feel a sense of purpose from doing just anything that we happen to find meaningful. It may feel meaningful to grow a company, but that doesn't mean growing a company is our life's purpose. To feel a sense of purpose we need to be doing what feels like the *most* meaningful thing we could do."[19]

"But what if accomplishing something that's only meaningful to you *is* what feels like the most meaningful thing you could do?" Ash asked.

## What Meaning Is the Most Meaningful?

In fact, research shows that what people find most meaningful in life varies by age, level of education, and gender. For example, younger people report finding personal growth more meaningful than helping others.[20] Older people, in contrast, find helping others more meaningful than personal growth.[21] Women find personal growth more meaningful than men,[22] and people with advanced degrees find helping others more meaningful than people without advanced degrees.[23]

Yet research also shows that almost everyone finds interpersonal relationships more meaningful than both personal growth *and* personal accomplishment.[24]

In other words, nothing is more meaningful to us than our interactions with other people. Given that other studies suggest, in the words of researcher Roy Baumeister, "that givers have more meaningful lives than takers,"[25] it's likely that contributing to the welfare of others—especially others we love—will feel in general more meaningful than contributing solely to our own welfare. What's more, contributing to the welfare of many people typically feels more meaningful to us than contributing to the welfare of only one person—even if that one person happens to be us. This is simply because the greater the number of people our actions impact, the more meaningful our actions feel. It's likely, therefore, that altruistic action creates more eudaimonic happiness than either personal accomplishment or personal growth.[26]

Not that this is true for everyone. And not that an action can't feel meaningful in more than one way. For example, when we think about writing a book and expressing our ideas in elegant, clear prose, we find ourselves in the world of Learning, delighting in the eudaimonic happiness that comes from personal accomplishment. But if in the next moment we think about our book's potential to impact readers in a positive way, we'll find ourselves in the world of Compassion, delighting in the eudaimonic happiness that comes from creating value for others.

Finally, as I detail in *The Undefeated Mind*, a focus on contributing to the welfare of others will also

> help sustain us through loss, improve our ability to endure stress, enhance our sense of self-worth, diminish our inclination to give up, make mundane tasks more enjoyable, help us to say no more easily, defend us against despair, and imbue the events of our lives with heightened significance. Few things, I concluded, had the same power to make us as resilient.[27]

So while exceptions will always exist, and many people may not find their greatest joy in contributing to the welfare of others, for most of us, doing so has the power to bring not only the most joy, but also the most strength. Thus, in the end, for most of us, the world of Compassion offers the greatest happiness possible that can be achieved from attachment.

Eventually, Louisa told Ash she thought she was ready to terminate therapy. The anger she felt at the men who'd killed Annabelle had receded enough that she was once again "able to find forgiveness for them in her heart."

When she told him this, an image of Annabelle hunched over a terrified Ben flashed through Ash's mind, her body then slumping over her son's and falling to the ground in front of him. He wondered how any attempt at forgiveness could succeed in the face of an image like that.

"Louisa, tell me something," Ash said. "Do you honestly feel that those men don't deserve to be punished?"

Louisa shook her head firmly. "No, Dr. Ash, they deserve to be punished. My Annabelle deserves justice. That is not what I'm saying. I don't forgive what they did. I forgive *them*."

Ash felt relieved to hear this. "So you condemn their actions—just not the men themselves."

"Yes."

"But how is it possible to forgive someone whose actions you refuse to forgive?"

"In my mind, I allow them to be more than just my daughter's murderers. They have done a terrible, terrible thing. But that doesn't mean that is all they have ever done. They, too, I am sure, want only to be happy. They have just gone horribly wrong in trying to get there."

"That's—that's an astounding perspective for you to have, Louisa."

"Don't you wonder about them, Dr. Ash? What their lives were like? What drove them to join a gang? Did they start out wanting to hurt people?" She shook her head in answer to her own question. "Don't all children begin wanting to be loved?"

"All children begin as self-centered takers," Ash said with a mischievous grin.

"That is true, too," Louisa said with a laugh. "It is up to us to teach them not to be. Perhaps these boys were never given a chance to learn this. Perhaps they have lived their entire lives in hopelessness and fear."

Ash wondered to what degree Louisa's desire to humanize her daughter's murderers was an attempt to make sense of her loss. Perhaps it comforted her to believe the men who killed Annabelle were simply misguided rather than evil. A world populated by misguided people seemed far safer. The misguided, at least, could be taught and the danger they represented neutralized.

Then again, Ash thought, maybe Louisa was right. Certainly there *were* genuinely evil people, true sociopaths who cared nothing for anyone but themselves and who harmed others without remorse. But who knew better than Ash just how misguided people could be?

"So how did you do it, Louisa?" Ash asked. "How did you find it in your heart to forgive them?"

"Do not think I am a saint, Dr. Ash. I am deeply hurt by what those boys did. Also, with my family I am often annoyed and disappointed. And I am busy. So busy I feel I do not have time to think of other people very often. But," she said, "I am also very interested in stories."

"Stories?"

Louisa nodded. "Everyone has a story, Dr. Ash. No one is only what we see. No one is only what they have done to us. When you learn a person's story, it is no longer so easy to dismiss them. When you learn a person's story, they become a person to you. I know you think I shouldn't care about those boys who killed my Annabelle. Carlos doesn't think I should, either. It makes him mad, like it made you mad"—and here she smiled at him—"but this tragedy did not start with the death of my daughter. It started with the stories of those boys. I know you do not understand. Carlos doesn't, either. There is only one person who I know would have, and she is no longer with us."

Ash smiled. "Annabelle?"

Louisa nodded. "As I told you before, she too felt the pain of others as if it were her own."

"It's entirely possible," Ash said, "that Louisa is the wisest person I've ever met."

"Why, because she found a way to let go of her anger?" I asked. "Or because she told you we all need to be interested in each other's stories and that we're all human beings who should love one another?"

"Because she doesn't just *say* those things," Ash said. "She lives them. Because she really does believe that for her to be happy she has to help everyone else become happy, too."

"Even the men who murdered her daughter," I marveled.

"That's a little more complicated. Figuring out how not to hate them isn't the same thing as wanting them to be happy. I don't know if she'd say she wants them to be happy."

"You did say she said she wants them to be punished," I remarked.

"Yeah, but out of desire for justice, not revenge. She still thinks they deserve her compassion."

"I'll tell you, I sure admire her for it," I said, "but you were right—I'm *not* sure I'd feel the same if it were my son. I'm not sure I would want to. I'm not even sure I *should* want to."

"I'm not either. But I also think there really is something she understands that we don't. I'm not sure if those gangbangers deserve it or not, but I admire her for having compassion for them."

"I don't know if she's the wisest person you've ever met, but she is remarkable."

"You have no idea," Ash said. "You know what she's been doing? It's unbelievable."

"What?"

"She's been visiting them in prison."

"The gangbangers?"

Ash nodded.

"Why?" I asked.

"She wants to hear their stories."

## Key Points

- Compassion is defined as the life-condition of love.

- In the life-condition of Compassion we care as much about the happiness of other people as we do our own.

- When we care about the happiness of others *more* than our own, we may neglect ourselves, become resentful, and begin to view altruistic action as a burden.

- For most of us, altruistic action creates the greatest sense of meaning and therefore the greatest amount of eudaimonic happiness.

- The core delusion of the world of Compassion is that to be happy we need to help other people become happy.

# 10

# Enlightenment

*There are only two ways to live your life. One is as though nothing is a miracle. The other is as though everything is a miracle.*

—Albert Einstein

Enlightenment is defined as the life-condition of awe. When we're in it, we remain in a continual state of wonder at the sublime order and beauty of the universe. In fact, being in the life-condition of Enlightenment changes our entire view of reality, making our previous experience of the world seem like nothing more than a dream from which we've finally awakened.

In the world of Enlightenment, we're neither all-knowing nor all-powerful. Enlightenment is neither a "supernatural state that enables us to perform super-human feats [nor] a transcendental state, divorced from the everyday reality of this world."[1] It's simply a life-condition human beings enter and leave like any other. To enter it is to remain as much ourselves as we do when we enter, for example, Anger or Tranquility.

There are, however, several important ways in which the world of Enlightenment is different from the other nine worlds. First and foremost, in the world of Enlightenment, the joy we experience is absolute. That is, it remains uninfluenced by circumstances or attachment. It wells up from our innermost being, making itself felt at every moment. It's not a euphoric joy that immobilizes and

289

addicts us, like the kind we might feel from a narcotic. That is, it doesn't make us passive and foolishly accepting of everything that comes our way, good or bad. Rather, it's a joy that activates us in the most positive and productive way, leaving us feeling like our best, most loving, and compassionate self. The joy of Enlightenment is literally the best good feeling human beings are capable of experiencing. It's better than all the other positive emotions combined; it's better than the joy we feel from attachment in the world of Rapture. It is the joy of all joys.

This isn't to say that in the world of Enlightenment we don't also feel pain. The loss of a valued possession, the death of a loved one, a decline in our health—all cause us as much pain when we're in the world of Enlightenment as they do when we're in any of the other nine worlds. Attaining enlightenment doesn't disconnect us from attachment. Far from it. In the world of Enlightenment, our attachments all become equally beautiful, equally precious to us.

What we do leave behind when we enter the world of Enlightenment, however, is suffering. There is simply no pain—not even the pain caused by awareness of our mortality—that can diminish the joy we feel in the world of Enlightenment.

To most of us, the idea that we could achieve such a state seems ludicrous. Indeed, upon attaining enlightenment, the historical Buddha, Siddhartha Gautama, immediately recognized just how difficult it would be for us "ordinary beings"—the term used in Buddhism to describe the unenlightened—to believe we have an enlightened nature at all. Further, even if we acknowledge that we might have an enlightened nature, so shrouded in mysticism has the whole notion of enlightenment been that most of us can't imagine how we could ever attain it ourselves.

Yet, as we'll see, evidence is beginning to accumulate not only that the life-condition of Enlightenment is a real state with neurological causes and correlates, but also that, just like all the other nine worlds, it's a life-condition available to us all.

## The Experience of Enlightenment

Though technically I no longer practice Buddhism, I was originally drawn to it, as I write in *The Undefeated Mind*, because of its claim that the state of enlightenment was a real thing, that there really was a truth to know that would in some way explain the ultimate nature of reality and my relation to it and that, once grasped, this truth would help me construct a life-condition of indestructible happiness.

I thought this because I'd once caught a glimpse of what I believed such a life-condition would feel like. I'd come home for the summer after my sophomore year in college and had been sitting in my bedroom watching and listening to the trees swaying in an afternoon breeze through an open window when I found myself suddenly and inexplicably filled with the strongest sense of connection to my surroundings I'd ever known. At the same time, I began to overflow with the most powerful feeling of goodwill and loving assent toward everyone and everything I'd ever experienced. I seemed somehow larger than myself, as if what I'd always considered to be "me" was in reality nothing more than a personality within a personality—like the protagonist in A. E. Van Vogt's short story "Asylum" who discovers to his amazement that he isn't a man with an IQ of 110 at all but instead a facet of an alien mind that possesses an IQ of 1,200, "an actor who'd been completely absorbed in his role, but who was now alone in his dressing room after the play was over removing the grease paint, his mood of the play fading, fading, fading. . . ." Wondrously, at that moment I felt as accepting of the idea of my dying as I was about the idea of the sun setting at the end of the day. And then, as many others who've described similar experiences have reported, within minutes the feeling faded away.[2]

Four years later, I had a similar experience at the end of my second year of medical school, shortly after I broke up with my first girlfriend, Melissa. I'd become so depressed that my classmates had stopped sitting near me. They recognized I was in pain but had no idea what to say to me or how to provide comfort. I felt this was a small mercy as I had little energy to speak and wouldn't have known how to respond even if they had reached out to me. I would come home at the end of every day feeling exhausted and humiliated. Sleep was the only thing I looked forward to because it was the only thing that brought me relief from my suffering.

This went on for three months. Then one night I found myself sitting on a beach on the shore of Lake Michigan. The moon was full and reflected a white cone of light over the water, a great undulating liquid carpet. The pier was quiet except for the gentle sloshing of waves on the shore. I found if I focused on that sound, I felt a little better. I told myself that I'd been wallowing in my suffering and that I should have begun to recover by then, but for some reason I felt as awful as I had the night Melissa ended our relationship. This only added to my self-loathing.

Then I heard a small splashing as something moved in the water. I looked more carefully. Fish were darting up near the surface. Gradually, my thoughts turned away from my suffering, and I began to look around me. The universe itself didn't know or care how I was feeling, and for some reason that thought soothed me. It was as it should be. All was as it should be, I thought.

And then there came a small burst in my chest, a sudden lightening of weight, and everything I saw was abruptly transformed. The stars were no longer the stars and the moon not the moon, but life—*life*—the very same life as me. Inexplicably, everything around me seemed heartbreakingly beautiful. I felt a profound sense of belonging and a sense of certainty that every single thing that had happened to me and that ever would happen to me was right and good and as it should be. My mind wasn't the small, limited thing I'd always believed it to be, but something as vast and flawless as the universe itself. In that moment I knew that the purest emotion I would ever experience was nothing but loving assent and egoless goodwill toward all things, which were as perfect and beautiful as I was. I swelled with a feeling of gratitude so sweet I would always, from that point forward, believe that it was ten times, a hundred times, a thousand times greater a gift to have felt it toward another than to have received it from someone else. My pain was abruptly transformed into something bittersweet, something to be enjoyed even, because it, too, was a part of the continual dance of perfect interdependent motion that was life. In that moment, I loved myself totally, free of the boundaries of my small-minded ego. I loved myself for my capacity to love. I loved my faults. I was love itself.

Then, as unexpectedly as this awareness dawned, it faded away. In minutes, my suffering returned. I felt as if I were suddenly back on the other side of a piece of paper, as if the epiphany I'd just experienced was that close—and that far—from the state to which I'd now returned. I was stunned. I tried to recapture the experience, to wrap my mind back around the thoughts that had created it.

But those very same thoughts now seemed powerless to create it again. How had this happened? What had happened?

I waited. But now the waves were just the waves and the sand just the sand. So I waited some more. Soon, though, I realized that the experience had moved beyond my grasp. Eventually, I stood up, went back to my car, and drove home.

After this second episode, even more powerful than the first, I wondered, just how common was this kind of experience? Did I know anyone else who'd ever had one?

It turned out, in fact, that I did.

Ash was working at his desk one morning when he received a phone call from his attorney. A legal issue he thought he'd long ago put to rest had abruptly resurfaced and was once again threatening his livelihood. Gripped by a debilitating fear, he felt a strange impulse to leave work. He took the elevator down to the ground floor and walked out into the street. He stumbled down the block and finally sat down against a fire hydrant. He began to cry. After a few minutes of staring aimlessly and hopelessly at nothing, his gaze landed on the Sears Tower standing several blocks away. It began to capture his attention with its tall chiral symmetry, its sleek upward thrust toward the sky, and suddenly he found he couldn't take his eyes off it. He had the thought then that this building wasn't just a series of bolts, drywall, glass, and steel but a miracle of human ingenuity. The thousands upon thousands of relationships and transactions and processes that had been required to bring it to life—too many for him to grasp all at once—overwhelmed and staggered him. And then he found himself abruptly aware of the sunlight warming his face, the breeze on his skin, the sounds of the city around him. Even the leaves on the trees lining the street seemed to become sharper, brighter, and he had the sudden thought that no matter what happened to him, it would pale in significance next to the miracle of architecture at which he was now gazing in awe. He felt then that whatever did happen, he'd survive it. He was no longer feeling fear but now wonderment and joy. He sat there for a few minutes basking in the feeling of being completely at peace, and then, as abruptly as it had come, the feeling disappeared only to be replaced once more by fear. He became aware that he was still sitting against the fire hydrant in the middle of the sidewalk, so he stood up. Then he walked back to his office.

In fact, it turns out that individuals in almost every culture and period of history—from the Buddha himself to the poet Walt Whitman to the writer Eckart Tolle—have reported having these kinds of experiences.[3] As psychologist Steve Taylor points out in his book *Waking From Sleep*:

> The vision of the world that Walt Whitman describes in *Leaves of Grass*, for example, is essentially the same as that of the Upanishads [treatises expounding the concepts of Hinduism] (the earliest of which were written down 2,500 years ago and probably originated centuries before then), of the third-century Greek philosopher Plotinus, of the medieval German mystic Meister Eckart, and so on.[4]

Taylor further references a study done in 1974 by sociologist Andrew Greeley in which 35 percent of the subjects who were asked if they had ever had the experience of being "very close to a powerful, spiritual force that seemed to lift [them] out of [themselves]" answered that they had. In fact, 21 percent said they'd had the experience several times, and 12 percent said that it happened to them often.[5] Neuroscientist Andrew Newberg, who's spent nearly three decades mapping what he calls "the neural correlates of spiritual experiences," has also documented (through web-based surveys he's been running since 2008) the surprising frequency with which people experience the life-condition of Enlightenment.[6]

Yet even more than their frequency, what's most striking about these "awakening experiences," as Taylor calls them, is their uniformity. Of course, individuals from different backgrounds and historical periods have used different language to describe them, typically explaining the meaning of their experiences in terms of their pre-existing beliefs.[7] Some, for example, have believed they communed with God. Others have called their experiences "spiritual" or even "mystic." But whatever specific labels are used, at their core, the descriptions are invariably the same, and consist of seven essential characteristics.

First and foremost is reported a powerful feeling of unity with one's surroundings. As Taylor writes:

> We realize that the underlying nature of all seemingly separate things is one and the same . . . that normally we are just aware of the surface reality of things. We become aware that, say, a tree and a river—or you or I—are only different in the

way two waves of the sea appear to be separate and distinct. In reality they—and we—are part of the same ocean of being.[8]

Second, perhaps as a result of this awareness, our sense of self dissolves as

we transcend . . . the seeming duality between ourselves and the world, our sense of being an "I" locked away inside our heads, detached from a world which is "out there," [and] we realize that we're part of the world, that in a sense we *are* [the world].

We don't just become one with other beings, but with all living and non-living things and with the world—or the universe—as a whole.[9]

Third, our newfound connection to the "world—or the universe—as a whole" engenders the sense that we posses a larger, truer self.

We realize that the ego-self which we always thought was our true self—the chattering "I" with its never-ending worries and desires—is only a kind of limited and false shadow self, a sort of imposter which has taken over our psyche. Now we become a much more stable, deep-rooted, and expansive self, which can't be damaged by rejection and doesn't constantly hanker for attention and is free of the anxieties that oppress the ego.[10]

Fourth, with the dissolution of our sense of self also comes a boundless compassion and love "for the people [we're] with, for the whole human race, and for the whole world."[11] We feel an empathy that can be so strong we almost feel as if we've *become* the people and things for which we feel it.

Fifth, as Newberg writes, we have a "feeling of profound clarity that some deeper insight or truth or wisdom has been reached,"[12] and feel, according to Taylor, a sense of rightness with the world,

a sense of *meaning*, a sense of an atmosphere of harmony and benevolence. We have the beginning of a sense that all is well, that in some strange way the world, far from being the coldly indifferent place that science tells us it is, does "mean well" by us and is a benign place. No matter what problems fill our life and how full of violence and injustice the world is, there's a sense that . . . everything *is* good, that the world is somehow perfect."[13]

Sixth, we experience an intense feeling of joy and well-being.

We feel that there's a new kind of power or energy running through us, an energy which can be still and intense and fill us with a glow of serenity or be wild and powerful and fill us with ecstasy. There's a feeling of being exalted.

Reports of awakening experiences often include phrases like "[there was] a feeling of absolute bliss . . . a feeling of intoxication, so great was the happiness" [and] "I was filled with a great surge of joy."

This isn't a joy *because* of something . . . it's just there, a natural condition of being.[14]

Finally, seventh, we lose our fear of death. As the poet Alfred Lord Tennyson describes:

Individuality itself seem[s] to dissolve and fade away into boundless being . . . this [isn't] a confused state but the clearest, the surest of the surest, utterly beyond words—where death [is] an almost laughable impossibility—the loss of personality (if so it were) seeming no extinction but the only true life.[15]

The reason that descriptions of awakening experiences are so uniform ends up being straightforward: the life-condition of Enlightenment is rooted neither in a widespread delusion nor in a mystic law or supernatural entity, but rather in the neurobiology of the human brain itself.[16] Enlightenment isn't a mystical phenomenon; it's a neurological phenomenon. It turns out that all the things that have been found to induce awakening experiences—from meditation[17] to seizures[18] to the use of psychedelic drugs like psilocybin[19]—induce measurably identical changes in the brain.[20]

When someone has an awakening experience, alterations occur predominantly in a neural system called the default mode network.[21] The default mode network switches on when we aren't distracted by external tasks and are instead focused inwardly—on ourselves—in some way. During awakening experiences, we see both a suppression of activity *in* key parts of the default mode network and a suppression of communication *between* these parts,[22] both to a degree that matches the intensity of the reported experience.[23] Further, in suppressing the default mode network, activity in and between *other*, more primitive brain structures seems to increase.[24] One of these structures in particular, the anterior insula, a key component of the brain's reward circuit, may in fact be the source of the transcendent joy we feel in the life-condition of Enlightenment.[25] In a case report of a patient about to undergo brain surgery for uncontrolled seizures, electrically stimulating the anterior insula produced feelings of intense bliss.[26]

Though woefully incomplete, this description of what happens in the brain during an awakening experience offers a compelling reason to believe that the life-condition of Enlightenment is a real, achievable state characterized by specific patterns of brain activity. What's more, descriptions of what it's like to be in the life-condition of Enlightenment offer compelling reasons to believe that the life-condition of Enlightenment is a supremely desirable state—in fact, the *most* desirable state—toward which we should be bending every resource we have to achieve.

Unfortunately, what this description doesn't do is make clear how such patterns of brain activity might be created consistently—how we might turn the life-condition of Enlightenment into our basic life tendency. While psychedelic drugs quickly and intensely induce awakening experiences, the experiences they induce are temporary (not to mention incapacitating). Though people do report sustained improvements in "attitudes about life" as well as "greater improvement in well-being" for up to six months after ingesting psilocybin when also pursuing some kind of spiritual practice,[27] these improvements don't seem to represent a full-blown manifestation of the life-condition of Enlightenment itself. Regrettably, meditation is also impractical as a means for attaining enlightenment. Not only do most people who have awakening experiences through meditation report that the experience is temporary as well, but also others have meditated for decades without ever having an awakening experience at all.

On the other hand, if we assume it will eventually be possible to map in exhaustive detail the patterns of brain activity induced by psilocybin, and further that those patterns are what *cause* us to experience the life-condition of Enlightenment, a fascinating possibility emerges: we might one day be able to manifest the life-condition of Enlightenment using biofeedback. A study done at Stanford University on controlling pain centers in the brain suggests this possibility.

Researchers there used functional MRI scanners to provide subjects real-time pictorial representations of activity in the area of the brain responsible for the perception of pain, the anterior cingulate cortex, which they embodied in the image of a flame. The subjects were then trained to decrease the level of activity in the anterior cingulate cortex using the same biofeedback techniques people have used to learn to reduce their heart rate. (This is done by getting continuous and immediate feedback from a heart monitor while trying out different mental images designed to slow the heart rate until by trial and error the most effective mental image is found.) When researchers then prodded the subjects with a painful stimulus and instructed them to focus on making the pictorial representation of the activity in the anterior cingulate cortex (the flame) smaller, the majority of subjects were able to reduce their pain by as much as 50 percent. In essence, by using real-time functional MRI machines, the subjects were able to learn to *consciously control a nonconscious brain process.*[28]

Theoretically, there's no reason we couldn't use this same technique to learn how to generate the brain activity patterns characteristic of an awakening experience, in essence enabling us to attain enlightenment at will. Exactly what thought process or imagery might prove most effective for achieving this—whether biofeedback training might simply make us better meditators or lead us to an even more reliable method for attaining enlightenment—remains an open question.

Unfortunately, the idea of attaining enlightenment through biofeedback remains only fanciful speculation for now. Still, the study raises the possibility that there might exist an approach that *is* more reliable than meditation—not to mention more durable than psilocybin—for manifesting the life-condition of Enlightenment. For it wasn't just one strategy that enabled subjects to lower the level of activity in the anterior cingulate cortex. It was multiple strategies, including trying to avoid paying attention to the pain, trying to perceive the pain as a neutral experience instead of a tissue-damaging experience, trying to perceive the pain as minor, and trying to control the pain.

So what might be a more reliable and durable approach to manifesting the life-condition of Enlightenment? Given the central thesis of this book, that all life-conditions are generated by beliefs, we advance the hypothesis that just as the nine worlds below the world of Enlightenment are brought into being by the core delusions, the world of Enlightenment is brought into being by a core truth. If this is true, and we can find a way to consistently stir up a belief in this core truth, we should not only be able to manifest the life-condition of Enlightenment but also be able to establish it as our basic life tendency.

# The Fundamental Cause of Enlightenment

The idea that stirring up a belief in a mere idea could induce the patterns of brain activity that generate the life-condition of Enlightenment isn't as farfetched as it might seem. We can, after all, achieve relief from depression with cognitive therapy, which studies suggest normalizes activity in areas of the brain that help us control our emotions by normalizing our beliefs.[29] In fact, the improvements in depression produced by cognitive therapy *outlast* those produced by antidepressant medication,[30] apparently because, unlike medication, normalizing our beliefs normalizes activity in control areas of the brain permanently.[31]

## The Sense of Self

So what belief might give rise to the life-condition of Enlightenment? A prime candidate—espoused by meditators all over the world—is that the self is an illusion. As Sam Harris writes in his book *Waking Up*:

> There is no discrete self or ego living like a Minotaur in the labyrinth of the brain. And the feeling that there is—the sense of being perched somewhere behind your eyes, looking out at a world that is separate from yourself—can be altered or entirely extinguished.[32]

At first glance, this claim seems absurd. We all *feel* as if we're a self—in fact, we feel as if we're the same self we've always been. We may look back into our past and remember wanting something we no longer want, like a doll house, or believing in something we no longer believe in, like Santa Claus. But as I write in *The Undefeated Mind*:

> We all carry with us a concrete yet paradoxically ineffable sense of self, a feeling of a coherent identity that we define as "us"—a core self that resides somewhere within our skulls amidst a chorus of peripheral selves all locked within the same small space. It remains this core sense of self to which we're all desperately attached and in great fear of having annihilated by death.[33]

It's this "ineffable sense of self" that makes us feel, if not identical to, at least linked to who we remember being as children. It's this sense of self that feels like the unique essence of who we are. That feels fixed. That feels like the thing that thinks our thoughts.

But this "ineffable sense of self" almost certainly *isn't* the thing that thinks our thoughts. Researchers David Oakley and Peter Halligan argue that "our thoughts [and] beliefs" are the "products of fast, efficient nonconscious systems" and that we only believe our conscious self has originated our thoughts and beliefs because we become consciously aware of our thoughts and beliefs the moment they appear.[34] Yet as Oakley and Halligan write, "We don't consciously choose our thoughts or feelings—we become aware of them." As evidence for this, they cite, among other things, studies showing that the conscious intention to move a limb occurs *after* the motor systems in the brain begin to fire.[35] Harris devotes an entire book, *Free Will*, to arguing this same point, concluding, "We do not know what we intend to do until the intention itself arises. To understand this is to realize that we are not the authors of our thoughts and actions in the way that people generally suppose."[36]

Nor, as Harris also argues, is the self fixed. We may think that who we are today represents the final evolution of who we're always going to be (what Daniel Gilbert calls the *end of history illusion*), yet we also discover every time we look back at our past selves that we *have* changed and often in profound ways.[37] The only thing about us that doesn't change is the *feeling itself* that our self doesn't change. Throughout our lives, what it *feels like* to be who we are remains the same. This sense of being unchanging then fools us into thinking that some part of us *is* unchanging. But when we look for that unchanging part we can't find it because it doesn't actually exist.

So is the self the illusion that Harris argues it is? Not quite. Though the self may not be the originator of our thoughts, and the perception that we have a fixed self *is* an illusion, the *feeling* itself of having a self—of *being* a self—is real. Researcher Antonio Damasio argues this is because the self *does* in fact exist. It's just not what we think it is. It's not an unchanging *thing* but rather a dynamic *process*.

Damasio argues that subjectivity—the feeling of having a perspective from which one goes through experience—develops only in a mind that generates a self. That self, he theorizes, is created in layers by three intertwined but ultimately separate neurological circuits that evolved one on top of the other. The first and most basic he calls the *protoself*. The protoself, he argues, produces the primordial feelings we discussed in the Introduction, feelings that "reflect the current state of the body along varied dimensions—for example, along the scale that ranges from pleasure to pain."[38] The protoself forms the foundation of selfhood. Upon it then is built the *core self*, which pulses into being every time something affects the protoself. The core self is what creates the feelings of subjectivity, of knowing, and of control. Yet it brings us awareness only of the present moment. The third, final, and most sophisticated layer of the self is the *autobiographical self*, which contains our personal biography. Unlike the core self, the autobiographical self is the self that's aware of our past and can envision our future. It's also the autobiographical self that "[deliberately seeks] well-being."[39]

How do we know these different layers of self exist? Because damage to the parts of the brain responsible for generating the uppermost layer of the self, the autobiographical self, leaves the lowermost layers of the self, the core self and the protoself, intact and observable. For example, children born with hydranen-cephaly, a condition in which the entire cerebral cortex is missing, still exhibit evidence of a protoself and a rudimentary core self. They still express emotion in their faces, smile at toys, laugh when tickled, and even "move toward an object or situation they crave—for example, crawl toward a spot on the floor where sunlight is falling and where [they] will bask in the sun and obviously draw benefit from the warmth."[40] But damage the part of the brain from which the protoself arises—the rear part of the brain stem[41]—and the result is coma, not only the absence of self, but the absence of consciousness. From this it's clear that the self is both layered and hierarchical: you can't have an autobiographical self without a core self and a protoself first, but you can have a core self and a protoself without an autobiographical self. This hierarchical organization will turn out to be crucial for generating the life-condition of Enlightenment, as we'll see.

## The Scope of the Self

So the *feeling* of being a self is real. But if the perception that we have a *fixed* self is an illusion, might grasping that truth somehow generate the life-condition of Enlightenment? Many of us already have an intuitive sense that minimizing the activity of the self—the ego—will diminish our propensity to feel negative emotions like anger, greed, and shame, which only arise when we have a sense of self to which we feel attached. So might severing that attachment entirely, or nearly entirely, be how meditation generates awakening experiences and how we might best be able to enter the life-condition of Enlightenment?

It just might. Evidence suggests, in fact, *that the autobiographical self is created by activity in the default mode network.*[42] Thus, to awaken to the illusion of the self might be exactly equivalent to suppressing the activity in the default mode network, which then sets off the cascade that produces the life-condition of Enlightenment.

Yet seeing that we don't actually have a fixed self is difficult, analogous to catching sight of our ocular blind spot. Our minds are constructed specifically to *prevent* us from seeing both, possibly explaining why meditation is so unreliable a means with which to attain enlightenment. Even Harris, who's spent decades meditating and interacting with communities of meditators, acknowledges that "most people never truly master the practice and don't reach a condition of imperturbable happiness."[43] To see that the fixed self is an illusion—to stir up a *belief* that it's an illusion in such a way that causes the life-condition of Enlightenment to manifest—just seems too hard for most of us to accomplish.

### *Flow as the Gateway to Enlightenment?*

Perhaps, though, to attain enlightenment we don't need to awaken to the illusion of the fixed self at all. Perhaps instead we only need to turn our attention away from the *feeling* of being a fixed self. The best way to not think about something, to lose our awareness of it, is, in fact, to think about something else.[44] So might deliberately focusing our attention somewhere other than on our sense of self produce the same effect as meditation and psilocybin, enabling us to lose the feeling of being a self enough to cause the life-condition of Enlightenment to manifest?

In fact, the *scope* of the self we experience diminishes, enlarges, and diminishes again in response to circumstances all the time. It moves, as Damasio writes,

> from a richly detailed and fully situated portrayal of who we are to an ever-so-
> faint hint that we do own our mind and our thoughts and our actions. That

scope constantly shifts up or down a scale as if it moved on a gliding cursor. The upward or downward shift can [even] occur *within* a given event, quite rapidly, as needed . . . For instance, when I took my eyes off the page to think [just now], and the dolphins that were swimming by caught my attention, I was not engaging the full scope of my autobiographical self because there would be no need for it . . . nor did I need an autobiographical self to cope with the thoughts that preceded my writing of the preceding sentences. However, when an interviewer sits across from me and wants to know why and how I became a neurologist and neuroscientist rather than an engineer or filmmaker, I do need to engage my autobiographical self, [and] my brain honors that need.[45]

It turns out that maintaining a sense of self is an energy-intensive process. So the idea that the brain would have a mechanism by which to diminish the scope of the self whenever possible makes good evolutionary sense.[46] Might there then be a way for us to take advantage of this regulatory mechanism? Might there be something in our environment to which we could turn our attention—or a *way* of attending to our environment in general—that diminishes the autobiographical self enough to enable us to enter the life-condition of Enlightenment?

In fact, there might be. For example, we know from studies on what psychologist Mihaly Csikszentmihalyi has famously termed *flow* that

when all a person's relevant skills are needed to cope with the challenges of a situation, that person's attention is completely absorbed by the activity. There is no excess psychic energy left over to process any information but what the activity offers. All the attention is concentrated on the relevant stimuli.

As a result, one of the most universal and distinctive features of optimal experience takes place: people become so involved in what they are doing that the activity becomes spontaneous, almost automatic; they stop being aware of themselves as separate from the actions they are performing.[47]

Many of us, in fact, have had this experience. I remember painting a portrait commission when I was home for the summer from college one year and being so engrossed in it that I would lose my sense of self for hours on end. I was deeply immersed in flow.

Indeed, studies show that when we're in a state of flow, our default mode network *is* suppressed.[48] In fact, flow may actually be one of the few things that slides Damasio's "gliding cursor" all the way down to its lowest setting, where our sense of self is so diminished we may not be fully aware we're feeling anything at all.

Unfortunately, diminishing the sense of self to such an extreme degree may actually *preclude* entry into the life-condition of Enlightenment. Though being fully immersed in the experience of painting did bring me joy, it didn't yield the *transcendent* joy that contemplating the trees outside my bedroom window had brought me the summer before or that contemplating the waves along Lake Michigan would bring me three years later. Diminishing the sense of self too much may, in fact, preclude a conscious awareness of being in any life-condition at all.

It seems that to generate the life-condition of Enlightenment, the scope of the self must diminish just enough to permit us to feel a powerful sense of unity with the world but not so much that we lose our awareness of feeling it. Unfortunately, whether because it diminishes the scope of the self too much or because it fails to do enough of something else (perhaps, for example, increase activity in the insula), focusing on an external task, no matter how engaging, doesn't appear to cause entry into the life-condition of Enlightenment. Even when experiencing a less intense degree of flow wherein the scope of the self is only somewhat diminished, the intensity of pleasure we feel, while significant, isn't transcendent. Nor are any of the other characteristics of the life-condition of Enlightenment present.

This doesn't mean, however, that turning our attention away from the self is the wrong strategy for attaining enlightenment. It only suggests that a *task* may be the wrong thing to turn our attention toward. After all, there must be *some* other way of generating the life-condition of Enlightenment. Otherwise, how could either Ash or I have done it even briefly without the help of meditation or psilocybin?

## Suppressing the Sense of Self

In the first few pages of his book *The Power of Now*, Eckhart Tolle describes the circumstances that led up to the moment he entered the life-condition of Enlightenment:

One night not long after my twenty-ninth birthday, I woke up in the early hours with a feeling of absolute dread. I had woken up with such a feeling many times before, but this time it was more intense than it had ever been. The silence of the night, the vague outlines of the furniture in the dark room, the distant noise of a passing train—everything felt so alien, so hostile, and so utterly meaningless that it created in me a deep loathing of the world. The most loathsome thing of all, however, was my own existence. What was the point in continuing to live with this burden of misery? Why carry on with this continuous struggle? I could feel that a deep longing for annihilation, for nonexistence, was now becoming much stronger than the instinctive desire to continue to live.

"I cannot live with myself any longer." This was the thought that kept repeating itself in my mind. Then suddenly I became aware of what a peculiar thought it was. "Am I one or two? If I cannot live with myself, there must be two of me: the 'I' and the 'self' that 'I' cannot live with." "Maybe," I thought, "only one of them is real."

I was so stunned by this strange realization that my mind stopped. I was fully conscious, but there were no more thoughts. Then I felt drawn into what seemed like a vortex of energy. It was a slow movement at first and then accelerated. I was gripped by an intense fear, and my body started to shake. I heard the words "resist nothing," as if spoken inside my chest. I could feel myself being sucked into a void. It felt as if the void was inside myself rather than outside. Suddenly, there was no more fear, and I let myself fall into that void. I have no recollection of what happened after that.

I was awakened by the chirping of a bird outside the window. I had never heard such a sound before. My eyes were still closed, and I saw the image of a precious diamond. Yes, if a diamond could make a sound, this is what it would be like. I opened my eyes. The first light of dawn was filtering through the curtains. Without any thought, I felt, I knew, that there is infinitely more to light than we realize. That soft luminosity filtering through the curtains was love itself. Tears came into my eyes. I got up and walked around the room. I recognized the room, and yet I knew that I had never truly seen it before. Everything was fresh and pristine, as if it had just come into existence. I picked up things, a pencil, an empty bottle, marveling at the beauty and aliveness of it all.

That day I walked around the city in utter amazement at the miracle of life on earth, as if I had just been born into the world.

For the next five months, I lived in a state of uninterrupted deep peace and bliss.[49]

What's most remarkable about this description is how commonly it's reported.[50] As was the case with Tolle, what's typically detailed is some degree of suffering, which then builds for a varying period of time, until finally there comes a sudden capitulation—a renunciation not of suffering *but of the effort to avoid feeling it.* This was what actually happened to both Ash and me. It wasn't the experience of suffering that we found exhausting but the work required to fight it. It was only at the moment we gave up trying that our awakening experiences began.

Could an abrupt surrender to suffering diminish the sense of self enough to induce an awakening experience? There might actually exist a mechanism by which it could. Acceptance of suffering is associated with a reduction in one of the signature signs of depression, depressive rumination,[51] which refers to the tendency to focus compulsively on the causes and consequences of one's depression. Depressive rumination, in turn, is thought by some researchers to be caused by an abnormal degree of connectivity between the prefrontal cortex and the default mode network.[52] So if we were to imagine that acceptance of suffering actually *causes* a reduction in depressive rumination—which, it's important to note, hasn't been proven—it's reasonable to assume it might do so by suppressing activity in and connections to the default mode network. And if an abrupt surrender to suffering has the power to suppress the default mode network, perhaps it also has the power to generate awakening experiences.

On the other hand, many awakening experiences—such as my first one— *aren't* preceded by suffering. In fact, it may not have been a surrender to suffering that caused Tolle to have his awakening experience either. It wasn't, after all, just the experience of suffering that he wanted to escape. "I cannot live with myself any longer," he repeated over and over. I, too, remember immediately prior to my second awakening experience feeling a strong sense of self-contempt. I was sick of suffering and sick of myself for feeling it. It wasn't just my suffering from which I wanted to be freed. It was from myself. From my sense of *being* a self.

Perhaps, then, to enter the life-condition of Enlightenment we don't need to awaken to the illusion of the self so much as take some kind of action to *reject* the self. Indeed, research suggests that prayer carried out with an intent to surrender oneself to a higher power also suppresses the default mode network.[53] Interestingly, unlike the surrender to suffering, the surrender of oneself *also seems to increase activity in the insula*.[54]

It may not be the thing we surrender to, however, that causes these effects so much as the act of surrender itself. I remember immediately prior to both of my awakening experiences explicitly trying to connect with and surrender to something other than a higher power: the beauty of nature as it spread out before me.

According to one survey, approximately 20 percent of awakening experiences appear to be triggered by an interaction with nature.[55] Might there be something about nature that grants it the power to suppress the default mode network in a way that mimics both the effects of psilocybin and meditation to produce the life-condition of Enlightenment?

Indeed, there just might be. Nature, it turns out, is uniquely capable of inducing awe.

### The Nature of Awe

Awe is defined as "a feeling of wonder and amazement at being in the presence of something vast that transcends one's current understanding."[56] Though no functional MRI studies have yet been done to show that awe suppresses the default mode network, studies do show that the feeling of awe significantly diminishes the scope of the self and induces joy.[57] Could awe then be another path to the life-condition of Enlightenment?

It certainly seemed to be so for me. In attempting to surrender myself to the beauty of nature as it spread out before me, I found myself abruptly looking at that beauty in a particular way—perceiving something *about* that beauty—that abruptly induced in me a feeling of awe. That feeling of awe then seemed to be what transported me into the life-condition of Enlightenment. Given that awe inclines us toward altruism,[58] enhances the sense that we're part of something larger than ourselves,[59] and makes us feel more connected to other people[60]—all of which are characteristics of the life-condition of Enlightenment—it could be argued that the life-condition of Enlightenment *is* awe. In other words, awe isn't just an alternative path to enlightenment. It's a core part of the *experience* of enlightenment.

So what did I see in the trees outside my window and in the waves lapping at the shores of Lake Michigan that induced awe? What was different about those two particular moments from the literally thousands upon thousands of other moments during which I looked at scenes of nature both before and since and felt nothing?

The answer is that in those two moments I wasn't seeing nature as merely beautiful. I was seeing it as *sublime*. In her book, *Plato at the Googleplex*, philosopher Rebecca Newberger Goldstein writes that one doctrine "to which Plato seems to have held firm through all the philosophical twists and turns with which he presents us is the intertwining of truth, beauty, and goodness. Call it the Sublime Braid."[61] The notion here is that the universe is constructed with the inherent elegance, perfection, and inevitability of a mathematical truth, and that this sublime order is something we're able to perceive as beautiful and good (by which is meant not morally good but valuable).

While different writers, from Longinus to Edmund Burke to Immanuel Kant, have approached the subject of the sublime from different perspectives, most have agreed that it revolves principally around the notion of vastness. This is likely why large vistas tend to feel sublime to us: such views remind us that the full scope of existence is literally beyond the ability of the human mind to contain. We simply have no personal experience with which to imagine it. This is perhaps also why trying to imagine it has the effect of making us feel small. And indeed, when subjects viewing pictures of nature report them as sublime, functional MRI scanners show a suppression of the default mode network—something they don't show when subjects report such natural views as merely beautiful.[62]

Kant especially understood the important point that "sublimity is not contained in anything in nature, but only in our mind."[63] At certain times, triggered by certain external causes, our mind *creates* the perception that the world is sublime. It's this perception then—that the world is sublimely vast, beautiful, and good beyond our ability to fully imagine—that induces awe.

The idea that perceiving the universe as sublime can induce awe and that awe is the true gateway to enlightenment goes at least as far back as Plato. As Goldstein points out:

> Socrates' speech in the Symposium is urging us on in the direction of an impersonal vision, promising us that, in losing our personal attachments, even our attachment to our own self, we will achieve a knowledge that will make us over in its light—the perfect proportions of [the Sublime Braid] assimilated into our knowing minds.[64]

So here at last, we believe, is the core truth of the life-condition of Enlightenment: *the entire universe and everything in it is sublime*. It's the stirring up of this belief—the active perception of our surroundings as sublime—that induces the feeling of awe and generates the life-condition of Enlightenment. As Harris writes:

> Is there a form of happiness beyond the mere repetition of pleasure and avoidance of pain? Is there a happiness that does not depend upon having one's favorite foods available, or friends and loved ones within arm's reach, or good book to read, or something to look forward to on the weekend? Is it possible to be happy before anything happens, before one's desires are gratified, in spite of life's difficulties, in the very midst of physical pain, old age, disease, and death?[65]

The answer, we would argue, is a resounding yes. And what makes that answer a yes is that the joy that emanates from the life-condition of Enlightenment doesn't come from having a particular attachment. Rather, it comes from perceiving the world in a particular way. And because that perception is available to us at every moment, the happiness that comes from the world of Enlightenment is truly absolute. Once we gain this perspective, nothing—absolutely nothing—can take it away from us.

## Making Enlightenment Our Basic Life Tendency

Unfortunately, though we may understand intellectually that the universe is sublime, stirring up that belief intensely enough to generate a feeling of awe, which then causes us to enter the life-condition of Enlightenment, is far from easy. It's entirely possible, and even likely, that some people have an easier time than others perceiving the universe as sublime because of the way they were born, much in the same way some people have an easier time than others dunking a basketball. But even people who are genetically gifted in this way may struggle to feel awe consistently.

On the other hand, we're no less capable of feeling awe than we are of feeling any other emotion. We only need to find the right external cause, or trigger. Indeed, in theory, generating enough awe to enter the life-condition of Enlightenment shouldn't be any harder than summoning up enough sadness to cry on command.

Unfortunately, there doesn't yet exist an evidence-based approach—a recipe with clearly ordered steps—to guide us. We can, however, speculate about how to purposely generate the feeling of awe based on research studies that have been done thus far. While sprawling natural vistas should probably be the first place we look for a reliable trigger of awe, other triggers are also available. Encountering people who "display virtuosity, magnanimity, or stature," viewing great art, listening to moving music, and encountering perspective-shifting ideas have all been found to trigger awe.[66] Even watching videos of colored droplets colliding in slow motion has been found to trigger it.[67] We might also induce awe by removing our thoughts from our day-to-day activities and contemplating the full span of our life as if from a great distance, purposely conceiving of it as a single event rather than as a series of days, months, and years. This can have a perspective-rocking effect, making our life seem far smaller than it does when we're looking at it up close and the days stretching in front of us appear to taper indefinitely into the future.

We need to keep in mind, however, that we can't force ourselves to feel awe any more than we can force ourselves to feel sad. We have to *discover* what triggers us to feel awe. Some of us, for example, may only need to look at a high-resolution picture of the earth to feel awe, while others may actually need to be looking down at the earth itself from orbit. Interestingly, as Michael Pollan writes in his book *How to Change Your Mind*:

The dozen or so Apollo astronauts who have escaped Earth's orbit and traveled to the moon . . . [have] reported that the experience changed them in profound and enduring ways. The sight of that "pale blue dot" hanging in the infinite black void of space erased the national borders on our maps and rendered Earth small, vulnerable, exceptional, and precious.

Edgar Mitchell, returning from the moon on Apollo 14, had what he has described as a mystical experience, specifically *savikalpa samadhi*, in which the ego vanishes when confronted with the immensity of the universe during the course of a meditation on an object—in this case, planet Earth.

"The biggest joy was on the way home," he recalled. "In my cockpit window, every two minutes: the earth, the moon, the sun, and the whole panorama of the heavens. That was a powerful, overwhelming experience.

"And suddenly I realized that the molecules of my body, and the molecules of my spacecraft, the molecules in the body of my partners, were prototyped, manufactured in some ancient generation of stars. [I felt] an overwhelming sense of oneness, of connectedness . . . And it was accompanied by an ecstasy, a sense of 'Oh my God, wow, yes'—an insight, an epiphany."[68]

The ultimate goal, however, is to learn to see the sublime in *everything*. It may require a certain quieting of the autobiographical self, a deliberate turning away from its worries and doubts and attempts at problem solving, and a focus on viewing everything as if seeing it for the first time, like a child. To do this we may need to focus back in on details in our environment that don't typically catch our attention: the texture of the clouds overhead, the dappling of sunlight on water, the fluttering of leaves in the wind, the sound of waves lapping against a shore, the smoothness of porcelain, the grain pattern in a hardwood floor. But if we purposefully and consistently seek to be astonished by the world, we may eventually learn to do so out of habit. Each successive experience of awe may then teach us how to feel awe more easily. Like an actor learning to summon up emotion on command, we may become proficient at stirring up the belief that the cosmos is sublime intensely enough to induce awe and enter into the life-condition of Enlightenment simply with consistent practice.

# Is the Core Truth Actually True?

Is the universe *objectively* sublime? In the sense that it *is* both vast beyond our ability to imagine and more perfectly ordered than we could ever make it ourselves, yes. The reason the word *buddha*, a Sanskrit term meaning "awakened one," is used to describe those who've attained enlightenment is because in the life-condition of Enlightenment we do, to a certain extent, perceive reality more accurately than we do when we're in any of the other nine worlds.

But that doesn't mean all the ideas that emerge from the life-condition of Enlightenment are equally valid. As Harris writes, "I believe we should be very slow to draw conclusions about the nature of the cosmos on the basis of inner experiences—no matter how profound they may seem."[69] While knowledge about how to be happy—wisdom—is indeed maximized when the feeling of being a self is minimized, knowledge about the workings of the cosmos is not.

Certainly, the idea that we're deeply embedded in and intertwined with our surroundings is a demonstrable fact. So is the idea that the feeling of being a fixed self is an illusion. But other feelings that are a part of the awakening experience and that have been codified through the millennia into religious cosmology—specifically Buddhist cosmology—remain highly suspect. For example, the notion that life is eternal, that we continually reincarnate as different people, as well as the notion of karmic retribution, that whatever we do today will be returned to us in some form one day in the future, defy our current understanding of the laws of biology and physics and almost certainly aren't real. The notion of reincarnation isn't even logical: if there's no fixed self that represents the unchanging core of our being, no unique psychic fingerprint, so to speak, that persists from even one *moment* to the next, what part of us could possibly persist from one *life* to the next? And even if such a thing *were* possible, in what way would we feel like—would we *be*—our past self without being able to remember that self as it once was?

Still, many people come away from awakening experiences absolutely convinced that ideas like these are true. This may be because they also come away with a "feeling of profound clarity that some deeper insight or truth or wisdom has been reached,"[70] something Dostoevsky, who famously suffered from temporal lobe seizures, described as the feeling "of [having achieved an] under-standing and awareness of the supreme principle of life."[71]

Yet the sense of having learned this "supreme principle" likely owes more to our neurology than to an accurate perception of the truth. One researcher, Michael Winkelman, hypothesizes that we may be unable to put our sense of this supreme principle into words because connections to the part of the brain involved in generating speech, Broca's area, are reduced during awakening experiences.[72] Further, researchers Fabienne Picard and Florian Kurth hypothesize that the insula, a part of the brain that also appears to be involved in judging the mismatch between our predictions about reality and reality itself, becomes less able to generate uncertainty and ambiguity when overstimulated by awakening experiences. This leads, they think, not just to the feeling of bliss as mentioned earlier, but also to a powerful feeling of certainty.[73] This then may explain the feeling that some kind of ultimate truth has been revealed, something the psychologist William James dubbed the *noetic* sense. This noetic sense then may be what gave rise to the Buddhist concept of *kyochi-myogo*, the idea that objective reality and the Buddha's wisdom are fused—in essence, that the way the Buddha saw reality is the way reality is.

But no matter how certain the Buddha may have felt that his enlightened perception of reality was accurate, he was still only a human being using a human brain, an apparatus that's since been proven not only to err frequently in its assessment of reality but also to be *systematically* prejudiced in the way it assesses. It turns out, as we alluded to in Chapter 8, that the number of cognitive biases discovered to affect our thinking amounts to no fewer than two hundred.[74]

Even most modern ideas about reality, when subjected to rigorous scientific testing, turn out to be wrong. So it's hard to imagine that subjective, intuitive insights, no matter how enlightened, could match the power of the scientific method, plodding and imperfect as it is, for verifying truths about the nature of the cosmos.[75] Though it's equally hard to imagine that anyone could know better how to maximize human flourishing and happiness than a person unbound by his small-minded ego, the Buddha never had even the tiniest inkling, for example, that time slows down for a body as it approaches the speed of light or that space-time is curved.

Without knowledge of the scientific method prompting him to question his noetic sense of certainty, the Buddha had no way of knowing, no reason even to imagine, that his new perception of the cosmos might be flawed. As a result, Buddhism, flowing directly from the Buddha's enlightenment, commingles verifiable truths about what it takes to be indestructibly happy with ideas about cosmology that are no more accurate than the principles of astrology. That the Buddha's view of cosmology was flawed, however, doesn't make his attaining enlightenment any less remarkable or the insights he gained into the workings of his own mind and how to become indestructibly happy any less valid. It does mean, however, that not every feeling we have about external reality when in the life-condition of Enlightenment will be true. As Harris concludes:

> It is quite possible to lose one's sense of being a separate self and to experience a kind of boundless, open awareness—to feel, in other words, at one with the cosmos. This says a lot about the possibilities of human consciousness, but it says nothing about the universe at large.[76]

# What Is It Like to Be Enlightened?

So the reason to spend our entire lives trying to enter the life-condition of Enlightenment isn't because doing so will awaken us to all fundamental truths about reality. It's because doing so will change the way we perceive our relationship to the world, and in doing so bring us the experience of absolute happiness.

If relative happiness is defined as the joy we feel when we think about our attachments, absolute happiness is defined as the joy we feel when we lose the feeling of being a self. Where relative happiness requires us to *have* something, absolute happiness requires us only to *see* something.

Yet just being able to enter the life-condition of Enlightenment doesn't by any means guarantee we'll be able to remain there. As with any life-condition, we'll only remain in the world of Enlightenment as long as the belief that creates it—in this case, the belief that the universe is sublime—remains stirred up.

## *Enlightenment and Suffering*

Though we don't suffer when we're deep in the life-condition of Enlighten-ment—the feeling of joy is just too strong—we certainly can and do feel pain. We can also feel frustrated, hurt, stressed, sad, and more. Nothing about being in the life-condition of Enlightenment prevents us from feeling multiple emo-tions at once. *Negative* emotions, however, are muted—colored by the feeling of transcendent joy—and transformed into experiences that can even be enjoyed.

The things that *trigger* negative emotions when we're in the life-condition of Enlightenment, on the other hand, are different from the things that trigger them when we're in any of the other nine worlds. For one thing, in the life-condition of Enlightenment our sense of self is greatly diminished, so emotions typically triggered by the ego, like shame, pride, greed, envy, and jealousy, tend not to be triggered at all. Other negative emotions like anger, sadness, and fear that might have been triggered by the ego are instead triggered by our concern for others. For example, when in the life-condition of Enlightenment, instead of becoming angry in response to feeling shame, we become angry in response to injustice. Instead of obsessing over money, power, or fame, we obsess about making a contribution to society. When we're in the life-condition of Enlight-enment, even our so-called negative emotions function in a positive way.

Not only that, but the life-condition of Enlightenment also prevents our positive emotions from functioning in a negative way. For example, only when we're in the life-condition of Enlightenment can we feel a desire for something without becoming consumed by greed in the world of Hunger. Or feel basic pleasure without becoming addicted to it in the world of Animality. Or feel the thrill of victory without feeling superior to others in the world of Anger. Or feel relief from the end of pain without becoming apathetic in the world of Tranquility. Or think about a possession without becoming overly attached to it in the world of Rapture. Or accomplish something meaningful without ignor-ing other important aspects of our lives in the world of Learning. Or improve ourselves without ceasing to care about the harm we may do to others in the world of Realization. Or create value for others without sacrificing ourselves in the world of Compassion. Because only when we enter the life-condition of

Enlightenment—even if only in the most superficial way—do we feel all those things without believing we *need* to feel them to be happy.

Indeed, when we're in the life-condition of Enlightenment, there's no need to free ourselves from the core delusions at all. Simply put, the more deeply we enter into the life-condition of Enlightenment, the harder it becomes for external causes to stir up the core delusions. And when we're fully immersed in the life-condition of Enlightenment and find ourselves bathing in transcendent joy, the core delusions can't be stirred up at all. But this only makes sense: why would we believe we need *any* attachment to be happy when we're already feeling a transcendent happiness that can't be destroyed?

Not that when we're in the life-condition of Enlightenment we *reject* attachment. Far from it. Money, shelter, friends, food, health, comfort, meaning, and more—all continue to matter to us a great deal. We're merely able to let our attachments go more easily when we must. This is even the case for the thing to which we feel the most attached, our own life.

## Overcoming the Fear of Death

In *The Undefeated Mind*, I describe the fear of death that rose up to confront me after suffering through a series of near-fatal medical mishaps:

> The anxiety that began to envelop me at that point was of an entirely different order than I'd ever experienced. It began to interfere with my ability to function, which made plain to me that what my brush with death—twice—had taken from me was *my ability to believe I would never die*. Knowing *intellectually* that death awaits us is quite clearly a different thing from *believing* it, much in the same way knowing intellectually gravity will make you fall is a different experience from actually swooning at the edge of a parapet at the top of a tall building. Ultimately, being ill brought me to the realization, contrary to what I'd always believed in my heart, that there was nothing special about me at all. Like everyone else, I was only a piece of meat that would eventually spoil.
>
> I felt like one of my long-time patients, Rita, who for as long as I'd known her had been consumed by a fear of death so great she'd become like a child in her need for constant reassurance that she would be all right. For Rita, every sore throat was cancer, every bout of chest pain was a heart attack, and an inability to

fall asleep meant she was dying. She'd been on almost every antidepressant and anti-anxiety medication known but continued to experience a fear so intense that at one point she became unable to leave her home. Her anxiety, in short, made her inconsolable and her life a joyless nightmare.

Which I now understood in a way I hadn't before. Now, like her, my fear of death would rise up at the smallest provocation: whether I'd feel a minor twinge in my chest, develop a rash on my arms, or my hand would shake, I would become paralyzed with fear. Even though I recognized intellectually that my reactions were overblown, every new symptom I felt caused my doctor's brain to leap to horrifying conclusions simply because I now knew in a way I hadn't before that bad things could actually happen to me.[77]

Since that time, mercifully, my fear of death has ceased to be so consistently stirred up. Yet when people struggling with their own fear of death have asked me how I was able to reduce mine, my answer has been that I haven't. I've just learned how to ignore it. The way I do that, I tell them, is by engaging so intensely in life that I literally *forget* about death. I keep myself so busy, so interested in what I'm doing, that the fact that one day I'm going to die almost never even enters my mind.

I've always thought this was a good solution. But recent evidence suggests that the life-condition of Enlightenment might offer an even better one. A study by Roland Griffiths showed that when psilocybin is given to terminally ill cancer patients, it largely diminishes—and in some cases even eliminates—the fear of death altogether. This effect appears to persist for up to six months or longer.[78] The study also suggested that this reduction in the fear of death is due specifically to the awakening experience itself. "Under the influence of hallucinogens," a researcher who conducted a similar study writes, "individuals transcend their primary identification with their bodies and experience ego-free states before the time of their actual physical demise, and return with a new perspective and profound acceptance."

There are several possibilities for why this "new perspective and profound acceptance" of death might develop after we've had an awakening experience. It may come from the feeling that death itself is illusory, as some people have reported coming to believe after having an awakening experience. It may come from being filled with such a transcendent joy that our fear of not being is simply blotted out, much in the same way the light of the stars is blotted out by the sun. It may come from realizing that the fixed self is an illusion, which then causes us to lose our sense of attachment to it—to our very life—and to begin identifying more with what feels like the larger life of the cosmos. It may come because in losing the feeling of being a self we "rehearse" our death in a way that makes death feel less frightening. Or it may come because awakening experiences simply shut down our fear response in the same way they shut down our feeling of being a self.

I remember during my first awakening experience feeling a strong sense of acceptance of my mortality as well. Yet that experience wasn't powerful enough to leave me permanently unafraid of death. Having had it did nothing, for example, to prevent the terror of death from rising up to grip me nearly two decades later when I got sick and thought I might actually be about to die.

Yet my awakening experiences have left me with the hope that I *can* solve the problem of death, that I can permanently free myself from the fear of it. Though many people come to believe in some kind of an afterlife after having an awakening experience, it's my strong sense that a newfound belief in an afterlife isn't the mechanism by which the life-condition of Enlightenment eliminates the fear of death. My own awakening experiences didn't for one moment lead me to believe that my life would continue after my death, but during them my fear of death completely abated. Others have reported a similar abatement of their fear of death after their awakening experiences without developing a belief in an afterlife either.[79] And if having an awakening experience can free us from our fear of death without requiring us to believe something for which there's no objective proof, I can think of no better reason to make pursuing the life-condition of Enlightenment our life's most pressing goal.

## World Peace

Except for one. To see that the world and everything in it is sublimely beautiful—to *feel* it and understand it with our life—isn't just to feel joy. It's also to feel love. As Goldstein writes, "The appropriate reaction to the beauty of the Sublime Braid can only be love."[80]

Sadly, though, to say that love is all that matters is more likely to elicit skeptical eye rolls than astonished agreement from anyone who isn't themselves inhabiting the life-condition of Enlightenment. But this makes the platitude no less true. As Pollan writes:

> The mystical journey seems to offer a graduate education in the obvious. Yet people come out of the experience understanding these platitudes in a new way; what was merely known is now felt, takes on the authority of a deeply rooted conviction. And, more often than not, that conviction concerns the supreme importance of love.[81]

If to live in the world of Compassion is to feel love for other people, to live in the world of Enlightenment is to feel love for *everything*. The kind of love we feel for the world when we're in the life-condition of Enlightenment isn't a romantic love, of course, but a selfless love best defined, as Armin Zadeh writes in his book *The Forgotten Art of Love* "as the urge and continuous effort for another person's happiness and well-being."[82] While we often have to "consciously . . . prioritize love over competing impulses"[83] to remain loving when we're in any of the other nine worlds, in the world of Enlightenment love isn't just effortless—it's inescapable. In this state, the love we have for the world and for other people admits no room for exclusion, condemnation, or demonization. It's the closest thing to divine love a human being can feel. It's a love that makes forgiveness of even the most heinous sinner not just possible but unavoidable.

This doesn't mean, however, in the life-condition of Enlightenment we accept the slings and arrows of outrageous fortune—or attacks on ourselves or others—with a blissful smile and a transcendent shrug. It's impossible to love the world with the fierceness of a buddha and stand by passively in the face of injustice or suffering. Rather, in diminishing the degree of attachment we feel to our self, we gain access to wisdom that tells us when we *should* fight, and when we should accept what can't be changed.

Because when we're in the life-condition of Enlightenment, what we care about more than anything else—more than even our own life—is figuring out how to help everyone else enter the world of Enlightenment, too. In fact, the only thing that matters to us more than the happiness of other individuals is the happiness of all humanity. When we're in the life-condition of Enlightenment, we love the world so much we'll do anything to save it.

For the world does indeed need saving. Though there's good evidence that people are safer, richer, healthier, freer, better educated, more literate, smarter, and even happier than at any other time in human history,[84] there still exists an almost overwhelming number of problems that we need to solve: climate change, political corruption, pandemics, terrorism, and more. Perhaps, though, no problem is more important to solve than the problem posed by the core delusions themselves. It's our lack of wisdom, our insistence on pursuing happiness in the most foolish of ways that gives rise to, among other things, every form of human conflict that exists, from fist fights between siblings to shouting matches between spouses to wars between countries.

When we're in the life-condition of Enlightenment, we love the world and everything and everyone in it so much that we find ourselves compelled to try to solve the problem of human conflict, the problem of human suffering, in the most fundamental way. We feel compelled, in other words, to help all people become indestructibly happy. For not only would that solve the problem of human suffering, it would also result in the greatest accomplishment of all: world peace.

Many argue that human nature itself precludes the possibility of world peace, that even the *idea* of world peace is a childish fantasy. Certainly, the human race will never lose its capacity to be led astray by the core delusions in its collective pursuit of happiness and will therefore always create conflict and misery for itself. But this only explains why the path to world peace won't ever be found in the passing of more laws or in diplomacy: we simply can't legislate or negotiate wisdom. But if wisdom *is* the key to happiness, world peace might yet be found in the life-condition of Enlightenment.

Because just imagine what the world would be like if enough people felt that the single most important thing they could do—that their most urgent personal need—was to help everyone around them achieve the same kind of happiness they themselves had found in the life-condition of Enlightenment.

World peace would indeed be within reach.

## Key Points

- Enlightenment is defined as the life-condition of awe.

- The life-condition of Enlightenment represents a real, attainable life state with defined neurological correlates.

- In the life-condition of Enlightenment we feel a sense of unity with our surroundings, lose our sense of self while gaining a sense of being a larger, truer self, develop a profound feeling of compassion and love for others, feel that we've awakened to a great truth that's beyond our ability to express in words, feel a transcendent sense of joy, and lose our fear of death.

- We enter the life-condition of Enlightenment by finding a way to reduce the sense of being a self.

- We can perhaps best reduce the sense of being a self by generating a feeling of awe.

- We generate the feeling of awe by learning to see the world as sublime.

- The core truth of the world of Enlightenment is that the universe and everything in it is sublime.

## HELL

**CORE DELUSION**
We're powerless to end our suffering.

*Characterized by...*
A state of despondency in which negativity and pessimism color all our experiences

## HUNGER

**CORE DELUSION**
To be happy we need to get what we want.

*Characterized by...*
A persistent feeling of yearning, restlessness, and emptiness

## ANIMALITY

**CORE DELUSION**
Happiness and pleasure are one and the same.

*Characterized by...*
An obsession with basic pleasure, often leading to impulsive and self-destructive behavior

## ANGER

**CORE DELUSION**
To be happy we need to be better than everyone else.

*Characterized by...*
An obsessive concern with how others view us, making us contemptuous, competitive, and jealous toward everyone

## TRANQUILITY

**CORE DELUSION**
To be happy we need to avoid pain.

*Characterized by...*
An excessive need to maintain the status quo, often leading to a reluctance to challenge even unhealthy and adverse circumstances

## RAPTURE

**CORE DELUSION**
Our happiness is dependent on specifi attachments.

*Characterized by...*
A state of joy, energy, and confidence in ou ability to achieve our goals and overcome obstacles

**HELL**
LIFE-CONDITION OF
**SUFFERING**

**HUNGER**
LIFE-CONDITION OF
**DESIRE**

**ANIMALITY**
LIFE-CONDITION OF
**INSTINCT**

**ANGER**
LIFE-CONDITION OF
**EGO**

**TRANQUILITY**
LIFE-CONDITION OF
**SERENITY**

**RAPTURE**
LIFE-CONDITION O
**JOY**

# LOWER WORLDS
Pursuit of Hedonic Happiness

# HIGHER WORLDS
## Pursuit of Eudemonic Happiness

**ABSOLUTE HAPPINESS**

**ENLIGHTENMENT**

LIFE-CONDITION OF
**AWE**

**COMPASSION**

LIFE-CONDITION OF
**LOVE**

**REALIZATION**

LIFE-CONDITION OF
**SELF-IMPROVEMENT**

**LEARNING**

LIFE-CONDITION OF
**MASTERY**

*ENLIGHTENMENT*

**CORE TRUTH**
**The universe**
**and everything in**
**it is sublime.**

*Characterized by...*
A sense of unity with our
surroundings and
transcendent joy

*COMPASSION*

**CORE DELUSION**
**To be happy we need to**
**make other people**
**happy.**

*Characterized by...*
An altruistic dedication
to creating value for
other people

*REALIZATION*

**CORE DELUSION**
**To be happy we need**
**to grow.**

*Characterized by...*
An obsession with
self-examination and
personal development

*LEARNING*

**CORE DELUSION**
**To be happy we need**
**to accomplish or**
**experience something**
**meaningful.**

*Characterized by...*
A relentless drive to
learn and create
meaning

THE **TEN**
core beliefs
*of* happiness

# AFTERWORD

Few things have as much power to affect the course of our lives as our beliefs about what we need to be happy. For those are the beliefs, we hope we've convinced you, that determine how happy we're able to be.

Those beliefs do this, we hope we've also convinced you, by giving rise to the Ten Worlds. From Hell to Enlightenment, which of the Ten Worlds—which life-condition—we inhabit determines not only the way we experience the events of our lives but also the level of happiness those events cause us to experience.

To figure out which of the Ten Worlds represents your basic life tendency, we invite you to consider which of the stories we've told in this book most resembles your own. Though you may have found some of them extreme, we hope you'll find at least one of them familiar.

And if you do find one of them familiar, we'd invite you to ask yourself if the core delusion that created it is a belief you often find stirred up in yourself. Do you often find yourself feeling, for example, that the most basic thing you need to be happy is to have all your desires fulfilled? Or to experience basic pleasure? Or to feel superior to everyone around you? Or to gain freedom from pain? Or to create something of value? Or to develop your potential? Or to help others become happy? Even if what you believe you need to be happy isn't one of the core delusions we've identified, to identify what you do believe you need to be happy represents the first step in understanding how to establish a happiness that lasts.

For by asking himself questions like these, Ash was able to recognize that he comes from the world of Tranquility, which then helped free him from the belief that he risks his happiness with every decision he makes. By asking myself questions like these, I was able to recognize that I come from the world of Learning, which helped me to understand why I'm so obsessed with creating important works. (It also showed me how often I come from the world of Anger, which made me aware of my need to feel superior to others and in so doing saved my marriage.)

Being able to look at your beliefs with a skeptical eye positions you to understand more objectively how they serve you—and how they don't. Not to say that things to which you're attached won't make you happy. And not that the happiness your attachments bring—relative happiness—is a happiness you don't want.

But if you're willing to entertain the notion that your beliefs about what you need to be happy will only ever bring you relative happiness, perhaps you might be willing to aim at a different kind of happiness altogether. Perhaps you might be willing to entertain the notion that it's your attachment to your sense of self that's narrowed the range of happiness you're able to feel. Perhaps you might also consider that by casting that sense of self aside, by being willing to feel small, you might paradoxically find yourself feeling bigger than you ever have before.

Because there really does exist a path to happiness that's indestructible. And if you're willing to make the effort to take it, to look for the sublime beauty in the world that surrounds you each and every minute, to breathe it in and surrender yourself to it, then you might just find yourself feeling a happiness you've never known. A happiness not dependent on attachment. A happiness that can't be destroyed by anything. A happiness that's absolute.

# Introduction

1. Alex Lickerman, *The Undefeated Mind* (Deerfield Beach: Health Communications, Inc., 2012), 14.

2. Antonio Damasio, *Self Comes to Mind* (New York: Pantheon Books, 2010), 57–59.

3. Daniel Gilbert, *Stumbling on Happiness* (New York, NY: Vintage Books, 2006), 38.

4. Steffen Nestler, "Belief Perseverance: The Role of Accessible Content and Accessibility Experiences," *Social Psychology* 41 (2010): 35–41.

5. Christine Wilson-Mendenhall, Lisa Feldman Barrett, and Lawrence Barsalou, "Neural Evidence that Human Emotions Share Core Affective Properties," *Psychological Science* 24 (2013): 947–956.

6. Antonio Damasio, *Self Comes to Mind* (New York: Pantheon Books, 2010), 21.

7. James Russell, "Core Affect and the Psychological Construction of Emotion," *Psychological Review* 110 (2003): 145–172; Antonio Damasio, *Self Comes to Mind* (New York: Pantheon Books, 2010), 21–22; Stefan Koelsch et al., "The Quartet Theory of Human Emotions: An Integrative and Neurofunctional Model," *Physics of Life Reviews* 13 (2015): 1–27.

8. George Loewenstein, "Hot-Cold Empathy Gaps and Medical Decision Making," *Health Psychology* 24 (2005): S49–S56; Judith Beck, *Cognitive Therapy: Basics and Beyond* (New York, NY: The Guilford Press, 1995), 1–2.

9. Christine Wilson-Mendenhall, Lisa Feldman Barrett, and Lawrence Barsalou, "Neural Evidence that Human Emotions Share Core Affective Properties," *Psychological Science* 24 (2013): 947–956.

10. Peter Kuppens, Dominique Champagne, and Francis Tuerlinckx, "The Dynamic Interplay Between Appraisal and Core Affect in Daily Life," *Frontiers in Psychology* 3 (2012): Article 380.

11. R. Barker Bausell et al., "Is Acupuncture Analgesia an Expectancy Effect? Preliminary Evidence Based on Participants' Perceived Assignments in Two Placebo-Controlled Trials," *Evaluation & the Health Professions* 28 (2005): 9–26.

12. Raul de la Fuente-Fernandez et al., "Expectation and Dopamine Release: Mechanism of the Placebo Effect in Parkinson's Disease," *Science* 293 (2001): 1164–1166.

13. Lewis Cohen, "A Current Perspective of Pseudocyesis," *The American Journal of Psychiatry* 139 (1982): 1140–1144.

14. Christine Scher, Rick Ingram, and Zindel Segal, "Cognitive Reactivity and Vulnerability: Empirical Evaluation of Construct Activation and Cognitive Diatheses in Unipolar Depression," *Clinical Psychological Review* 25 (2005): 487–510.

15. Paul Salkovskis et al., "Responsibility Attitudes and Interpretations are Characteristic of Obsessive Compulsive Disorder," *Behaviour Research and Therapy* 38 (2000): 347–372.

16. Stefan Koelsch et al., "The Quartet Theory of Human Emotions: An Integrative and Neurofunctional Model," *Physics of Life Reviews* 13 (2015): 1–27.

17. Édouard Claparède, "Recognition et Moïté," *Archives of Psychology* 11 (1911): 79–90.

18. Justin Feinstein, Melissa Duff, and Daniel Tranel, "Sustained Experience of Emotion After Loss of Memory in Patients with Amnesia," *Proceedings of the National Academy of Sciences of the United States of America* 107 (2010): 7674–7679.

19. Eugenie Georgaca, "Factualization and Plausibility in Delusional Discourse," *Philosophy, Psychiatry, & Psychology* 11 (2004): 13–23.

20. Jamie Leeser and William O'Donohue, "What is a Delusion? Epistemological Dimensions," *Journal of Abnormal Psychology* 108 (1999): 687–694.

21. Corey Guenther and Mark Alicke, "Self-Enhancement and Belief Perseverance," *Journal of Experimental Social Psychology* 44 (2008): 706–712.

22. Raymond Nickerson, "Confirmation Bias: A Ubiquitous Phenomenon in Many Guises," *Review of General Psychology* 2 (1998): 175–220.

23. Matthew Tyler Boden and Howard Berenbaum, "The Bidirectional Relations Between Affect and Belief," *Review of General Psychology* 14 (2010): 227–239; Raymond Nickerson, "Confirmation Bias: A Ubiquitous Phenomenon in Many Guises," *Review of General Psychology* 2 (1998): 175–220.

24. Craig Anderson, Mark Lepper, and Lee Ross, "Perseverance of Social Theories: The Role of Explanation in the Persistence of Discredited Information," *Journal of Personality and Social Psychology* 39 (1980): 1037–1049.

25. Steffen Nestler, "Belief Perseverance: The Role of Accessible Content and Accessibility Experiences," *Social Psychology* 41 (2010): 35–41.

26. Christine Scher, Rick Ingram, and Zindel Segal, "Cognitive Reactivity and Vulnerability: Empirical Evaluation of Construct Activation and Cognitive Diatheses in Unipolar Depression," *Clinical Psychological Review* 25 (2005): 487–510.

27. Amy Wenzel (Modification of Core Beliefs in Cognitive Therapy), *Standard and Innovative Strategies in Cognitive Behavior Therapy* Ed: Irismar Reis de Oliveira (New York, NY: InTech, 2012), http://www.intech open.com/books/standard-and-innovative-strategies-in-cognitive-behavior-therapy/modification-of-core -beliefs-in-cognitive-therapy.

## Chapter 1

1. Ulrich Orth, Richard Robins, and Laurenz Meier, "Disentangling the Effects of Low Self-Esteem and Stressful Events on Depression: Findings from Three Longitudinal Studies," *Journal of Personality and Social Psychology* 97 (2009): 307–321.

2. Edmund Rolls et al., "Representations of Pleasant and Painful Touch in the Human Orbitofrontal and Cingulate Cortices," *Cerebral Cortex* 13 (2003): 308–317.

3. Andrew Chen et al., "Human Pain Responsivity in a Tonic Pain Model: Psychological Determinants," *Pain* 37 (1989): 143–160.

4. Diane Zelman et al., "The Effects of Induced Mood on Laboratory Pain," *Pain* 46 (1991): 105–111.

5. Richard Stephens and Claire Allsop, "Effect of Manipulated State Aggression on Pain Tolerance," *Psychological Reports: Disability and Trauma* 111 (2012): 311–321.

6. Ibid.

7. Arnoud Arntz and Lily Claassens, "The Meaning of Pain Influences its Experienced Intensity," *Pain* 109 (2004): 20–25.

8. Kurt Gray and Daniel Wegner, "The Sting of Intentional Pain," *Psychological Science* 19 (2008): 1260–1262.

9. Ethan Kross et al., "Social Rejection Shares Somatosensory Representations with Physical Pain," *Proceedings of the National Academy of Sciences* 108 (2011): 6270–6275.

10. C. Nathan DeWall et al., "Acetaminophen Reduces Social Pain: Behavioral and Neural Evidence," *Psychological Science* 21 (2010): 931–937.

11. Irvin Yalom, *Love's Executioner* (New York: Pantheon Books, 2011), 81–82.

12. Jeroen Swart et al., "Exercising with Reserve: Exercise Regulation by Perceived Exertion in Relation to Duration of Exercise and Knowledge of Endpoint," *The British Journal of Sports Medicine* 43 (2009): 775–781.

13. Mark Litt, "Self-Efficacy and Perceived Control: Cognitive Mediators of Pain Tolerance," Journal of *Personality and Social Psychology* 54 (1988): 149–160.

14. Henry Beecher, "Relationship of Significance of Wound to Pain Experienced," *Journal of the American Medical Association* 161 (1956): 1609–1613.

15. John Abela et al., "Negative Cognitive Style and Past History of Major Depressive Episodes in University Students," *Cognitive Therapy and Research* 36 (2012): 219–227.

16. Patricia Murphy and George Fichett, "Belief in a Concerned God Predicts Response to Treatment for Adults with Clinical Depression," *Journal of Clinical Psychology* 65 (2009): 1000–1008.

17. George Papakostis et al., "Hopelessness as a Predictor of Non-Response to Fluoxetine in Major Depressive Disorder," *Annals of Clinical Psychiatry* 19 (2007): 5–8.

18. Lyn Abramson, Gerald Metalsky, and Lauren Alloy, "Hopelessness Depression: A Theory-Based Subtype of Depression," *Psychological Review* 96 (1989): 358–372; Judy Garber and Steven Hollon, "Universal vs. Personal Helplessness in Depression: Belief in Uncontrollability or Incompetence?" Journal of Abnormal Psychology 89 (1980): 56–66.

19. Stefan Koelsch et al., "The Quartet Theory of Human Emotions: An Integrative and Neurofunctional Model," *Physics of Life Reviews* 13 (2015): 1-27.

20. Edi Frei et al., "Localization of MDMA-Induced Brain Activity in Healthy Volunteers Using Low Resolution Electromagnetic Tomography (LORETA)," *Human Brain Mapping* 14 (2001): 152–165.

21. Kent Berridge and Morten Kringelbach, "Building a Neuroscience of Pleasure and Well-Being," *Psychology of Well-Being: Theory, Research and Practice* 1 (2011): Kent Berridge and Morten Kringelbach, "Building a Neuroscience of Pleasure and Well-Being," *Psychology of Well-Being: Theory, Research and Practice* 1 (2011): http://www.psywb.com/content/1/1/3.

22. Jutta Joormann et al., "Neural Correlates of Automatic Mood Regulation in Girls at High Risk for Depression," *Journal of Abnormal Psychology* 121 (2012): 61–72.

23. Qing-sen Ming et al., "Interaction Between A Serotonin Transporter Gene Promoter Region Polymorphism and Stress Predicts Depressive Symptoms in Chinese Adolescents: A Multi-Wave Longitudinal Study," *BMC Psychiatry* 13 (2013): 142; Guilherme Polanczyk et al., "Protective Effect of CRHR1 Gene Variants on the Development of Adult Depression Following Childhood Maltreatment," *Archives of General Psychiatry* 66 (2009): 978–985.

24. Jerry Guintivano et al, "Identification and Replication of a Combined Epigenic and Genetic Biomarker Predicting Suicide and Suicidal Behaviors," *American Journal of Psychiatry* 171 (2014): 1287–1296.

25. R Crupi and S Cuzzocrea, "Neuroinflammation and Immunity: A New Pharmacological Target in Depression," *CNS & Neurological Disorders–Drug Targets* 15 (2016): 464–476.

26. John Kelly et al., "Brain-Gut-Microbiota Axis: Challenges for Translation in Psychiatry," *Annals of Epidemiology* 26 (2016): 366–372.

27. Felice Jacka et al., "A Randomized Controlled Trial of Dietary Improvement for Adults with Major Depression (the 'SMILES' Trial)," *BMC Medicine* 15 (2017): 1–13.

28. George Loewenstein, "Hot-Cold Empathy Gaps and Medical Decision Making," *Health Psychology* 24 (2005): S49–S56.

29. Morton Kringelbach and Kent Berridge, "The Neuroscience of Happiness and Pleasure," *Social Research (New York)* 77 (2010): 659–678.

30. Lisa Martin, Harold Neighbors, and Derek Griffith, "The Experience of Symptoms of Depression in Men vs. Women," *JAMA Psychiatry* 70 (2013): 1100–1106.

## Chapter 2

1. Andrew Mathews, "Why Worry? The Cognitive Function of Anxiety," *Behaviour Research and Therapy* 28 (1990): 455–468.

2. Frank Pittman, *Man Enough* (New York: The Berkley Publishing Group, 1993), 130.

3. Ibid., 271.

4. Timothy Wilson and Daniel Gilbert, "Affective Forecasting: Knowing What to Want," *Advances in Experimental Social Psychology* 35 (2003): 345–411.

5. Adam Shriver, "The Asymmetrical Contributions of Pleasure and Pain to Subjective Well-Being," *The Review of Philosophy and Psychology* 5 (2014): 135–153.

6. Daniel Gilbert and Timothy Wilson, "Miswanting: Some Problems in the Forecasting of Future Affective States," in *Feeling and Thinking: the Role of Affect in Social Cognition*, ed. J. Forgas (Cambridge: Cambridge University Press, 2000), 178–197.

7. Ed Diener, Richard Lucas, and Christie Scollon, "Beyond the Hedonic Treadmill: Revising the Adaptation Theory of Well-Being," *American Psychologist* 61 (2006): 305-314.

8. Sonja Lyubomirsky, Laura King, and Ed Diener, "The Benefits of Frequent Positive Affect: Does Happiness Lead to Success?" *Psychological Bulletin* 131 (2005): 803–855.

## Chapter 3

1. Kent Kiehl, "A Cognitive Neuroscience Perspective on Psychopathy: Evidence for a Paralimbic System Dysfunction," *Psychiatry Research* 142 (2006): 107–128; James Blair, "Neurobiological Basis of Psychopathy," *British Journal of Psychiatry* 182 (2003): 5–7.

2. Fazil Aliev et al., "Genes Associated with Alcohol Outcomes Show Enrichment of Effects with Broad Externalizing and Impulsivity Phenotypes in a Independent Sample," *Journal of Studies of Alcohol and Drugs* 76 (2015): 38–46.

3. Yvonne Ulrih-Lai et al., "Pleasurable Behaviors Reduce Stress via Brain Reward Pathways," *Proceedings of the National Academy of Sciences* 107 (2010): 20529–20534.

4. Walter Mischel and Nancy Baker, "Cognitive Appraisals and Transformations in Delay Behavior," *Journal of Personality and Social Psychology* 31 (1975): 254–261.

5. Kent Berridge and Morten Kringelbach, "Neuroscience of Affect: Mechanisms of Pleasure and Displeasure," *Current Opinion in Neurobiology* 23 (2013): 294–303.

6. Janice Froelich, "Opioid Peptides," *Neurotransmitter Review* 21 (1997): 132–135.

7. Jill Littrell, "How Addiction Happens, How Change Happens, and What Social Workers Need to Know to Be Effective Facilitators of Change," *Journal of Evidence-Based Social Work* 8 (2011): 469–486.

8. Gabor Egervari et al., "Striatal K3K27 Acetylation Linked to Glutamatergic Gene Dysregulation in Human Heroin Abusers Holds Promise as Therapeutic Target," *Biological Psychiatry* 81 (2017): 585–594; Ryan LaLumiere and Peter Kalivas, "Glutamate Release in the Nucleus Accumbens Core is Necessary for Heroin Seeking," *The Journal of Neuroscience* 28 (2008): 3170–3177.

## Chapter 4

1. Ronald Fischer and Diane Boer, "What is More Important for National Well-Being: Money or Autonomy? A Meta-Analysis of Well-Being, Burnout, and Anxiety Across 63 Societies," *Journal of Personality and Social Psychology* 101 (2011): 164–184; Louis Tay and Ed Diener, "Needs and Subjective Well-Being Around the World," *Journal of Personality and Social Psychology* 101 (2011): 354–365.

2. Richard Schwartz, *Internal Family Systems Therapy* (New York: The Guilford Press, 1995).

3. Richard Ryan and Edward Deci, "Self-Determination Theory and the Facilitation of Intrinsic Motivation, Social Development, and Well-Being," *American Psychologist* 55 (2002): 68–78.

4. Colin Wastell, "Exposure to Trauma: The Long-Term Effects of Suppressing Emotional Reactions," *The Journal of Nervous and Mental Disease* 190 (2002): 839–845.

5. Rachel Barnes and Stacey Tantleff-Dunn, "Food for Thought: Examining the Relationship between Food Thought Suppression and Weight-Related Outcomes," *Eating Behaviors* 11 (2010): 175–179; Laura Campbell-Sills et al., "Effects of Suppression and Acceptance on Emotional Responses of Individuals with Anxiety and Mood Disorders," *Behaviour and Research Therapy* 44 (2006): 1251–1263.

6. Colin Wastell, "Exposure to Trauma: The Long-Term Effects of Suppressing Emotional Reactions," *The Journal of Nervous and Mental Disease* 190 (2002): 839–845.

## Chapter 5

1. James Gross and Oliver John, "Individual Differences in Two Emotion Regulation Processes: Implications for Affect, Relationships, and Well-Being," *Journal of Personality and Social Psychology* 85 (2003): 348–362.

2. Jillian Scott, et al., "Negative Urgency and Emotion Regulation Strategy Use: Associations with Displaced Aggression," *Aggressive Behavior* 41 (2015): 502–512.

3. Irvin Yalom, *Love's Executioner and Other Tales of Psychotherapy* (New York: Perennial Classics, 2000), 122.

4. James Gross and Robert Levenson, "Hiding Feelings: The Acute Effects of Inhibiting Negative and Positive Emotion," *Journal of Abnormal Psychology* 106 (1997): 95–103.

5. John Blackledge and Steven Hayes, "Emotion Regulation in Acceptance and Commitment Therapy," *Psychotherapy in Practice* 57 (2001): 243–255; Jessica Flynn, Tom Hollenstein, and Allison Mackey, "The Effect of Suppressing and Not Accepting Emotions on Depressive Symptoms: Is Suppression Different for Men and Women?" *Personality and Individual Differences* 49 (2010): 582–586; Laura Campbell-Sills et al., "Effects of Suppression and Acceptance on Emotional Responses of Individuals with Anxiety and Mood Disorders," *Behaviour and Research Therapy* 44 (2006): 1251–1263.

6. Paul Szasz, Aurora Szentagotai, Stefan Hofmann, "The Effect of Emotion Regulation Strategies on Anger," *Behavior Research and Therapy* 49 (2011): 114–119.

7. John Blackledge and Steven Hayes, "Emotion Regulation in Acceptance and Commitment Therapy," *Psychotherapy in Practice* 57 (2001): 243–255; Jessica Flynn, Tom Hollenstein, and Allison Mackey, "The Effect of Suppressing and Not Accepting Emotions on Depressive Symptoms: Is Suppression Different for Men and Women?" *Personality and Individual Differences* 49 (2010): 582–586; Laura Campbell-Sills et al., "Effects of Suppression and Acceptance on Emotional Responses of Individuals with Anxiety and Mood Disorders," *Behaviour and Research Therapy* 44 (2006): 1251–1263.

8. James Gross and Oliver John, "Individual Differences in Two Emotion Regulation Processes: Implications for Affect, Relationships, and Well-Being," *Journal of Personality and Social Psychology* 85 (2003): 348–362.

9. Ibid.

10. James Gross and Oliver John, "Individual Differences in Two Emotion Regulation Processes: Implications for Affect, Relationships, and Well-Being," *Journal of Personality and Social Psychology* 85 (2003): 348–362.

11. Ibid.

12. Marion Underwood, John Coie, and Cheryl Herbsman, "Display Rules for Anger and Aggression in School-Age Children," *Child Development* 63 (1992): 366–380.

# Chapter 6

1. Lysann Damisch, Barbara Stoberock, and Thomas Mussweiler, "Keep Your Fingers Crossed! How Superstition Improves Performance," *Psychological Science* 21 (2010): 1014–1020.

2. Sonja Lyubomirsky, Laura King, and Ed Diener, "The Benefits of Frequent Positive Affect: Does Happiness Lead to Success?" *Psychological Bulletin* 131 (2005): 803–855; Barbara Fredrickson et al., "What Good are Positive Emotions in Crises? A Prospective Study of Resilience and Emotions Following the Terrorist Attacks on the United States on September 11th, 2001," *Journal of Personality and Social Psychology* 84 (2003): 365–376.

3. Marco Loggia, Jeffrey Mogil, and M. Catherine Bushnell, "Experimentally Induced Mood Changes Preferentially Affect Pain Unpleasantness," *The Journal of Pain* 9 (2008): 784–791.

4. Ed Diener, Richard Lucas, and Christie Scollon, "Beyond the Hedonic Treadmill: Revising the Adaptation Theory of Well-Being," *American Psychologist* 61 (2006): 305–314.

5. Alex Lickerman, *The Undefeated Mind* (Deerfield Beach: Health Communications, Inc., 2012), 159.

6. Sonja Lyubomirsky, Laura King, and Ed Diener, "The Benefits of Frequent Positive Affect: Does Happiness Lead to Success?" *Psychological Bulletin* 131 (2005): 803–855.

7. William Tov and Huey Woon Lee, "A Closer Look at the Hedonics of Everyday Meaning and Satisfaction," *Journal of Personality and Social Psychology* 111 (2016): 585–609.

8. Ibid.

9. Stefan Koelsch et al., "The Quartet Theory of Human Emotions: An Integrative and Neurofunctional Model," *Physics of Life Reviews* 13 (2015): 1–27.

10. Kent Berridge and Morten Kringelbach, "Pleasure Systems in the Brain," *Neuron* 86 (2015): 646–664.

11. Stefan Koelsch et al., "The Quartet Theory of Human Emotions: An Integrative and Neurofunctional Model," *Physics of Life Reviews* 13 (2015): 1-27.

12. Ibid.

13. Ibid.

14. Ibid.

15. Jeffery Miller et al., "Anhedonia after a Selective Bilateral Lesion of the Globus Pallidus," *The American Journal of Psychiatry* 163 (2006): 786–788.

16. Stefan Koelsch et al., "The Quartet Theory of Human Emotions: An Integrative and Neurofunctional Model," *Physics of Life Reviews* 13 (2015): 1-27.

17. Guillaume Sescousse, Jerome Redoute, and Jean-Claude Dreher, "The Architecture of Reward Value Coding in the Human Orbitofrontal Cortex," *The Journal of Neuroscience* 30 (2010): 13095–13104

18. Stefan Koelsch et al., "The Quartet Theory of Human Emotions: An Integrative and Neurofunctional Model," *Physics of Life Reviews* 13 (2015): 1-27.

19. Ibid.

20. Daniel Kahneman, *Thinking, Fast and Slow* (New York: Farrar, Straus and Giroux, 2011), 405.

21. Richard Lucas et al., "Reexamining Adaptation and the Set Point Model of Happiness: Reactions to Changes in Marital Status," *Journal of Personality and Social Psychology* 84 (2003): 527–539.

22. Roy Baumeister et al., "Some Key Differences Between a Happy Life and a Meaningful Life," *The Journal of Positive Psychology* 8 (2013): 505–516.

23. Dianne Vella-Brodrick, Nansook Park, and Christopher Peterson, "Three Ways to be Happy: Pleasure, Engagement, and Meaning–Findings from Australian and US Samples," *Social Indicators Research* 90 (2009): 165–179.

24. William Tov and Huey Woon Lee, "A Closer Look at the Hedonic of Everyday Meaning and Satisfaction," *Journal of Personality and Social Psychology* 111 (2016): 585–609.

25.  Sonja Lyubomirsky, Laura King, and Ed Diener, "The Benefits of Frequent Positive Affect: Does Happiness Lead to Success?" *Psychological Bulletin* 131 (2005): 803–855.

26.  William Tov and Huey Woon Lee, "A Closer Look at the Hedonic of Everyday Meaning and Satisfaction," *Journal of Personality and Social Psychology* 111 (2016): 585–609.

27.  Daniel Kahneman, *Thinking, Fast and Slow* (New York: Farrar, Straus and Giroux, 2011), 409.

28.  Ibid., 200–201.

29.  Shelley Taylor, "Adjustment to Threatening Events: A Theory of Cognitive Adaptation," *American Psychologist* 38 (1983): 1161–1173.

30.  Daniel Gilbert, *Stumbling on Happiness* (New York, NY: Vintage Books, 2006), 167.

31.  Ibid., 111–115.

32.  Ibid., 177.

33.  Ibid., 55–57.

34.  Jordi Quoidbach et al., "Money Giveth, Money Taketh Away: The Dual Effect of Wealth on Happiness," *Psychological Science* 21 (2010): 759–763.

35.  Kennon Sheldon and Sonja Lyubomirsky, "The Challenge of Staying Happier: Testing the Hedonic Adaptation Prevention Model," *Personality and Social Psychology Bulletin* 38 (2012): 670–680.

36.  Daniel Gilbert, *Stumbling on Happiness* (New York, NY: Vintage Books, 2006), 56.

37.  Christopher Reeve, *Still Me* (New York, NY: Ballantine Books, 1999), 295.

38.  Ibid., 295.

39.  https://en.wikipedia.org/wiki/Christopher_Reeve#cite_note-79

40.  Richard Schulz and Susan Decker, "Long-Term Adjustment to Physical Disability: The Role of Social Support, Perceived Control, and Self-Blame," Journal of *Personality and Social Psychology* 48 (1985): 1162–1172.

41.  Roy Baumeister et al., "Some Key Differences Between a Happy Life and a Meaningful Life," *The Journal of Positive Psychology* 8 (2013): 505–516.

42.  Yang Yang, "Social Inequalities in Happiness in the United States, 1972 to 2004: An Age-Period-Cohort Analysis," *American Sociological Review* 73 (2008): 204-226.

43.  Kennon Sheldon and Sonja Lyubomirsky, "The Challenge of Staying Happier: Testing the Hedonic Adaptation Prevention Model," *Personality and Social Psychology Bulletin* 38 (2012): 670–680.

44.  Sonja Lyubomirsky and Kennon Sheldon, "Pursuing Happiness: The Architecture of Sustainable Change," *Review of General Psychology* 9 (2005): 111–131.

45.  Ibid.

46.  Ibid.

47.  Ibid.

48.  Stefan Koelsch et al., "The Quartet Theory of Human Emotions: An Integrative and Neurofunctional Model," *Physics of Life Reviews* 13 (2015): 1-27.

49.  Kent Berridge and Morten Kringelbach, "Building a Neuroscience of Pleasure and Well-Being," *Psychology of Well-Being: Theory, Research and Practice* 1 (2011): http://www.psywb.com/content/1/1/3.

50. Camile Wortman and Roxane Silver, "The Myths of Coping with Loss Revisited," in *Handbook of Bereavement Research: Consequences, Coping, and Care*, ed. Margaret Stroebe, Robert Hansson, Wolfgang Stroebe, and Henk Schut (Washington, DC: American Psychological Association, 2001), 405–429.

51. Joan Arnold, Penelope Buschman, and Linda Cushman, "Exploring Parental Grief: Combining Quantitative and Qualitative Measures," Archives of Psychiatric Nursing 19 (2005): 245–255.

52. Ibid.

53. Daniel Kahneman, *Thinking, Fast and Slow* (New York: Farrar, Straus and Giroux, 2011), 405.

54. Dennis Klass, Phyllis Silverman, and Steven Nickman, "Preface," in *Continuing Bonds: New Understandings of Grief*, ed. Dennis Klass, Phyllis Silverman, and Steven Nickman (New York: Taylor & Francis, 1996), xviii.

55. Wendy Lichtenthal and Dean Cruess, "Effects of Directed Written Disclosure on Grief and Distress Symptoms Among Bereaved Individuals," *Death Studies* 34 (2010): 475–499.

56. Stefan Koelsch et al., "The Quartet Theory of Human Emotions: An Integrative and Neurofunctional Model," *Physics of Life Reviews* 13 (2015): 1-27.

57. Nichiren Daishonin, "The Eight Winds" in *The Writings of Nichiren Daishonin*, vol. 1 (Japan: Soka Gakkai, 1999), 794.

## Chapter 7

1. Richard Ryan and Edward Deci, "On Happiness and Human Potentials: A Review of Research on Hedonic and Eudaimonic Well-Being," *Annual Review of Psychology* 52 (2001): 141–166.

2. Carol Ryff and Burton Singer, "Know Thyself and Become What You Are: A Eudaimonic Approach to Psychological Well-Being," *Journal of Happiness Studies* 9 (2008): 13–39.

3. Richard Ryan and Edward Deci, "On Happiness and Human Potentials: A Review of Research on Hedonic and Eudaimonic Well-Being," *Annual Review of Psychology* 52 (2001): 141–166.

4. Navjot Bhullar, Nicola Schutte, and John Malouff, "The Nature of Well-Being: The Roles of Hedonic and Eudaimonic Processes and Trait Emotional Intelligence," *The Journal of Psychology* 147 (2013): 1–16; Matthew Gallagher, Shane Lopez, and Kristopher Preacher, "The Hierarchical Structure of Well-Being," *Journal of Personality* 77 (2009): 1025–1050; Dianne Vella-Broderick, Nansook Park, Christopher Peterson, "Three Ways to Be Happy: Pleasure, Engagement, and Meaning–Findings from Australian and US Samples," *Social Indicators Research* 90 (2009): 165–179; Michael Steger, Todd Kashdan, and Shigehiro Oishi, "Being Good by Doing Good: Daily Eudaimonic Activity and Well-Being," *Journal of Research in Personality* 42 (2008): 22–42.

5. Feng Kong et al., "Brain Regions Involved in Dispositional Mindfulness During Resting State and their Relation with Well-Being," *Social Neuroscience* 11 (2016): 331–343.

6. Feng Kong et al., "Different Neural Pathways Linking Personality Traits and Eudaimonic Well-Being: A Resting-State Functional Magnetic Resonance Imaging Study," *Cognitive, Affective, and Behavioral Neuroscience* 15 (2015): 299–309.

7. Ibid.

8. Ibid.

9. Ibid.

10. Feng Kong et al., "Different Neural Pathways Linking Personality Traits and Eudaimonic Well-Being: A Resting-State Functional Magnetic Resonance Imaging Study," *Cognitive, Affective, and Behavioral Neuroscience* 15 (2015): 299–309; Lewis et al., "Neural Correlates of the 'Good Life': Eudaimonic Well-Being is Associated with Insular Cortex Volume," *Social Cognitive and Affective Neuroscience* 9 (2014):615–618.

11. Stefan Koelsch et al., "The Quartet Theory of Human Emotions: An Integrative and Neurofunctional Model," *Physics of Life Reviews* 13 (2015): 1-27.

12. Mario Livio, *Why?* (New York: Simon and Schuster, 2017), 100.

13. Eva Telzer et al., "Neural Sensitivity to Eudaimonic and Hedonic Rewards Differentially Predict Adolescent Depressive Symptoms Over Time," *Proceedings of the National Academy of Sciences* 111 (2014): 6600-6605; Aaron Heller et al., "Sustained Striatal Activity Predicts Eudaimonic Well-Being and Cortisol Output," *Psychological Science* 24 (2013): 2191–2200.

14. Eva Teller et al., "Gaining While Giving: An fMRI Study of the Rewards of Family Assistance Among White and Latino Youth," *Society for Neuroscience* 5 (2010): 508–518; Tristen Inagaki and Naomi Eisenberger, "Neural Correlates of Giving Support to a Loved One," *Psychosomatic Medicine* 74 (2012): 3–7.

15. Dianne Vella-Broderick, Nansook Park, Christopher Peterson, "Three Ways to Be Happy: Pleasure, Engagement, and Meaning–Findings from Australian and US Samples," *Social Indicators Research* 90 (2009): 165–179.

16. Ibid.

17. Navjot Bhullar, Nicola Schutte, and John Malouff, "The Nature of Well-Being: The Roles of Hedonic and Eudaimonic Processes and Trait Emotional Intelligence," *The Journal of Psychology* 147 (2013): 1–16.

18. Eva Telzer et al., "Neural Sensitivity to Eudaimonic and Hedonic Rewards Differentially Predict Adolescent Depressive Symptoms Over Time," *Proceedings of the National Academy of Sciences* 111 (2014): 6600-6605.

19. Stacey Schaefer et al., "Purpose in Life Predicts Better Emotional Recovery from Negative Stimuli," *PLOS One* (2103): http://journals.plos.org/plosone/article?id=10.1371/journal.pone.0080329.

20. Carol Ryff et al., "Purposeful Engagement, Health Aging, and the Brain," *Current Behavioral Neuroscience Reports* 3 (2016): 318–327.

21. Viktor Frankl, *Man's Search for Meaning* (Boston: Beacon Press, 2006), 113.

## Chapter 8

1. Daniel Kahneman, *Thinking, Fast and Slow* (New York: Farrar, Straus and Giroux, 2011), 21.

2. A Selsignore et al., "Perceived Responsibility for Change as an Outcome Predictor in Cognitive-Behavioural Group Therapy," *British Journal of Clinical Psychology* 47 (2008): 281–293.

3. Ibid.

4. Viktor Frankl, *Man's Search for Meaning* (Boston, MA: Beacon Press, 1959), 112.

5. Ibid., 21–22.

6. Carola Salvi et al., "Sudden Insight is Associated with Shutting Out Visual Inputs," *Psychonomic Bulletin and Review* 22 (2015): 1814–1819.

7. Ap Dijksterhuis and Teun Meurs, "Where Creativity Resides: The Generative Power of Unconscious Thought," *Consciousness and Cognition* 15 (2006): 135–146.

8. Claire Zedelius and Jonathan Schooler, "Mind Wandering 'Ahas' Versus Mindful Reasoning: Alternative Routes to Creative Solutions," *Frontiers in Psychology* 17 (2015): https://www.frontiersin.org/articles/10.3389/fpsyg.2015.00834/full.

9. Ap Dijksterhuis and Teun Meurs, "Where Creativity Resides: The Generative Power of Unconscious Thought," *Consciousness and Cognition* 15 (2006): 135–146.

10. Marc-Andre Reinhard, Rainer Greifeneder, and Marin Scharmach, "Unconscious Processes Improve Lie Detection," *Journal of Personality and Social Psychology* 105 (2013): 721–739.

11. Ibid.

12. Amor Danek and Jennifer Wiley, "What About False Insights? Deconstructing the Aha! Experience Along its Multiple Dimensions for Correct and Incorrect Solutions Separately," *Frontiers in Psychology* 20 (2017): https://www.frontiersin.org/articles/10.3389/fpsyg.2016.02077/full.

13. Carola Salvi et al., "Sudden Insight is Associated with Shutting Out Visual Inputs," *Psychonomic Bulletin and Review* 22 (2015): 1814–1819.

14. Benjamin Baird et al., "Inspired by Distraction: Mind Wandering Facilitates Creative Incubation," *Psychological Science* 23 (2012): 1117–1122.

15. Ibid.

16. Carola Salvi et al., "Sudden Insight is Associated with Shutting Out Visual Inputs," *Psychonomic Bulletin and Review* 22 (2015): 1814–1819.

17. Ellen Lee et al, "Altered States of Consciousness During an Extreme Ritual," *PLoS One* 11 (2016): http://journals.plos.org/plosone/article?id=10.1371/journal.pone.0153126.

18. Arne Dietrich, "Functional Neuroanatomy of Altered States of Consciousness: The Transient Hypofrontality Hypothesis," *Consciousness and Cognition* 12 (2003): 231–256.

19. Arne Dietrich and Phillip Sparling, "Endurance Exercise Selectively Impairs Prefrontal-Dependent Cognition," *Brain and Cognition* 55 (2004): 516–524.

20. Marily Appezzo and Daniel Schwartz, "Give Your Ideas Some Legs: The Positive Effect of Walking on Creative Thinking," *Journal of Experimental Psychology: Learning, Memory, and Cognition* 40 (2014): 1142–1152.

21. Arne Dietrich, "Functional Neuroanatomy of Altered States of Consciousness: The Transient Hypofrontality Hypothesis," *Consciousness and Cognition* 12 (2003): 231–256; Bangalore Kalyani et al., "Neurohemodynamic Correlates of 'OM' Chanting: A Pilot Functional Magnetic Resonance Imaging Study," *International Journal of Yoga* 4 (2011): 3–6.

22. Alex Lickerman, *The Undefeated Mind* (Deerfield Beach: Health Communications, Inc., 2012), 3–5.

23. Haiyang Yang et al., "Unconscious Creativity: When can Unconscious Thought Outperform Conscious Thought?" *Journal of Consumer Psychology* 22 (2012): 573–581; David Engelman, *Incognito* (New York: Vintage Books, 2011), 69–74.

### Chapter 9

1. Alex Lickerman, *The Undefeated Mind* (Deerfield Beach: Health Communications, Inc., 2012), 195.

2. Ibid., 196.

3. Ibid., 196.

4. Ibid., 196.

5. Olga Klimecki et al., "Differential Pattern of Functional Brain Plasticity after Compassion and Empathy Training," *Social, Cognitive, and Affective Neuroscience* 9 (2014): 873–879.

6. Ibid.

7. Ibid.

8. Olga Klimecki et al., "Functional Neuroplasticity and Associated Changes in Positive Affect After Compassion Training," *Cerebral Cortex* 23 (2013): 1552–1561.

9. Paul Miller and Nancy Eisenberg, "The Relation of Empathy to Aggressive and Externalizing/Antisocial Behavior," *Psychological Bulletin* 103 (1988):324–344.

10. Harma Meffert et al., "Reduced Spontaneous but Relatively Normal Deliberate Vicarious Representations in Psychopathy," *Brain* 136 (2013): 2550–2562.

11. Carolyn Schwartz and Meir Sendor, "Helping Others Helps Oneself: Response Shift Effects in Peer Support," *Social Science and Medicine* 48 (1999): 1563–1575.

12. Stephanie Brown et al., "Coping with Spousal Loss: Potential Buffering Effects of Self-Reported Helping Behavior," *Personality and Social Psychology Bulletin* 34 (2008): 849–861.

13. Alex Lickerman, *The Undefeated Mind* (Deerfield Beach: Health Communications, Inc., 2012), 207.

14. Bruce Headey, "The Set-Point Theory of Well-Being Has Serious Flaws: On the Eve of a Scientific Revolution?" *Social Indicators Research* 97 (2010): 7–21.

15. Sonja Lyubomirsky, Kennon Sheldon, and David Schkade, "Pursuing Happiness: The Architecture of Sustainable Change," *Review of General Psychology* 9 (2005): 111–131.

16. Alex Lickerman, *The Undefeated Mind* (Deerfield Beach: Health Communications, Inc., 2012), 28–29.

17. Soyoung Park et al., "A Neural Link between Generosity and Happiness," *Nature Communications* 8 (2017): 1–10.

18. Christopher Peterson et al., "Strengths of Character, Orientations to Happiness, and Life Satisfaction," *The Journal of Positive Psychology* 2 (2007):149–156.

19. Alex Lickerman, *The Undefeated Mind* (Deerfield Beach: Health Communications, Inc., 2012), 34–41.

20. Nathaniel Lambert et al., "Family as a Salient Source of Meaning in Young Adulthood," *The Journal of Positive Psychology* 5 (2010): 367–376.

21. Melissa Grouden and Paul Jose, "How Do Sources of Meaning in Life Vary According to Demographic Factors?" *New Zealand Journal of Psychology* 43 (2014): 29–38.

22. Ibid.

23. Ibid.

24. Ibid.

25. Roy Baumeister et al., "Some Key Differences Between a Happy Life and a Meaningful Life," *The Journal of Positive Psychology* 8 (2013): 505–516.

26. Melissa Grouden and Paul Jose, "How Do Sources of Meaning in Life Vary According to Demographic Factors?" *New Zealand Journal of Psychology* 43 (2014): 29–38.

27. Alex Lickerman, *The Undefeated Mind* (Deerfield Beach: Health Communications, Inc., 2012), 38.

## Chapter 10

1. Richard Causton, *The Buddha in Daily Life* (Parktown: Rider Books, 1995), 74.

2. Alex Lickerman, *The Undefeated Mind* (Deerfield Beach: Health Communications, Inc., 2012), 237–238.

3. Steve Taylor, *Waking From Sleep* (Carlsbad: Hay House, 2010), xiii.

4. Ibid., xiii.

5. Ibid., xiii–xiv.

6. Andrew Newberg and Mark Robert Waldman, *How Enlightenment Changes Your Brain* (New York: Avery, 2016), 18.

7. Andrew Newberg and Mark Robert Waldman, *How Enlightenment Changes Your Brain* (New York: Avery, 2016), 31–40, 47–52.

8. Steve Taylor, *Waking From Sleep* (Carlsbad: Hay House, 2010), 15.

9. Ibid., 16–18.

10. Ibid., 18.

11. Ibid., 10.

12. Andrew Newberg and Mark Robert Waldman, *How Enlightenment Changes Your Brain* (New York: Avery, 2016), 14.

13. Steve Taylor, *Waking From Sleep* (Carlsbad: Hay House, 2010), 9.

14. Ibid., 18.

15. Ibid., 107.

16. Michael Winkelman, "The Mechanisms of Psychedelic Visionary Experiences: Hypotheses from Evolutionary Psychology," *Frontiers in Neuroscience* 11 (2017): https://www.frontiersin.org/articles/10.3389/fnins.2017.00539/full.

17. Andrew Newberg et al., "The Measurement of Regional Cerebral Blood Flow During the Complex Cognitive Task of Meditation: A Preliminary SPECT Study," *Psychiatry Research: Neuroimaging Section* 106 (2001): 113–122; Andrew Newberg et al., "A Case Series Study of the Neurophysiological Effects of Altered States of Mind During Intense Islamic Prayer," *The Journal of Physiology–Paris* 109 (2015): 214–220; John Castro, "Meditation Has Stronger Relationships with Mindfulness, Kundalini, and Mystical Experiences than Yoga or Prayer," *Consciousness and Cognition* 35 (2015): 115–127.

18. Fabienne Picard and Florian Kurth, "Ictal Alterations of Consciousness During Ecstatic Seizures," *Epilepsy and Behavior* 30 (2014): 58–61.

19. Roland Griffiths, et al., "Psilocybin Can Occasion Mystical-Type Experiences and Sustained Personal Meaning and Spiritual Significance," *Psychopharmacology* 187 (2006): 268–283.

20. Michael Winkelman, "The Mechanisms of Psychedelic Visionary Experiences: Hypotheses from Evolutionary Psychology," *Frontiers in Neuroscience* 11 (2017): https://www.frontiersin.org/articles/10.3389/fnins.2017.00539/full.

21. Ibid.

22. Michael van Elk and Andre Aleman, "Brain Mechanisms in Religion and Spirituality: An Integrative Predictive Processing Framework," *Neuroscience and Biobehavioral Reviews* 73 (2017): 359–378.

23. Robin Carhart-Harris et al., "Neural Correlates of the Psychedelic State as Determined by fMRI Studies with Psilocybin," *Proceedings of the National Academy of Sciences* 109 (2012): http://www.pnas.org/content/109/6/2138; Cosimo Ugesi et al., "The Spiritual Brain: Selective Cortical Lesions Modulate Human Self-Transcendence," *Neuron* 65 (2010): 309–319; Irene Cristofori et al., "Neural Correlates of Mystical Experience," *Neuropsychologia* 80 (2016): 212–220.

24. Michael Winkelman, "The Mechanisms of Psychedelic Visionary Experiences: Hypotheses from Evolutionary Psychology," *Frontiers in Neuroscience* 11 (2017): https://www.frontiersin.org/articles/10.3389/fnins.2017.00539/full; Irene Cristofori et al., "Neural Correlates of Mystical Experience," *Neuropsychologia* 80 (2016): 212–220.

25. Fabienne Picard and Florian Kurth, "Ictal Alterations of Consciousness During Ecstatic Seizures," *Epilepsy and Behavior* 30 (2014): 58–61.

26. Fabienne Picard, Didier Scavarda, and Fabrice Bartolomei, "Induction of a Sense of Bliss by Electrical Stimulation of the Anterior Insula," *Cortex* 49 (2013): 2935–2937.

27. Roland Griffiths et al., "Psilocybin-Occasioned Mystical-Type Experience in Combination with Meditation and Other Spiritual Practices Produces Enduring Positive Changes in Psychological Functioning and in Trait Measures of Prosocial Attitudes and Behaviors," *Journal of Psychopharmacology* 32 (2018): 49–69.

28. R. Christopher deCharms et al., "Control Over Brain Activation and Pain Learned by Using Real-Time Functional MRI," *Proceedings of the National Academy of Sciences* 102 (2005): 18626–18631.

29. Robert DeRubeis, Greg Siegle, and Steven Hollon, "Cognitive Therapy vs. Medications for Depression: Treatment Outcomes and Neural Mechanisms," *Nature Reviews Neuroscience* 9 (2008): 788–796; Zhen Yang et al., "Cognitive Behavioral Therapy is Associated with Enhanced Control Network Activity in Major Depression and Posttraumatic Stress Disorder," *Biological Psychiatry: Cognitive Neuroscience and Neuroimaging* 3 (2018): 311–319; Anjali Sankar et al., "Neural Effects of Cognitive-Behavioural Therapy on Dysfunctional Attitudes in Depression," *Psychological Medicine* 45 (2015): 1425–1433.

30. Ibid.

31. Ibid.

32. Sam Harris *Waking Up* (New York: Simon and Schuster, 2014), 9.

33. Alex Lickerman, *The Undefeated Mind* (Deerfield Beach: Health Communications, Inc., 2012), 235.

34. David Oakley and Peter Halligan, "Chasing the Rainbow: The Non-Conscious Nature of Being," *Frontiers in Psychology* 8 (2017): https://www.frontiersin.org/articles/10.3389/fpsyg.2017.01924/full.

35. Ibid.

36. Sam Harris, *Free Will* (New York: Free Press, 2012), 13.

37. Jordi Quoidbach, Daniel Gilbert, and Timothy Wilson, "The End of History Illusion," *Science* 339 (2013): 96–98.

38. Antonio Damasio, *Self Comes to Mind* (New York: Pantheon Books, 2010), 229.

39. Ibid., 29.

40. Ibid., 85–86.

41. Ibid., 21.

42. Antonio Damasio, *Self Comes to Mind* (New York: Pantheon Books, 2010), 229.

43. Sam Harris, *Waking Up* (New York: Simon and Schuster, 2015), 30.

44. Daniel Wegner, et al., "Paradoxical Effects of Thought Suppression," *Journal of Personality and Social Psychology* 53 (1987): 5–13.

45. Antonio Damasio, *Self Comes to Mind* (New York: Pantheon Books, 2010), 180–181.

46. Ibid., 241.

47. Mihaly Csikszentmihalyi, *Flow* (New York: Harper Perennial Modern Classics, 2008), 53.

48. Martin Ulrich, Johannes Keller, and Georg Gron, "Neural Signatures of Experimentally Induced Flow Experiences Identified in a Typical fMRI Block Design with BOLD Imaging," *Social Cognitive and Affective Neuroscience* 11 (2016): 496–507.

49. Eckhart Tolle, *The Power of Now* (Novato: New World Library, 1999), 3–5.

50. Steve Taylor, *Waking From Sleep* (Carlsbad: Hay House, 2010).

51. Brett Ford et al., "The Psychological Health Benefits of Accepting Negative Emotions and Thoughts: Laboratory, Diary, and Longitudinal Evidence," *Journal of Personality and Social Psychology* http://psycnet.apa.org/doiLanding?doi=10.1037%2Fspsp0000157.

52. Paul Hamilton et al., "Depressive Rumination, the Default-Mode Network, and the Dark Matter of Clinical Neuroscience," *Biological Psychiatry* 78 (2015): 224–230.

53. Andrew Newberg et al., "A Case Series Study of the Neurophysiological Effects of Altered States of Mind During Intense Islamic Prayer," *The Journal of Physiology–Paris* 109 (2015): 214–220.

54. Ibid.

55. Steve Taylor, *Waking From Sleep* (Carlsbad: Hay House, 2010), 123.

56. Jennifer Stellar et al., "Awe and Humility," *Journal of Personality and Social Psychology* 114 (2018): 258–269.

57. Ibid.

58. Paul Piff et al., "Awe, the Small Self, and Prosocial Behavior," *Journal of Personality and Social Psychology* 108 (2015): 883–899.

59. Ibid.

60. Patty Van Cappellen and Vassilis Saroglou, "Awe Activates Religious and Spiritual Feelings and Behavioral Intentions," *Psychology of Religion and Spirituality* 4 (2012): 223–236.

61. Rebecca Newberger Goldstein, *Plato at the Googleplex* (Vintage Books: New York, 2015), 50.

62. Tomohiru Ishizu and Semir Zeki, "A Neurobiological Enquiry into the Origins of Our Experience of the Sublime and Beautiful," Frontiers in Human Neuroscience 2014: https://www.frontiersin.org/articles/10.3389/fnhum.2014.00891/full.

63. Ibid.

64. Rebecca Newberger Goldstein, *Plato at the Googleplex* (Vintage Books: New York, 2015), 258.

65. Sam Harris, *Waking Up* (New York: Simon and Schuster, 2014), 12.

66. Ibid.

67. Paul Piff et al., "Awe, the Small Self, and Prosocial Behavior," *Journal of Personality and Social Psychology* 108 (2015): 883-899.

68. Michael Pollan, *How to Change Your Mind* (Penguin Press: New York, 2018), 258–259.

69. Sam Harris, *Waking Up* (New York: Simon and Schuster, 2015), 192.

70. Andrew Newberg and Mark Robert Waldman, *How Enlightenment Changes Your Brain* (New York: Avery, 2016), 14.

71. Fabienne Picard and Florian Kurth, "Ictal Alterations of Consciousness During Ecstatic Seizures," *Epilepsy and Behavior* 30 (2014): 58–61.

72.  Michael Winkelman, "The Mechanisms of Psychedelic Visionary Experiences: Hypotheses from Evolutionary Psychology," *Frontiers in Neuroscience* 11 (2017): https://www.frontiersin.org/articles/10.3389/fnins.2017 .00539/full.

73.  Fabienne Picard, "State of Belief, Subjective Certainty and Bliss as a Product of Cortical Dysfunction," *Cortex* 49 (2013): 2494–2500.

74.  https://en.wikipedia.org/wiki/List_of_cognitive_biases

75.  Jerry Coyne, *Faith vs. Fact* (Viking: New York, 2015).

76.  Sam Harris, *Waking Up* (New York: Simon and Schuster, 2014), 43–44.

77.  Alex Lickerman, *The Undefeated Mind* (Deerfield Beach: Health Communications, Inc., 2012), 229–230.

78.  Roland Griffiths et al., "Psilocybin Produces Substantial and Sustained Decreases in Depression and Anxiety in Patients with Life-Threatening Cancer: A Randomized Double-Blind Trial," *Journal of Psychopharmacology* 30 (2016): 1181–1197.

79.  Michael Pollan, *How to Change Your Mind* (Penguin Press: New York, 2018), 345.

80.  Rebecca Newberger Goldstein, *Plato at the Googleplex* (Vintage Books: New York, 2015), 55.

81.  Michael Pollan, *How to Change Your Mind* (Penguin Press: New York, 2018), 71.

82.  Armin Zadeh, *The Forgotten Art of Love* (Novato: New World Library, 2017), 33.

83.  Ibid., 50.

84.  Steven Pinker, *Enlightenment Now* (Viking: New York, 2018), 322–324.

# ABOUT THE AUTHORS

**Alex Lickerman, M.D.**, is a primary care physician, former assistant professor of medicine, former director of primary care, and former assistant vice president for Student Health and Counseling Services at the University of Chicago. He currently leads a direct primary care practice in Chicago called ImagineMD.

Alex's first book, *The Undefeated Mind: On the Science of Constructing an Indestructible Self,* received numerous favorable reviews from many sources, including *Publishers Weekly.* A noted speaker and media expert, he has been quoted in Crain's *Chicago Business, The Chicago Tribune, Men's Health, The New York Times,* and *TIME,* and has had articles appear in *Psychology Today, Crain's Chicago Business, USA Today, Slate, The Huffington Post, Counselor Magazine,* and *Medicine on the Midway.*

He's also been a guest on NPR's *On Point.* He's also written a television pilot called *Sessions* that was optioned by DreamWorks Television, as well as several movie screenplays, including an adaptation of Milton's *Paradise Lost.* Alex lives in Chicago with his wife, Rhea, and son, Cruise. Alex comes from the world of Learning.

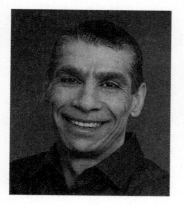

**Ash ElDifrawi, Psy.D.**, has built a reputation as a thought leader in clinical, social, and consumer psychology. He began his career as a clinical psychologist before transitioning into work as a marketing executive for some of the most prestigious and innovative companies in the world.

Ash received his bachelor's degree in biology and master's degree in social science from the University of Chicago, where he also conducted clinical research in the areas of neurology and bio-psychology. He earned his doctorate in clinical psychology from the Chicago School of Psychology, completed his internship at the world-renowned Family Institute at Northwestern, and then went on to be the inaugural fellow at the Center for Family Health at the University of Chicago. Ash is still a licensed clinical psychologist.

After transitioning to a career in marketing, he has held senior positions at companies including Google, McKinsey, Wrigley, Gogo, and currently Redbox. He's been featured in *The Economist, Forbes, Bloomberg, Fast Money, WSJ, NY Times,* CNBC, Mashable, *Crain's Chicago Business,* MarketWatch, and Re/Code. Ash also co-wrote a television pilot called *Sessions* that was optioned by Dream-Works Television. Ash lives in Hinsdale, Illinois, with his wife, Amy, and two children, Aidan and Allison. Ash comes from the world of Tranquility.

# INDEX

## A

AA. *See* Alcoholics Anonymous (AA)
Absolute happiness, 185, 314–320, 325
  fear of death, 316–318
  vs. relative happiness, 314
  suffering, 315–316
  world peace, 318–320
Alcohol and Tranquility, 161
Alcoholics Anonymous (AA), 96–97
Alcoholism and Animality, 85–86
Altruism 278
Analytic problem solving, 252
Analytic thinking and Realization, 235
Anderson, Craig, 13–14
Anger, 99–136
  arrogance as reaction formation, 128–136
    insecurities, 129–130, 132
    narcissism, 130–131
  autonomy, 108–116
    ego and self-importance, 108
    Internal Family Systems Therapy (Parts Model), 111–113
  competence, appearance of, 116–118
  core delusion, 129–130
  discrimination and, 100
  ego protection, 124–128
  life-condition, 99–100
  power of, 118–123
    shame, 119–120, 135
  reaction formation, 102–108
    definition, 103
    provocation, 105
Animality, 73–98
  core delusion, 90–91
  freedom, 83–89
    alcoholism, 85–86
    brain processing, 84
  impulsivity, 80, 83, 84, 90
  life condition, 73–74

nature's motivation of animals, 89–91
neurology and psychology, 93–97
  dopamine-induced cravings, 94
  rationalizing choices, 95
pleasure as basic drive and delusion, 91–93
  brain chemistry, 92
  indulgence and overindulgence, 92
self-centeredness, 79–83
  and sociopathy, 79–80, 83–84
  unrestrained id, 80
Anterior cingulate cortex and suffering, 26
Anterior insula of reward circuit and experience of Enlightenment, 297
Antidepressants and core delusion of learned helplessness, 30
Anxiety
  anxiety-reducing cognitive and behavioral strategies, 192
  attachment, 47
  distress, 47
  as event, 48–53
  obsession and, 49–50, 69
  regression as defense mechanism, 51
  and relative happiness, 187
Anxiety-reducing cognitive and behavioral strategies, 192
Appearance of change, 248
Arrogance as reaction formation, 128–136
  insecurities, 129–130, 132
  narcissism, 130–131
Associative processing, 253
Atlas and Hercules myth, 11–12
Attachments
  and anxiety, 47
  as conduit for joy, 205
  conflation of attachments, 204
  grief about loss of, 206
  as incidental, 204–209
  and joy, 181
  love as response to attachment, 202

neurology, 202
noticing and appreciating, 195
personal preferences in, 201
as pleasure, 203
recovery from loss of, 206
to self, 325
specificity of, 201
temporary nature of, 196
Authentic self and Tranquility, 165
Autobiographical self, 301
Autonomy and Anger, 108–116
ego and self-importance, 108
Internal Family Systems Therapy (Parts Model), 111–113
Avoidance of conflict and Tranquility, 149
Awe and Enlightenment, 293, 307–309
and experience of Enlightenment, 293
sublime vs., 308
Sublime Braid of truth, beauty, and goodness, 308

**B**

Basic pleasures and basic drives, 178
Behavioral activation therapy, 193
Beliefs
consequences of ignoring, 9
delusions, 12–14
in God, effect on core delusion of learned helplessness, 30
about happiness, 11–12
perseverance of, 13
power of, 7
rationalization, 13–14
and relative happiness, 325
stirring up of, 8–9
Biofeedback and experience of Enlightenment, 297
Boundless compassion and love and experience of Enlightenment, 295
Brain chemistry and Animality, 92
Brain processing and Animality, 84
Brain's machinery of mood generation, 36–37
Buddhism, 146, 184, 251, 254, 313–314

**C**

Change and Realization, 243–247
Changing self, not circumstances, 250
Claparède, Édouard, 9–10
Clarity of insight and experience of Enlightenment, 295
Cognitive biases, 314
Cognitive reappraisal and Tranquility, 166
Comfort with status quo and Tranquility, 150
Compassion, 261–287
core delusion, 277
empathy, 271–277
forgiveness, 271–272
grief, 275
relationship, Compassion and empathy, 276–277
therapeutic use of, 272
happiness and Compassion, 277–281
altruism 278
reward circuit of brain, 278
life-condition, 261–262
life stories, 285–286
love and life satisfaction studies, 281–282
meaning, 282–283
nature of Compassion, 266–271
*jihi*, 266
unconditional positive regard, 266–267
Competence, appearance of and Anger, 116–118
Conscious control of nonconscious brain process and experience of Enlightenment, 298
Conscious vs. unconscious problem solving and Realization, 251–253
analytic, 252
through insight, 252
Continuous positive airway pressure (CPAP) machine, 2
Core affect, 5
Core beliefs of happiness (chart), 322–323
higher worlds, 323
lower worlds, 322
Core delusions, 14–16
cognitive therapy, 14
core beliefs, 15
Core delusions of Ten Worlds
Anger—happiness comes from superiority, 129–130
Animality—pleasure and happiness are the same, 90–91
Compassion—happiness depends on happiness of others, 277
Hell—powerlessness to end suffering, 32
Hunger—we need to get what we want for happiness, 67
Learning—happiness comes from meaningful accomplishment, 222
Rapture—happiness and attachment, 184–185
Realization—happiness comes from personal growth, 257
Tranquility—happiness requires avoidance of pain, 159–160
Core self, 301
Core truth and experience of Enlightenment, 298–299
Core truth that the universe is sublime, 309, 312–314
cognitive biases, 314
*kyochi-myogo*, 312
noetic sense, 313
Cotard delusion, 13
CPAP machine. *See* Continuous positive airway pressure (CPAP) machine
Creation of value, 221–222
Csikszentmihalyi, Mihaly, 303

**D**

Default mode network and Enlightenment, 296, 302, 304, 306–308
Delusions as obstacles to happiness, 12–14
    fixed false ideas, 12
    thought process vs. content of delusion, 12–13
Denial of desire and Tranquility, 145–149
    isolation, 147
    suffering, 146
Depression
    brain's machinery of mood generation, 36–37
    condition of, 22–25
    despair, 199
    diminished capacity for pleasure, 176
    powerlessness, 198
    and Tranquility, 157–158
    true cause of, 36–42
Discrimination and Anger, 100
Distress and anxiety, 47
Dopamine-induced cravings and Animality, 94
Dysfunctional belief abandonment, 258

**E**

Ego and self-importance and Anger, 108
Ego protection and Anger, 124–128
Emotional maturity and Tranquility, 167
Empathy, 271–277
    forgiveness, 271–272
    grief, 275
    relationship to Compassion, 276–277
    therapeutic use of, 272
End of history illusion, 300
Enlightenment, 289–321
    absolute happiness, 314–320
        fear of death, 316–318
        vs. relative happiness, 314
        suffering, 315–316
        world peace, 318–320
    awe, 307–309
        sublime vs., 308
        Sublime Braid of truth, beauty, and goodness, 308
    core truth that the universe is sublime, 309, 312–314
        cognitive biases, 314
        *kyochi-myogo*, 312
        noetic sense, 313
    experience of, 290–299
        anterior insula of reward circuit, 297
        awe, 293
        biofeedback, 297
        boundless compassion and love, 295
        clarity of insight, 295
        conscious control of nonconscious brain process, 298
        core truth of, 298–299
        default mode network, 296

feeling of unity with surroundings, 294–295
loss of fear of death, 296
MRI scans, 298
neurological phenomenon, 296
possession of larger self, 295
psychedelic drugs, 297
self dissolving into transcendence, 295
well-being, 296
wonderment and joy, 293, 296
    fundamental cause of, 299–309
        flow experience and unity with the world, 302–304
        renunciation of effort to avoid suffering, 306
        scope of self, 301–302
        self as illusion, 299–301. *See also* Self, illusion of
        surrender of self and increase of insula activity, 307
    life condition, 289–290
    as life tendency, 309–311
        practicing to see sublime in everything, 311
        triggers for, 310
Erroneous beliefs as roadblocks to happiness, 4
Eudaimonia from creating value, 217–221, 223–227
    brain physiology of, 224
    as hedonic happiness, 224
Eudaimonic happiness. *See* Hedonic happiness vs. Eudaimonic happiness
Eudaimonic happiness and learning, 227–232
    joy through meaning, 231
    as type of hedonic happiness, 231
Eudaimonic happiness emergence, 191
Experience stretching, 190–191
    hedonic happiness diminishment, 190–191
    risk of loss, 191

**F**

Fear of conflict and Tranquility, 141–145
Fear of death and absolute happiness, 316–318
Feeling emotions and Tranquility, 165–170
    authentic self, 165
    cognitive reappraisal, 166
    emotional maturity, 167
    relief, 170
Feeling of unity with surroundings and experience of Enlightenment, 294–295
Feeling safe and Tranquility, 149–153
    avoidance of conflict, 149
    comfort with status quo, 150
Fixed false ideas, 12
Flow experience and unity with the world, 302–304
Forgiveness and empathy, 271–272
Frankl, Viktor, 228–229, 252
Freedom and Animality, 83–89
    alcoholism, 85–86
    brain processing, 84

Freedom from problems and Tranquility, 153–159
    depression, 157–158
    silence, 157
*Free Will* (Harris), 300
Future focus, 191–194
    anxiety-reducing cognitive and behavioral strategies, 192
    behavioral activation therapy, 193
    eudaimonic happiness emergence, 191

**G**

Gastric bypass, 2
Genogram, 54–58
Gilbert, Daniel, 3–4, 64, 67, 189, 190, 191, 300
Goldstein, Rebecca Newberger, 308
Gradual vs. sudden change and Realization, 247–249
    appearance of change, 248
    human revolution, 248
    intentionality, 247
    internal cause stirred up by external cause, 247
Grief
    and empathy, 275
    about loss of attachments, 206

**H**

Happiness
    absolute, 185
    and Compassion, 277–281
    delusions as obstacles to, 12–14
    erroneous beliefs as roadblocks to, 4
Happiness and Compassion, 277–281
    altruism 278
    reward circuit of brain, 278
Harris, Sam, 299
Hedonic adaptation, 67–68, 181–182
    baselines, 182
    diminishing returns, 181
Hedonic happiness and pleasure, joy, 182–183
    final intensity, 183
    misremembering, 183
    peak intensity, 183
    satisfaction, 183
Hedonic happiness vs. eudaimonic happiness, 177–178
Hell, 21–43
    core delusion, 32
        antidepressants and, 30
        belief in God and, 30
        learned helplessness, 29
        pessimistic self-explanatory style, 30
    depression
        brain's machinery of mood generation, 36–37
        condition of, 22–25
        true cause of, 36–42
    entrenchment in distorted views, 34
    life condition of social isolation, 21
    and self-worth, 33

suffering as response to pain, 25–29
    anterior cingulate cortex and, 26
    pain tolerance, differences in, 26, 29
    power of acceptance, 31
    severity of related to need to solve, 37
wisdom, 35–36
Hercules and Atlas myth, 11–12
Higher-order pleasures vs. joy, 180
Hippocampus
    and cognition, 179
    and joy, 179
    and memory, 10
*How to Change Your Mind* (Pollan), 310–311
Human revolution, 248
Hunger, 45–72
    and anxiety
        attachment, 47
        distress, 47
        as event, 48–53
        obsession and, 49–50, 69
        regression as defense mechanism, 51
    core delusion, 67
    life-condition, 45–46
    love, desire for, 58–60
    miswanting, 67–71
        hedonic adaptation, 67–68
        wanting vs. liking, 67
        wanting vs. needing, 68
    satisfaction, 71
    universal/existential anxiety, 60–64
        disproportionate wanting, 64
        dissatisfaction and meaning, 65
    validation, need for, 53–58
        genogram to analyze, 54–58
        low self-esteem, 54

**I**

Impulsivity and Animality, 80, 83, 84, 90
Indulgence and overindulgence and Animality, 92
Insecurities and Anger, 129–130, 132
Insight and Realization, 235
Insightful problem solving, 252
Intentionality of change, 247
Internal cause stirred up by external cause, 247
Internal Family Systems Therapy (Parts Model), 111–113
Isolation and Tranquility, 147

**J**

*Jihi*, 266
Joy. *See also* Pleasure vs. joy
    and attachments, 181, 205
    through meaning, 231

**K**

Kahneman, Daniel, 182, 205, 235
*Kyochi-myogo*, 312

**L**

Learning, 211–233
    core delusion, 222
    creation of value, 221–222
    eudaimonia from creating value, 217–221, 223–227
        brain physiology of, 224
        as hedonic happiness, 224
    eudaimonic happiness
        benefits, 227–232
        joy through meaning, 231
        as type of hedonic happiness, 231
    life-condition, 211–212
    mastery, 216–217
Life-condition
    beliefs
        dysfunctionality of, 16
        about happiness, 11–12
        power of, 7
        stirring up of, 8–9
    core delusions, 14–16
        cognitive therapy, 14
        core beliefs, 15
    definition, 5–6
    determinants of, 6–7
    happiness
        delusions as obstacles to, 12–14
        erroneous beliefs as roadblocks to, 4
    internal causes, 7
    shifting of, 9
Life-conditions of the Ten Worlds
    Anger, 99–100
    Animality, 73–74
    Compassion, 261–262
    Enlightenment, 289–290
    Hell, 21
    Hunger, 45
    Learning, 211–212
    Rapture, 173–174
    Realization, 235–236
    Tranquility, 137–138
Life stories and empathy, 285–286
Life without pain and Tranquility, 157–164
    alcohol, 161
    safety, 159
    suppression, 160
Loss of fear of death and experience of Enlightenment, 296
Love
    desire for, 58–60
    and life satisfaction studies, 281–282
    as response to attachment, 202
*Love's Executioner* (Yalom), 27
Low self-esteem and Hunger, 54

**M**

Mandela, Nelson, 192, 228–229

*Man Enough* (Pittman), 59
Mastery and learning, 216–217
Meaning and Compassion, 282–283
Mindset, 5
Mind wandering, 253
Misremembering, 183
Miswanting, 67–71
    hedonic adaptation, 67–68
    wanting vs. liking, 67
    wanting vs. needing, 68
Mood-generating machinery, 36–37, 39, 77, 196
MRI scans and experience of Enlightenment, 298
Myth of Hercules and Atlas, 11–12

**N**

Narcissism and Anger, 130–131
Nature's motivation of animals, 89–91
Neurological phenomenon and experience of
        Enlightenment, 296
Neurology and psychology and Animality, 93–97
    dopamine-induced cravings, 94
    rationalizing choices, 95
Newberg, Andrew, 294
Noetic sense, 313

**O**

Obsession and Hunger, 45–46, 49, 58, 60, 67, 69
Obstructive sleep apnea, 1–2

**P**

Pain tolerance, differences in, 26, 29
Parts Model. *See* Internal Family Systems Therapy
        (Parts Model)
Peak intensity, 183
Pessimistic self-explanatory style and core delusion of
        learned helplessness, 30
Pittman, Frank, 59
*Plato at the Googleplex* (Newberger), 308
Pleasure and pain as core incentives, 2
Pleasure as basic drive and delusion and Animality, 91–93
    brain chemistry, 92
    indulgence and overindulgence, 92
Pleasure as true cause of joy, 200–204
    attachment as pleasure, 203
    attachments, specificity of, 201
    neurology of attachment, 202
    love as response to attachment, 202
    personal preferences, 201
    as trigger to joy, 180
Pleasure vs. joy, 178–181
    attachment and joy, 181
    basic pleasures and basic drives, 178
    higher-order pleasures vs. joy, 180
    hippocampus and cognition, 179
    hippocampus and joy, 179
    homeostatic, 178

pleasure as trigger to joy, 180
reward circuit of hypothalamus and pleasure, 178–179, 180
satiation of pleasure, 181
Pollan, Michael, 310–311
Positive emotion, 176–177
Possession of larger self and experience of Enlightenment, 295
Power of acceptance to alleviate suffering, 31
Power of Anger to cause shame, 119–120, 135
*Power of Now, The* (Tolle), 304–306
Primordial feelings, 5
Protoself, 301
Provocation and Anger, 105
Psychedelic drugs and experience of Enlightenment, 297
Psychological immune system, 189

**R**

Rapture, 173–210
attachments as incidental, 204–209
attachments as conduit for joy, 205
conflation of attachments, 204
grief, 206
recovery, 206
as basic life tendency, 195–200
attachment, temporary nature of, 196
mood-generating machinery, 196
noticing and appreciating, 195
core delusion, 185–186
experience stretching, 190–191
hedonic happiness diminishment, 190–191
risk of loss, 191
future focus, 191–194
anxiety-reducing cognitive and behavioral strategies, 192
behavioral activation therapy, 193
eudaimonic happiness emergence, 191
hedonic adaptation, 181–182
baselines, 182
diminishing returns, 181
hedonic happiness and pleasure, joy, 182–183
final intensity, 183
misremembering, 183
peak intensity, 183
satisfaction, 183
hedonic happiness vs. eudaimonic happiness, 177–178
life-condition, 173–174
pleasure as true cause of joy, 200–204
attachment as pleasure, 203
attachments, specificity of, 201
neurology of attachment, 202
love as response to attachment, 202
personal preferences, 201
pleasure vs. joy, 178–181

attachment and joy, 181
basic pleasures and basic drives, 178
higher-order pleasures vs. joy, 180
hippocampus and cognition, 179
hippocampus and joy, 179
homeostatic, 178
pleasure as trigger to joy, 180
reward circuit of hypothalamus and pleasure, 178–179, 180
satiation of pleasure, 181
positive emotion, 176–177
relative happiness, 184–190
absolute happiness, 185
anxiety, 187
psychological immune system, 189
Rationalization for dysfunctional beliefs, 13–14
Rationalizing choices and Animality, 95
Reaction formation and Anger, 102–108
definition, 103
provocation, 105
Realization, 235–259
analytic thinking, 235
change, 243–247
conscious vs. unconscious problem solving, 251–253
analytic, 252
through insight, 252
core delusion, 257
gradual vs. sudden change, 247–249
appearance of change, 248
human revolution, 248
intentionality, 247
internal cause stirred up by external cause, 247
insight, 235
life-condition, 235–236
self-development, 238–240
self-reformation as path to happiness, 240–243
transient hypofrontality, 253–254
associative processing, 253
mind wandering, 253
wisdom acquisition, 250–258
changing self, not circumstances, 250
conscious vs. unconscious problem solving, 251–253
dysfunctional belief abandonment, 258
relative happiness and attachment, 258
transient hypofrontality, 253–254
Recovery from loss of attachments, 206
Reeve, Christopher, 191, 205–206, 228
Regression as defense mechanism with anxiety, 51
Relative happiness, 184–190, 325
vs. absolute happiness, 185, 314
anxiety, 187
and attachment, 258, 325
psychological immune system, 189
Relief and Tranquility, 170

Renunciation of effort to avoid suffering, 306
Reward circuit of hypothalamus and pleasure, 178–179,
      180, 276, 278, 297

**S**

Safety and Tranquility, 159
Satiation of pleasure, 181
Satisfaction, 183
Schizophrenia, 13
Schwartz, Richard, 112
Scope of self, 301–302
Self-centeredness and Animality, 79–83
      and sociopathy, 79–80, 83–84
      unrestrained id, 80
Self-development and Realization, 238–240
Self dissolving into transcendence and experience of
      Enlightenment, 295
Self, illusion of
      autobiographical self, 301
      core self, 301
      end of history illusion, 300
      feeling of being a self, 300–301
      illusion of, 300
      protoself, 301
Self-reformation as path to happiness, 240–243
Shame and Anger, 119–120, 135
Silence and Tranquility, 157
Sociopathy and Animality, 79–80, 83–84
Still Me (Reeve), 191
Stumbling on Happiness (Gilbert), 3–4
Sublime Braid of truth, beauty, and goodness, 308
Sublime vs. awe, 308
Suffering and absolute happiness, 315–316
Suffering and Tranquility, 146
Suffering as response to pain, 25–29
      anterior cingulate cortex and, 26
      pain tolerance, differences in, 26, 29
      power of acceptance, 31
      severity of related to need to solve, 37
Suppression and Tranquility, 160
Surrender of self and increase of insula activity, 307

**T**

Taylor, Steve, 294
Therapeutic use of empathy, 272
Thinking, Fast and Slow (Kahneman), 182
Thought process delusion vs. content of delusion, 12–13
360-degree feedback evaluation, 215
Tolle, Eckart, 294, 304–306
Tranquility, 137–171
      core delusion, 159–160
      denial of desire, 145–149
            isolation, 147
            suffering, 146
      fear of conflict, 141–145

feeling emotions, 165–170
      authentic self, 165
      cognitive reappraisal, 166
      emotional maturity, 167
      relief, 170
feeling safe, 149–153
      avoidance of conflict, 149
      comfort with status quo, 150
freedom from problems, 153–159
      depression, 157–158
      silence, 157
life-condition, 137–138
      core affect, 138
      neurotic resistance to change, 137
life without pain, 157–164
      alcohol, 161
      safety, 159
      suppression, 160
Transient hypofrontality and Realization, 253–254
      associative processing, 253
      mind wandering, 253

**U**

Unconditional positive regard, 266–267
Undefeated Mind, The (Lickerman), 3, 251, 266, 283, 290,
      299, 316
Universal/existential anxiety, 60–64
      disproportionate wanting, 64
      dissatisfaction and meaning, 65
Unrestrained id and Animality, 80

**V**

Validation, need for, 53–58
      genogram to analyze, 54–58
      low self-esteem, 54

**W**

Waking from Sleep (Taylor), 294
Waking Up (Harris), 299, 300
Well-being and experience of Enlightenment, 296
Wisdom acquisition and Realization, 250–258
      changing self, not circumstances, 250
      conscious vs. unconscious problem solving, 251–253
      dysfunctional belief abandonment, 258
      relative happiness and attachment, 258
      transient hypofrontality, 253–254
Wonderment and joy and experience of Enlightenment,
      293, 296
World peace and absolute happiness, 318–320

**Y**

Yalom, Irvin, 27

**Z**

Zen Buddhism, 146